HOW TO GET INTO HARVARD LAW SCHOOL

INVALUABLE ADVICE ON APPLYING
AND A LOOK AT SUCCESSFUL
APPLICATION ESSAYS FROM
CURRENT STUDENTS
AND RECENT GRADS

Willie J. Epps, Jr.

Foreword by Charles J. Ogletree, Jr.

CB
CONTEMPORARY BOOKS

Library of Congress Cataloging-in-Publication Data

Epps, Willie J.
    How to get into Harvard Law School : invaluable advice on applying and a
look at successful application essays from current students and recent grads /
Willie J. Epps, Jr..
        p.   cm.
    ISBN 0-8092-3252-9
    1. Harvard Law School—Admission.   2. Law schools—Massachusetts—
Cambridge—Admission.   I. Title.
KF292.H34E67   1996
340′.071′17444—dc20   95-40914
                                                                            CIP

Cover design by Amy Nathan
Front cover photograph by Mary Reilly

Published by Contemporary Books
A division of NTC/Contemporary Publishing Group, Inc.
4255 West Touhy Avenue, Lincolnwood (Chicago), Illinois 60712-1975 U.S.A.
Copyright © 1996 by Willie J. Epps, Jr.
Printed in the United States of America
International Standard Book Number: 0-8092-3252-9
    01 02 03 04 05 QP 21 20 19 18 17 16 15 14 13 12 11 10 9 8 7 6 5 4

For Mom, Dad, and Beatryx,
with all my love,
with all my gratitude.
I thank God for blessing me with your wisdom and support.
My world revolves around you . . . and it always will. . . .

Contents

Foreword

The question that perplexes both successful and unsuccessful applicants to Harvard Law School is, "How is it possible to be admitted to such an outstanding and prestigious institution?" In his comprehensive, anecdotal, and often humorous book, *How to Get into Harvard Law School*, Willie Epps, Jr., has offered a compelling answer to that question. It is a must-read for anyone who is interested in trying to negotiate the maze that is known as the admissions process at Harvard Law School.

I am particularly interested in this book for two reasons. First, Willie Epps, Jr., was one of my favorite students at Harvard Law School. I had the pleasure of meeting him before he started at Harvard and knew that he would make many exceptional contributions to the legal profession. He has never let me down. Second, this book is important because it takes a very commonsense approach to what many think is an archaic process—getting into law school. It is important because it makes all of those who are thinking about entering a place like Harvard Law School recognize the challenge and the opportunities such a pursuit can offer. It also reflects the fact that Willie Epps, Jr., like so many who have gone before him, realize that there is a special responsibility that goes along with attending law school. This book will hopefully encourage future generations of law students to not only pursue a legal career but also to have a special sense of responsibility to use their training to improve the social fabric of our society. It is also an important document in helping students to understand the human qualities of integrity, honesty, and fairness that are essential to our legal profession if it is ever to meet the high standards that the public imposes on it.

My only regret is that this book was not available when I applied to Harvard Law School in 1975. It certainly would have made the process a lot easier, increased my level of confidence, and made the three years of hard work more understandable. However, this book is forward looking for all those who will now take it upon themselves to consider Harvard Law School and will hopefully represent the future generation of great lawyers who will change the system forever.

While we must salute Willie Epps, Jr., for his outstanding work, we must also salute the future generation of lawyers who are willing to take this challenge and pursue a legal career.

—*Charles J. Ogletree, Jr.*

Acknowledgments

The idea for this book was cultivated greatly during a telephone conversation that I had with my Harvard Law School classmate, Jason Grumet, during our first year at the Law School. I am thankful for Jason's imagination, encouragement, and friendship.

The manuscript for this book was written by me during the spring semester of my final year at Harvard Law School (HLS) to satisfy Harvard's written work requirement. My thanks to Professor Charles J. Ogletree, Jr., for serving as my faculty advisor for this project. Professor Ogletree is arguably the busiest and most popular member of the faculty at Harvard. He takes an interest in all of his students and serves as a role model to young people from all racial and economic backgrounds. I am a better person today because of Professor Ogletree's intellect, mentoring, and compassion.

My thanks to the many Harvard Law School students who either participated in my survey or gave me the rights to publish their personal statements. Your reflections on the HLS admissions process will benefit thousands of future applicants to our Law School. Thank you for making this book the most informative and comprehensive publication of any on the market pertaining to Harvard Law School admissions.

The following classmates of mine (whether their material is printed in this book or not) helped me a great deal in their own very special way: Eulas Boyd, David Buckner, Clarke Camper (1994–95 student government vice president), Helen Cantwell (1994–95 president of the Harvard Legal Aid Bureau), Catherine Caporusso, Diane Cardona, Brooke Deratany, Mike Epstein, Don Esposito, Burt Fealing, John Freedman, Vivian Hamilton, Matt Henshon (class of 1995 marshal), Jessica Herrera, Caroline Lewis, Erik Lindseth, Chantal Kordula, Jonathan Levey, Sam Liccardo, Erin McPherson, Robert Musslewhite, Polly Nyquist, Michele Pinder, Elizabeth Rowe, Ted Ruger (1994–95 president of the *Harvard Law Review*), Shirly Su, Tania Tetlow, Jon Unger (first class of 1995 marshal), Scott Weiner, and Terry Wood.

I appreciate HLS Dean of Admissions Joyce Curll's willingness to meet with me on a few occasions in her office to discuss her selection process. I am also grateful to Dean Curll, JoAnn DiSalvo, Todd Morton, and the rest of the Law School's admissions staff for allowing me to serve as a Law School admissions student recruiter during my three years at HLS. I very much enjoyed representing the Law School at the following colleges: Amherst (my alma mater), Smith, Mount Holyoke, Bates, Colby, and Bowdoin, among others. During those trips, I gained a greater appreciation for what HLS applicants want to know and need to know about our admissions policies.

The HLS Registrar's Office cooperated fully with this project. Many thanks to Ms. Allana Pollard and her colleagues in Griswold 100 for honoring, in a timely manner, every student request for a copy of their personal statement.

To my dear friends and co-founders of Phaze III, Robert E. James, II (1994–95 president of the Harvard Black Law Students Association) and Rory E. Verrett (class of 1995 marshal), thanks for "sleeping" on the project. Your words of discouragement only encouraged me—just as you two had intended.

To my Amherst–HLS mentor Chaka M. Patterson, Esq., I will return that fictitious bottle of No-Doz™ to you later this year. Thanks for paving the way!

To my heart, Kathleen Mary O'Connor, I appreciate the many hours you spent both editing this manuscript and providing valued advice, and the years of unconditional support and love you have given to me.

This manuscript would never have been published if I had not had Mrs. Denise Stinson (of the Stinson Literary Agency in Detroit, Michigan) in my corner. Denise, thank you for pushing me to make this book better. Thank you also for honoring the two most important obligations that an agent has to her client: the duty of loyalty and the duty to care.

Thanks to Mrs. Maggie Rodgers of Southern Illinois University–Edwardsville (East St. Louis Campus) for her invaluable assistance with revisions of the manuscript.

A big thanks to Contemporary Books, Inc., and my editor, Kara Leverte, for believing in this project and giving me my first book deal.

And finally, thanks to all the teachers and administrators who encouraged me along the way, from kindergarten through law school. A special acknowledgment to the Amherst College crew—Professor Tom Dumm, Professor David Wills, and Dean Ben Lieber—for writing the recommendations to get me into Harvard Law School in the first place.

Introduction

My first class at Harvard Law School opened with a prophetic statement from Professor David Wilkins. He said: "Congratulations on your acceptance to Harvard. You've won the lottery! You are now guaranteed access to the good life. If you're worried about failing at Harvard, don't be. Time passes and so will you."

Professor Wilkins's allusion to the concepts of "the lottery," the "good life," and "time passes" stuck with me.

The Lottery

Receiving an acceptance letter from Harvard Law School is indeed analogous to winning the lottery. For every member of my Law School class, which numbers 557, there were perhaps a dozen other accomplished and talented applicants from around the world who could not only have survived but excelled at this school. Were my classmates and I just the lucky ones to be admitted? Maybe. But I would like to think that getting into Harvard is more than luck.

Getting admitted to Harvard Law School is about long hours of developing your intellectual capacity, demonstrating a passion for and mastery of various extracurricular activities, holding interesting jobs and leadership positions, having a sense of purpose and unwavering dedication, and doing the most with the opportunities available. Just as important, it is about receiving, along the way, intangible things such as encouragement, guidance, love, and support. For no one, no matter how self-sufficient, wins the Law School lottery without some assistance through the years from a parent, teacher, mentor, or friend.

I entered college realizing that law school would be my next stop in preparations for a career utilizing law, government, and private organizations to enrich the lives of those outside the economic and political mainstream. At Amherst College, I built a strong academic record. I majored in political science, taking classes on American government, public policy, race, and gender. In addition, I wrote a senior honors thesis examining the use of racial "code words" in presidential politics.

Outside of class, I served as student body president my junior year, and class president my freshman, sophomore, and senior years. I was a high-ranking Air Force ROTC cadet and an active member of the Black Students' Union. I also worked part-time as a research assistant to a professor and as a campus student security assistant.

During my college summers, I interned in Washington, D.C. for one of my U.S. senators; in East St. Louis, Illinois, for the U.S. Attorney; and at Patrick Air Force Base, Florida, for the Staff Judge Advocate.

My undergraduate academic honors include *cum laude*; the Samuel Wally Brown Scholarship for character, class leadership, and scholarship; Air Force ROTC Scholarship; United States Senate Youth Program Scholarship; Beth Overton Memorial Award for public speaking; and Air Force ROTC Honors ribbons.

Despite these accomplishments, I knew when I began the law school application process during my senior year of college, that I would not be guaranteed an admissions letter from Harvard Law School. On one hand, I understood that many of my peers from across the country would apply to Harvard with better grades, more impressive work experiences, and letters of recommendation just as supportive. On the other hand, I reasoned that I, too, was more than capable of submitting a compelling application. In other words, I knew that it would be difficult to get accepted at HLS. Completing Harvard's application, however, was worth my time and effort since my record clearly indicated that I had done the most with the opportunities given to me.

Feeling that I would be "competitive" but not a shoe-in, I sensed that I had no room for error when applying to Harvard Law School. Therefore, I decided that it was critical for me to do the application process the right way or not at all. The right way to play the Law School admissions game is to find out all you can about the process and to learn what works and what doesn't work. To find the answers to these mysteries, I turned to friends who were already attending Harvard Law. They told me what they did when applying, the good and bad, and then urged me not to repeat their mistakes. This book, *How to Get into Harvard Law School*, is my attempt to relay to you what works and what doesn't work.

Chapter 1 describes what life is like for students at Harvard Law School. The topics addressed include the first-year curriculum, second- and third-year electives, clinical placements, faculty/student interaction inside and outside the classroom, classroom dynamics among students, work load, Law School facilities, extracurricular activities, financial aid, intramural athletics, student housing, dining facilities, the social life, job placement, student diversity, and faculty diversity.

Chapter 2 examines whether Harvard Law School is right for you by outlining the positives and negatives of attending HLS.

Chapter 3 discusses the application process, application strategies, and time-management techniques during the process. Commonsense advice is also given so that you will be able to avoid the typical applicant mistakes.

Chapter 4 goes behind the scenes to examine how admissions committee decisions are made each year at Harvard. This chapter will walk you through each step of the process, from the application's arrival at the Law School to the final decision-making stage.

Chapter 5 is a compilation of profiles and questionnaires completed by fifty Harvard Law students. The students are profiled so that you can get a sense of the unbelievably diverse talent that studies at the Law School—from the straight A scholar to the well-rounded politico-jock to the former actress or actor. The school often looks beyond the numbers to find talented leaders.

The following information is included in each profile:

> Name (optional)[1]
> Harvard Law School class
> Undergraduate Institution
> Undergraduate GPA
> Graduate Institution (if applicable)
> LSAT Score
> Hometown and High School
> Types of Recommenders (professors or employers)
> Race, Sex, and Class
> Major Undergraduate Activities
> Major Scholastic or Academic Honors
> Work Experience
> Parents' Occupations
> Legacy Factor

Student questionnaires are available in this chapter in their unedited form so that you can get a sense of how Harvard Law School students approached the admissions process. The questionnaire consists of the following questions:

1. When and why did you apply to Harvard Law School? Was your application completed early, late, or in the middle of the process?

2. How would you describe the undergraduate institution that you attended? Does it have a strong reputation and a solid track record of sending lots of its graduates to Harvard Law School?

3. Did you think, prior to being accepted, that you had a decent chance of being admitted to Harvard Law School?

---

[1]Most questionnaires in this book are printed with names attached. Many others are printed with names withheld. Students who elected to have their questionnaire printed with no name attached did so because of one of the following two reasons: (1) Privacy—many students did not want their privacy or the privacy of their families invaded by the publication of this book. (2) Modesty—other students did not want to appear to be bragging about their undergraduate grades, past extracurricular activities, LSAT score, or admissions to Harvard Law School.

4. Did you take any time off prior to applying or matriculating at HLS? If so, why did you take time off and what did you do?

5. What were your strongest assets when applying to Harvard Law School? Grades? LSAT score? Extracurriculars? Personal statement? Recommendations? Family connections? Personal background? Work experience?

6. What types of courses did you take as an undergraduate to prepare yourself for Harvard Law School?

7. What was your LSAT score(s)? How did you prepare for the test? If you took an LSAT prep course, which one, and did it help?

8. How long did you spend on your personal statement? What did you write about and how did you decide on the topic? Did anyone help you with your statement? If so, who?

9. Who wrote your recommendations for Harvard Law School and how did you choose them? How much notice did you give your recommenders and when were your recommendations completed?

10. What type of extracurricular activities did you participate in during your undergraduate years that you feel were beneficial to your being admitted to Harvard Law School, and why?

11. Do you feel that your race, sex, or class played a role in the admissions process? If so, explain.

12. Do you think your political ideology played a role in the admissions process? If so, explain.

13. Did you see the Harvard Law School campus prior to applying or being admitted? If so, what arrangements did you make for the visit, what were your initial impressions, and have your initial impressions changed very much? If you didn't visit the campus prior to being accepted, why not?

14. When did you receive your letter of acceptance from the Dean of Admissions and what were you doing?

15. How are you paying for Harvard Law School? Parents? Loans? Savings? Work?

16. What do you plan to do in the immediate years following graduation? What are your long-term career goals?

And finally, to get you to begin thinking about the all-important personal statement, Chapter 6 is composed of more than seventy essays that worked!

The Good Life

Since you are reading this book, I will assume that you are a privileged person, living in a privileged community. My concept of privilege in this instance is not monetarily based. Rather, my use of the word "privilege" refers to the opportunity that you have been given to study, to learn, to think, and to grow.

Now you are considering furthering your education through law school. This is a privilege, and should be thought of as such. Regardless of admission to any law school, because of your current level of education, you most likely will be fortunate enough to live what Professor Wilkins calls the *good life*. For many of us it means the security of corporate America. For some of us it means community activism, teaching, or government service. And for others, it means more education at the next prestigious stop along the way to the good life.

Whatever your concept of the *good life* may be—happiness and family, great health or comfort—we should strive, as lawyers or laypersons, to dialogue across differences and propose bold ideas to complex problems. As time passes in the coming years, we should work to enrich those communities in need and serve as a door-opener for those without access to a support system. From first-hand experience we realize that chances of success increase dramatically when someone who cares lends a hand.

If you attend law school at Harvard or not, enjoy the good life and take a few less fortunate people with you. Because in the end, life is not about your accomplishments. It's about how your accomplishments have affected the lives of others. After all, *time passes* and so will you.

Good luck as you begin your quest to determine whether Harvard Law School is a place worth pursuing!

1
Life at Harvard Law School Today

The Harvard Law School (HLS) is considered by many to be the most prestigious academic institution on the face of this earth. It is the oldest existing law school in the United States[1] and one of the world's largest. Since its inception in 1817, Harvard Law School has served as the model by which all other law schools were created and the standard by which all others are judged.

The Law School's mission is to prepare its graduates to serve as lawyers and in law-related roles. Its goal is to provide comprehensive and enlightened training for law practice; for public service at the local, state, federal, and international levels; and for law teaching and legal scholarship.[2] The school's strongest assets today are its unparalleled national and international reputation and its diverse and talented student body. Accordingly, graduates of the school work in many different settings during their professional lives.

---

[1] A proprietary law school in Litchfield, Connecticut, was older by thirty-three years.

[2] Harvard Law School, *1994–1995 Catalog* (Cambridge, Massachusetts) p. 17.

e Law School is located in Cambridge, Massachusetts, just across the Charles River from Boston. Cambridge is considered to be intellectual, urban, clean, liberal, and upscale. The Law School campus is situated just north of historic Harvard Yard at Harvard University. There are seventeen buildings at the Law School for classrooms, student housing, libraries, faculty offices, and student/administrative services. Most buildings are connected by an underground tunnel that is used during blustery New England winters. The Law School campus is shaded by beautiful old trees and has ample grassy areas that invite students (in the fall and spring) to engage in a game of catch after class or an outdoor lunch with friends.

First-Year

Each year, about 550 students enter Harvard Law School on a three-year quest that ends with the attainment of the Doctor of Jurisprudence (J.D.) degree. These 550 first-year students are randomly divided into four sections of approximately 140. In these sections, students attend five of their six first-year required courses: Contracts, Civil Procedure, Criminal Law, Property, and Torts.[3] Four of these required courses will be taught with the entire section of 140 students enrolled. For the remaining class, each section is divided into thirds so that the subject can be taught by professors to groups of less than 50. The sixth required course, Introduction to Lawyering, is taught one afternoon a week in the fall semester. This course, designed to assist students in developing legal skills, is taught in small groups of twenty. In addition to the six first-year required courses, students select one elective course: Constitutional Law, Corporations, Federal Litigation, International Law, Lawyering, or Negotiations Workshop.

In a first-year classroom, there will be very few "right" or "wrong" answers. Professors lead classes by analyzing and interpreting with students actual court cases. This case-method teaching involves presenting students with a narrative-fact pattern, and

---

[3]These courses may be taught throughout the year or offered complete in the fall or spring semester.

then allowing the students to decide how the parties in each case should argue and how courts should decide the particular case. The cases often turn on social, economic, or political factors. Debates are usually lively, even though class participation, for better or for worse, does not affect a student's final grade.

First semester can be intimidating at HLS. Most students are unfamiliar with how to read or brief cases. The reading load is heavy and dense, and students tend to put pressure on themselves to do well. During the first semester, most students are still trying to figure out what they must do to survive, then excel, at Harvard.

First-year students at the Law School must take the initiative to participate in class. While two or three professors will still cold-call on students using the Socratic method, most professors teaching first-level (1L) classes at Harvard today prefer volunteers. Many Harvard students are reluctant to talk in class because they do not want to spout a wrong answer, fearing embarrassment. Students must also take the initiative to form study groups outside of class. The professors do not organize these for students.

Student apprehensions climax during exam time in the first semester. Those living in the cramped quarters of the Law School's Gropius complex are known to internalize a disproportionate amount of stress by hanging around too many uptight law students. Once first-semester exams have been taken, however, Harvard Law becomes a much less stressful place for 1Ls. Moreover, there is a feeling after first-semester grades are released that the hard part of HLS is over.

During the second semester of first-year, all students are required to participate in the first-year Ames Moot Court Competition. 1Ls also are encouraged to compete in the Williston competition.

Upper Years

In the second and third years, students are expected to complete fifty-two credits. This can be achieved by taking three to four classes a semester, or two to three classes a semester in conjunction with a clinical placement. Second- and third-year courses and seminars are completely elective. "However, the Faculty strongly recommends that students take Accounting, Constitutional Law, Corporations and Taxation, in the second year, as these courses are prerequisite to much advanced work, and one or more courses with substantial clinical component in the second and third years."[4] Almost all students take at least one course in their second or third year that involves a clinical placement.

Unlike first-year classes, second- and third-year classes are not taken within sections. Classes are smaller and better mixed, ranging from twenty-five to fifty students for seminars. Second- and third-year electives are offered in the areas of administrative law, business organization and finance, commercial law, comparative law, conflict of laws, constitutional law and theory, criminal law, family law, federal law, government regulation, human rights, international legal studies, jurisprudence, law and other disciplines, legal history, legal practice (clinical and non-clinical), legal profession, local government and urban planning, property (wealth and resources), taxation and public finance, and torts.

Most second- and third-year classes are intellectually stimulating. Others are downright boring. The Socratic method in the upper classes also has been replaced in most cases by voluntary participation or a panel system.[5] Class time per week varies from ten to fifteen hours.

The most popular and oversubscribed courses include Constitutional Law with Professor Charles Fried or Professor Lawrence Tribe, Corporations with Professor Reinier Kraakman, Taxation with Professor Alvin Warren, Copyright with Professor Arthur Miller, Labor Law with Professor Paul Weiler, Trial Advocacy Workshop (criminal) with Professor Charles Ogletree, Evidence with Professor Charles Nesson, and Legal Professions with Professor David Wilkins.

Officially, regular class attendance and participation are expected of all students. In reality, class attendance is taken in only one class at the Law School (Trial Advocacy Workshop). Accord-

---

[4]Harvard Law School, *1994–1995 Catalog* (Cambridge, Massachusetts) p. 17.

[5]"Panel system" refers to a group of students being placed on notice by the professor that they are mainly responsible for class discussion for a period from one day to one week. A student usually serves on panel once during a given semester.

ingly, some students take advantage of their freedom by skipping classes regularly to work for a Boston law firm, run their own small business, concentrate on extracurricular activities, travel, or generally goof off.

During either the second or third year, students must satisfy the written work requirement by writing a two-credit paper either under the individual supervision of a faculty member or in connection with a Law School seminar. All students also must complete a course instruction on the legal profession and issues of professional responsibility.

Schedule

The Law School is on the traditional semester system (fall and spring) for all students, and manages to squeeze-in a winter term for 2Ls and 3Ls for three weeks in January. During winter term, most students take one course that meets weekdays for three hours a day. Other students take advantage of clinical placements and independent study. Courses at the Law School are for full-time students only. Courses at HLS are offered days only.

Grades

The grading system is bearable. Harvard has a nine-category system, ranging from A+ to F. The Law School seems to have a strong B curve. A grades are not unusual. C's, D's, and F's are virtually nonexistent. Again, class participation is not factored into final grades in any class. Exams take place at the end of the course; three-hour in-class exams (open-book) or eight-hour take-home exams are the most popular forms of examination. It is virtually impossible to fail a course at Harvard today.

The competition at Harvard Law School, contrary to popular opinion, is not cutthroat. Although students strive to excel academically, most are willing to help out a classmate in need. Class outlines are produced by groups of students working together. Almost everyone joins a voluntary study group during his or her first year.

Students who complete their course work with distinction receive their degree *cum laude*, *magna cum laude*, or *summa cum laude. Cum laude* distinctions are made for those graduating with an average in the B+ range. *Magna cum laude* signifies those graduating with a strong A– average. *Summa cum laude*, which is rarely awarded, is reserved for those Harvard Law School students who have maintained slightly better than an A average. About half of all students graduate with some form of distinction.

Cross Registration

Students are allowed to cross-register for courses in other faculties of Harvard without additional charge. It is not unusual for second- and third-year students to supplement their Law School education with classes at Harvard's John F. Kennedy School of Government or the Harvard Business School. Cross-registration is also available at the Massachusetts Institute of Technology and the Fletcher School of Law and Diplomacy at Tufts University.

Degree Options

The following joint degrees may be earned while in residence at the Law School: Juris Doctor/Master of Business Administration (J.D./M.B.A.) with the Harvard Business School; Juris Doctor/Master of Public Policy (J.D./M.P.P) or Juris Doctor/Master of Public Administration (J.D./M.P.A.) with Harvard's John F. Kennedy School of Government; Juris Doctor/Master of Arts in Law and Diplomacy (J.D./M.A.L.D.) with the Tufts University Fletcher School; and Juris Doctor/Doctor of Philosophy (J.D./Ph.D.) and Juris Doctor/Masters (J.D./M.A.) with any program offered at the Harvard Faculty of Arts and Sciences, the Graduate School of Design, the Divinity School, or graduate programs at Massachusetts Institute of Technology.

Bar Exam

Students do not expect Harvard to prepare them to pass a state bar. The legal education at Harvard is national, intentionally not focusing on any one state's law. Almost all Harvard students take a bar review course (usually Bar/Bri Bar Review Course) in the summer immediately following graduation to prepare for their state's bar.

Students

The student body is composed of approximately 1,850 people, including Masters of Law (LL.M.) and Doctor of Juridical Science (S.J.D.) candidates. J.D. students come from all fifty states, more than twenty countries and more than three hundred undergraduate schools. Over sixty countries are represented in the LL.M. program. The student body is 59 percent male, 41 percent female, 11 percent black, 8 percent Asian, 5 percent Hispanic, and 1 percent Native American. The student body is one of the most diverse student bodies of any law school. Harvard graduates more African-American lawyers each year than any other law school, excluding Howard University in Washington, D.C., and Texas Southern University in Houston.

Harvard's desire to have a diverse and interesting student body is an educational bonus. Students learn as much from each other as they do from professors and casebooks. In addition, it is one of the school's goals to have all aspects of society represented at HLS so that the legal profession in turn will be enriched. Thus all elements of American society can receive well-educated representation.

Harvard Law students major in a wide range of subjects at the undergraduate level and represent almost 200 colleges and universities. More than 30 percent of HLS students have advanced degrees in another discipline.

Faculty

The Law School has a capable, competent, and busy full-time faculty of sixty-seven and part-time faculty of fifty. Each professor is required to teach three courses a year. Unlike many other universities, professors actually teach the courses at Harvard Law; teaching assistants are rare. Faculty–student interaction in class is healthy, but could be improved with smaller class sizes. Interaction outside of class needs refinement. Students can easily schedule lunches with professors and visit during office hours, but it is difficult to see a professor on short notice or outside of office hours. Some professors enjoy students and make teaching and mentoring a priority. Others are distant, more involved with their own intellectual and monetary pursuits.

Professors at Harvard Law School, in addition to preparing for class and advising students, spend a great deal of time researching and writing books and articles, conducting their own private practice, serving as consultants, appearing on television and radio programs, and serving on internal faculty–student committees.

Faculty diversity is a major issue on campus. Harvard prides itself on being a leader in all areas of the law. But in terms of faculty diversity, Harvard is "bringing up the rear."[6] The core faculty (professors and assistant professors) is now at sixty-eight, the highest in Harvard Law School history. Percentage of women faculty members (nine of sixty-eight, or 13 percent) is also highest, but well below national average. While the percentage of African-American professors (five of sixty-eight, or 7.4 percent) is above the national average, no woman of color, no Asian American, no Hispanic, and no openly homosexual person currently sits on the faculty at Harvard Law School. In fact, no woman of color, no Asian American, no Hispanic, and no openly homosexual person has ever served as a member of Harvard Law School's core faculty.

Student Organizations

Student organizations at the Law School range from clinical practice for academic credit, professional interest groups, and service societies to social activities, student publications, and special interest and ethnic groups. Through student organizations, most students are able to greatly enhance their quality of life while at HLS. The following is a list of organizations representing the breadth of student activities[7]:

ABA, Law Student Division. An affiliate of the American Bar Association; represents students as members of the legal profession.

La Alianza. Provides academic and social support for members of the Hispanic/Latino community.

---

[6]See author quoted on the issue of HLS faculty diversity in "2 Books Raise Anew Questions of Bias at Harvard Law" by Alice Dembner, *The Boston Globe*, October 11, 1994, City Edition, Metro/Region, p. 17.

[7]Harvard Law School, *Student Organizations 1994–1995* (Cambridge, Massachusetts) and Harvard Law School, *Application 1995* (Cambridge, Massachusetts) p. 6–8.

Amnesty International. Concentrates on urgent-action campaigns involving participation by the student body, helps other AI chapters with their prisoner-of-conscience campaigns, and sponsors relevant informational events.

Armenian Students Association. Aims to promote interest and understanding of Armenian history, culture, and current affairs at HLS.

Asian American Law Students Association. Serves to address the needs and concerns of the Asian American community at Harvard.

Battered Women's Advocacy Project. Explores the issues surrounding domestic violence and trains members to act as lay-court advocates for women seeking temporary restraining orders for their abusers.

Big Brother/Big Sister Organization. Provides students the opportunity to help the community through helping a less-fortunate child.

Black Law Students Association. Implements programs designed to enhance the academic, political, and cultural experience for African Americans at Harvard.

BlackLetter Law Journal. A student-operated journal dedicated to the dissemination of legal literature, thought, and ideas that have a direct impact on the minority community.

Board of Student Advisers. Administers the Ames Moot Court Competition, assists with planning and administering first-year orientation, compiles the *Course Evaluation Guide*, and sponsors a series of speakers.

Catholic Law Students Association. Serves and strengthens the Catholic community at the Law School through frequent Masses, weekly prayer, fellowship, retreats, speakers programs, service projects, and issue debates.

Children and Family Rights Project. Brings together students interested in a wide range of children and family rights issues, including juvenile justice, child and spouse abuse, day care, child support and custody, and education.

Chinese Law Association. Brings together students interested in all issues relating to Chinese culture and the Asia-Pacific region.

Christian Fellowship. Composed of Christian law students from diverse church backgrounds and traditions who meet weekly; hold small Bible-study groups; work at shelters; sponsor clothing and food drives; and hold parties, short trips, retreats, and other informal social gatherings.

Civil Liberties Union. A multifaceted organization for those concerned with civil rights and civil liberties, promoting campus and community awareness, as well as student involvement in ensuring rights and liberties through the application of law.

Civil Rights–Civil Liberties Law Review. A journal profoundly committed to social change; publishes articles by lawyers, professors, and students in a broad range of areas such as constitutional theory, poverty law, due process, and equal protection.

Coalition for Civil Rights. United students and student organizations seeking to diversify the faculty, student body, and curriculum of HLS.

Committee on Sports and Entertainment Law. Provides an environment in which students can meet, exchange ideas, and learn about legal practice in sports and entertainment fields from attorneys, agents, professors, and professional organizations.

Crew. An athletic organization for students who wish to take a break from the books, make new friendships, increase physical strength and stamina, and partake in the camaraderie and competition of one of the university's oldest sports.

Defenders. Helps its members gain practical litigation experience through a wide range of criminal matters, from show-cause hearings to full bench and/or jury trials alleging misdemeanors and minor felonies.

Democrats. Seeks to energize, amplify, and channel Democratic political interest, and to promote and develop the policies of the Democratic Party.

Dormitory and Student Affairs Council. The primary social planning organization for HLS; sponsors social recreational activities and participates in policy decisions affecting dormitories.

Drama Society. Offers opportunities for people interested in singing, acting, dancing, writing, choreography, lighting, sound, makeup, costumes, props, stage-managing, directing, or producing through four full-scale productions.

Environmental Law Review. Includes articles by lawyers, policymakers, and students addressing all aspects of environmental law, ranging from energy and urban land use to hazardous wastes and wilderness preservation.

Environmental Law Society. Undertakes research and litigation support for national and regional environmental groups, local environmental lawyers, and state agencies.

European Law Association. Promotes a better understanding of European cultures, politics, and legal systems among members of the HLS community.

Federalist Society for Law and Public Policy. Committed to bringing conservative and libertarian perspectives on the law to Harvard.

Forum. Brings to HLS noteworthy individuals from all fields of endeavor to engage in an enlightening and wide-ranging exchange of ideas.

Forum on Law and Education. Brings together future lawyers, educators, and policy makers to explore ways to improve our schools.

Harvard Association for Law and Business. For students interested in learning more about how law and business interact.

Harvard Law Couples Association. Exists primarily to enrich the experience of the "significant others" (i.e. spouses, girlfriend/boyfriend, children) of HLS students.

Harvard Law Record. A student-owned and -operated newspaper covering Law School activities, personalities, and matters of general interest to the legal community.

Harvard Law Review. A general legal periodical that serves judges, lawyers, professors, students, and the legal profession as a whole, while training its members in legal research and writing.

Human Rights Journal. Publishes articles by leading scholars in the field as well as student-written notes on human rights issues in U.S. foreign policy, book reviews, and reports on internships sponsored by the school's Human Rights Program.

International Law Journal. The oldest and most frequently cited student-edited review of international law in the United States.

International Law Society. An academic and social meeting ground for students interested in international law, international affairs, and human rights.

J.D./M.B.A Association. Represents the interests of J.D./

M.B.A. students in academic and administrative matters.

Jewish Law Students Association. Offers a wide range of political, cultural, social, and religious programs.

Journal of Law and Public Policy. The only student-run conservative or libertarian law journal in the country.

Journal of Law and Technology. Keeps up with legal implications of developments in a wide range of emerging technologies.

Journal on Legislation. Examines the current state of the law, discusses trends in and theoretical underpinnings of legislation, presents detailed statements of how the law should be changed, and proposes specific model acts for adoption by legislatures.

Korean Association. Fosters awareness about the Korean community among members and in HLS as a whole.

Labor Law Project. Brings together students with an interest in labor and employment law and such related issues as union democracy, employment discrimination, negotiation, and collective bargaining.

Lambda. Focuses on legal, political, and social issues of interest to students concerned about discrimination that is based upon sexual orientation and preference, through speakers and discussions; works with community legal and political rights groups; and serves as a support group for lesbian, gay, and bisexual students.

Law and Health Care Society. Attempts to address issues of interest to students who are considering careers in health law.

Law and Philosophical Society. Offers students and faculty an opportunity to explore more fully many of the philosophical issues they confront in class, in independent study, and in informal conversation.

Law and Technology Society. Promotes awareness of legal issues and opportunities at the cutting edge of technology.

Law School Council. The student government of the Law School.

Legal Aid Bureau. Provides litigation experience for students and legal services in civil matters to low-income people in the greater Boston area.

Legislative Research Bureau. Researches and drafts legislation to be introduced in local city councils, in state legislatures across the country, and in Congress.

Lincoln's Inn Society. A social club.

Mediation Program. Trains student volunteers in mediation theory and technique and provides local courts and litigants with an alternative method for settling small claims disputes.

Middle Eastern Law Students Association. Addresses the concerns of all students interested in the social, political, and cultural aspect of the region.

National Lawyers Guild. The on-campus chapter of the National Lawyers Guild, a nationwide network of progressive lawyers.

Native American Law Students Association. Working to foster an atmosphere of enlightenment for the Law School community on unique Native American legal issues.

Phi Alpha Delta. A legal service organization that is dedicated to the principles of integrity, compassion, courage, and professional service.

Poetry Club. Meets to share poetry and prose that members have written or read.

Roscoe Pound Society. For students who are studying law after having been away from school or college for a period of time.

Prison Legal Assistance Project. Through student attorneys, represents Massachusetts prisoners in administrative hearings.

Real Estate and Urban Development Forum. Provides educational information and activities in the areas of real estate, urban planning, architecture, historic preservation, community development, housing, project finance, environmental planning, zoning, tax policy, public development, landscape architecture, and related fields.

Republicans. Encourages debate and discussion; is involved in the political process, and fosters general awareness of the Republican perspective.

Scales of Justice. An a capella singing group.

Small Owners Assistance Program. Represents the interests of low- and moderate-income property owners at the Cambridge Rent Control Board.

Soccer Club. For men and women interested in playing soccer.

Society for Law, Life and Religion. An organization for students concerned with the defense of First Amendment liberties and the dignity of life.

Softball Club. Organizes weekly games for men and women.

South Asian Law Students Association. Promotes an understanding and appreciation of South Asian culture at HLS.

Southern Union. Promotes collegiality among members who share an interest in the southern region of the United States.

Student-Funded Fellowships. Funds HLS students who work at low- and non-paying public interest jobs.

Student Public Interest Network. Addresses the concerns of students seeking alternatives to private corporate-law practices.

Tenant Advocacy Project. A clinical organization that represents Cambridge tenants in hearings before the Cambridge Rent Control Board.

Veterans Association. Provides social support for former, present, and future military men and women, and establishes a foundation for veterans' interest at HLS.

Volunteer Income Tax Assistance Program. Student volunteers provide low-income, elderly, and disabled residents in Boston, Cambridge, and Somerville with free, confidential tax assistance in preparing state and federal forms.

Women of Color Collective. Addresses issues concerning African-American, Asian American, Latina, and Native American women at HLS and in the society at large.

Women's Law Association. Addresses issues of concern to women students at HLS and tries to improve the position of women in the traditionally male legal profession.

Women's Law Journal. Devoted to the development of a feminist jurisprudence; seeks to explore the impact of the law on women and women on the law.

Yearbook. Captures the moods and methods of legal education at Harvard in more than 200 pages of artwork, photographs, and prose.

Social Life

Much of the value of the Law School degree is in the friendships and contacts students make. Therefore, students make it a point to get to know their classmates outside the classroom.

Students at Harvard Law School have to take control of their social lives, meaning, a social life does not exist unless someone steps forward to make it happen. The quality of the Law School's social life has been rated very poor by numerous surveys. This reflects on those students who do not make an effort. For those who do make an effort, the sky is the limit.

Students at HLS, on the whole, work and play hard. Students at the Law School take the opportunity to socialize informally during lunch in Harkness Dining Commons, after class by the Backbench Pub and Harkboxes, and during the evenings in the Law School dorms. It is not unusual for students to debate legal ideas and theories while hanging out. If you walk through the dorms late at night, it is not odd to find groups of students struggling with the great public policy decisions of the day regardless of whether they are watching "ER," "Seinfeld," CNN, or C-SPAN.

Students at HLS find time to read the newspaper during morning coffee. The *New York Times*, the *Wall Street Journal*, and the *Boston Globe* are the most popular newspapers at the school. A small minority of students read *USA Today* for its excellent national sports coverage.

Prominent speakers frequent the campus. Receptions for visiting speakers are well attended. "Saturday School," a program designed by Professor Charles Ogletree to bring diverse speakers to campus, is responsible for getting some of the bigger names to visit. The Harvard Law School Forum is also active in recruiting national leaders and policymakers to HLS for speaking engagements.

Intramural athletics are alive and well at Harvard. Softball, volleyball, crew, basketball, soccer, and flag football are all co-ed sports. Students occasionally go jogging in the afternoons on the banks of the Charles River or attend an aerobics class held in our run-down Hemenway Gymnasium.

Major campus social events include the 1L "Booze Cruise" on the Boston Harbor in September, the Ames Moot Court Competition Finals in November during which a U.S. Supreme Court Justice presides, the Dean's Holiday Party in December, the Public Interest Auction in March, the Annual Law School Parody in April, BLSA Spring Conference and the Annual Law School Semi-Formal in April, and the Graduation Dinner and Dance in May. In addition, the "Salsa" and "Go South" parties are always well attended.

Cambridge is a wonderful city for shopping, strolling, dining, and drinking. There are diverse and interesting shops in Harvard Square. During the day, Law Students can be spotted hanging at Au

Bon Pain. At night, law students occasionally frequent the Bow and Arrow, Hong Kong, and Spaghetti Club. The more popular restaurants in the Square include California Pizza Kitchen, the House of Blues, the Bombay Club (Indian cuisine), Shilla (Japanese and sushi), Chili's, Border Cafe (Mexican), and Grindell's (traditional food/bar).

Boston is accessible by train or bus from Harvard Square. It is a city that can be experienced fully when walking. The Freedom Trail is a "must do," as is Newbury Street and Faneuil Hall on a sunny day. Boston's nightlife is unlimited with its bars, clubs, theaters, and professional sports teams: Red Sox baseball, Bruins hockey, and Celtics basketball. Coffee and dessert at one of Boston's many cafes, such as Sonsie, is a wonderful way to cap off an evening downtown.

When students get bored with the Boston metropolitan area, they can take a road trip to New York, Vermont, or Maine for sightseeing, shopping, and skiing.

Law School Facilities[8]

The main campus includes ten structures.

1. Austin Hall (1883) is one of the oldest buildings in continuous use for law teaching in the country. It was designed by Henry Hodson Richardson in the Romanesque Revival architectural style. The first floor contains three large classrooms, in which students learn the law while sitting under the portraits of white, male, wealthy English judges. On the second floor is the Ames Courtroom, named for former Dean James Barr Ames. The Courtroom serves as the sight where second- and third-year students argue moot court cases before panels of practicing judges. A justice of the United States Supreme Court presides over the final round of the Ames Moot Court Competition. The Criminal Justice Institute, founded and directed by Professor Charles J. Ogletree, Jr., occupies the third floor of Austin, sharing space with Morgan Courtroom. Several student organizations have offices in the building, including the Har-

---

[8]Entire discussion of facilities is based heavily on Ellen Miller and Steven Smith, "A Walking Tour of the Harvard Law School" (Special Collections Department, Harvard Law Library and Harvard Law School Publications Center).

vard Defenders, Prison Legal Assistance Project and the Mediation Program.

2. Gannett House (1838) is the oldest surviving building on the Law School campus. It is a three-story, white, porticoed, Greek Revival building that stands out on a campus which is predominantly brick-built. Since 1925, Gannett House has been home to the Harvard Legal Aid Bureau and the *Harvard Law Review*.

3. Hemenway Gymnasium (1940), while owned and operated by Harvard University and not the Law School, is used a great deal by law students, faculty, and staff for basketball, squash, aerobics, weight-lifting, and general exercise. Students frequently complain, and rightfully so, that the gym is not adequately maintained.

4. Hastings Hall (1889) provides living quarters for 96 students in 60 suites. The lower level houses the Publications Center, where most administrative publications are produced; nine scholarly journals edited by Law School students; and various student organizations including the Black Law Students Association and Women's Law Association.

5. Griswold Hall (1969) was dedicated in the fall of 1979 to Erwin Griswold (1904–1994), former dean of the school (1946–1967) and former United States solicitor general, on the occasion of his seventy-fifth birthday. Griswold houses the Dean's Office, faculty offices, the Registrar's Office, a small classroom, and other administrative offices.

6. Langdell Hall (1906), the massive structure which serves as the center of the Law School campus, is named after Christopher Columbus Langdell, the first dean of Harvard Law School (1870–1895) and father of the case method of teaching law. The Harvard Law Library occupies a major portion of Langdell Hall. It is the largest law library in the world. The book collections, which include more than 1.5 million bound volumes, support the teaching and research of the Law School and serve as a resource for legal scholars throughout the world. The main reading level is on the fourth floor. At the north end of the reading room is the Treasure Room, where rare books, manuscripts, and the most valuable paintings in the art collections are displayed. The library has 32 full-time librarians and seats 901 patrons. Langdell Hall, closed for renovation during the 1996–97

academic year, contains a number of faculty offices.

7. Reginald F. Lewis International Law Center (1958) houses the International Legal Studies Library, consisting of approximately one-third of the Law Library's large international law collection. The Lewis Center is also the home of the graduate program to which approximately 150 lawyers and scholars from around the world come to Harvard each year to pursue an LL.M. or S.J.D. degree. The Lewis Center was dedicated in 1993 to the late Reginald F. Lewis (class of '68), chairman and CEO of TLC Beatrice. Shortly before his untimely death in 1992, Mr. Lewis gave Harvard Law School a $3 million gift which, at the time, was the largest gift ever received by the school. Lewis is the first major facility at Harvard named in honor of an African American.

8. Pound Hall (1970) is named for Roscoe Pound, former dean of the school (1916–1936). There are several large classrooms on the first floor, and some smaller classrooms on the first and second floors. The walls of the second and third floors are covered with photographic portraits of the Law School faculty. A portion of the first floor is an exhibition on women in the law. The second floor also has a large conference area called the Ropes/Gray Room. Job fairs, school plays, formal dinners, and Law School receptions are held in Ropes/Gray. Administrative offices, including the Admissions Office, are located on the third, fourth, and fifth floors. A faculty dining room is situated on the third floor.

9. Harkness Graduate Center (1950) was designed by Walter Gropius. This complex includes student dormitories, a cafeteria, the Harkbox Cafe (small coffee shop), student mailboxes, the Backbench Pub, pool tables, television rooms, the Law School Coop (small convenience store), and general social and study space. Murals in the Harkness Commons (the main building) are by Joan Miró, Josef Albers, Jean Arp, and Herbert Bayer. Students consider the main building and the attached five Law School dormitories—Ames, Dane, Holmes, Shaw, and Story—to be architectural disasters. Nevertheless, the U.S. Historical Society says otherwise, recognizing the complex as a historical landmark. Unfortunately for current and future students, Gropius can never be destroyed or extensively altered.

10. Hauser Hall (1994) is the Law School's newest building. It is named after alumni Gustave and Rita Hauser[9] to honor their $13 million gift to the Law School, the largest cash gift ever donated to a law school. The building, incorporating some architectural elements of Austin Hall, won the American Institute of Architects 1994 Achievement Award. Hauser Hall contains thirty-five faculty offices, three conference rooms, three seminar rooms, and two classrooms. The School's student computer lab is located in the basement of the building. Students call Hauser "the new faculty playground" as most space in this five story building is devoted to faculty offices.

Other buildings on campus include Baker House, a charming Victorian building that houses the Alumni Center; Wyeth Hall, a student dormitory next to Baker House to the north; and North Hall, formerly a Quality Inn, now the newest residential building on campus.

Off campus is the Hale and Dorr Legal Services Center in Jamaica Plain, the Law School's primary teaching clinic.

Costs

Tuition for students is over $19,000 per academic year. The required university health service fee is $650 a year. Dormitory charges, if you live on campus, range from $2,770 to $7,725. The student activity fee is $225. Books and supplies are close to $800, while personal expenses average $2,430.

Financial Aid

A Law School graduate's debt can be enormous. The average Harvard Law student borrows close to $20,000 a year through the combination of federal, institutional, and private loans.

---

[9]Gustave M. Hauser, J.D. (class of '53) is chairman and CEO of Hauser Communications Inc. He is a pioneer of the modern cable television industry, responsible for developing MTV Music Television, Nickelodeon television networks, pay-per-view programming, and other advanced interactive services. Rita E. Hauser (class of '58) is of counsel to the New York firm of Stroock & Stroock & Lavan, specializing in international legal matters. She is engaged in philanthropic activities as president of the Hauser Foundation. "Harvard Law School," a supplement to the Harvard University Gazette (Spring 1995) p. 1.

Recognizing that most students graduate with a considerable amount of debt and that careers in the public sector do not pay enough to cover projected loan payments, the Law School in 1978 established the Low Income Protection Plan (LIPP). This program, the first of its kind in the country, helps student repay debt while they work in low-paying law-related jobs.

Some students say that they will benefit greatly from LIPP. Other students call the program "LIPP service," since it is perceived as underfunded, unable to truly subsidize careers in public service. Once accepted by the Admissions Committee, potential students should examine the intricate details of LIPP before accepting Harvard's offer.

Placement

Harvard Law students do not have to knock on doors and pound the pavement to find employment. HLS students are accustomed to employers seeking them out for jobs. Over 600 law firms, corporations, and governmental entities interview students on campus in October of each year. This process can be grueling for students who, as a group, go through 15,000 interviews in a four-week period.

Most employers like what they see when they come to Harvard and often invite students to visit their offices for follow-up interviews. To cut down on the number of classes that are missed by students during firm interview season, the Law School implemented a Fly-out Week. Fly-out Week takes place at the beginning of November. During this period, students travel to cities all across America, at the expense of the firms, to determine where they would like to work in the coming summer. The average Law School student receives multiple offers of employment from many of the country's most elite firms.

Over half (62 percent) of the class goes directly to a law firm following graduation. About 28 percent of the graduating class accepts a one- or two-year judicial clerkship. Close to 5 percent of HLS graduates pursue public interest or government. Three percent work in business while 1 percent pursues academic careers immediately. The average starting salary for HLS graduates approaches $70,000 a year.

2

Is Harvard Law School Right for You?

Despite being one of the most prestigious institutions on the face of this earth, Harvard Law School is not the ideal place for everyone. This chapter outlines the positives and negatives of attending Harvard Law School to help you determine for yourself whether Harvard would be a good place to spend three years and close to $100,000.

Before beginning the Law School application process, figure out why you want to attend Harvard. Think seriously about what you would want to get out of your Law School education. Think seriously about the investment in time and money that you would have to make to attend Harvard. Reflect on your life's ambitions and goals and see whether Harvard Law School could help you achieve those things.

A lot of talented men and women enter Harvard not wanting to pursue legal careers. Some enter Harvard wanting to go into politics. Others want to start businesses, teach at the college or high school level, become sports agents, or become actors or actresses. They nevertheless matriculated at Harvard because they figure the Law School degree will always be something to "fall back on." They can initially give their dream profession a try, they figure, and if unsuccessful, they can always practice law.

Once third-year rolls around, many of these same students are in debt in excess of $90,000 and finally realize that they must begin to make payments on these loans six months following graduation. Looking ahead to career options, many of them believe that they have no choice but to practice law to pay off the loans. It makes no sense, they reason, to try to attempt starting a business or an acting career with $90,000 of debt (a $1,200 monthly payment for ten to fifteen years).

In a sense, some students choose to become "indentured servants" at the prestigious law firms across the country. The students to which I am referring, as I mentioned, do not want to be lawyers. But they figure they must in order to pay off their loans. They think to themselves that later in life—like five to seven years down the road—"I'll do what I really want to do."

My point is simple. Life is short. You should not have to spend so many years doing something that you do not find enjoyable. Lots of people like to practice law. If you anticipate that you'll be one of those people, then you have nothing to worry about. HLS is worth strongly considering. If, on the other hand, you anticipate not wanting to practice law, take a close look at all your options before you decide to apply. Ask yourself: After graduating from HLS, will you be able to do something that you want to do? Will you be able to immediately pursue your dreams following an HLS education? Are you willing to defer your dreams and work as a lawyer for a period of time after Harvard to gain additional experiences and to pay off your debt? Does working for a prestigious law firm fit into long-term goals? In short, take control of the process before it begins. If you are thinking seriously about Harvard Law, you need to start, if you have not already, plotting your life and destiny.

If law school fits into your career plan, HLS still may not be the place for you. Harvard Law School is for self-starters who will take control of their educational experience. No one at HLS can make you happy or make your time at the Law School enjoyable. Students who grow at HLS are those who take advantage of all the opportunities that exist at this major institution.

Harvard Law School is not for the passive learner. If you are the type of person who wants your schedule planned and dictated by someone else, HLS is not right for you. If you just expect interesting lectures, sight-seeing tours of Boston, and happy hours with students to just happen without making an effort to plan these events, then HLS is not right for you. If you expect a Law School professor to approach you after class to see if you have questions about the material or to see if you would like to have lunch at some point, then HLS is definitely not the right place for you.

Positives of Harvard Law School

Reputation

Harvard enjoys a strong international and national reputation. With a Harvard Law degree, you can attain employment in an unlimited number of areas: corporate law, judicial clerkships, consulting, banking, public interest, government, and academia. In the 1990s, starting salaries for HLS graduates in New York can approach the six-figure mark. The average starting salary for Harvard graduates is around $70,000.

Placement

The typical Harvard Law student has many employment options during the summers while enrolled in law school and certainly in the years that follow graduation. HLS lawyers are well represented at every major law firm in the country, in the Fortune 500 companies, in high-ranking government posts, and in the public-interest community.

Flexibility of HLS Degree

HLS graduates pursue many career options. Law, business, finance, entertainment, politics, writing, and teaching are all viable options.

Financial Aid

Harvard Law School has a need-blind admissions policy. Once admitted, Harvard uses its resources to provide qualified students with grants and loans. Seventy percent of all students receive some type of financial assistance, almost always in the form of loans.

Speaker Series

During three years at Harvard, students are guaranteed exposure to national and international decision-makers. Many of them are invited to speak at the Law School and at Harvard's John F. Kennedy School of Government. Recent speakers include Vice President Al Gore, Reverend Jesse Jackson, Dan Rather, President Jean Bertrand Aristide, Professor Lani Guinier, Professor Charles Murray, Ice T, Spike Lee, Dr. Ruth Westheimer, countless numbers of U.S. senators and congresspersons, at least half of the current Supreme Court, and notorious or well-established business leaders.

Student Body

Harvard Law School is 59 percent men, 41 percent women, 11 percent black, 8 percent Asian, 5 percent Hispanic, and 1 percent Native American. Students come from all 50 states and 27 foreign countries. Students are graduates of the Ivy League schools, Little Three institutions (Amherst, Williams, and Wesleyan), large state schools, small liberal arts colleges, historically African-American colleges and universities, women's colleges, and military academies. There is a range of economic classes within the student body.

Course Selection

The size and breadth of the courses offered at Harvard Law School is unrivaled by any other law school in the United States. Classes are offered in every imaginable area of the law.

Class Size

Some students like the large classes so that they can be somewhat "anonymous" when busy with other activities. If they cannot attend class for a couple of weeks, no one will miss them.

HLS Student Interaction with Other Schools

Students often take advantage of activities planned by students at the other area schools.

Famous and Talented Professors

The lot of professors include Charles Ogletree, Alan Dershowitz, Phil Heymann, Charles Fried, Lawrence Tribe, Martha Minow, Arthur Miller, Christopher Edley, Martha Field, and David Wilkins.

The faculty is intelligent. It is fairly easy to work for the professor of your choice. Professors have plenty of money to pay students assisting with research. Most students do not take advantage of the opportunities to work with professors outside of class. So if you want to work with a given professor, he or she will undoubtedly have an assignment for you to tackle.

Classroom Space
Classroom space is plentiful and modern.

Clinical Placements
Clinical programs enrich the student experience at the Law School. It is an opportunity to do something for others and to give back. Some 500 students a year participate in fieldwork programs. These programs involve placement of students in dozens of organizational settings: legal services offices, state and federal agencies, district attorneys' and public defenders' offices, public interest organizations, private law firms, and others. Harvard sponsors three in-house clinics where students work on actual cases, interacting with their clients, while enrolled in classroom courses. The in-house placements include the Criminal Justice Institute, Immigration and Refugee Clinic at Cambridge–Somerville Legal Services, and Hale and Dorr Legal Services Center. The Harvard Defenders, Harvard Legal Aid Bureau, Harvard Mediation Program, Prison Legal Assistance Project, and Tenant Advocacy Project are considered voluntary extracurricular clinical placements for course credit.

Grading
Strong B curve. It is not too hard to survive.

Housing in Cambridge
There are plenty of available apartments in the neighborhoods surrounding the Law School. They are on the pricey side, but better than the dorms at the Gropius complex.

Langdell Library
The Law School library is the largest law library in the world, with over 1.5 million volumes. Extensive renovations are planned for the 1996–97 academic year.

Alumni Association[1]

The list of graduates reads like *Who's Who*. Bruce Babbitt '65, Secretary of the Interior, former Governor of Arizona; Janet Reno '63, U.S. Attorney General; Deval Patrick '83, Assistant Attorney General for Civil Rights; Dr. William J. Bennett '71, former U.S. Secretary of Education; current U.S. Supreme Court Justices Stephen G. Bryer '64, Ruth Bader Ginsberg 1956–'58,[2] David H. Souter '66, Antonin Scalia '60, and Anthony M. Kennedy '61; former Supreme Court Justices Harry A. Blackmun '32, Lewis F. Powell, Jr. '32 and William J. Brennan, Jr. '31; U.S. Senators John H. Chafee '50 (R-RI), Carl Levin '59 (D-MI), Russ Feingold '79 (D-WI), Bob Graham '62 (D-FL), James Jeffords '62 (R-VT), Spencer Abraham '78 (R-MI), Ted Stevens '50 (R-AR), Paul Sarbanes '60 (D-MD), William Roth '49 (R-DE), and Larry Pressler '71 (R-SD); Congressmen Christopher Cox '76 (R-CA), Barney Frank '77 (D-MA), William J. Jefferson '72 (D-LA), Charles Schumer '74 (D-NY), Sander M. Levin '57 (D-MI), and Patricia Schroeder '64 (D-CO); Professor Archibald Cox '37, former U.S. Solicitor General and Watergate special prosecutor; William Weld '70, Governor of Massachusetts; Bruce Sundlun '48, Governor of Rhode Island; Elizabeth Hanford Dole '65, former U.S. Secretary of Labor and U.S. Secretary of Transportation; Ray Mabus, Jr. '75, former Governor of Mississippi; Henry A. Kissinger '55, former Secretary of State; Michael Dukakis '60, former Governor of Massachusetts, 1988 Democratic nominee for President; Kurt Schmoke '76, Mayor of Baltimore; Xavier Suarez '75, Mayor of Miami; Michael H. Brown '88, founder of City Year; Ralph Nader '58, public advocate; Randall Robinson '70, founder of TransAfrica; Robert W. Bennett '65, Dean of Northwestern University School of Law; Paul A. Brest '65, Dean of Stanford Law School; Colin S. Diver '68, Dean of University of Pennsylvania Law School; John R. Kramer '62, Dean of Tulane University School of Law; John Sexton '78, Dean of NYU Law School; Christopher F. Edley, Sr. '00, former President and CEO of United Negro College Fund; James O. Freedman '60,

---

[1]Unofficial list of famous Law School graduates provided by Mr. Randy W. Lakeman, Director of Development Research, Baker House, Harvard Law School.

[2]Attended Harvard Law School for two years. Member of the *Harvard Law Review*. Transferred to Columbia Law School for third year to be with husband. Received Columbia's J.D.

President of Dartmouth College; Robert H. Edwards '61, President of Bowdoin College; Timothy J. Sullivan '69, President of College of William and Mary; Daniel P. Davidson '52, Chairman and CEO of U.S. Trust Company; Domenico DeSole '72, President and CEO of Gucci America; Doug Geoga '80, President of Hyatt Hotels Corporation; Leonard H. Goldson '30, Chairman of Capital Cities/ABC; Gerald Grinstein '57, Chairman, CEO and President of Burlington Northern Corp.; Jim Koch '78, founder of Boston Beer Company (Samuel Adams Beer); John F. McGillicuddy '55, Chairman and CEO of Chemical Bank; John D. Ong '57, Chairman of B. F. Goodrich Company; David S. Paresky '63, CEO and President of Thomas Cook Travel; David Rockefeller, Jr. '66; Michael Roach, Founder of America West Airlines; Herbert B. Shapiro '63, President of Serta Mattress Company; Bruce Slovin '60, President of Revlon Group; Harold R. Somerset '67, CEO and President of C&H Sugar Company; Laurence A. Tisch '49, Chairman, CEO, and President of CBS, Inc.; Harold M. Williams '49, President and CEO of J. Paul Getty Trust; Robert F. Erburu '55, Chairman of Times Mirror Company; Leland H. Faust '71, founder of Career Sports International (which manages the investment portfolios of more than 100 sports stars); Bertram H. Fields '52, "most feared lawyer in Hollywood" whose clients include Michael Jackson, Dustin Hoffman, David Geffen, and Warren Beatty; Michael E. Kinsley '77, Editor of *The New Republic* and co-host of CNN's "Crossfire"; Anthony Lewis '57, columnist for the *New York Times*, Pulitzer Prize winner for national correspondence; Douglas I. McHenry '77, film producer for *New Jack City*, *House Party 2*, and director of *Jason's Lyric*; Debora M. de Hoyos '78, first female managing partner in a major U.S. law firm; Ruth E. Fitch '83, first African-American woman to be named partner in a large law firm; Ronald J. Bass '67, Academy Award winning screenwriter of *Rain Man*, screenwriter of *Sleeping with the Enemy*, and co-writer of the film *The Joy Luck Club*; Scott Turow '78, author of *One L*, *Presumed Innocent*, and *The Burden of Proof*; Glenn A. Padnick '73, partner of Castle Rock Entertainment, producers of the television show *Seinfeld*, and films such as *A Few Good Men*, *Misery*, and *When Harry Met Sally*; William A. Rusher '48, publisher of the *National Review*; and Hershel Shanks '56, actively trying to free the Dead Sea Scrolls from the control of a small group of scholars and make them available to all researchers and the public.

Location

Cambridge is a wonderful small city, clean, urban, and liberal. It is right across the Charles River from Boston. The entire metropolitan area is fully accessible by subway. The major sections of downtown Boston are within walking distance. Harvard Law School is less than four hours by car from New York City. HLS is located less than two hours from vacation and recreational spots in Vermont, New Hampshire, and Maine.

Weather

Cambridge gets all four seasons. The fall and spring seasons are especially beautiful. Despite the harsh winters, many students manage to enjoy the snow and ice by playing snow football in the Cambridge Commons on Sundays, ice skating in the Boston Commons on Saturday afternoons, skiing in Vermont or western Massachusetts, or starting snow fights between classes.

Negatives of Harvard Law School

Class Size

Because of the high student to faculty ratio, many find the Law School to be impersonal and cold. The large classroom environment, some argue, detracts from true intellectual legal discourse that is more apparent at Yale, Chicago, and Stanford law schools.

Student Body

"Everyone graduated from Harvard College or Princeton!" Despite the racial and ethnic diversity of Harvard Law School, the school tends to be overrepresented by graduates of Ivy League schools, the Little Three, Stanford, Duke, Wellesley, and a few large selective state universities such as the University of Michigan, Rutgers, the University of Virginia, and the University of North Carolina. There needs to be more outreach to women's colleges, other state universities, and historically African-American colleges and universities.

Homogeneous Faculty

The Law School's faculty also lags behind other top law schools in terms of racial and gender diversity. No woman of color, no Asian American, no Hispanic, no openly gay person, no physically challenged person has ever been a member of HLS' core faculty. Each year in the spring, student members of the Coalition for Civil Rights organizes "Strike Day," a day-long protest to call attention to the lack of faculty diversity at HLS. In past years, people typically boycotted classes on "Strike Day." More recently, however, students have been committed to the issue of diversity without skipping classes.

Faculty Inaccessibility

Members of the faculty will not hold your hand. Most are very busy; students are often secondary. Teaching is not a major priority.

Tuition Cost

Many students graduate with $90,000 of debt from their law school experience. Harvard Law School needs to be more generous with its grant money. LIPP is lip service.

HLS Student Interaction with Other Schools

While many take advantage of the activities at other institutions within the Boston area, most students restrict themselves to the Law School campus. Students on the whole are not assertive.

Arrogance

With a strong reputation comes arrogance. Some students are definitely narrow-minded in their outlook on other quality law schools and graduates of those schools.

Weather

Summers in Cambridge are ideal: 80 degree days, low humidity, cool nights. Unfortunately, the Law School is closed then. Winters in Cambridge are too cold and too long for most. If weather is important to you, try Stanford.

Location

New England. See "Weather."

Nonresponsive Administration

The administration at Harvard rarely concerns itself with student sentiment and student concern.

Poor Student Services
See "Nonresponsive Administration."

Low Quality of Student Life
See "Nonresponsive Administration."

Grading
Intellectual growth of students can be stunted at HLS. There is no ongoing dialogue between professor and student, no exchange of ideas on a daily basis. Good thinking is devalued in numerous ways. In Law School, you do not write papers to be graded or commented on by professors. Instead, there is one exam for each class at the end of the semester (probably an unfair system for the amount of material students must cover), geared toward quick, spur of the moment responses. Fast thinking is valued more than good thinking.

Grading also tends to be random. Students feel that they can either work hard or blow off the semester and still get the same grade.

Placement
Since it is so easy to get a job as a Harvard Law School graduate, many students do not think about what they are doing with their lives before accepting a law firm position. They merely drop off their résumé at the career placement center and wait for the big firms to come knocking at their door. If students had to expend more energy seeking out employers, not so many would get on the corporate fast track.

Campus Housing
The Gropius complex at the Law School is reminiscent of 1960s architecture, with dated buildings and small cramped rooms. If you cannot live on campus in Hastings or North Hall, live off campus in an apartment.

Campus Food
Although the food is not bad during the first month of your first year, it gets old very quickly.

The Gymnasium
The gym is a dump. Technically owned by the University, it is used mainly by the law students. Use other Harvard athletic facilities or get a membership at Bally's.

Poor Facilities Compared to Other Harvard Schools
Law students are envious of the Business School facilities.

Lack of Community
HLS is sometimes divisive along the lines of race and interests. But this happens at every school, right?

3
The Application Process

The Law School application process can be very difficult and time-consuming. In this chapter, I describe aspects of the application process, discuss application strategies, and suggest time management techniques. I also attempt to give commonsense advice so that you can avoid typical applicant mistakes.

Overview

The Harvard Law School Admissions Committee recommends that you submit your application as soon as possible after October 15 of a given admissions cycle. Applications will be considered roughly in the order received. Each application is guaranteed a full reading if submitted by the February 1 deadline. Although no applications will be considered before early December, and only a few applicants will receive a decision before January, it is still in your best interest to beat the crowd of applicants. After all, Harvard Law School, which has "rolling admissions," receives a third of its applications on the February 1 deadline after most of the class has been filled! Do you think your chances of admission are good if your application arrives so late with so many others for so few spots?

To get a jump on the application process, a potential applicant should set up a schedule which will enable him or her to have a complete application by mid-November of a given admissions cycle. If you plan to attend Harvard Law School directly after college, take the LSAT at the end of your junior year; work on your personal statement; call Harvard Law School for an application during the summer after you complete the LSAT; at the beginning of the senior year, visit the professors who will be writing your letters of recommendation, inform them of Harvard's rolling admissions policy and tell them that you would like to have their recommendations by early November; fill out the application in the fall; and ask the college's dean or administrative officer for the College Certification letter as soon as possible your senior year. If you stay on this timetable, you will hear from Harvard by mid-January at the latest.

The Law School Admission Test (LSAT)

The LSAT is a half-day standardized test required for admission to Harvard Law School. It consists of five 35-minute sections of multiple-choice questions. Four of the five sections are scored. These sections include one analytical reasoning section, one reading comprehension section, and two logical reasoning sections. The fifth section is an experimental one used to pretest new test items and forms. A 30-minute writing sample is administered at the end of the test. The score scale for the LSAT is 120 to 180, with 120 being the lowest possible score and 180 being the highest.

Taking the LSAT should be your first affirmative step in the admissions process. It is best to take the LSAT at the end of your junior year in college or at the beginning of your senior year, either the June or October administrations. LSAT scores for successfully admitted students in the past years have ranged from below 154 to a perfect score of 180, but the better the score the better your chances. Take an LSAT prep course if you have the time and money or buy an LSAT prep book and study for at least a month before the test.

Do not let a less-than-stellar LSAT score discourage you from applying to HLS. The LSAT score is only one of a number of criteria at which the Admissions Committee will look.

You should register with the Law School Data Assembly Service (LSDAS) at the same time you register for the LSAT.[1] LSDAS prepares a report containing much of the information Harvard Law School will need to make a decision on your application: an undergraduate academic summary; copies of all undergraduate, graduate, and law school/professional school transcripts; and LSAT scores and writing sample copies.

The LSAT registration fee is $78. Late registration fee is an additional $47. LSDAS subscription fee is $79 for twelve months of service, including reporting to one law school. Additional LSDAS law school reports are $7 each when ordered at initial registration. Additional LSDAS law school reports are $10 each when ordered after you subscribe to LSDAS initially. You may request a fee waiver through Law Services or Harvard Law School. The basic criterion for granting a waiver is inability to pay for the service. Your inability to pay will be validated by the LSAC Fee Waiver Application Form, supported by federal income tax forms and other documents requested by Law Services or Harvard Law School.

The Application

After you get the LSAT and LSDAS out of the way, it is time to concentrate on the application. You can request an application from Harvard Law School beginning mid-August through January of each year by calling (617) 495-3109 or (617) 495-3179. You can also write directly to the Admissions Committee for an application: Harvard Law School, Admissions Office, Pound Hall 300, Cambridge, Massachusetts 02138. You should probably allow two weeks for delivery.

The application that you receive from Harvard will contain a

---

[1]Both the Law School Admission Test (LSAT) and Law School Data Assembly Service (LSDAS) are services provided by the Law School Admissions Council. The Law School Admissions Council (LSAC or Law Services) is a nonprofit corporation whose members are 192 law schools in the United States and Canada. It was founded in 1947 to coordinate, facilitate, and enhance the law school admissions process.

brief introduction to the Law School; an explanation of the J.D. curriculum; a list and description of student organizations; information regarding concurrent degree programs, public interest law, housing, facilities for the disabled, and smoking policy; the admissions policy; and, most importantly, the application materials.

The application materials are used by the Admissions Committee to help evaluate your qualifications for acceptance. Materials for you to complete include: (1) the application form, (2) your personal statement, (3) cards and labels, (4) the appropriate application fee, (5) a college certification, and (6) two recommendations.

The Application Form

The application form should be filled out completely. Give as much information as possible in the space provided. If more space is needed, feel free to attach additional pages. Answer all questions and sign the form. Typewritten answers are best for neatness, but the Committee does understand that typewriters are becoming technologically extinct, i.e., hard to find.

The application form requires routine information: your full name;[2] social security number; date of birth; citizenship; present mailing address; permanent mailing address; high school name, location, and year of graduation; list of colleges, universities, graduate and professional schools attended on a full-time basis; a list and brief description of non-academic activities that have been important to you; list of employment positions held and hours worked during your undergraduate academic years; list of full-time employment, including summer employment; list of scholastic or academic honors including scholarships, fellowships, prizes, honor societies, etc.; list of dates you have taken or will take the LSAT; date(s) registered with LSDAS; names of the two people submitting recommendations for you; name of school(s) submitting college certification; and your race, which is optional.

In addition, you will be asked to answer yes or no to the following questions:

---

[2]Be sure to use exactly the same name on all application, LSDAS, and GAPSFAS (Graduate and Professional School of Financial Aid Service) materials.

Has your academic career been interrupted for one
or more terms?

In an academic setting, have you been subject to
disciplinary sanctions, or are charges
pending?

Have you ever been expelled, suspended, placed
on probation, or given an academic warning?

Have you ever been convicted of a felony?

Have you ever been convicted of a misdemeanor
(except drunkenness, simple assault,
speeding, minor traffic violations, affray or
disturbing the peace) within the last five
years?

Are any charges pending which, if you were to be
convicted, would require your answer to
either of the two previous questions to be
yes?

Are you currently deferring enrollment at a law
school that requires a commitment not to
apply elsewhere?

Have you ever attended a law school?

If any answer to the above questions is yes, additional details
must be provided on a separate sheet.

The application form is straightforward, but it is nevertheless
important to pay attention to each question and answer it completely.
Grammatical errors and typos are not ignored by the committee. I
recommend supplementing the application form with an up-to-date
copy of your résumé.

Your Personal Statement

The personal statement is your opportunity to present yourself to
the Admissions Committee, highlighting your background, experiences, and ideas. According to the Committee, "the personal
statement can be an opportunity to illuminate your intellectual
background and interests." This may be accomplished by writing
about a course, academic project, book, research assistantship,

artistic endeavor, or cultural experience that has been important to you. The personal statement can also be used to clarify or elaborate on the information that you provided on the application form.

Chapter 6 of this book is composed of numerous personal statements that were submitted to the Law School in recent years by applicants who were accepted and matriculated at Harvard Law School. As you will notice by reading many of those statements, each one gives the reader a sense of the person as a potential student and graduate of Harvard Law School. Those statements share a commonality in candidness and thoughtfulness about past accomplishments and personal background.

Regardless of the content, the personal statement should be limited to two pages, typed and double-spaced. Your name and signature should be placed on the statement.

Cards and Labels

It is important for you to complete the cards and labels that will be enclosed with your application materials. Complete the acknowledgment cards and provide postage. The Admissions Committee will then acknowledge receipt of your application when it arrives at the Law School. After your LSDAS report arrives at Harvard and is matched with your file, the Committee will notify you with one of the cards if any material requested has not been received. Also, the Committee will use one of the cards to tell you that your application has been completed and submitted to the Admissions Committee.

Once a decision has been reached regarding your application, the address labels that you have completed will be used to inform you of their decision. Other labels will be used to send additional information to you at a later date if you are fortunate enough to be accepted, wait-listed, or placed in the "hold" category.

Application Fee

Your application will not be considered without the appropriate application fee. If your application is postmarked before December 1, the $50.00 early fee is required. If your application is postmarked between December 2 and February 1, the $65.00 standard fee is required. All applications that are postmarked after the February 1 deadline must be accompanied with the $75.00 late fee. The application process is expensive for applicants and expensive for Harvard Law School. Therefore, the application fee structure, according to the Committee, is intended to provide incentives to applicants to apply early, and reflects the variability in the real cost of processing applications.

If you receive (or received) substantial financial aid as an undergraduate, you may be eligible for an application fee waiver. Each year, 400 to 500 economically disadvantaged applicants are granted a fee waiver by the Admissions Committee. To determine your eligibility, contact your undergraduate financial aid officer or college dean and ask them to provide Harvard Law School with your financial aid transcript.

College Certification

The college certification is a fairly simple form required from each academic institution that has granted or is expected to grant you a degree and from any institution at which you are currently enrolled. The first portion of the form must be completed by you, the applicant, with basic information such as your name, address, college, degree received or to be obtained, and date/expected date of degree. You are also required to either waive or retain your right of access to this certification. The form must be dated and signed by you.

Once you have completed your portion of the Harvard Law School College Certification, take (or mail) the form and envelope to the current dean or administrative officer at each educational institution that has awarded or is expected to award you a degree. You can photocopy the form if you will have received more than one degree.

Your institution(s) will provide the following information about you: degree you are seeking or have obtained, date awarded or expected, your cumulative GPA, your rank, and the size of your class. In addition, the following questions about you will be answered:

>Has the applicant been subject to any disciplinary actions?
>
>Are any disciplinary actions pending?
>
>Has the applicant been expelled, suspended, placed on probation, required to withdraw, or given an academic warning?

If the answer is yes to any of the questions above, the dean or current administrative officer will be asked to explain further. Once the certification has been completed, the dean or administrative officer of your school(s) should place the form in the envelope provided by you, seal and sign the back flap of the envelope, and then return the envelope to you. This form will be submitted unopened by you with the rest of your application materials.

The certification is commonly referred to on many campuses as "the Dean's Letter." The purpose of this form is not to request a recommendation. Rather, the certification is an official statement from your educational institution(s) that you are a student in good standing.

Any dean or pre-law advisor of your school can fill out this form. If you know an administrative officer personally, it is to your advantage to ask him or her to complete this form for you. This will give that same administrator the opportunity to write an additional letter of recommendation for you and to enclose such letter in the certification envelope. You should give your educational institution(s) a couple of weeks to one month response time in filling out this form.

Two Recommendations

Your application will not be categorized as "complete" until you submit two letters of recommendation on your behalf. Although more than two recommendations can be submitted with your application materials, the admissions committee strongly encourages applicants to limit the number of recommendations to two unless there are extenuating circumstances.

You should ask two people who know you and your academic work well to write your recommendations. Ask a professor who has advised you or hired you as a research assistant. You may also consider asking your favorite professor to write for you regardless of your performance in his or her class; after all, it is not necessary to have earned an A in a class before approaching the professor for a recommendation, but it helps! Avoid asking the "big name" professor who barely knows you and cannot remember that you were a student in his or her class.

Recommendations should be asked for at least two months before you plan to mail your completed application to Harvard Law School. If you are applying during your senior year, tell professors in September of your senior year, or tell them your junior year before you leave for the summer that you are applying to law school and would greatly appreciate a recommendation.

If you have taken time off before applying to Harvard, consider having an employer or immediate supervisor write a letter of recommendation. If you have worked indirectly for someone famous or powerful—like the President, a senator, or a CEO—but have not interacted with that person very much, it is not to your advantage to secure a recommendation from him or her. Ask someone who knows you and your work well. Mediocre and impersonal recommendations from famous people will not help your admission chances at Harvard Law School.

Once you have selected your recommenders, you must complete the first part of the Harvard Law School Recommendation forms. The following information will be required from you: your name, social security number, name of recommender, name of undergraduate college, your signature, and date. You will also be required to either waive or retain your right of access to the recommendation.[3]

When the top portion of each form has been completed, deliver the forms and envelopes to the recommenders. Ask each recommender to enclose the recommendation letter, seal the envelope, sign

---

[3]Federal legislation provides you with a right of access to the recommendation which may be waived, but neither Harvard Law School nor any person can require you to waive this right. HLS does not care whether you waive your right or not. Most applicants, however, waive their rights to view the recommendations at a later date so that the individual recommenders will feel that they can be more candid about the applicant. The choice is yours.

across the seal, and return it to you when completed. Do not open the envelopes or break the seal. Submit the envelopes with your application materials. Remember to send your recommenders thank-you cards (or expensive gifts!) after they have completed their recommendation for you.

Mailing Your Application

Send all your application materials together if possible. This includes the (1) application form, (2) your personal statement, (3) cards and labels, (4) the appropriate application fee, (5) a college certification, and (6) two recommendations. Keeping the materials together greatly accelerates the processing of your application and increases the Committee's ability to issue a rapid response. If it is impossible to send all of your materials together, send as many parts of your application as possible at the same time.

   For peace of mind, it is perfectly acceptable to send your application by registered or certified mail. It is perfectly unacceptable, however, to request an interview with the Admissions Committee (interviews are never given!) or to harass Committee staff for a quick admissions decision, by telephone or in person.

4

How Admission Decisions Are Made at Harvard Law School

The process of selecting each year a class of 550 students from an applicant pool of over 8,000 can be a grueling undertaking. In this chapter, I go "behind the scenes" to examine how Admissions Committee decisions are made during each admissions cycle at Harvard Law School. Based on the information ascertained through interviews with HLS Dean of Admissions Joyce Curll, I disclose each step of the admissions process, from the application's arrival at the Law School to the final decision-making steps.

The Committee begins considering complete applications in early December. Because of the volume of applications, it takes several weeks for a completed application to be considered. Applications submitted prior to January usually receive a decision four to eight weeks after submission. Decisions on applications submitted within three weeks of the February 1 deadline may take longer than eight weeks from the date of completion.

Once your application has been considered, you will receive a prompt decision: admit, wait-list, hold, or deny. Admitted students have until April 15 to accept Harvard's offer. Wait-listed applicants may not know the final result of their application until the end of the summer. Those in the hold category are students who are being strongly considered for admission, but more comparison is needed between the applicant and the rest of the applicant pool. A student in the hold category can receive an admit, deny, or wait-list letter at any time during the process.

1. Receipt of Application/Request for LSDAS Report

Once your application materials are received by the Harvard Law School admissions office, an admissions office staff member will access a summary of your Law School Data Assembly Service (LSDAS) Law School Report from Law Services. This communication is facilitated by business computers and modems. In a matter of seconds, your LSDAS profile summary appears on the computer screen in the admissions office and is then down-loaded by staff. The profile summary includes your name, GPA, LSAT score, educational institutions, etc. Unfortunately, such a profile summary does not include a duplicate of your academic transcript(s) which are used by Harvard to analyze and examine the trend in your grades, the range of your grades, and the classes in which your grades were received. Since it is important for the Committee to evaluate your actual transcript, the office puts in a request to Law Services for a printed copy of your full LSDAS Law School Report. It takes about one week for the law school report to arrive at Harvard when it is requested early in the admissions process (November and December). Later in the process (January, February, and March) when lots of law schools are requesting reports, it may take up to three weeks for LSDAS to honor Harvard's requests.

2. Assemble File/Assign Ranking

Once your full LSDAS law school report has been received by the Admissions Committee, a staff member will assemble your complete application in packet-style. The packet will be assembled in the following manner:

a. Summary Sheet

The top cover sheet of your packet is called a summary sheet. The summary sheet, which is produced by Harvard for each applicant, contains your demographic information such as name, age, race, addresses, educational institutions, hometown, year by year analysis of grades, LSAT score, social security number, etc. The summary sheet also has space reserved for comments from the readers of your application.

b. LSDAS Report

The full LSDAS Law School Report includes an undergraduate academic summary; copies of all undergraduate, graduate, and law-school or professional-school transcripts; and LSAT scores and writing sample copies.[1] Essentially, the LSDAS Law School Report is the vehicle through which every law school applicant's undergraduate record is evaluated, then centralized and standardized under one uniform system. The conversion of grades under one uniform system allows law schools such as Harvard to better compare applicants' grades earned at any undergraduate school. Grades are converted to a standard 4.0 system. Law Services makes no attempt to access the value of grades earned at different colleges. Harvard Law School admissions committee members understand that a particular grade earned at one college may not have the same meaning as the identical grade at another. In all cases, a copy of your transcript accompanies the LSDAS law school report. Interpretation of your grade-point average is left to Law School admissions personnel.

c. Application Form

This includes routine information such as your full name, social security number, date of birth, citizenship, mailing addresses, list of extracurricular activities, list of educational institutions attended, employment history, academic honors, and responses to the character questions.

---

[1]Law School Admissions Council, LSAT/LSDAS *Registration and Information Book 1995–96* (Newtown, PA, 1995) p. 22.

d. Personal Statement
Limit two pages.

e. Letters of Recommendation
At least two required.

f. College Certification.

g. Any Additional Information.
Based on your grade point average, LSAT score, and undergraduate institution,[2] your newly assembled file will be assigned some index number.[3] The higher the index number, the greater your chances for admission. The lower the index number, the lower your chances for admission. Your application will be given to a member of the Admissions Committee staff based on its index number. The higher indexed applications are sent directly to Dean for Admissions Joyce Curll for her reading. Lower ranked applications are sent to her assistants, and lately funneled to Dean Curll.

3. Initial Readings (Highly Ranked Applications)

Highly ranked applications are read first by Dean Joyce Curll. After her first reading, she rates the application in one of the following seven ways: sure admit, likely admit, possible admit, neutral, likely denial, probable denial, or will deny.[4] Each application in this strong pool is then sent to at least one faculty member of the Admissions Committee.[5]

---

[2]Undergraduate institutions are ranked by the HLS Admissions Committee on the basis of the average LSAT score of its students.

[3]Much like the LSAT, the index number ranges from 120 to 180. Your academic record, however, is given twice the weight of your LSAT score.

[4]About two-thirds of all applications received are initially given the rating of "possible admit" or better.

[5]The Admissions Committee is composed of four tenured Harvard Law School faculty members plus Dean of Admissions Joyce Curll. Mr. Todd Morton, the Assistant Dean for Admissions, serves the Committee in somewhat of an *ex officio* capacity.

The faculty component of the Admissions Committee receives 2,000 applications a year, about a quarter of the total applications received by the Admissions Committee staff each year. Each faculty member of the Committee reads about 600 to 800 applications each year. Dean Joyce Curll personally reads or skims virtually every application.

4. Decisions on Highly Ranked Applications

If a faculty member of the Admissions Committee receives your application from Dean Curll (and her staff) and it has been rated as "sure admit" or "likely admit," you will be automatically admitted if the Admissions Committee faculty member agrees. This means that an acceptance letter will be mailed to you by the school when you get a strong rating from Dean Curll and a strong second by one faculty member on the Committee. If Dean Curll rates your application as "possible admit" or "neutral," it will take at least two faculty members of the Committee to strongly back your application before you can be accepted.

5. Initial Readings (Lower-Ranked Applications)

Lower-ranked applications go directly to other staff members in the Admissions Office.[6] Their job is to look beyond the raw numbers to find talented and qualified students who may have otherwise been overlooked. If your application is ranked lower and it catches the eye of one of the staffers, it will be assigned a rating of "sure admit," "likely admit," or "possible admit" and then passed on to Dean Curll.

---

[6]Lower-ranked applications usually are read first by Assistant Dean Todd Morton, Director of Financial Aid Sally Donahue, or an experienced Admissions Committee staff reader.

6. Decisions on Lower-Ranked Applications

If Dean Curll assigns a similar rating of "sure admit," "likely admit," or "possible admit" to your application, your file goes to a faculty member or members of the Committee for analysis. If your application has been rated as "sure admit" or "likely admit," you will automatically be admitted if a faculty member of the Admissions Committee agrees. If your application is sent to the faculty members of the Committee with a rating of "possible admit," it will take at least two Committee members to strongly back your application before you can be accepted.

Most applications in the lower-ranked pile receive ratings along the lines of "likely denial," "probable denial," and "will deny." Therefore, lower-rated applications usually die among Dean Curll and her staffers, never actually reaching the faculty members of the Admissions Committee.

The faculty members who serve on the Admissions Committee do so by invitation from the Dean of the Law School. Between December and April, each faculty member of the Committee reads about ten applications a day. In the end, 800 applicants will be accepted. The yield will be around 550.

Interviews are not part of the admissions process. Harassing the Admissions Office staff for an admissions decision, by telephone or in person, can only hurt your chances for admission. If for some reason you absolutely have to communicate with the Admissions Office staff during the application process, write to them at Harvard Law School, 1563 Massachusetts Avenue, Cambridge, MA 02138. The office does not accept faxes.

7. Financial Aid

Financial aid files are reviewed only after you have been admitted to Harvard Law School, to ensure that an application for financial aid will in no way affect a decision for admission.

In order to receive a financial aid award decision in time to meet admission-deposit deadlines, you need to file both your Free

Federal Form and your College Scholarship Service financial aid form by mid-February. You can obtain a federal form through your college financial aid office, or by calling the United States Department of Education at 1-800-4FEDAID. Financial aid forms can be ordered by calling 1-609-771-7725. You can also obtain those forms in your college or university financial aid office.

5

Advice from Fifty Students Who Successfully Survived the Admissions Process

Profile

Name: Raquel E. Aldana
Harvard Law School class: 1997
Undergraduate institution: Arizona State University
Undergraduate GPA listed by category—3.75+, 3.50–3.74,
3.25–3.49, 3.00–3.24, below 3.00: 3.75+
Graduate institution and GPA, if applicable: N/A
LSAT Score listed by percentile—99–95, 94–90, 89–85, 84–80,
79–75, 74–70, 69–65, below 64: 84–80
Hometown and high school: Phoenix, AZ; South Mountain
High School
Types of recommenders, i.e., professors or employers: Both
professors and employers
Race, sex, and class: Central American/Latina; female; lower
Major undergraduate activities: English tutor and teacher, resident
assistant, and peer advisor in a program for minority students for
four years; LSAT and other entrance-exam instructor, English and
Spanish tutor, and peer advisor for the academic resource center at
the university; Latino organizations: Spanish Club, MECha, and

Hispanic Leadership Project; Intern for an organization working with documenting INS abuse for six months

Major scholastic or academic honors: Graduated *summa cum laude*; member of the Phi Kappa Phi and recipient of their fellowship

Work experience (including summer) prior to HLS: Mentor and counselor for at-risk junior-high-school students for six months; Bilingual instructor for a Central-American and Mexican community organization of women; Spanish teacher to professional adults doing business in Latin America; Law library clerk in major law firm in Phoenix.

Parents' occupations: Father is a security guard and my mother works as a distributor of advertisements.

Legacy factor: N/A

Questionnaire

1. When and why did you apply to Harvard Law School? Was your application completed early, late, or in the middle of the rolling admissions process?

I applied to Harvard simply to follow the encouragement of friends who thought I had a good chance of being accepted. I had no inclinations to coming here. In fact, once I did receive my acceptance, I struggled with my ultimate decision to come here. There was a lot of fear that I would find myself surrounded by elitists who more than likely were not sympathetic to the issues that touched my heart. I have been proven both right and wrong.

I completed the process early, I think before December.

2. How would you describe the undergraduate institution that you attended? Does it have a strong reputation and a solid track record of sending lots of its graduates to Harvard Law School?

Definitely not. That is, I knew of no one from Arizona State who had come to Harvard. I received little guidance in that regard from my institution. In fact, my decision to apply was independent of any encouragement from my professors and/or peers at the school.

Arizona State does not have a strong academic reputation, though I would argue that for students who are interested in learning, the opportunities are there.

3. Did you think, prior to being accepted, that you had a decent chance of being admitted to Harvard Law School?

Not really. My acceptance came somewhat as a surprise. Not that I felt unqualified. In fact, I considered myself a strong candidate more because of me as a person than my academic record alone, though [it was] exceptional in my own community.

I was scared rather that my personal statement would not be what Harvard, with its reputation for corporate law, would welcome. I wasn't sure how receptive Harvard would be to non-mainstream accomplishments.

4. Did you take any time off prior to applying or matriculating at HLS? If so, why did you take time off and what did you do?

Yes, I took a semester off. I worked three jobs in the community as a bilingual instructor, Spanish teacher, and counselor to young kids at risk of dropping out of school. A lot of what I did was also to render social services to my students and their family members.

5. What were your strongest assets when applying to Harvard Law School? Grades? LSAT score? Extracurriculars? Personal statement? Recommendations? Family connections? Personal background? Work experience?

I think I brought a combination of factors, though I am the first to admit that my academic record alone would not have secured me a place at Harvard. I had quite a bit of community work; my personal story as an immigrant was appealing, and my recommendations quite tear-jerking.

6. What type of courses did you take as an undergraduate to prepare yourself for Harvard Law School?

I double majored in literature, both English and Spanish. In addition, I took lots of history courses. I wanted to do a lot of reading and writing before I got here, but I also wanted to come with a strong sense of my history and culture.

7. What was your LSAT score(s)? How did you prepare for the test? If you took an LSAT prep course, which one, and did it help?

Funniest story. I both took the course and ended up teaching it. I was a much better teacher than a taker of the exam. I ended up performing at about ten points less than I had been averaging on my practice exams. I think I received 157.

8. How long did you spend on your personal statement? What did you write about and how did you decide on the topic? Did anyone help you with your statement? If so, who?

A lot of time. I revised quite a bit and had lots of friends look at it. I decided to just tell my story, as I saw it. Most of my friends always said, however, that it sounded like I wanted to be a social worker and not a law student. Maybe I thought the two were not necessarily exclusive.

I decided to write about my story because I knew not too many people coming to Harvard would share it. I do consider myself unique in my experiences, at least in the sense that I have been singled out by Americans as the immigrant ideal.

9. Who wrote your recommendations for Harvard Law School and how did you choose them? How much notice did you give your recommenders and when were the recommendations completed?

I had two professors and an employer write my recommendations. I chose them because they knew me well and had a strong commitment to help me. I didn't have to give them much. I was lucky in that they knew me personally and liked me a great deal. I only provided them with a form and a self-addressed envelope.

10. What type of extracurricular activities did you participate in during your undergraduate years that you feel were beneficial to your being admitted to Harvard Law School, and why?

Definitely my community involvement. I did not do too much at the school. I didn't run for office. I simply was always a mentor, teacher, and counselor to children, youths, and adults—sharing my life with them and teaching them what I knew, to make sure they also got a piece of the pie.

11. Do you feel that your race, sex, or class played a role in the admissions process? If so, explain.

I would only hope so. I don't say that facetiously. I don't have a problem with admitting to people that being a Central American female immigrant helped me to get here, but only because that experience, weighed against my accomplishments, said a great deal about my commitment, about my work ethic, and my value as an individual who could give lots of herself to society.

It's all about questioning the assumptions. I didn't go to a better undergrad school because I didn't know I could have. So, no regrets nor embarrassment.

12. Do you think that your political ideology played a role in the admissions process? If so, explain.

I kind of felt maybe it would hurt me. But then again Harvard prides itself, if not in the faculty, in the idiosyncracies of its student body. I can't complain about that. Certainly I am most definitely a minority in many regards, including my way of looking at the world, but I am not alone here.

13. *Did you see the Harvard Law School campus prior to applying or being admitted? If so, what arrangements did you make for the visit, what were your initial impressions, and have your impressions changed very much? If you didn't visit the campus prior to being accepted, why not?*

Yes. Very few. I actually mostly interacted with people from the Kennedy School. I had very little contact with Harvard law students. A lot of it had to do with fearing that if I didn't like anyone I met I would be deterred too quickly from coming. So I went to classes I thought I would enjoy, and liked what I saw. Asked a few questions of a few minority students and felt OK, not thrilled, about being able to be here.

14. *When did you receive your letter of acceptance from the Dean of Admissions and what were you doing?*

I was working as a counselor when I received it. I was debating between Boalt and University of Chicago Law School. I'm afraid the name of Harvard carries a lot of weight, and I came a little scared and reluctant.

15. *How are you paying for Harvard Law School? Parents? Loans? Savings? Work?*

I had a fellowship this year for $7,000. I also received a school grant of about $5,000. The rest is all loans.

16. *What do you plan to do in the immediate years following Law School graduation? What are your long-term career goals?*

Probably clerk for a judge or work for the Department of Justice. I'm not sure what I will be doing long-term, but I want to be in a good position with resources and influence to affect some changes in low-income communities and third-world countries.

Profile

Name Withheld
Harvard Law School class: 1995
Undergraduate institution: Rutgers

Undergraduate GPA listed by category—3.75+, 3.50–3.74, 3.25–3.49, 3.00–3.24, below 3.00: 3.75+

Graduate institution and GPA, if applicable: N/A

LSAT Score listed by percentile—99–95, 94–90, 89–85, 84–80, 79–75, 74–70, 69–65, below 64: 94–90

Hometown and high school: Edison, NJ; Edison High School

Types of recommenders, i.e., professors or employers: One professor; one internship supervisor

Race, sex, and class: White, female, middle

Major undergraduate activities: Founder and president of women's social/community group; Hillel; student at local ballet school; various part-time jobs

Major scholastic or academic honors: College honors program/full scholarship; Phi Beta Kappa, Junior Year inductee; Foreign language honor society and proficiency awards; misc. departmental awards for academic merit; college fellowship for graduating senior bound for law school

Work experience (including summer) prior to HLS: Jack-of-all-trades: Production/research assistant and policy intern at university television station (semester internship for credit, leading to paid summer position); Substitute teacher for public school system; Legal secretary/receptionist; Lifeguard/swim teacher; Creative dramatics instructor at local YWCA; Dental assistant/receptionist.

Parents' occupations: Father—Professor of mathematics, Kean College of N.J., Mother—Elementary school art teacher

Legacy factor: N/A

Questionnaire

1. When and why did you apply to Harvard Law School? Was your application completed early, late, or in the middle of the rolling admissions process?

I applied to HLS because my college boyfriend made me. I never thought I would get in, did not want to leave New York, and did not want to waste time doing a second essay. (I think I had already been accepted to Columbia at the time, which was my first choice.) But my boyfriend at the time had high expectations and really pushed me. It was truly an afterthought, so the application came in very late: I think in February (I remember having to FedEx™ it to make a deadline).

2. How would you describe the undergraduate institution that you

attended? Does it have a strong reputation and a solid track record of sending lots of its graduates to Harvard Law School?

I went to a "good state school." Rutgers gets a small handful into HLS each year, probably two to five students. I think there are four of us in the class of '95.

3. Did you think, prior to being accepted, that you had a decent chance of being admitted to Harvard Law School?

As I explained in question 1, I did not think I had any chance of getting in and almost didn't bother applying.

4. Did you take any time off prior to applying or matriculating at HLS? If so, why did you take time off and what did you do?

No.

5. What were your strongest assets when applying to Harvard Law School? Grades? LSAT score? Extracurriculars? Personal statement? Recommendations? Family connections? Personal background? Work experience?

Grades: I had like a 3.99.

Extracurrics: I started and ran my own student organization.

Writing: I think my essays helped a lot.

6. What type of courses did you take as an undergraduate to prepare yourself for Harvard Law School?

None intentionally because I never expected to go to law school, but I think a lot of courses wound up helping anyway. I took a ton of English courses, which were great for reading skills. Microeconomics helped a lot. The greatest prep of all I think was, rather surprisingly, a six-student graduate seminar in theater criticism. It was an intensive writing class in which we wrote weekly theater reviews under tight time- and page-constraints. Our work was sharply critiqued and we were forced to edit regularly. It was the best writing training I ever got, something lawyers could generally use a lot more of.

7. What was your LSAT score(s)? How did you prepare for the test? If you took an LSAT prep course, which one, and did it help?

43 (old scale).

I prepped by reading books and taking practice exams; I did not take a course.

8. How long did you spend on your personal statement? What did you

write about and how did you decide on the topic? Did anyone help you with your statement? If so, who?

For my personal statement I wrote about my experience founding a women's organization and, as it turned out, my general philosophy of feminism as well (though I did not really realize what I was saying at the time). Choosing the topic was completely obvious: it was, hands-down, the most important and influential thing in my life at the time. I have zero recollection of how long it took to write. On the other hand, I remember very well that I wrote my second essay in two days flat because I was rushing to meet the application deadline. The topic for that one was already suggested by the application ("world of ideas") and I focused it by taking an original poem I had written and expanding the ideas in it. No one really helped me with either essay, though I shared them with some close friends and got some generally positive feedback.

9. *Who wrote your recommendations for Harvard Law School and how did you choose them? How much notice did you give your recommenders and when were the recommendations completed?*

Both my recommendations were completed long in advance of my application process. The chairman of my department offered to write me one after I had completed a course with him the beginning of my sophomore year, so I figured I might as well get it and put it on file with the university career-services office. Similarly, my other recommender offered to write for me after I had completed a credit-bearing internship under her supervision during my junior year. She actually later became my summer employer and updated the recommendation after I completed that position. Neither were geared toward law school.

10. *What type of extracurricular activities did you participate in during your undergraduate years that you feel were beneficial to your being admitted to Harvard Law School, and why?*

As I mentioned in the question about my personal statement, I feel like my extracurricular experience was probably the one thing that shaped me more than anything else prior to law school, and probably gave me the best preparation for law school I could possibly get. It was also probably a huge factor in my getting admitted. As a sophomore I founded a women's social, community, and cultural organization. The group actually drew a lot of heat from the school administration and the Greek students organizations on campus for a whole lot of complicated reasons, not the least of which was the fact that the group of women I started it with were all Jewish. (We were instantly pegged as discriminatory and exclusionary and a whole hullabaloo ensued—oddly similar to the BALSA issue that hit the fan last year.) The experience gave me an incredible perspective on issues of multiculturalism. Actually, though, I didn't write about that, per se, in my personal statement about the experience, but instead wrote about the related gender implications of founding a women's group, which had been my interest in starting the group to begin with. The organization was a vehicle for exploration of my feminist ideas, which I was just beginning to understand at the time.

11. Do you feel that your race, sex, or class played a role in the admissions process? If so, explain.

No. I think if anything, being a white Jewish middle-class girl from New Jersey could only have hurt me.

12. Do you think that your political ideology played a role in the admissions process? If so, explain.

Yes. Though I wasn't really aware of it at the time, as I mentioned, my personal statement partly reflected a feminist ideology that probably helped me somewhat. Basically, all the stuff I wrote was novel and half-baked to me because I was struggling with it at the time. Now having studied that kind of thing, I see that my ideas fit into one of the standard "molds" of feminism. But I think my essay reflected a genuine search and sensitivity toward feminist issues that probably helped me.

13. Did you see the Harvard Law School campus prior to applying or being admitted? If so, what arrangements did you make for the visit, what were your initial impressions, and have your impressions changed very much? If you didn't visit the campus prior to being accepted, why not?

I had visited Harvard University several times through high school and college. I applied and was admitted to the law school very late, so I didn't have time to make any huge visit once accepted, especially since I'd been here before. I came up for one afternoon, sort of a spontaneous road trip, with no prior arrangements. While I was here I basically did logistics: put down my deposit, picked out a dorm, etc. One thing I do remember though that influenced me was that it was final exam period and at the end of the day I saw a bunch of students congregating outside the Hark. (I think they had all just handed in take-homes and some might have been finished.) They all looked happy and friendly, and I thought that HLS might be a nice place to be.

14. When did you receive your letter of acceptance from the Dean of Admissions and what were you doing?

I got it real late, in May, and it came with the whole info pack, so it was this huge envelope that didn't fit in the mailbox, just sitting on my porch when I came home. I don't remember what I was doing at the time. I think I was toward the end of my final exams, or maybe done with them, and beginning the process of moving out of my apartment. I was pretty shocked, and I had already put down a deposit and made all my arrangements to go to Columbia months before, so I remember thinking instantly that I had a tough decision to make.

15. How are you paying for Harvard Law School? Parents? Loans? Savings? Work?

Loans.

16. What do you plan to do in the immediate years following Law School graduation? What are your long-term career goals?

I am clerking next year; beyond that I don't know. Long-term I think, theoretically I would like to work for a women's rights organization or a D.A.'s office. Definitely litigation. Although lately I've been thinking I should have gone to med school . . .

Profile

Name: Stephanie Barnes
Harvard Law School class: 1997
Undergraduate institution: Tougaloo College
Undergraduate GPA listed by category—3.75+, 3.50–3.74, 3.25–3.49, 3.00–3.24, below 3.00: 3.75+
Graduate institution and GPA, if applicable: N/A
LSAT Score listed by percentile—99–95, 94–90, 89–85, 84–80, 79–75, 74–70, 69–65, below 64: 74–70
Hometown and high school: Greenville, MS; Greenville High School
Types of recommenders, i.e., professors or employers: Professors
Race, sex, and class: African American, female, lower-middle
Major undergraduate activities: Mississippi State University Famous Maroon Band, MSU Majorette Squad, Sigma Tau Delta (English Honor Society), Tougaloo College Readers Group, Student Government Association, and *La Societé Française* (a French Class community service organization)

Major scholastic or academic honors: Dean's List, President's List,
   Phi Kappa Phi, and Senior Poet of the Year
Work experience (including summer) prior to HLS: Sonic's Drive-In,
   1992; Mississippi State University Math Department, 1992; Gayfer's
   Department Store, 1992–93; Structure, 1993–94; Baskin-Robbins,
   1993–94; Cleary, Gottlieb, Steen & Hamilton, summer 1994;
   Greenville High School, summers 1991–93.
Parents' occupations: Mother—Fifth-grade teacher, Father—
   Superintendent
Legacy factor: N/A

Questionnaire

1. When and why did you apply to Harvard Law School? Was your application completed early, late, or in the middle of the rolling admissions process?
   Middle.

2. How would you describe the undergraduate institution that you attended? Does it have a strong reputation and a solid track record of sending lots of its graduates to Harvard Law School?
   Tougaloo is a small, private, historically black college. I was the first student to get accepted to Harvard since 1974.

3. Did you think, prior to being accepted, that you had a decent chance of being admitted to Harvard Law School?
   No.

4. Did you take any time off prior to applying or matriculating at HLS? If so, why did you take time off and what did you do?
   No.

5. What were your strongest assets when applying to Harvard Law School? Grades? LSAT score? Extracurriculars? Personal statement? Recommendations? Family connections? Personal background? Work experience?
   Grades, personal statement, recommendations, and extracurriculars.

6. What type of courses did you take as an undergraduate to prepare yourself for Harvard Law School?
   I took an Introduction to Business Law course, a Pre-Law Seminar, and several analytical courses.

7. *What was your* LSAT *score(s)? How did you prepare for the test? If you took an* LSAT *prep course, which one, and did it help?*

157. I prepared myself for the LSAT by doing practice LSATs during my spare time. The semester I took the LSAT, I was working three jobs.

8. *How long did you spend on your personal statement? What did you write about and how did you decide on the topic? Did anyone help you with your statement? If so, who?*

I spent a good two weeks writing, revising, and developing my personal statement. I got several professors to read and critique it after I had written it.

9. *Who wrote your recommendations for Harvard Law School and how did you choose them? How much notice did you give your recommenders and when were the recommendations completed?*

My English professor, Dr. Horvath, who was also the one who encouraged me to apply to Harvard wrote my recommendation letter. Although I gave him the recommendation letter form in early September, he did not complete it until late November because a jealous classmate took the form from his papers and destroyed it, so I had to find another one to give to him to fill out. My second recommendation letter came from my French instructor, who was also supervising the community service group for which I was president. I got the application to her in early September and she completed it within two weeks.

10. *What type of extracurricular activities did you participate in during your undergraduate years that you feel were beneficial to your being admitted to Harvard Law School, and why?*

Because of my heavy work schedule, I was unable to participate in many extracurricular activities. I suppose the community service projects were the most helpful.

11. *Do you feel that your race, sex, or class played a role in the admissions process? If so, explain.*

I think the fact that there were so few applicants from Mississippi and historically black colleges and universities may have played a factor, but I sincerely hope that I was admitted because the admissions committee saw that I had potential and a history of hard work and dedication.

12. *Do you think that your political ideology played a role in the admissions process? If so, explain.*

No.

13. *Did you see the Harvard Law School campus prior to applying or being admitted? If so, what arrangements did you make for the visit, what were your initial impressions, and have your impressions changed very much? If you didn't visit the campus prior to being accepted, why not?*

No, I didn't visit the campus prior to being accepted because, first of all, I didn't think I'd get in and secondly, it was too expensive and it was difficult to get time off. I did visit after being accepted and attended the BLSA [Black Law Students Association] Spring Conference and New Admit Day.

14. *When did you receive your letter of acceptance from the Dean of Admissions and what were you doing?*

March 7, 1993. My boyfriend and I were drinking beer listening to Bob Marley when my mother called and read the letter to me (it had gone to my home address).

15. *How are you paying for Harvard Law School? Parents? Loans? Savings? Work?*

Loans and grants.

16. *What do you plan to do in the immediate years following Law School graduation? What are your long-term career goals?*

To be perfectly honest with you, I have no idea. All of the plans that I had when I first came to Harvard have been all washed away. This place can be very detrimental to the spirits. At this point, I am just trying to keep myself and my soul intact. However, I am thinking about tax or corporate or international law. I recently realized that I do not want to be a lawyer. My long-term goals are very uncertain, but my ultimate goal is either to own my own business or be in a high management position of a major corporation.

Profile

Name Withheld
Harvard Law School class: 1996
Undergraduate institution: Cornell University
**Undergraduate GPA listed by category—3.75+, 3.50–3.74,
     3.25–3.49, 3.00–3.24, below 3.00:** 3.25–3.49
Graduate institution and GPA, if applicable: N/A
**LSAT Score listed by percentile—99–95, 94–90, 89–85, 84–80,
     79–75, 74–70, 69–65, below 64:** 94–90

Hometown and high school: Syracuse, NY; Nottingham High School

Types of recommenders, i.e., professors or employers: Professors, college administrators

Race, sex, and class: African American, male, middle

Major undergraduate activities: tutoring, empathy and referral service, Tae Kwon Do Club, Black Students United

Major scholastic or academic honors: National Merit Scholar recipient, Cornell Federation Scholarship Recipient, Cornell Outstanding Communication Student Scholarship recipient (Ken Bissett Award), Dean's list six semesters

Work experience (including summer) prior to HLS: Mechanical engineering intern, summer 1989; Peer counselor for Lemoyne College's Higher Education Preparation Program, summer 1990; Administrative assistant for student services and admissions, 1991–93; Management communication researcher, 1992–93.

Parents' occupations: Mother—Nurse, Father—College administrator

Legacy factor: N/A

Questionnaire

1. When and why did you apply to Harvard Law School? Was your application completed early, late, or in the middle of the rolling admissions process?

I applied to Harvard Law School in late December. Doing all of my applications was such an administrative burden that I waited until one of the secretaries in the office where I worked had time to help me type them.

I applied to Harvard Law School because it seemed like the logical thing to do. I originally wanted to go to Georgetown Law School, but my pre-law advisor (an HLS alumnus) said that Harvard was the prototype of law schools and I should start there and work my way down.

2. How would you describe the undergraduate institution that you attended? Does it have a strong reputation and a solid track record of sending lots of its graduates to Harvard Law School?

Most Cornell students that go on to law school studied Industrial and Labor Relations (ILR) as undergraduates. I was a communications major, but I still think that ILR provided a very strong pre-law preparatory curriculum with undergraduate labor law courses, and a strong conceptual bias toward economic reasoning.

3. Did you think, prior to being accepted, that you had a decent chance of being admitted to Harvard Law School?

Yes. Once I made up my mind to apply, I thought I would be accepted because of the trend in my grades (I started out as an engineering student with poor grades, then showed five consecutive semesters of marked improvement), and the tremendous support of college administrators who were writing my recommendations.

4. Did you take any time off prior to applying or matriculating at HLS? If so, why did you take time off and what did you do?

No.

5. What were your strongest assets when applying to Harvard Law School? Grades? LSAT score? Extracurriculars? Personal statement? Recommendations? Family connections? Personal background? Work experience?

I think my personal statement, personal background, and recommendations were my strongest assets. I think the work I did as a communication management researcher, my grades, and my LSAT scores, were at least enough to let an admissions person know that I probably wasn't too risky an admit decision.

6. What type of courses did you take as an undergraduate to prepare yourself for Harvard Law School?

As a communications major I took many public speaking and business speaking courses to prepare me for life as a litigator. I also took writing courses of all kinds: courses that required research, creative writing courses, or science writing courses. (Science writing courses force you to communicate complex ideas in simple ways, i.e., explain atomic fission in three sentences or less.)

7. What was your LSAT score(s)? How did you prepare for the test? If you took an LSAT prep course, which one, and did it help?

I took Kaplan, but I did not go to the classes. I used it because it forced me to take at least two practice tests under test conditions, something I was unlikely to do myself. I scored a 163 which was 91st percentile.

8. How long did you spend on your personal statement? What did you write about and how did you decide on the topic? Did anyone help you with your statement? If so, who?

I spent one full day on my personal statement. I wrote about my personal approach to life. I explained how I conceive of life as a series of games and explained how I saw law as the most incredible set of rules for a game that I had ever seen, and that my desire to win the game required me to study the rules. I had a friend edit it for spelling and grammar.

9. Who wrote your recommendations for Harvard Law School and how did you choose them? How much notice did you give your recommenders and when were the recommendations completed?

I gave my recommenders two months' notice and two of them were still late. My employers in the office of student services and admissions were my most potent recommenders because they could speak as employers and academicians. I also got a recommendation from my faculty advisor in the communication program who just happened to be my supervisor for the communication management research that I had worked on. I chose them because they had the right answer to the question "Are you comfortable writing me a good recommendation?"

10. What type of extracurricular activities did you participate in during your undergraduate years that you feel were beneficial to your being admitted to Harvard Law School, and why?

I worked on a literary magazine and participated on the speech team for a short period, but I think my tutoring in the community and my work with an empathy-and-referral service, probably marked me as a person that, at least occasionally, thought about someone else, and I like to think that helped to get me in.

11. Do you feel that your race, sex, or class played a role in the admissions process? If so, explain.

I think that an intelligent admissions person should read my accomplishments in light of the distance I had to travel to achieve them, but I just don't know how big a part of my admit decision those types of factors played.

12. Do you think that your political ideology played a role in the admissions process? If so, explain.

Yes. My personal statement also explained that I had studied communication to learn how to affect people, and that I needed to study law to learn how to affect institutions and that if I could add economic strength I might be able to make a difference for African-American people. That concept combined with my participation in predominantly African-American organizations probably indicated that I might bring a particular perspective to HLS discourse.

13. Did you see the Harvard Law School campus prior to applying or being admitted? If so, what arrangements did you make for the visit, what were your initial impressions, and have your impressions changed very much? If you didn't visit the campus prior to being accepted, why not?

I didn't visit the campus because I knew that if I got in I would go regardless of how I felt about the campus.

14. When did you receive your letter of acceptance from the Dean of Admissions and what were you doing?

I was drinking beer and watching a basketball game. My friends had hid the envelope from me until all of my housemates had returned from their classes. I do not remember the date.

15. How are you paying for Harvard Law School? Parents? Loans? Savings? Work?

I am borrowing most of the money, I am working part time for the Boston law firm that I worked for after my 1L year, and my mother is helping when she is able.

16. What do you plan to do in the immediate years following Law School graduation? What are your long-term career goals?

I intend to work for a law firm until I can pay back my loans, after that I just don't know.

Profile

Name: David Buckner
Harvard Law School class: 1995
Undergraduate institution: Rutgers College, Rutgers University
Undergraduate GPA listed by category—3.75+, 3.50–3.74, 3.25–3.49, 3.00–3.24, below 3.00: 3.75+
Graduate institution and GPA, if applicable: John F. Kennedy School of Government
LSAT Score listed by percentile—99–95, 94–90, 89–85, 84–80, 79–75, 74–70, 69–65, below 64: 99–95

Hometown and high school: Miami, FL; Palmetto Senior High
Types of recommenders, i.e., professors or employers: Professors
Race, sex, and class: Caucasian, male, middle
Major undergraduate activities: President of the class of 1991,
    newspaper columnist, Rutgers College Fellows, Cap and Skull,
    Rutgers College Governing Association
Major scholastic or academic honors: Harry S Truman Scholar,
    Phi Beta Kappa, Eagleton Institute of Politics, Rutgers College
    Honors Program
Work experience (including summer) prior to HLS: Lifeguard
    (Dade County Parks), summer 1990; Foliage Design Systems
    (landscaping), summer 1989; University of Miami (research-
    medical), summer 1988.
Parents' occupations: Father—Professor of pediatric surgery,
    University of Miami, Mother—educator
Legacy factor: N/A

Questionnaire

1. When and why did you apply to Harvard Law School? Was your application completed early, late, or in the middle of the rolling admissions process?

I applied to HLS in the fall of my senior year of college, and had my application in and complete by the end of November (which I believe is relatively early in the process). I applied because I wanted a career in public service, and a law degree seemed the most appropriate route to that career.

2. How would you describe the undergraduate institution that you attended? Does it have a strong reputation and a solid track record of sending lots of its graduates to Harvard Law School?

Rutgers has a solid reputation, and is regarded as one of the better state schools in the country. On average, about three to five people get into HLS from Rutgers each year, which is not a large number compared with the number of people admitted from the Ivy League.

3. Did you think, prior to being accepted, that you had a decent chance of being admitted to Harvard Law School?

I thought that I had an even chance of being accepted, but was fully conscious of the fact that only a limited number of Rutgers students get into HLS each year.

4. Did you take any time off prior to applying or matriculating at HLS? If so, why did you take time off and what did you do?

No, I did not take any time off.

5. What were your strongest assets when applying to Harvard Law School? Grades? LSAT score? Extracurriculars? Personal statement? Recommendations? Family connections? Personal background? Work experience?

I believe that my grades, LSAT score, extracurriculars, and recommendations were the strongest parts of my application. I do not know which, if any of these, was the decisive factor in my being admitted.

6. What type of courses did you take as an undergraduate to prepare yourself for Harvard Law School?

I did not take any particular courses to prepare myself for HLS. I was a political science major.

7. What was your LSAT score(s)? How did you prepare for the test? If you took an LSAT prep course, which one, and did it help?

My LSAT score was a 46 (old scale). I prepared for the test by reading prep books and taking practice tests. I did not take a prep course.

8. How long did you spend on your personal statement? What did you write about and how did you decide on the topic? Did anyone help you with your statement? If so, who?

I believe that I spent about one week on the statement. I wrote about my experience in college, because that is what I thought personal statements were about. No one helped me with my statement.

9. Who wrote your recommendations for Harvard Law School and how did you choose them? How much notice did you give your recommenders and when were the recommendations completed?

Professor Michael Shafer, Dean James Reed, and Professor Gerald Pomper wrote my recommendations for HLS. I chose them because I had an opportunity previously to work with each of them in both academic and non-academic settings (like university political issues), and I felt that they could best comment on my abilities and aptitudes, both good and bad. I gave them at least one month's notice, and the recommendations were completed and received by HLS by the end of November.

10. What type of extracurricular activities did you participate in during your undergraduate years that you feel were beneficial to your being admitted to Harvard Law School, and why?

I was president of my class for four years, a member of the Dean's Cabinet, a Rutgers College Fellow, on the Rutgers College Governing Association and a political columnist for two campus newspapers. I am not sure if any of these were particularly important to my admission at HLS.

11. Do you feel that your race, sex, or class played a role in the admissions process? If so, explain.

No, I do not feel that these played a role.

12. Do you think that your political ideology played a role in the admissions process? If so, explain.

No, I do not think that HLS even really knew about my political ideology.

13. Did you see the Harvard Law School campus prior to applying or being admitted? If so, what arrangements did you make for the visit, what were your initial impressions, and have your impressions changed very much? If you didn't visit the campus prior to being accepted, why not?

No, I did not visit the campus prior to applying or being admitted. I'm not sure why I did not visit.

14. When did you receive your letter of acceptance from the Dean of Admissions and what were you doing?

I received my letter of acceptance while I was at home on winter break. I believe I was concentrating on getting a suntan.

15. How are you paying for Harvard Law School? Parents? Loans? Savings? Work?

I am paying for HLS through a combination of parental support, the Truman scholarship, savings, and work.

16. What do you plan to do in the immediate years following Law School graduation? What are your long-term career goals?

I plan to clerk for a judge immediately after graduating, and then to seek work as a prosecutor. Eventually, I want to enter electoral politics.

Profile

Name: Craig Buckser
Harvard Law School class: 1997
Undergraduate institution: Cornell University (School of Industrial and Labor Relations)
Undergraduate GPA listed by category—3.75+, 3.50–3.74, 3.25–3.49, 3.00–3.24, below 3.00: 3.50–3.74
Graduate institution and GPA, if applicable: N/A
LSAT Score listed by percentile—99–95, 94–90, 89–85, 84–80, 79–75, 74–70, 69–65, below 64: 99–95
Hometown and high school: Smithtown, NY; Smithtown High School East
Types of recommenders, i.e., professors or employers: One professor and one employer
Race, sex, and class: White, male, upper-middle
Major undergraduate activities: Cornell Civil Liberties Union (president), WVBR-FM (disk jockey), Residence Hall Government
Major scholastic or academic honors: Dean's List, Golden Key Honor Society, Ives Award Finalist, Summer Research Assistantship
Work experience (including summer) prior to HLS: Paralegal for a civil rights attorney; Circulation desk worker at a library; Research guide writer at school archives; Intramural sports referee.
Parents' occupations: Father—Electrical engineer, Mother— Computer programmer
Legacy factor: N/A

Questionnaire

1. When and why did you apply to Harvard Law School? Was your application completed early, late, or in the middle of the rolling admissions process?

I sent my application in October 1993. I applied to Harvard largely because of its reputation, the strength of its faculty, and the quality of its students.

2. How would you describe the undergraduate institution that you attended? Does it have a strong reputation and a solid track record of sending lots of its graduates to Harvard Law School?

The Industrial and Labor Relations School at Cornell is a small, trade-oriented school in the middle of a large university. It has a solid reputation as the leader in its field. Also, it has a fine track record of sending students to Harvard Law School.

3. Did you think, prior to being accepted, that you had a decent chance of being admitted to Harvard Law School?
Yes.

4. Did you take any time off prior to applying or matriculating at HLS? If so, why did you take time off and what did you do?
No.

5. What were your strongest assets when applying to Harvard Law School? Grades? LSAT score? Extracurriculars? Personal statement? Recommendations? Family connections? Personal background? Work experience?
This may seem cynical, but I think that the single biggest factor in my admission to Harvard Law School was my LSAT score. Before I began preparing for the LSAT, I never considered applying to Harvard. After I completed my first practice test, I realized that I had a good chance of getting accepted here. Perhaps I emphasize the LSAT because I took my grade point average as a given. (My GPA after my first semester was a 3.74. My GPA at graduation was a 3.74.) I believe that my extracurricular activities, recommendations, and personal statement did not hurt me. On the other hand, if my LSAT or grades were significantly worse, I would not be completing this survey now.

6. What type of courses did you take as an undergraduate to prepare yourself for Harvard Law School?
I took no specific pre-law course for the sake of preparing myself for law school. I did take a course in Labor Law as a required course. I also took a class in Employment Discrimination Law as an elective within my major. The plurality of my coursework was in labor economics and labor history.

7. What was your LSAT score(s)? How did you prepare for the test? If you took an LSAT prep course, which one, and did it help?
I got a 174 out of 180. I did not take any prep courses. I only prepared for about two weeks. I read a Barron's book in order to familiarize myself with the types of questions on the exam. Then, I took about five practice exams, which I had purchased from the Educational Testing Service (or its LSAT subsidiary). I took only one exam in full during a single

sitting. For the other ones, I would take two sections at a time.

8. How long did you spend on your personal statement? What did you write about and how did you decide on the topic? Did anyone help you with your statement? If so, who?

I spent about six or seven weeks on the personal statement (from notes to final product). Obviously, I never spent too long working on the personal statement on any specific day. I wrote about why I wanted to go to law school and why I wanted to become a law school professor after I graduated. I decided on the topic by talking to a couple of people, including a professor, about potential topics. I did have a few people review my statement, including friends, family members, and two professors.

9. Who wrote your recommendations for Harvard Law School and how did you choose them? How much notice did you give your recommenders and when were the recommendations completed?

I chose my recommenders on the basis of their ability to judge and their knowledge of my qualifications. My employer is a civil rights attorney for whom I have intermittently worked since my senior year of high school. The professor I chose taught my employment discrimination law class. I spoke regularly in that class, and I knew that she thought highly of me.

10. What type of extracurricular activities did you participate in during your undergraduate years that you feel were beneficial to your being admitted to Harvard Law School, and why?

My key extracurricular activity was the Cornell Civil Liberties Union. Since I was secretary for one semester and president for five semesters, I was able to demonstrate my leadership characteristics. Also, my involvement with the ACLU was an outgrowth of my interest in law.

11. Do you feel that your race, sex, or class played a role in the admissions process? If so, explain.

No.

12. Do you think that your political ideology played a role in the admissions process? If so, explain.

No.

13. Did you see the Harvard Law School campus prior to applying or being admitted? If so, what arrangements did you make for the visit, what were

your initial impressions, and have your impressions changed very much?
If you didn't visit the campus prior to being accepted, why not?

I did not visit the law school campus until after I was admitted. I did not think it was necessary for me to visit before I was accepted because my decision to apply was an easy one. My decision to attend Harvard was a little more difficult, so I wanted to visit and speak to students about their experiences at the law school.

My impressions of Harvard Law School have changed significantly. Initially, I thought that attending Harvard Law would be a miserable experience, especially for the first year. I chose to go here anyway because of the quality of education and my enhanced chances for securing a job in academia after I graduate.

Now, I think that Harvard is a great place to spend three years. The quality of life is much better than I had expected. Students are friendly. Professors are often available for lunch. Gropius complex is socially active. Conversations with students are often stimulating. Cambridge is a terrific place.

14. *When did you receive your letter of acceptance from the Dean of Admissions and what were you doing?*

I received my letter on January 14, 1994. I was in Florida visiting my aunt and uncle at the time. My roommate called me and gave me the news that night.

15. *How are you paying for Harvard Law School? Parents? Loans? Savings? Work?*

I am paying through loans. I am relying on the Low Income Protection Plan in order to pay for the loans with my anticipated low salary. My parents would be available to help me if their financial situation would allow it. Nonetheless, all of the loans ($29,500 this year) are in my name, and I would prefer that they not assist me.

16. *What do you plan to do in the immediate years following Law School graduation? What are your long-term career goals?*

I plan on clerking for about two years. Afterward, I hope to practice law for at least a couple of years. I would love to work for an ACLU affiliate, but I predict that my first post-clerkship job will be at a public defender's office. My long-term career goal is to become a law school professor.

Profile

Name Withheld

Harvard Law School class: 1995

Undergraduate institution: Stanford University

Undergraduate GPA listed by category—3.75+, 3.50–3.74, 3.25–3.49, 3.00–3.24, below 3.00: 3.75+

Graduate institution and GPA, if applicable: Kennedy School of Government, Harvard University, approx. 3.6 GPA

LSAT Score listed by percentile—99–95, 94–90, 89–85, 84–80, 79–75, 74–70, 69–65, below 64: 84–80

Hometown and high school: Milwaukie, OR; Clackamas High School

Types of recommenders, i.e., professors or employers: One former professor, one Kennedy School Associate Dean, and one former employer (city council member from Seattle, WA) (I submitted three letters since I had been out of school for a long period of time)

Race, sex, and class: White, male, middle

Major undergraduate activities: Stanford Jazz Ensemble; I.M.s (basketball); Editor, *Approaching Stanford*, an annually published book for newly admitted students; research assistant for a couple of professors

Major scholastic or academic honors: Graduated Stanford "with distinction," which is Stanford's highest academic honor; Kennedy Fellow at the Kennedy School, 1984–85 and 1985–86; master's thesis was voted one of the most outstanding by K-School professors

Work experience (including summer) prior to HLS: English teacher, Vietnamese refugee camp, Hong Kong, 1984; Legislative aide to Jane Noland, council member, Seattle, 1986–88; Budget associate, House Budget Committee, and legislative assistant, Rep. Charles Schumer, U.S. House of Representatives, 1989–91; Manager of congressional relations, Federal Home Loan Mortgage Corp. (Freddie Mac), 1991–92.

Parents' occupations: Father—Baptist minister and bishop, Mother—Musician and homemaker

Legacy factor: N/A

Questionnaire

1. When and why did you apply to Harvard Law School? Was your application completed early, late, or in the middle of the rolling admissions process?

I applied to HLS primarily because I had decided that I would only go to law school if I could go to a "name" school. Harvard and Yale were the only two schools which I considered belonged to this category; I did not get into Yale! Moreover, I had attended Harvard previously and knew and liked Cambridge.

I applied to HLS relatively early; I think that my application was complete shortly after Thanksgiving.

2. How would you describe the undergraduate institution that you attended? Does it have a strong reputation and a solid track record of sending lots of its graduates to Harvard Law School?

Stanford sends tons of students to HLS.

3. Did you think, prior to being accepted, that you had a decent chance of being admitted to Harvard Law School?

Yes, I thought that I had a good shot, given my knowledge of the qualifications of many of my buddies who were HLS alums. I had strong grades (3.94 GPA undergrad, roughly 3.6 grad), a strong GRE score from my K-School days (something like 98th and 99th percentiles in math and verbal), I had good work experience, I worked hard on my essays, and I expected to have very strong recommendations. But I was concerned that my LSAT would ding me—it was 81st percentile.

Still, I was fairly confident that HLS would, despite my LSAT, at least give me a hard look, given my other strengths.

4. Did you take any time off prior to applying or matriculating at HLS? If so, why did you take time off and what did you do?

Yes, see my work experience answer.

5. What were your strongest assets when applying to Harvard Law School? Grades? LSAT score? Extracurriculars? Personal statement? Recommendations? Family connections? Personal background? Work experience?

I believe that my strongest assets were: grades (3.94 undergrad, roughly 3.6 grad); a strong and relatively interesting personal statement; a strong work experience; very strong recommendations.

My greatest weakness was my LSAT score (81st percentile).

6. *What type of courses did you take as an undergraduate to prepare yourself for Harvard Law School?*

I was a political science/public policy major undergrad, so I took lots of political science, economics, policy, sociology, statistics classes.

7. *What was your LSAT score(s)? How did you prepare for the test? If you took an LSAT prep course, which one, and did it help?*

I had an 81 percentile score. I took a Kaplan prep course, and took it fairly seriously. I still don't know why I did so poorly; I had never scored below 90th percentile on my practice tests.

8. *How long did you spend on your personal statement? What did you write about and how did you decide on the topic? Did anyone help you with your statement? If so, who?*

I spent probably a total of twenty-five hours on my personal statement. My philosophy is that you have to write a personal statement that will catch the eye of the reader, and one that is intriguing, so that the reader will want to read beyond the first several sentences. I also believe that it is helpful if the personal statement is fairly personal, so that the reader gets a better feel for what makes me tick as a person.

I asked several friends to read it and got feedback from them.

9. *Who wrote your recommendations for Harvard Law School and how did you choose them? How much notice did you give your recommenders and when were the recommendations completed?*

I had three recommendations (since I was older, I submitted an extra one): one from a former political science professor, one from a former employer (a member of the Seattle City Council), and one from the former Associate Dean of the Kennedy School. I chose these people to represent the various facets of my experience: undergrad, grad, and work. I gave them plenty of notice, probably two to three months.

10. *What type of extracurricular activities did you participate in during your undergraduate years that you feel were beneficial to your being admitted to Harvard Law School, and why?*

Drummer, Stanford Jazz Band; Editor, *Approaching Stanford*, an annual guide for incoming freshmen; reporter, *Stanford University Campus Report*, the newspaper for faculty and staff.

11. *Do you feel that your race, sex, or class played a role in the admissions process? If so, explain.*

I thought that my age might help me get admitted (I was thirty when I applied).

I also tried to stress my middle-class background when I applied, prominently noting that my dad is a Baptist minister and my mom was a church organist. I thought that there might be something to HLS liking someone who'd come from a non-affluent background.

12. Do you think that your political ideology played a role in the admissions process? If so, explain.

Not that I know of.

13. Did you see the Harvard Law School campus prior to applying or being admitted? If so, what arrangements did you make for the visit, what were your initial impressions, and have your impressions changed very much? If you didn't visit the campus prior to being accepted, why not?

I used to live in one of the wonderful Gropius dorms during my K-School first year, so I had seen the campus before!

14. When did you receive your letter of acceptance from the Dean of Admissions and what were you doing?

I received my letter sometime in late January 1992; I was working as a lobbyist at that time.

15. How are you paying for Harvard Law School? Parents? Loans? Savings? Work?

All of the above except for parents. I had saved enough to pay for a little more than one year of school, and the rest of the time I've been doing the financial aid thing, racking up about $45,000 in loans.

16. What do you plan to do in the immediate years following Law School graduation? What are your long-term career goals?

Immediate years: practice law in Washington, D.C.

Long-term: most likely stay in Washington, practice law if I enjoy myself and return to more lobbying-related activities if I don't like law.

Profile

Name: Helen Virginia Cantwell
Harvard Law School class: 1995
Undergraduate institution: Wellesley College

Undergraduate GPA listed by category—3.75+, 3.50–3.74, 3.25–3.49, 3.00–3.24, below 3.00: 3.75+. Double major in economics and music.

Graduate institution and GPA, if applicable: N/A

LSAT Score listed by percentile—99–95, 94–90, 89–85, 84–80, 79–75, 74–70, 69–65, below 64: 94–90

Hometown and high school: Greenwich CT; Greenwich High School

Types of recommenders, i.e., professors or employers: 1. Chip Case, economics professor and my advisor; 2. Marty Brody, music professor and my advisor

Race, sex, and class: White, female, upper

Major undergraduate activities: President of Organization for Charitable Giving, a group that threw parties and gave money to charity; elected class officer designated to get graduation speaker (Hillary Rodham Clinton); played the organ (for $$) at local church and took lessons all four years; economics department tutor (for $$); music department teaching assistant and tutor (for $$); president of Wellesley College Cap and Gown Organization (i.e., ordered graduation regalia for my classmates); computer consultant on campus (for $$); volunteered at following at different points during school: Newton-Wellesley Hospital, City Year team leader, tutored Chinese Americans in English in Chinatown.; intramural crew team (sat seat #2!); played squash, did aerobics, and ran; co-music director of the Junior Show, an original musical comedy (I wrote and directed the music for the show—and had a role, too!)

Major scholastic or academic honors: Phi Beta Kappa, Durant Scholar, *magna cum laude*, First Year Student Distinction

Work experience (including summer) prior to HLS: High school: worked at local restaurant; Senior year summer and January of first year of college: worked at a dress store in the mall as salesperson; Summer after first year in college: worked as office manager and salesperson for a china, silver, and crystal shop (office manager means did inventory, accounting, and accounts receivable/payable); Summer after second year in college: paid internship with the Research and Statistics Division at the Board of Governors of the Federal Reserve in Washington, D.C. Helped section chief do research for regression analyses on various economic questions; Summer after third year in college: field manager, trainer, and canvasser for CONNPIRG [Connecticut Public Interest Research Group] and MASSPIRG [Massachusetts]. Worked on campaign for

Clean Water Act/RCRA strengthening; Summer after final year in college: research analyst for a small financial services company in Stamford, CT. Did research on different bond markets; During college: I had several jobs.

Parents' occupations: Father—Attorney; former general counsel for Colgate–Palmolive, Co. In his retirement, my father has become a town legislator and has weaseled himself onto several important committees which set policy/distribute funds for the town. Mother—Homemaker (with college education), town legislator. While my mother is not on the more powerful committees, she gets more votes than my father.

Legacy factor: N/A

Questionnaire

1. When and why did you apply to Harvard Law School? Was your application completed early, late, or in the middle of the rolling admissions process?

I applied to HLS in early January, so about the middle of the application process.

Why? Because my advisor made me (see below) and because it can get you places. I had very instrumental feelings about this place then (and still do). I saw Harvard as a means to achieving what I want to achieve and little more (with the marked exception, of course, of the Harvard Legal Aid Bureau).

2. How would you describe the undergraduate institution that you attended? Does it have a strong reputation and a solid track record of sending lots of its graduates to Harvard Law School?

Wellesley College is the best educational institution in the United States, in my humble opinion. I mean it. It certainly was the best place for me and every day I appreciate the education that I received and the relationships that were formed there. The fact that it is a women's college, while not the foremost factor in my mind when I decided to attend Wellesley, certainly made the education special once I arrived. Wellesley has a pretty simple mission: prepare and strengthen women so that they can overcome any obstacle that they choose. A simple mission has its flaws—there are other things outside that mission that Wellesley does not pay attention to (and perhaps it should). But I think that overall, by paying attention to women's education and really working to strengthen women, Wellesley provides an unparalleled environment for women to learn, grow, and take charge.

In terms of a strong reputation, certainly among employers and graduate education, the statistics are higher for women coming from women's colleges in general and Wellesley in specific. Lots of Wellesley women are in my HLS class.

3. Did you think, prior to being accepted, that you had a decent chance of being admitted to Harvard Law School?

Short answer: Yes. Long answer: I did not want to come here and did not want to apply. In fact, I threw the application in the garbage at one point. But, my economics advisor said that he would not write my recommendation to any school unless I applied here (he has this idea that no other school compares). I needed his recommendation, both because he was my advisor and knew me/my work really well and because he has a reputation for writing very long and detailed (and good) recommendations. So, I applied to Harvard. I guess I knew I could get in, but I thought that it was still a crap shoot and that I might not.

4. Did you take any time off prior to applying or matriculating at HLS? If so, why did you take time off and what did you do?

No.

5. What were your strongest assets when applying to Harvard Law School? Grades? LSAT score? Extracurriculars? Personal statement? Recommendations? Family connections? Personal background? Work experience?

From my perspective, my strongest assets were my extracurriculars (a "straight from college" person's substitute for work experience, although I sort of count my summer jobs in with this category) and my personal goals for my education. In short, I guess I saw what I hoped to achieve in the public sector with my education as my strongest asset. It was what was most important to me in the application process.

From an "objective" or "numbers" perspective, my strongest assets were my grades and to some extent, my LSAT. I had very good grades in college which translated into very strong (so I am told, though I have never seen them) recommendations. I thought, and continue to think, that my personal statement was grossly inarticulate and I am sure that it had no bearing on my admission to Harvard.

6. What type of courses did you take as an undergraduate to prepare yourself for Harvard Law School?

All courses prepared me (and yet none really did . . .). I was an economics/music double major—because I truly loved studying both subjects. I also took science classes, computer science, religion, writing, French, political science, and art history. All classes were small and therefore I got a lot of attention and learned how to think critically. This skill has been quite helpful here at HLS.

7. What was your LSAT score(s)? How did you prepare for the test? If you took an LSAT prep course, which one, and did it help?

I think I was in the 91st or 92nd percentile. I took an LSAT prep course, Princeton Review, and thought it was horrible, a terrible waste of money. I took the class because I thought everyone else did and it was a dumb move. In fact, I think it hurt me because I did not really study for the test—I just did what was expected in the class without really thinking ahead to the test. But all turned out fine.

8. How long did you spend on your personal statement? What did you write about and how did you decide on the topic? Did anyone help you with your statement? If so, who?

I spent a lot of time thinking about it and little time writing it. Initially, I wrote it all about playing the organ and did not mention law school at all. Then my Dean read it (I asked her to) and she said that while it was a fine essay about Baroque organ music, she thought I had put the wrong essay in the wrong envelope. *So*, I rewrote it, making it a much duller and straightforward piece about where I had come from and why I wanted to go to law school. Although I still consider it one of my most inarticulate pieces of writing and quite dull, the core ideas are still with me; my interest in law remains "questioning who is being served by our judicial system," the "inefficient political and legal process," and the "great need for reform in the public sector [with] lawyers playing a constructive role."

Then, my economics advisor read it, thought it was good (maybe just fine and inoffensive) and away it went.

I made a conscious decision not to allow any of my peers to read my statement. While I usually have no trouble spouting off on my opinions on various subjects, even myself, for some reason I have always had difficulty writing personal statements.

9. Who wrote your recommendations for Harvard Law School and how did you choose them? How much notice did you give your recommenders and when were the recommendations completed?

Marty Brody, music advisor. A good friend (still), mentor, all-around cool dude. Marty is a really smart guy and musician who almost played at

Woodstock with Joe Cocker and is still wondering where he would be had he gone along (he is pretty sure that he would not be chair of the music department at Wellesley). I chose Marty because he knew me as a friend (I used to dog-sit for him when he was on sabbatical) and I had done well in his class and gotten to know him through academics. Marty, as I recall, was a little slow in producing the recommendation, but everything got straightened out after one or two reminders.

Chip Case, economics advisor. When I got to college, everyone was raving about this Chip Case guy—"the guy" in the economics department. Also teaches at Harvard and works at the Federal Reserve Bank in Boston. Really nice, invites classes over to his house for dinner and singing (he plays the guitar). Very influential professor both within and without the Wellesley community. I was told that he wrote me a lengthy and impressive recommendation.

10. What type of extracurricular activities did you participate in during your undergraduate years that you feel were beneficial to your being admitted to Harvard Law School, and why?

My extracurriculars were terrific and really helped make my experience. The Junior Show was a highlight, because it was something that a group of us came together and wrote everything for—to be able to write the music was a real honor and a terrific experience.

My other activities were also good—I think it is especially important to have a job in college. It was good to earn the cash, but also to learn responsibility and, in my case, to provide service to the Wellesley community and help others learn (tutoring and computer consulting).

I'm not sure, however, that Harvard really looks beyond the numbers and so I do not know that the school really cared about what I cared about, namely these activities. So, they influenced me, but I am not sure if they influenced Harvard.

11. Do you feel that your race, sex, or class played a role in the admissions process? If so, explain.

Tough to say. My socioeconomic class probably did to the extent that those reading my application were probably of my class and could readily identify with my experiences and background. In addition, on paper (especially my senior year) I still look(ed) like a Greenwich girl, with a "nice" Wellesley education (although let me make clear that I think that is a misguided perception for anyone to think that Wellesley provides a "nice" education—it's just been something I've run into among the older, whiter, maler folks).

As for sex, I think it probably helped. A common comment at Wellesley regarding gender and admissions was very specific to our school. People would say, "Wellesley women are admitted because they are women who can do the work." Statistics were also bandied about that at HBS [Harvard Business School] the women who did well and stayed were from women's colleges and specifically Wellesley.

Bottom line—I think that all of these factors always count and can be used to justify anything; they all can cut both ways. I think that the most important influence was that my class (upper) and race (white) insured that I got a first-class education in order to prepare me for law school. Then maybe one extra thing was that I was a woman in the sort of traditional affirmative action way.

12. Do you think that your political ideology played a role in the admissions process? If so, explain.

Not really. Although I was already quite left-wing by the time I graduated from college, my ideas were not as focused as they are now. Consequently, my application—personal statement—is marked by a general commitment to public interest work, but not with a very strong ideological bend. Perhaps, given the time (spring 1992), that was a plus-factor to my admission to Harvard ("here's a public-minded person who's not going to 'sit in' at my office—grab her"). Again, I think everything is political, so it played a role, but my application in my opinion did not put forward a very strong political perspective.

13. Did you see the Harvard Law School campus prior to applying or being admitted? If so, what arrangements did you make for the visit, what were your initial impressions, and have your impressions changed very much? If you didn't visit the campus prior to being accepted, why not?

Yes, many times. I thought it was ugly, especially Gropius, and I knew not to live there (I had been to parties there—they were gross!). I also came to Admitted Students' Day and was generally unimpressed, although I did meet Jessica Rosenbaum, who I was impressed by! I thought the students seemed disgruntled and the class I went to was boring.

My impressions, generally speaking, have not changed and have become, like my political beliefs, more focused. It is still ugly and students are disgruntled for good reasons. Some classes have been good, but many more have been boring.

14. When did you receive your letter of acceptance from the Dean of Admissions and what were you doing?

I had been away for the first half of Spring Break with my friends and was stopping by school to pick up stuff before driving home for Easter. I got the package and was really happy. Then, I got into a *huge* fight with my roommate who was driving me crazy, almost crashed the car because of her, and by the time I called my boyfriend with the good news, I was in a foul mood. He remarked that I seemed to be the most unhappy person who had just gotten into Harvard Law School.

15. *How are you paying for Harvard Law School? Parents? Loans? Savings? Work?*

My parents and the continued high price of Colgate–Palmolive stock are footing the bill. This accident of birth has allowed me great freedom in my choice of careers.

16. *What do you plan to do in the immediate years following Law School graduation? What are your long-term career goals?*

Manhattan DA's office. Long-term, I'd like to stay there for a while, maybe even forever, maybe do federal criminal work, sex-crimes work. Ultimately, I'd love to be a judge.

Profile

Name Withheld
Harvard Law School class: 1997
Undergraduate institution: Stanford University
Undergraduate GPA listed by category—3.75+, 3.50–3.74, 3.25–3.49, 3.00–3.24, below 3.00: 3.25–3.49
Graduate institution and GPA, if applicable: Columbia Teachers College—3.6
LSAT Score listed by percentile—99–95, 94–90, 89–85, 84–80, 79–75, 74–70, 69–65, below 64: 94–90
Hometown and high school: Atlanta, GA; Westminster High School
Types of recommenders, i.e., professors or employers: Both
Race, sex, and class: Black, male, middle
Major undergraduate activities: Alpha Phi Alpha Fraternity, Rugby Team
Major scholastic or academic honors: National Achievement Scholar, Alpha Phi Alpha Fraternity Scholarship
Work experience (including summer) prior to HLS: High school history teacher; Analyst, New York City Office of Management and Budget–Urban Fellows Program.

Parents' occupations: Father—President, College Board,
Mother—Executive director, Girls, Inc.
Legacy factor: N/A

Questionnaire

1. When and why did you apply to Harvard Law School? Was your application completed early, late, or in the middle of the rolling admissions process?

I applied in January 1992 and deferred until 1994. I applied at a whim. I had only intended to apply to Yale, Georgetown, and Boalt, but, as I was throwing out all of my other applications, I saw Harvard's at the bottom of the pile. The application process was so easy and Harvard's name was so big that I decided to go for it. I didn't even want to go because of the negative experience my brother had in undergrad. However, I was rejected from Yale and couldn't choose Boalt over Harvard because of the weather and locale.

2. How would you describe the undergraduate institution that you attended? Does it have a strong reputation and a solid track record of sending lots of its graduates to Harvard Law School?

Stanford was an excellent experience and a great school. It has a very strong reputation and is the third-most represented school in my class here.

3. Did you think, prior to being accepted, that you had a decent chance of being admitted to Harvard Law School?

I thought that I had a decent, if outside, chance.

4. Did you take any time off prior to applying or matriculating at HLS? If so, why did you take time off and what did you do?

Yes, I did the Urban Fellows Program with the New York City government. It was a nine-month fellowship in which I worked for one agency (OMB) while learning about all the others and taking trips to Albany and D.C. to learn about the relationship between state/city and city/federal.

5. What were your strongest assets when applying to Harvard Law School? Grades? LSAT score? Extracurriculars? Personal statement? Recommendations? Family connections? Personal background? Work experience?

I believe that my work experience helped a lot, especially the fact that I was interested in education and the law. Also, my grades in grad school were better than my undergraduate grades. I like to think that I had good recommendations and a good personal statement but I have no basis for comparison. I am sure that my ethnicity helped as well.

6. *What type of courses did you take as an undergraduate to prepare yourself for Harvard Law School?*

None. I did not know that I was going to law school in undergrad.

7. *What was your LSAT score(s)? How did you prepare for the test? If you took an LSAT prep course, which one, and did it help?*

I got a 162. I used Kaplan and I think that it helped.

8. *How long did you spend on your personal statement? What did you write about and how did you decide on the topic? Did anyone help you with your statement? If so, who?*

I spent a couple of weeks. My parents read it, as well as my brother, and a friend who was a lawyer. I wrote about exactly why I wanted to go to law school, which was to further my career in education reform and policy.

9. *Who wrote your recommendations for Harvard Law School and how did you choose them? How much notice did you give your recommenders and when were the recommendations completed?*

I had an old recommendation from undergrad that I had used several times for other applications and I used one from the chairman of the history department. They were completed well before the deadline.

10. *What type of extracurricular activities did you participate in during your undergraduate years that you feel were beneficial to your being admitted to Harvard Law School, and why?*

I imagine that it helped that I played rugby and made the Northern California All-Star Team. They probably want something other than just academics. My fraternity helped too because it was community-service oriented and gave me ample opportunities to do public service.

11. *Do you feel that your race, sex, or class played a role in the admissions process? If so, explain.*

I think that my race played a factor. I think that most schools want to prove that they are diverse and are eager for black applicants. Black men are in an especially dire situation in America and are even scarcer than black women. This is obvious in the lopsided ratio of black women to black men in most predominantly white schools, both secondary and higher ed. I don't think class played a factor at all.

12. Do you think that your political ideology played a role in the admissions process? If so, explain.

Not particularly. I am not radical one way or another that would make me stand out from the crowd.

13. Did you see the Harvard Law School campus prior to applying or being admitted? If so, what arrangements did you make for the visit, what were your initial impressions, and have your impressions changed very much? If you didn't visit the campus prior to being accepted, why not?

Yes, I stayed with a friend who was already in the law school. My impressions were not favorable. It was cold, not as pretty as Stanford, and very unfamiliar. I had also just broken up with my girlfriend, so that added to my funk.

14. When did you receive your letter of acceptance from the Dean of Admissions and what were you doing?

I got it after work sometime in March or April.

15. How are you paying for Harvard Law School? Parents? Loans? Savings? Work?

Mostly loans with a little bit of help from my parents.

16. What do you plan to do in the immediate years following Law School graduation? What are your long-term career goals?

I would like to clerk for a judge. Then maybe work at a public interest firm or a private firm that will allow me an opportunity to work in the public sector somehow. Government is attractive to me in the long-run. Idealistically, I would love to be secretary of education one day (if that department still exists by the time I get there!).

Profile

Name: Michael L. Castellano
Harvard Law School class: Class of 1998 (joint degree); came in with the class of 1997

Undergraduate institution: Johns Hopkins
**Undergraduate GPA listed by category—3.75+, 3.50–3.74,
   3.25–3.49, 3.00–3.24, below 3.00:** 3.50–3.74
Graduate institution and GPA, if applicable: N/A
**LSAT Score listed by percentile—99–95, 94–90, 89–85, 84–80,
   79–75, 74–70, 69–65, below 64:** 99–95
Hometown and high school: Catonsville, MD; Catonsville
   High School
Types of recommenders, i.e., professors or employers: All
   professors
Race, sex, and class: White, male, middle
Major undergraduate activities: Lacrosse club team, Cambridge
   University American Football Team, Tau Epsilon Phi fraternity
   Philanthropy Coordinator, tutored a local 6th grader, Senior Class
   Gift, Clinton/Gore Campaign
Major scholastic or academic honors: Dean's List, National Merit
   Scholar, Beneficial–Hodson Scholar, Maryland Distinguished
   Scholar, Phi Beta Kappa, Pi Sigma Alpha, Golden Key
Work experience (including summer) prior to HLS: Not much:
   Busboy at Phillips' Restaurant; Valet parker, University of Maryland
   Law School Alumni Office; U.S. Senate—Senator Sarbanes,
   Committee on Small Business of the U.S. House of Reps.
Parents' occupations: Father—Airport safety administrator, Federal
   Aviation Administration, Mother—Lay ministry coordinator,
   Archdiocese of Baltimore
Legacy factor: N/A

Questionnaire

1. When and why did you apply to Harvard Law School? Was your application completed early, late, or in the middle of the rolling admissions process?

   I applied to Harvard in December 1993. I applied here for a couple of reasons. Number 1: it is Harvard Law, that speaks for itself. Number 2: I wanted to do a joint degree with an International Studies School and Harvard has such a program with the Fletcher School of Law and Diplomacy. I still cannot explain why I wanted to go to law school at all, but when I was figuring out what I wanted to do last year, I knew that I wanted to go to a graduate International Studies program, and then I figured it was my duty as a poli sci major to apply to law schools. Since I wasn't even sure that I wanted to go to law school, I only applied to the top schools, so if I didn't get in [it was] no big deal and if I did it would be like a bonus. Which it has been.

I had everything in by mid- to late December. I think that is relatively early, though not very early, in the process.

2. How would you describe the undergraduate institution that you attended? Does it have a strong reputation and a solid track record of sending lots of its graduates to Harvard Law School?

Hopkins had two people come to Harvard Law last year. I am not sure in what year the other guy graduated from Hopkins, though. So I would say that Hopkins doesn't do a very good job of getting people here. We do OK with other law schools, but not with Harvard.

3. Did you think, prior to being accepted, that you had a decent chance of being admitted to Harvard Law School?

Yes, I aced the LSAT, I had good grades, good recommendations, and I have always been blessed with good fortune.

4. Did you take any time off prior to applying or matriculating at HLS? If so, why did you take time off and what did you do?

Came straight from college.

5. What were your strongest assets when applying to Harvard Law School? Grades? LSAT score? Extracurriculars? Personal statement? Recommendations? Family connections? Personal background? Work experience?

LSAT was very strong. Grades were solid. I think my recs were very good. I think I conveyed the impression of seeking admission from an academic and not a professional perspective, which I think was what helped them decide to admit me.

6. What type of courses did you take as an undergraduate to prepare yourself for Harvard Law School?

I didn't take anything to prepare myself for law school. The courses I did take were a lot of political science courses (that was my major) mostly with an international focus; a bunch of economics courses, one or two philosophy courses; a smattering of history—western civ., U.S. history.

7. What was your LSAT score(s)? How did you prepare for the test? If you took an LSAT prep course, which one, and did it help?

I got a 176. I did a lot to prepare for the test. I didn't take Kaplan or Princeton Review, but I did take a course at a local college that met four times and went over strategies. I think a course, any kind of course, is helpful just to expose you to the test, give you some good advice you wouldn't think of on your own, and make you feel more confident when going into the test. I think the most valuable preparation I did was taking the old LSATs. Material from Kaplan and Princeton Review just is not the same as the actual LSAT and you can tell the difference when you use them (I had a bunch of these materials from friends who had taken those prep courses). Definitely take practice exams and definitely time yourself and definitely try different techniques to see what works best.

8. How long did you spend on your personal statement? What did you write about and how did you decide on the topic? Did anyone help you with your statement? If so, who?

I spent forever on my personal statement. I hate writing about myself like that. I seriously spent two solid weeks working on different ideas. I had input from my parents and from the pre-law advisor at Hopkins.

I wrote about myself, not about what I have done or any work experience, or why I wanted to go to law school, but just about why I think I am a neat person.

9. Who wrote your recommendations for Harvard Law School and how did you choose them? How much notice did you give your recommenders and when were the recommendations completed?

All professors from Hopkins. One professor was my thesis advisor and I had a very good relationship with him. One was a professor whom I also had a good relationship with from an independent study course that he had supervised and from having done some work on one of his books. The third professor was just nice enough to write a good rec based on a grade that I had gotten in one of his classes. I barely knew him.

I gave all the recommenders probably one-and-a-half-months' notice for the law school recs. Then I got all the materials to them probably with one month before I wanted it in.

10. What type of extracurricular activities did you participate in during your undergraduate years that you feel were beneficial to your being admitted to Harvard Law School, and why?

The Clinton/Gore campaign, various athletics, the Mock Trial team. I think the fact that I wrote poetry helped, too.

11. Do you feel that your race, sex, or class played a role in the admissions process? If so, explain.

No, I think being a white, middle-class male could only have hindered my chances of being admitted.

12. *Do you think that your political ideology played a role in the admissions process? If so, explain.*

I doubt it. Besides the fact that I worked on Clinton/Gore, it never figured into my application.

13. *Did you see the Harvard Law School campus prior to applying or being admitted? If so, what arrangements did you make for the visit, what were your initial impressions, and have your impressions changed very much? If you didn't visit the campus prior to being accepted, why not?*

Didn't visit. Once I got the acceptance letter I knew I was going here and I saw no need to spend the money to come up here to check it out.

14. *When did you receive your letter of acceptance from the Dean of Admissions and what were you doing?*

It was late April. I had just returned from a lacrosse game and a friend of mine and one of my roommates were waiting on my front stoop with "a very thick envelope from Harvard Law."

15. *How are you paying for Harvard Law School? Parents? Loans? Savings? Work?*

All loans so far; this summer I'll be working for a firm which should help me out.

16. *What do you plan to do in the immediate years following Law School graduation? What are your long-term career goals?*

Immediate years: work for a big firm that pays well in D.C. or New York so that I can get the experience and training, and make money to pay back some of my loans. Then I would like to work for a firm or an organization, or the government, that works on international economic issues—treaty negotation, investment by multinational corporations, investigating the relationship between law and economic development.

Profile

Name: Laura R. Cheng
Harvard Law School class: 1997
Undergraduate institution: Harvard
Undergraduate GPA listed by category—3.75+, 3.50–3.74, 3.25–3.49, 3.00–3.24, below 3.00: 3.50–3.74

Graduate institution and GPA, if applicable: Northeastern University, 3.75+

LSAT Score listed by percentile—99–95, 94–90, 89–85, 84–80, 79–75, 74–70, 69–65, below 64: 99–95

Hometown and high school: Opelousas, LA; 9th–10th grades: Westminster Christian Academy, Opelousas; 11th–12th grades: Phillips Exeter Academy

Types of recommenders, i.e., professors or employers: Two professors, one from Harvard and one from Northeastern

Race, sex, and class: White, female, middle

Major undergraduate activities: Work-study jobs, Bible study

Major scholastic or academic honors: No major ones

Work experience (including summer) prior to HLS: During undergrad I worked at the Harvard International Office. Summers I often spent teaching: advanced junior high students through a Duke program, refugee students through a Harvard public service program. During my year of grad school at Northeastern I worked in the English Language Center there. The summer before HLS I spent teaching English at a hospital in China.

Parents' occupations: My father is a minister/counselor/teacher. (He holds several jobs.) My mother was the co-founder (with my father) of Westminster Christian Academy and its administrator for 12 years. Since my parents moved to Florida in 1989, she has held several other jobs in administration and marketing.

Legacy factor: N/A

Questionnaire

1. When and why did you apply to Harvard Law School? Was your application completed early, late, or in the middle of the rolling admissions process?

After being away from Harvard for a year, I found that I missed its academic rigor and intellectual challenge. The grad program I was in did not provide that. In general, I also felt that the populations I most wished to work with (immigrant and international families) would probably not go see a counselor on their own; I needed more practical skills to be able to serve them effectively.

Somehow my husband kept egging me on to go to law school. My undergrad degree was in linguistics, which is probably the most useful degree for rocking on the LSAT (whatever else it's good for, who knows).

So at his insistence, I took the LSAT. After that he kept on me to apply to law school. He is in medical school right now, so we wanted to coordinate our careers. Because I like Boston, we made a deal that if I got into Harvard he would stay in Boston for his residency. Otherwise I would wait until after he graduated and apply to law schools according to his residency choices. So I only applied to one law school—Harvard.

Even though I started the law school admissions process late, since I only applied to one school, it was easy to get the materials in by December.

2. How would you describe the undergraduate institution that you attended? Does it have a strong reputation and a solid track record of sending lots of its graduates to Harvard Law School?

Harvard undergrad—I suppose it speaks for itself.

3. Did you think, prior to being accepted, that you had a decent chance of being admitted to Harvard Law School?

I was a little worried about my GPA from undergrad—it was solid but not perfect. After talking with a counselor from the Office of Career Services, we decided my chances were 50/50. I was hoping that my multicultural leanings would help my application stand out.

4. Did you take any time off prior to applying or matriculating at HLS? If so, why did you take time off and what did you do?

For a year after undergrad, I studied counseling psychology at Northeastern University. I also worked at their English Language Center, organizing cultural programs and field trips for the many international students there. Fortunately, this job came with tuition remission, so I felt no regrets about leaving the psychology program (without finishing) to come to HLS. The summer before HLS my husband and I were in China; he was doing a medical elective at the Shashi First Hospital in Hubei province, and I was the English teacher for fifty doctors and nurses.

5. What were your strongest assets when applying to Harvard Law School? Grades? LSAT score? Extracurriculars? Personal statement? Recommendations? Family connections? Personal background? Work experience?

Honestly, I think my LSAT and personal statement were the strongest assets. The personal statement shares a lot of my heart and vision for the future. Also, perhaps my cross-cultural marriage has given me a perspective on life a little different from the typical law student.

6. What type of courses did you take as an undergraduate to prepare yourself for Harvard Law School?

None. I didn't even know I would be going to law school. I took absolutely no economics, government, political science, or political theory classes whatsoever. Now I'm paying for it.

Of course, the linguistics classes did help me quite a bit on the LSAT, but the LSAT is not like law school.

7. What was your LSAT score(s)? How did you prepare for the test? If you took an LSAT prep course, which one, and did it help?

My LSAT score was 176. In my opinion, the prep courses are a waste of time. I took the suggestion of my college counselor and bought copies of six of the old LSAT exams. Then I took all six of them. After that, I was ready to roll.

8. How long did you spend on your personal statement? What did you write about and how did you decide on the topic? Did anyone help you with your statement? If so, who?

I began one personal statement, but my husband thought it sounded weak, so that one was scrapped and I started over. Once I got going the statement took me only a day or two, but I had been thinking about it for about a month.

My statement revolved around a multicultural/international theme, and also wove in my desire to help these populations. I chose that theme because it was one of the strongest influences from my past and motivating factors for the future.

9. Who wrote your recommendations for Harvard Law School and how did you choose them? How much notice did you give your recommenders and when were the recommendations completed?

When I applied to grad school I had a terrible time with recommenders—I had to call them at all kinds of exotic locations and remind them to complete my recommendations. One recommender completed hers the morning the application was due.

The second time around, for HLS, I tried to choose my recommenders more wisely. One was a professor at Northeastern whom I respected a lot. I gave her about two months' notice, but she finished the letter within a week or two. The other recommender was a professor from the Linguistics department. He was the only professor I really knew at Harvard undergrad, and even then I felt shy about asking him. His letter took a little longer—perhaps I bugged him about it too much, being paranoid from my previous experience—but it was also completed about a month or two after I asked him.

10. What type of extracurricular activities did you participate in during your undergraduate years that you feel were beneficial to your being admitted to Harvard Law School, and why?

Besides my work-study job and church activities, I was not involved in many extracurriculars. However, I did get married the summer before my junior year—and my husband was the one who encouraged me to apply to HLS. So perhaps dating him was the most beneficial extracurricular!

11. Do you feel that your race, sex, or class played a role in the admissions process? If so, explain.

Although white by birth, because of my marriage and life experiences I sometimes see myself as more multicultural/Asian. Perhaps this made my application stand out a little bit.

12. Do you think that your political ideology played a role in the admissions process? If so, explain.

I'm usually pretty quiet when it comes to politics, so I doubt that played a role.

13. Did you see the Harvard Law School campus prior to applying or being admitted? If so, what arrangements did you make for the visit, what were your initial impressions, and have your impressions changed very much? If you didn't visit the campus prior to being accepted, why not?

Because I went to Harvard undergrad and lived in Boston, I never made any special arrangements to visit the campus, although I passed by it many times.

14. When did you receive your letter of acceptance from the Dean of Admissions and what were you doing?

I received the letter in February. After I got it, I beeped my husband at the hospital two or three times until he left his meeting to call me back. Of course, we were both very excited and grateful.

15. How are you paying for Harvard Law School? Parents? Loans? Savings? Work?

Since marriage, my parents have not contributed to our finances. The first year was paid through loans and part-time jobs. For the next two years,

I have received a Harvey Fellows Scholarship which will pay for a large chunk of tuition. (This scholarship is co-funded by the Coalition of Christian Colleges and Universities and the Mustard Seed Foundation, both in D.C.)

16. What do you plan to do in the immediate years following Law School graduation? What are your long-term career goals?

Short-term, my only goal is to pay back my educational loans, along with my husband's for med school. Long-term, I think we would like to move to China and work there. Right now we are just taking it one day at a time, trusting God to show his will for our future.

Profile

Name: Tim Corriero
Harvard Law School class: 1997
Undergraduate institution: Colgate University
Undergraduate GPA listed by category—3.75+, 3.50–3.74, 3.25–3.49, 3.00–3.24, below 3.00: 3.50–3.74
Graduate institution and GPA, if applicable: N/A
LSAT Score listed by percentile—99–95, 94–90, 89–85, 84–80, 79–75, 74–70, 69–65, below 64: 99–95
Hometown and high school: Ilion, NY; Ilion High School
Types of recommenders, i.e., professors or employers: One professor, two employers
Race, sex, and class: White, male, middle
Major undergraduate activities: Intramural sports, fraternity
Major scholastic or academic honors: Phi Beta Kappa
Work experience (including summer) prior to HLS: Renting real estate to foreigners in Rome, Italy; working as a legal assistant in a law firm in Washington, D.C.
Parents' occupations: Father—Artist, Mother—Schoolteacher
Legacy factor: N/A

Questionnaire

1. When and why did you apply to Harvard Law School? Was your application completed early, late, or in the middle of the rolling admissions process?

I applied because it's Harvard. Why else? I sent my application in on one of the few days before it was due. This is because I got my LSAT score back in mid-January and realized I had a good shot at admission. Plus filling out all those forms for all those schools is something that is easy to procrastinate on.

2. How would you describe the undergraduate institution that you attended? Does it have a strong reputation and a solid track record of sending lots of its graduates to Harvard Law School?

Colgate is not a good "feeder" school. It doesn't send many people to Harvard Law. Maybe one a year. It has a decent rep, but can't funnel people in like the big Ivys.

3. Did you think, prior to being accepted, that you had a decent chance of being admitted to Harvard Law School?

I thought I had a good chance. My numbers were pretty high. And I have had some interesting work and study experience abroad.

4. Did you take any time off prior to applying or matriculating at HLS? If so, why did you take time off and what did you do?

I took two years off after college working in Italy and in D.C. See job descriptions. I didn't have much of a plan to go to law school after graduation, but the job market sucked and if I could get into Harvard Law or work at some mediocre job, there was no choice to be made.

5. What were your strongest assets when applying to Harvard Law School? Grades? LSAT score? Extracurriculars? Personal statement? Recommendations? Family connections? Personal background? Work experience?

LSAT score and work experience.

6. What type of courses did you take as an undergraduate to prepare yourself for Harvard Law School?

None. I majored in philosophy and religion. You can't "prepare" for law school. Poli sci is bullshit.

7. What was your LSAT score(s)? How did you prepare for the test? If you took an LSAT prep course, which one, and did it help?

174. I took that Princeton review and really loved it. I took a practice exam with a hangover and an attitude and didn't even get 160. This woke me up and I practiced the games until I could do them backwards.

Everything else came by itself, but I really needed some guidance on how to tackle those ridiculous games.

8. How long did you spend on your personal statement? What did you write about and how did you decide on the topic? Did anyone help you with your statement? If so, who?

I wrote about my work experience in Italy because I thought it was unique. It was a page long but I spent 20-plus hours on it.

9. Who wrote your recommendations for Harvard Law School and how did you choose them? How much notice did you give your recommenders and when were the recommendations completed?

Professor: the only one who still remembered me well after two years out of school. And the one I enjoyed most.

Employers: the attorneys I worked most closely with at the law firm when I worked as a paralegal.

I gave them both a couple of months. They were completed mostly toward the deadline that I gave them.

10. What type of extracurricular activities did you participate in during your undergraduate years that you feel were beneficial to your being admitted to Harvard Law School, and why?

Zippo.

11. Do you feel that your race, sex, or class played a role in the admissions process? If so, explain.

Nope. If anything it might have worked against me because I am a white male. And there are plenty of us who apply.

12. Do you think that your political ideology played a role in the admissions process? If so, explain.

How could it? They don't know my political bent upon admissions.

13. Did you see the Harvard Law School campus prior to applying or being admitted? If so, what arrangements did you make for the visit, what were your initial impressions, and have your impressions changed very much? If you didn't visit the campus prior to being accepted, why not?

I didn't visit the campus because to me it's immaterial. Harvard could be located in New Haven (God forbid), and I'd still go. Plus I knew Boston from having lived here before and having seen at least the under-grad campus.

14. *When did you receive your letter of acceptance from the Dean of Admissions and what were you doing?*

August 1, 1994, and I was planning on attending the University of Virginia.

15. *How are you paying for Harvard Law School? Parents? Loans? Savings? Work?*

Loans, loans, and more loans.

16. *What do you plan to do in the immediate years following Law School graduation? What are your long-term career goals?*

Pay back all my loans working for a private firm. I would like to be a partner in a firm in ten years.

Profile

Name: Brooke Melisse Deratany
Harvard Law School class: 1996
Undergraduate institution: University of Virginia
**Undergraduate GPA listed by category—3.75+, 3.50–3.74,
    3.25–3.49, 3.00–3.24, below 3.00:** 3.75+
Graduate institution and GPA, if applicable: University of Florida,
    Center for Latin American Studies, 3.25–3.49
**LSAT Score listed by percentile—99–95, 94–90, 89–85, 84–80,
    79–75, 74–70, 69–65, below 64:** 94–90
Hometown and high school: Indialantic, FL; Melbourne High School,
    Melbourne, FL
Types of recommenders, i.e., professors or employers: Professors
Race, sex, and class: White: mother descended from Russian Jews,
    father's parents born in Syria and Lebanon, female, upper-middle
Major undergraduate activities: Officer, Cavalier Kickers dance and
    drill team; president, Spanish Club; officer, Alpha Chi Omega
    sorority; Peer Major Advisor; Inter-Sorority Council; "Be a Hero"
    volunteer at Clark Elementary School; dance instructor for
    University Union Short Courses (Lambada); Semester in Valencia,
    Spain (fall 1989); Summer in Fortaleza, Brazil (summer 1990)
Major scholastic or academic honors: Rotary Scholar in Buenos
    Aires, Argentina (March–December 1992); Fulbright–Hays
    fellowship in a group project abroad in Belo Horizonte, Brazil
    (January–March 1992); graduate assistantship (University of

Florida); Phi Beta Kappa; Golden Key Honor Society; vice president
of Sigma Delta Pi Spanish Honor Society; Echols Scholar

Work experience (including summer) prior to HLS:
Translator/hostess for Florida International Agribusiness Trade
Show (May 1993); Graduate Assistant, University of Florida Center
for Latin American Studies; Ran Tuesday Evening Latin American
Film Series, organized Conference on "Black Brazil," coordinated
Black Brazilian Vision photography exhibit, translated a Latin-
American database, translated documents from Spanish and
Portuguese into English (spring 1993); Gathered information for
two University of Florida professors (fall 1991); English teacher for
executives at advertising agencies in Buenos Aires, Argentina
(April–November 1992); Administrative assistant for Andrea
Deratany, a licensed psychologist (summer 1991); Sales
representative for Jostens Class Rings at the University of Virginia
(spring 1991); One-week "externship" with Amnesty International
in Washington, D.C. (May 1990); Waitress/hostess for Alumni Hall
at Darden Business School of University of Virginia (summer
1989); Copyroom manager for Reinman, Harrell Law Offices,
Melbourne, Florida (summer 1988).

Parents' occupations: Mother—Currently a psychologist in private
practice in Indialantic, Florida, after a 10-year political career: city
council, mayor, county commissioner. Before that, a full-time mom
and part-time student.
Father—Currently a political consultant/lobbyist in private practice
in Indialantic, Florida, after a 21-year political career: city council,
mayor, state representative, state senator. Started out as a barber
and cut hair for 30 years in his own shop, also dabbled in real
estate in a business he owned with his two brothers.

Legacy factor: N/A

Questionnaire

*1. When and why did you apply to Harvard Law School? Was your appli-
cation completed early, late, or in the middle of the rolling admissions
process?*

I applied to HLS over Christmas 1993, as soon as I got back from
Argentina; mailed application in early January, but letter of recommenda-
tion from director of Center for Latin American Studies not sent in until
March. Heard from HLS one week after that letter sent in.

2. *How would you describe the undergraduate institution that you attended? Does it have a strong reputation and a solid track record of sending lots of its graduates to Harvard Law School?*

UVA was an all-around school. It had its sports, its fraternities and sororities, with a reputation as a party school coupled with a reputation as an Ivy League with a state-school price tag. It was pretty homogenous— relatively upper-middle class, mildly conservative, mildly southern, with enough international students (a lot of diplomats' kids) to keep it interesting. It sends its share to HLS, but not "lots."

3. *Did you think, prior to being accepted, that you had a decent chance of being admitted to Harvard Law School?*

I thought that I would have more of a chance to get into HLS than in other top-rung schools because HLS seemed to be a place that looked at you more for who you were and what you did rather than your LSAT score or GPA. Turns out that Harvard took me right away and all those comparable schools wait-listed me (including University of Virginia!). Yale, however, flat-out rejected me. Luckily, I had heard from HLS first. I had hoped I would get in, and part of me thought I had a decent chance, but most of me thought it would just be too good to be true.

4. *Did you take any time off prior to applying or matriculating at HLS? If so, why did you take time off and what did you do?*

I had wanted to take a year off before going to law school in order to do something extraordinary. Travel, but how? I had known about the Rotary scholarship to spend a year studying anything anywhere since high school. That would be the way to finance something different. When I actually won it, I decided to go as far away as I possibly could (and stay in Latin America), so I picked Argentina. When I found out that the school year didn't start until mid-March, I thought about getting paid to go to school. I was lucky enough to win a graduate assistantship at the University of Florida. Actually, they told me I had won a fellowship, and I didn't realize until I actually got there that I would have to work one-third time in order to earn my keep. While there I found out about and applied for a Fulbright program in Brazil from January to mid-March of 1992. This was too good to be true! I would have been twiddling my thumbs for two and a half months had I not been chosen to be one of twelve graduate students to study Brazilian culture and language in Belo Horizonte, Brazil. Here, I was able to experience my first Brazilian Carnaval and dance with a samba school through the streets of a little town called Caxambu.

As I had spent the last of my savings the summer of 1991 on a trip through Europe as a present to myself for graduating from college, I was fortunate to be able to support myself with scholarships and the assistantship for the next two years. Although I had only planned on taking one year "off" before starting law school, it ended up being two. I even entertained the idea of making it three years in order to leisurely finish up my master's degree, and maybe pick up Haitian Creole (I thought to apply for a Title VI Area Studies fellowship), but my parents talked me out of it. They were afraid that if I waited another year that I would never end up applying for law school, which I had wanted to do since I was eleven years old. Although I still haven't polished up that M.A., I got an all-expenses-paid year in South America sandwiched by some interesting experiences in the Center for Latin American Studies at the University of Florida. Time off had turned into two more years of school. Although it wasn't much of a rest, it made me more confident about who I am, what I want to do with my life, and what issues matter most to me.

5. What were your strongest assets when applying to Harvard Law School? Grades? LSAT score? Extracurriculars? Personal statement? Recommendations? Family connections? Personal background? Work experience?

I think that my strongest assets were my Rotary and Fulbright experiences as well as my language abilities and interest in international law. HLS prides itself on being the best school for international law there is. HLS is also currently trying to develop its Latin American program, and my background screamed of that. My grades and scores were good enough so that I would be taken seriously, but they were by no means stellar, and I had no family connections whatsoever. I think my diverse extracurricular activities and my propensity toward leadership positions helped out.

6. What type of courses did you take as an undergraduate to prepare yourself for Harvard Law School?

I wasn't an Echol's Scholar at first at UVA because my SAT score was only 1310, and the cut-off had been more like 1400. I specifically applied for the program once I got to UVA and I became an Echol's Scholar in my second year. I had agonized my first year because I wasn't one of the "smart" people. Being an Echols Scholar was cool because you didn't have to pick a major, you had no requirements, and you got priority into any class that you wanted. This explains what I was doing in that statistics class my first year and why I never got a B– or below again at UVA. At first I wasn't going to pick a major. My first year, I had taken Introduction to just about everything. I took a couple psych classes, a couple rhetoric and communications classes, intro to sociology, intro to government, and on and on. I continued taking Spanish because I had been anticipating spending a semester in Spain since my 7th grade Spanish class, but I didn't want to major in a language because that didn't "look good" I had heard. I ended up doing an interdisciplinary Latin American studies major (and doubling in Spanish anyway). I was one class short of an international relations minor. I took a lot of classes in Portuguese language and literature, both at UVA and one summer in Brazil. My last semester I took French as well. I also had two semesters' worth of thesis writing, and I wrote on the Brazilian women's movement.

7. What was your LSAT score(s)? How did you prepare for the test? If you took an LSAT prep course, which one, and did it help?

I think my LSAT score was a 41 (the old system that was on a scale of 12 to 48). That put me at the 90th or 91st percentile. I had taken Stanley Kaplan. My diagnostic score had been a 39 and you were supposed to be able to raise your score an average of 9 points. Needless to say, I was a bit disappointed, but I couldn't complain. I had done another short course as well but I don't remember the name. Maybe I could have prepared better independently, but I remember not feeling like it.

8. How long did you spend on your personal statement? What did you write about and how did you decide on the topic? Did anyone help you with your statement? If so, who?

I spent a couple of days on my personal statement. I wrote about my life since graduating from UVA because I felt I had done some things that would make me stand apart from the applicant pool. Besides, UVA had a file on me that I had put together before I had graduated in 1991, complete with recommendations. I felt that I had changed a lot since graduation and that my personal statement would be the place to describe these changes. My parents proofread my personal statement and discussed with me what they thought would make it better. Their input was insightful.

9. Who wrote your recommendations for Harvard Law School and how did you choose them? How much notice did you give your recommenders and when were the recommendations completed?

I chose three people while in my fourth year at UVA. I picked people whom I felt knew me and my work pretty well. They had several weeks to write them. My first was this great lecturer who taught my two favorite classes at UVA: foreign policy of the United States, and international law. His name was Robert F. Turner, and he was director of the Center for National Security Law at UVA. I had talked to him about my dream of a career in international law. I remember him telling me to stay away from Harvard because it was a political minefield and was in decline (this was in late 1990). He wrote me a congratulatory letter when he found out that I got into HLS, saying that I would probably get a decent education here and he could understand why I would accept, but that he really preferred UVA. He obviously didn't realize that UVA had only wait-listed me! His assistant at the Center for National Security Law was my teaching assistant for his international law class, and I had him write a letter for me because I had worked with him closely on my paper for that class and I felt I had done a good job. I also had my thesis advisor—a female professor in the English Department—write a recommendation because she knew my writing intimately and seemed positive about my work. I knew that good writing was essential for law school.

When I actually applied to law schools in December 1992, I got a recommendation from Terry McCoy, the director of the Center for Latin American Studies. He had been supportive of me before I even arrived at the University of Florida, and had worked with my doing a semester and then leaving for a year and then coming back again. He only had a short period of time to do the recommendation and actually got around to doing it about a month after I gave it to him.

10. What type of extracurricular activities did you participate in during your undergraduate years that you feel were beneficial to your being admitted to Harvard Law School, and why?

I think my study-abroad experiences helped most.

11. Do you feel that your race, sex, or class played a role in the admissions process? If so, explain.

I don't think so. Although I had heard that HLS was looking to admit more women, the year I got in, women were still only about 40 percent of the entering class, and Dean Clark said that that was proportional to the percentage of applications. The fact that I'm Jewish couldn't have had any effect because I had not affiliated myself with any religious organizations at UVA, I don't have a "Jewish" name, and didn't participate in any organized religion even in high school.

12. *Do you think that your political ideology played a role in the admissions process? If so, explain.*

My ideology? I think the fact that I was interested in international relations and economic integration may have been attractive.

13. *Did you see the Harvard Law School campus prior to applying or being admitted? If so, what arrangements did you make for the visit, what were your initial impressions, and have your impressions changed very much? If you didn't visit the campus prior to being accepted, why not?*

No. After all, it's *Harvard*. It had to be beautiful, right? Ivy, New England charm. Well, as soon as I was admitted, Mom and Dad hustled me up here one not-so-fine typically gray and ugly April day. We stayed at the Radisson, ate at Legal Seafoods, shopped at Copley Plaza, paid my tuition, and side-tripped to Salem to see the witches. Ah, New England— sure if you're touring in style with the rents. Living here is something else.

I wasn't at all impressed with *the* Harvard Law School, at least as far as decor. I didn't want to leave my beautiful subtropical Florida greenery and sunshine for this ugly cold and gray, uh . . . place, but I knew that HLS was my destiny and I was going to put up with grayness, snow, the North-eastern personality, and this dreary campus to have the "Harvard Experience" that would secure my future. All I needed was a change in attitude and woolens, I thought. My first year I was in total denial about the ugliness of the buildings and the type-A-ness of the people, until around May. Drama Society and Scales of Justice and other activities kept me too busy to notice the cold. And, I told everyone sincerely how I *loved* it here and how it was *so much fun*. Even Gropius: "My hall is like my family and the rooms let in a lot of natural sunlight." Thank God I live in Wyeth this year and that I'll be there 3L year too, but how many more meals in the Hark can I take?

14. *When did you receive your letter of acceptance from the Dean of Admissions and what were you doing?*

I was a graduate student working on a conference called "Black Brazil" at the University of Florida. I was hap-hap-happy, calling Brazilians and making their travel plans and accommodations, creating posters. Enjoying the prestige among my peers from having actually been to the places that we were studying at the Center for Latin American Studies. My mother called me one night in mid-March with the news. I was dumbfounded. I jumped for joy! My dreams all coming true! Harvard! The Law School, especially for international law! The door was open, my future bright! I was in shock. I was beside myself with glee. This was it! Then a Brazilian guy I had met in Rio de Janeiro came to visit me in Florida. He said he had come to take me back to Brazil with him, that he wanted to marry me. I told him as soon as he got off the plane that I had gotten into Harvard Law School. By the end of his visit he had determined that an international lawyer wouldn't make a good mother to his children. He went back to Brazil and that was that. I started to worry for the first time that I was choosing my Harvard dream over *everything* else and this tradeoff made me a little glum, but I knew I was doing the right thing.

15. How are you paying for Harvard Law School? Parents? Loans? Savings? Work?

My father is generous enough to give me $20,000 a year for three years to help pay for law school. The rest I'm borrowing. I didn't work last summer, in fact I went further into debt by going to Paris to study French and European community law. This summer I'm working in Brazil with Baker & McKenzie and I have no idea what I will be paid, if anything. I'm expecting to owe about $30,000 in loans when I graduate.

16. What do you plan to do in the immediate years following Law School graduation? What are your long-term career goals?

I want to go back to Florida. My family is in central Florida, but I plan to live in Miami. Maybe I'll work for a law firm in their Latin American practice. Steel, Hector, and Davis would be nice, but they didn't give me an offer for this summer, maybe because they suspected (and they were right) that I would be in Brazil. But, I didn't know that for sure until December 27, 1994. I would ultimately like to deal with international issues in state and local government. Next winter I expect to do independent clinical work with the Florida International Affairs Commission in the Governor's Office. I think I'd like to lobby for international clients after learning the lobbying trade from my dad. I'd like to put my background to use in south Florida.

I feel there are a lot of multicultural issues—including immigration—that need negotiating. I feel both patriotic to my state and concerned for those who come to the U.S. to escape persecution or to make a better life. There's got to be a way to integrate people into the American system, without forcing them to give up their identities or their cultures, and, for goodness sake, why rob them of work authorization and education for their children? I guess my career will be largely political, but I don't know if that will include running for office.

Profile

Name: Donald R. Esposito, Jr.
Harvard Law School class: 1995
Undergraduate institution: University of North Carolina at
    Chapel Hill
**Undergraduate GPA listed by category—3.75+, 3.50–3.74,
    3.25–3.49, 3.00–3.24, below 3.00:** 3.75+
Graduate institution and GPA, if applicable: N/A
**LSAT Score listed by percentile—99–95, 94–90, 89–85, 84–80,
    79–75, 74–70, 69–65, below 64:** 99–95
Hometown and high school: Clemmons, NC; West Forsyth
    High School
Types of recommenders, i.e., professors or employers: Professors
Race, sex, and class: White, male, upper-middle
Major undergraduate activities: Student government; Carolina Union;
    NC Fellows Program; Office of Leadership Development Task
    Force; Campus Y Big Buddy; social fraternity; intramural sports
Major scholastic or academic honors: Graduated with Highest
    Honors and with Highest Distinction; Phi Beta Kappa; Phi Eta
    Sigma; National Merit Scholar; John Motley Morehead Scholar
Work experience (including summer) prior to HLS: Henry Luce
    Scholar, Japan Center for International Exchange; Institute of
    Government Intern, North Carolina Department of Public
    Instruction, Division of External Affairs; Counselor, North Carolina
    Close-Up Program; Research Analyst, Donaldson, Lufkin &
    Jenrette; substitute teacher, Winston–Salem/Forsyth County
    Schools; Intern, Charleston, South Carolina City Police
    Department; Youth soccer referee, Winston–Salem Optimist Club;
    Student columnist, the *Clemmons Courier.*
Parents' occupations: Mother—High school English teacher, West
    Forsyth High School; Father—Business executive, RJR Tobacco Co.
Legacy factor: N/A

Questionnaire

1. When and why did you apply to Harvard Law School? Was your application completed early, late, or in the middle of the rolling admissions process?

I was a history major, and was considering graduate school in history, but I wasn't certain that I wanted an academic career. I was also interested in government and public policy, and therefore considered law school as well. After I received my LSAT scores, I decided to apply to Harvard Law School, especially because it had a joint degree program with the Kennedy School of Government. I applied early in the admissions process during my senior year of college.

2. How would you describe the undergraduate institution that you attended? Does it have a strong reputation and a solid track record of sending lots of its graduates to Harvard Law School?

UNC has a strong academic reputation, largely because of the Morehead program. It usually sends five to six people a year to HLS, approximately half of whom are Moreheads. However, UNC sends most of its graduates to the law schools at UNC, Duke, and Virginia, rather than HLS.

3. Did you think, prior to being accepted, that you had a decent chance of being admitted to Harvard Law School?

Yes.

4. Did you take any time off prior to applying or matriculating at HLS? If so, why did you take time off and what did you do?

I deferred my admission to HLS for one year after receiving a Henry Luce Scholarship to work in East Asia. I had applied to the Luce program because I was not certain what I wanted to do after completing my undergraduate degree, and I saw it as an opportunity to stall having to make a final decision. It was also a "once in a lifetime" opportunity that I would later regret passing up if I did not go when I was young and largely free of heavy responsibilities. Finally, I was also tired of school and had just completed my senior honors thesis, and didn't think that I was ready to cope with the stress of law school right away.

5. What were your strongest assets when applying to Harvard Law School? Grades? LSAT score? Extracurriculars? Personal statement? Recommendations? Family connections? Personal background? Work experience?

I felt that my strongest asset in applying was well-roundedness: none of my credentials was overwhelming, but all were solid. I didn't feel as if I could point to any particular deficiency and say that that shortcoming would doom my application. I had good grades, a good LSAT score, and had been very involved on campus. I also thought that my summer experiences would strengthen my application, in that they would differentiate my application from the multitude that HLS would receive.

6. What type of courses did you take as an undergraduate to prepare yourself for Harvard Law School?

I didn't take any courses particularly to prepare myself for law school. As a history major, I took many history classes, and I also took a large number of political science and English classes. As a general rule, I would take anything that wasn't math or science.

7. What was your LSAT score(s)? How did you prepare for the test? If you took an LSAT prep course, which one, and did it help?

I had a 47 on a 48 scale. I took the Kaplan's prep course, and definitely felt that it helped. I really believe that the LSAT, at least in its format then, was too teachable.

8. How long did you spend on your personal statement? What did you write about and how did you decide on the topic? Did anyone help you with your statement? If so, who?

I spent several hours on my personal statement, largely because I would use it in some form for practically all law school, grad school, and fellowship applications. In addition, I completed my applications for "safety" schools first, so as to enable me to refine my statement as I went. Therefore, I deliberately applied to HLS after other schools, so that I would have more time to revise the statement.

9. Who wrote your recommendations for Harvard Law School and how did you choose them? How much notice did you give your recommenders and when were the recommendations completed?

My recommenders were all professors in whose classes I had done well, so far as I can remember. I gave my recommenders a lot of notice in that all of them completed multiple recommendations for me, and HLS was again one of the last applications that I completed.

10. What type of extracurricular activities did you participate in during your undergraduate years that you feel were beneficial to your being admitted to Harvard Law School, and why?

Once again, I didn't feel that any one activity made my application stand out, but I was involved in a wide range of activities and felt that I had demonstrated an ability to contribute in a wide variety of ways. My primary activity was my involvement in student government, both as an elected representative, a Student Congress officer, and as an appointed member of other boards. In addition, I worked on other, more specialized projects that dealt with single issues, such as on a proposal to include the Office of Leadership and Development in a proposed "Center for Undergraduate Excellence" that an alumnus was considering funding.

11. Do you feel that your race, sex, or class played a role in the admissions process? If so, explain.

I was worried that being an upper-middle-class white male from the suburbs would mean that my application would be boring and would not stand out from others, and I felt that the law school undoubtedly was looking for qualified female and minority students. While I think that it probably played a role, the admissions process seems so arbitrary and subjective that it seems impossible to identify any one factor that outweighed all others.

12. Do you think that your political ideology played a role in the admissions process? If so, explain.

No, I don't even know if my political ideology was obvious, or if even I could identify my political ideology with any accuracy. While my activities may have offered a suggestion of my political orientation if an admissions officer really wanted to know, I was not involved in any blatantly partisan activities.

13. Did you see the Harvard Law School campus prior to applying or being admitted? If so, what arrangements did you make for the visit, what were your initial impressions, and have your impressions changed very much? If you didn't visit the campus prior to being accepted, why not?

I didn't visit because I didn't have the time or the money to make the trip. I had applied to six law schools, and knew that I would never be able to visit them all. Therefore, I only visited UNC, although I had visited Virginia when I was considering undergraduate institutions.

14. When did you receive your letter of acceptance from the Dean of Admissions and what were you doing?

I received my letter of acceptance in late March or early April of my senior year, and had already received a Luce Scholarship to spend a year in Asia. I had been waiting to hear from Harvard, Yale, or Stanford so that I could defer my admission as soon as possible, in that I was afraid deferment was a first-come, first-served process. Otherwise, I was finishing my senior honors thesis, taking minimal classes, and enjoying my last few weeks in Blue Heaven.

15. How are you paying for Harvard Law School? Parents? Loans? Savings? Work?

I have taken out Stafford and SLS loans for each of the past three years. In addition, because my parents did not have to pay anything for my undergraduate education, they gave me the money that they would have spent on UNC, and have also given me $5,000/year. Finally, I have also worked for private firms after both my first and second years of law school, and have used summer earnings to help pay for law school.

16. What do you plan to do in the immediate years following Law School graduation? What are your long-term career goals?

I will be working for a private firm in North Carolina. In the long-term, I would like to become involved in public affairs in North Carolina, and maybe move over to a state government position, especially in the education area.

Profile

Name Withheld
Harvard Law School class: 1995
Undergraduate institution: Stanford University
Undergraduate GPA listed by category—3.75+, 3.50–3.74, 3.25–3.49, 3.00–3.24, below 3.00: 3.75+
Graduate institution and GPA, if applicable: N/A
LSAT Score listed by percentile—99–95, 94–90, 89–85, 84–80, 79–75, 74–70, 69–65, below 64: 94–90
Hometown and high school: Penn Valley, PA; Episcopal Academy, Merion, PA
Types of recommenders, i.e., professors or employers: One employer, one professor, one undergraduate advisor
Race, sex, and class: White, male, upper-middle
Major undergraduate activities: Study and work overseas; freshman advising; sports; board member of a national student government association; acting
Major scholastic or academic honors: Phi Beta Kappa; graduated with distinction in my major
Work experience (including summer) prior to HLS: After college, three years on Capitol Hill working for personal staffs of House members.

Parents' occupations: Both are physicians.
Legacy factor: N/A

Questionnaire

1. When and why did you apply to Harvard Law School? Was your application completed early, late, or in the middle of the rolling admissions process?

I applied probably in the early to middle part of the application season. I think HLS received my application in mid-December, and as I recall they were not due until well after Christmas (actually at the beginning of February, I think).

Why I decided to apply to HLS is a more difficult question, the hard part being the decision to go to law school, not the decision to apply to Harvard. I was very uncertain whether I wanted to become a lawyer at all. But I knew that if I was going to go to school for the education per se, as opposed to going for the status of being a lawyer, Harvard would be one of the schools I would apply to.

When the time came, I applied jointly both to law schools and to master's programs in public policy, and I was admitted to both HLS and the Kennedy School. During my first year at HLS, I decided not to attend the K-School.

2. How would you describe the undergraduate institution that you attended? Does it have a strong reputation and a solid track record of sending lots of its graduates to Harvard Law School?

Stanford has, I think, a good track record of graduates at HLS.

3. Did you think, prior to being accepted, that you had a decent chance of being admitted to Harvard Law School?

I definitely did not expect to be admitted to HLS, nor to Yale Law School (and I was only half wrong).

4. Did you take any time off prior to applying or matriculating at HLS? If so, why did you take time off and what did you do?

Yes. I spent nearly three years following college working on Capitol Hill in Washington, on the personal staffs of two members of Congress from California. At the end of college, I was definitely undecided as to what type of graduate school I would eventually go to. I wanted to delay further schooling until I had decided exactly what to study at the graduate level and why. (Unfortunately, this epiphany has yet to arrive.)

5. What were your strongest assets when applying to Harvard Law School? Grades? LSAT score? Extracurriculars? Personal statement? Recommendations? Family connections? Personal background? Work experience?

My strongest asset, I believe, was my three years of work experience in Washington, which gave me additional maturity and "real world" (if you can refer to Congress that way) experience, plus some personal insight into the legislative and political processes. Other than that, my background probably did not stand out in the pool of HLS applicants—my grades were good, my LSAT score and extracurriculars were competitive, I think I probably had one or two strong recommendations, and I had enough experience in foreign affairs and languages to show considerable knowledge in that one area. But I doubt that my application had outstanding features beyond good balance and, in particular, the three years of work experience.

6. What type of courses did you take as an undergraduate to prepare yourself for Harvard Law School?

I did not know I would go to law school, so I did not select courses with that in mind. But I did wind up choosing many relevant courses, mostly in political science, history, and economics.

7. What was your LSAT score(s)? How did you prepare for the test? If you took an LSAT prep course, which one, and did it help?

Forty-three out of a possible 48. I took an LSAT prep course offered through the federal government in D.C. (it offers courses through a sort of extension school). I believe the course was quite helpful inasmuch as it forced me to practice for the test more than I would have on my own.

8. How long did you spend on your personal statement? What did you write about and how did you decide on the topic? Did anyone help you with your statement? If so, who?

I don't recall how long I spent on the personal statement (probably a couple of weeks). For HLS, of course, we had the option of submitting two essays. For the personal statement, I wrote a general summary of my diverse experiences and reasons for wanting joint degrees in law and public policy (including a humorous, truthful opening quotation). For the other essay, I wrote a sort of opinion article on a topic with which I had been engaged at that time in my job.

Several personal friends in Washington helped me with editing and proofreading.

9. *Who wrote your recommendations for Harvard Law School and how did you choose them? How much notice did you give your recommenders and when were the recommendations completed?*

I submitted three recommendations. They were from: 1) the congressman who was my employer for two-and-a-half years, and who is himself an HLS grad; 2) my freshman advisor from college, an administrator at Stanford who has remained a close personal friend; and 3) a college professor of mine in political science/European relations.

Of these, my employer and my adviser were obvious, easy choices. The professor, on the other hand, I selected because I thought I should have one recommendation from a person who knew me in an academic context (although I actually didn't know him very well personally).

I don't remember how much notice I gave or when the recommendations were completed.

10. *What type of extracurricular activities did you participate in during your undergraduate years that you feel were beneficial to your being admitted to Harvard Law School, and why?*

None that played a crucial role, maybe my study and work experiences overseas during my junior year.

11. *Do you feel that your race, sex, or class played a role in the admissions process? If so, explain.*

No. HLS has seen my type before; if anything, we're overrepresented here, and I don't think it made a difference one way or the other.

12. *Do you think that your political ideology played a role in the admissions process? If so, explain.*

No. I worked for a Democrat on Capitol Hill, but again, I don't think this made any difference.

13. *Did you see the Harvard Law School campus prior to applying or being admitted? If so, what arrangements did you make for the visit, what were your initial impressions, and have your impressions changed very much? If you didn't visit the campus prior to being accepted, why not?*

I only visited HLS after I had been accepted. I had been to Harvard several years before, I didn't expect to be admitted, and I knew I would visit if the time came.

14. *When did you receive your letter of acceptance from the Dean of Admissions and what were you doing?*

I don't remember the date, but it was in the spring, in plenty of time to visit the campus on the official visiting day for admitted students, i.e., I guess I heard in March sometime. At the time I was still in my job in Washington and I continued in that job until the summer.

15. How are you paying for Harvard Law School? Parents? Loans? Savings? Work?

Mostly loans. In addition, I have used up the savings I accumulated while working after college. For this year, my 3L year, I reduced my borrowing a little bit, and my parents are making up the difference. But I will graduate with a very heavy loan debt.

16. What do you plan to do in the immediate years following Law School graduation? What are your long-term career goals?

After taking the California bar exam this summer, I intend to spend the fall months in Europe pursuing further language and legal studies. When I return to the States in the winter, I will resettle in the San Francisco Bay Area, where I hope to work in a legal job related to nonprofit organizations, education, and/or philanthropy—in other words probably a law job in tax, trusts, and/or estate planning. Whether that job will be in a private law firm, a government office, or an organization in the independent sector I don't yet know. In the longer run, I might imagine myself working for a nonprofit organization such as a foundation or a university.

Profile

Name Withheld
Harvard Law School class: 1995
Undergraduate institution: University of Michigan at Ann Arbor
Undergraduate GPA listed by category—3.75+, 3.50–3.74, 3.25–3.49, 3.00–3.24, below 3.00: 3.75+
Graduate institution and GPA, if applicable: N/A
LSAT Score listed by percentile—99–95, 94–90, 89–85, 84–80, 79–75, 74–70, 69–65, below 64: 99–95
Hometown and high school: Grosse Pointe Shores, MI; Our Lady Star of the Sea High School
Types of recommenders, i.e., professors or employers: Eliana Moya–Raggio (American culture professor, University of Michigan) and Keletso Atkins (African history professor, University of Michigan)

Race, sex, and class: Latina (Paraguayan), female, upper-middle

Major undergraduate activities: Founder and vice-president of Sigma Lambda Gamma (the first Latina sorority at the U of M); events coordinator and member of Amnesty International Chapter; member of Alpha Phi Omega (service fraternity); student mentor in the Mentorship Program

Major scholastic or academic honors: William J. Branstrom Freshman Prize; Dean's List; General Sophomore Honors Award; James B. Angell Scholar; Mortar Board; Phi Alpha Theta; Phi Beta Kappa

Work experience (including summer) prior to HLS: Telemarketer, Leukemia Society of Michigan; Intern, Washington Office on Latin America; Cook, South Quad Snackbar; Resident Assistant, South Quad Dorm.

Parents' occupations: My father is a doctor and my mother is a beautician.

Legacy factor: N/A

Questionnaire

1. When and why did you apply to Harvard Law School? Was your application completed early, late, or in the middle of the rolling admissions process?

I sent in my application on January 3, 1992. I applied to Harvard because of the prestige factor. As a Paraguayan immigrant, my father always said "In Paraguay, we knew the most prestigious schools in the world. There are seven: in the United States, Harvard, Yale, and MIT (for engineering); in England, Oxford and Cambridge; in France, the Sorbonne; and in Germany, the Heidelberg. And now my daughter may go to one of them." Although I had no real desire to come to Harvard, I applied out of respect for my parents and to see if I could get into the school.

2. How would you describe the undergraduate institution that you attended? Does it have a strong reputation and a solid track record of sending lots of its graduates to Harvard Law School?

I thought University of Michigan was the ideal well-rounded school. It had a strong academic reputation but also allowed its students to relax and enjoy life. Given the fact that about twenty of my fellow Wolverines are in my HLS class, I think that U of M has a pretty solid track record.

3. Did you think, prior to being accepted, that you had a decent chance of being admitted to Harvard Law School?

I guess I thought I had a chance or I wouldn't have applied. But I really thought that it was hit-or-miss. The standard "it's Harvard, it's tough to get in. I'm certainly not impressive enough" attitude. Now I that I look back, I think that I seriously underestimated the chances of my admission.

4. Did you take any time off prior to applying or matriculating at HLS? If so, why did you take time off and what did you do?

No.

5. What were your strongest assets when applying to Harvard Law School? Grades? LSAT score? Extracurriculars? Personal statement? Recommendations? Family connections? Personal background? Work experience?

I think my strongest assets were my grades, LSAT score, extracurriculars, and personal statement (personal background). Since I waived my right to see my recommendations, I have no idea exactly what they said. I do remember worrying that they weren't from sufficiently prestigious professors. The entire law school application process among history majors at Michigan has you convinced that if you don't get a recommendation from Professor Sidney Fine then you have no hope. Thankfully, I went to professors whom I felt comfortable with and that I knew actually knew something about me (versus the "she got an A in my course, I think" type of recommendation). Since I have zero family connections in the United States, I think I can safely say that they played no part in my admission.

I believe that my work experience was rather minimal and therefore not a very significant factor.

6. What type of courses did you take as an undergraduate to prepare yourself for Harvard Law School?

I had no intention of coming to Harvard Law School or any law school for that matter. Until I decided to take the LSAT in June of my junior year, I was intending to get a Ph.D. in Latin American history. I did not select any courses with the intention of preparing for law school until my senior year when some U of M 1Ls told me that economics would be helpful. I registered for Econ. 201 and found that advice was completely misguided (I still have nightmares about those ridiculous supply-and-demand curves).

7. What was your LSAT score(s)? How did you prepare for the test? If you took an LSAT prep course, which one, and did it help?

My LSAT score was a 168. I took Stanley Kaplan's prep course. I found it rather useless except for the fact that since I paid so much money for the course, I felt compelled to study. As I tell any undergraduate, there's no need to take those courses if you're focused enough to study on your own.

8. How long did you spend on your personal statement? What did you write about and how did you decide on the topic? Did anyone help you with your statement? If so, who?

Being the standard procrastinator type, I waited until the week before my self-determined application deadline and wrote it in one day. I wrote about being bicultural and struggling to find a comfortable identity in both my "worlds." I decided on that topic because I had spent the whole year starting a Latina sorority at U of M. That commitment made me realize that I wasn't alone in trying to define and maintain my Latina identity at a university setting. Realizing that, I thought it was the topic that said the most about me. No one helped me with my statement—it was just me and my computer during an all-nighter.

9. Who wrote your recommendations for Harvard Law School and how did you choose them? How much notice did you give your recommenders and when were the recommendations completed?

My recommenders were two women of color professors I had taken courses with at U of M. Eliana Moya Raggio taught me a Latina/American culture course. Keletso Atkins taught me African history. I selected both of them because I felt comfortable approaching them and I felt that they knew me. Originally, I felt a lot of pressure from my fellow history majors/law school applicants to ask a "prestigious" history professor. Since African history wasn't sufficiently "prestigious," people seemed to think I was crazy. I'm really glad that I ignored that pressure and asked these professors. I can't remember exactly when I gave my recommenders their forms but I would say around late November or early December.

10. What type of extracurricular activities did you participate in during your undergraduate years that you feel were beneficial to your being admitted to Harvard Law School, and why?

I believe that my extracurricular activities demonstrated a substantial and real commitment to the community around me. I was heavily involved in service projects and mentoring activities. One of my most important activities (at least to me) was founding the Latina sorority. I think the fact that I had taken some initiative to start an organization played some role in my being admitted (I assume that says something about my personality).

11. *Do you feel that your race, sex, or class played a role in the admissions process? If so, explain.*

I'm sure that being Latina played into the admission decision. Although I don't completely understand the role of race in HLS admissions, I'm sure that my race and gender made me different from other applicants and therefore played a positive role. As I've told students when recruiting for Harvard, my philosophy is that HLS can choose from a large pool of highly qualified students (obviously I include minority students in this pool of highly qualified applicants). The applicant has the burden of demonstrating what makes them special and different. How can he or she add to the HLS community and the legal world? I think that in my personal statement I conveyed that my commitment to the Latino community made me "special." The way that I see it is that by admitting you, HLS is giving you a benefit. They want to see what different skills and characteristics you have to make the most of it. (Of course, I could be completely wrong about the HLS application process.) I have no idea how being from a "non-traditional" Latino group might have made a difference. Needless to say, there are not a plethora of Paraguayans running around HLS.

12. *Do you think that your political ideology played a role in the admissions process? If so, explain.*

I'm not clear that my political ideology was apparent in my application. I think it was clear that I was committed to Latino issues (an ideology of sorts) and that I was fairly liberal (if one relies on the Amnesty International stereotype). I think like any factor, it contributed to what made me "different" (diversity in the broad sense).

13. *Did you see the Harvard Law School campus prior to applying or being admitted? If so, what arrangements did you make for the visit, what were your initial impressions, and have your impressions changed very much? If you didn't visit the campus prior to being accepted, why not?*

I did not visit Harvard Law School prior to beginning classes. After I was accepted at Stanford Law School, I intended to matriculate there. When my dad offered to send me to visit HLS, I declined. Instead, I asked to go visit Stanford. Since my father was very pro-Harvard, he said he didn't think it was worth it. In the end, I didn't visit either school.

14. When did you receive your letter of acceptance from the Dean of Admissions and what were you doing?

I was on my way to my afternoon class. I believe that I heard back from Harvard during the first few days of February. I went to class and afterwards called my parents. They were more thrilled than I was. To them, Harvard epitomized the attainment of the American dream.

15. How are you paying for Harvard Law School? Parents? Loans? Savings? Work?

Parents.

16. What do you plan to do in the immediate years following Law School graduation? What are your long-term career goals?

I have a clerkship with Judge Duff, Northern District of Illinois. I have an offer with Jenner & Block following my clerkship. I would like to be able to follow through with my original goal to do public interest work within the Latino community (maybe with an organization like MALDEF or AYUDA).

Profile

Name Withheld
Harvard Law School class: 1997
Undergraduate institution: Columbia College, Columbia University
Undergraduate GPA listed by category—3.75+, 3.50–3.74, 3.25–3.49, 3.00–3.24, below 3.00: 3.75+
Graduate institution and GPA, if applicable: N/A
LSAT Score listed by percentile—99–95, 94–90, 89–85, 84–80, 79–75, 74–70, 69–65, below 64: 89–85
Hometown and high school: West Orange, NJ; West Orange High School
Types of recommenders, i.e., professors or employers: Employers
Race, sex, and class: White, female, middle
Major undergraduate activities: Singing in the Columbia University Glee Club and a female a cappella group
Major scholastic or academic honors: Phi Beta Kappa (elected after junior year); *summa cum laude*
Work experience (including summer) prior to HLS: MASSPIRG,

summer '94; The Population Council, 1992–94; Frank Salomon Associates (classical music management agency), 1988–92; New York Philharmonic, 1987–88; National Foundation for Jewish Culture, part-time during 1986–87 and full-time summer of '86; Singer Kearfott Division (secretary), summer '85; lifeguard/swim instructor, summer of '84 and '83.

Parents' occupations: Father—professor of electrical engineering, Mother—musician (pianist and piano/music teacher)

Legacy factor: N/A

Questionnaire

1. When and why did you apply to Harvard Law School? Was your application completed early, late, or in the middle of the rolling admissions process?

I applied in early to mid-December of 1993. I applied to Harvard for many reasons, but the primary one (honestly) is that at that time, I was living in New York and my boyfriend was living in Boston and we decided we wanted to try to live in the same city so that put Harvard at the top of my list.

2. How would you describe the undergraduate institution that you attended? Does it have a strong reputation and a solid track record of sending lots of its graduates to Harvard Law School?

It's Ivy League, with a fairly strong reputation (but not as competitive as the big three). It does seem to send a lot of graduates here, perhaps more in recent years (it has become more competitive since it went co-ed, which was my freshman year).

3. Did you think, prior to being accepted, that you had a decent chance of being admitted to Harvard Law School?

I thought I had a decent chance, but not better than that (nor worse). I knew that my grades were strong enough but that my LSAT scores were a little weak, so that it would be determined by other factors, which seems to be hard to predict.

4. Did you take any time off prior to applying or matriculating at HLS? If so, why did you take time off and what did you do?

Yes! (See job experience above) I did not "take time off," but rather pursued a career in arts administration after graduating from college. After five years in that field, I decided that I needed to make a major change, and figured that some sort of grad school might be in order. It took another year or so to decide to try law school, and it was not until I actually started that I decided I had made the right choice.

5. What were your strongest assets when applying to Harvard Law School? Grades? LSAT score? Extracurriculars? Personal statement? Recommendations? Family connections? Personal background? Work experience?

I would guess that it was my unusual background, i.e., seven years out of college, and not having worked in traditional pre-law jobs in between. I also think that the fact that my personal statement indicated an interest in public interest law, which was easily backed up by my job experience (and probably recommendations too), might have played a role also.

6. What type of courses did you take as an undergraduate to prepare yourself for Harvard Law School?

I was an economics major, but this was *not* in preparation for law school, because law school was not something I was considering at that time. I would certainly say that these classes were useful for law school, as were my Columbia College core classes in political philosophy, literature, etc., but this is a happy coincidence, and was not planned.

7. What was your LSAT score(s)? How did you prepare for the test? If you took an LSAT prep course, which one, and did it help?

162. I prepared through the Princeton Review's book, and had a few review sessions with a friend who used to teach for them.

8. How long did you spend on your personal statement? What did you write about and how did you decide on the topic? Did anyone help you with your statement? If so, who?

I spent many weeks working on my personal statement—it would be impossible to calculate the total hours! I wrote about why I had made such dramatic career moves and how I wound up deciding to go to law school. Specifically, I wrote about why I initially wanted to work in the music business, why I left, and then focused on how my work at the Population Council had helped me decide that I wanted to be a lawyer in order to be a part of positive social developments. It was suggested that I write about my unusual career track, since that would be what the admissions staff would wonder about. From there, it seemed logical to use this explanation as a forum to talk about what values are important to me and how they played a role in my decision to go to law school and what I want to do when I graduate. Many people read my statement toward the end, when I was polishing it, but my then-boyfriend also read it many, many times as I was working and re-working the drafts.

9. Who wrote your recommendations for Harvard Law School and how did you choose them? How much notice did you give your recommenders and when were the recommendations completed?

My two former employers (one of whom was my boss at that time) wrote my recommendations. I chose them because it had been a long time since I had been in school and really did not have any professors who would have remembered me well enough to write a meaningful recommendation. I also knew that both of them would write favorable references. My boss at the Population Council has a Ph.D. and that organization is a research organization, so I also thought that being quasi-academic, it would not be so far from an academic reference. I don't remember how much notice I gave them. Note: My previous boss (at the place before the Population Council) had me draft the recommendation for him, and then I gave it to him on diskette for him to make any changes. That was the only way he had time to do it.

10. What type of extracurricular activities did you participate in during your undergraduate years that you feel were beneficial to your being admitted to Harvard Law School, and why?

At Columbia, my main activity was singing, which probably didn't help me in the admissions process. During my junior year in Israel, however, I was involved in an Arab-Jewish coexistence dialogue group, and tutored adult immigrants in a Hebrew literacy program. These two activities may have helped, in showing some commitment to public service-type work.

11. Do you feel that your race, sex, or class played a role in the admissions process? If so, explain.

No.

12. Do you think that your political ideology played a role in the admissions process? If so, explain.

I don't think so, although some cynical friends of mine postulated that my being liberal and talking about women's issues in my personal statement was helpful to me.

13. Did you see the Harvard Law School campus prior to applying or being admitted? If so, what arrangements did you make for the visit, what were

your initial impressions, and have your impressions changed very much? If you didn't visit the campus prior to being accepted, why not?

Yes. The aunt of my then-boyfriend is a good friend of Danny Greenberg's (the former head of the clinical program). I called him and arranged to speak to him when I was in Boston for a weekend in October (of 1993). We spoke about law school in general, whether it would be a good idea for me, etc., and he gave me some of his personal impressions about what he thought I would find good and bad about being at Harvard. Some of the benefits he pointed out, and the fact that he was so nice, gave me a more favorable impression than I had had before that visit. (I also went to an information session given by the admissions office.)

14. When did you receive your letter of acceptance from the Dean of Admissions and what were you doing?

I received my letter in mid-March. If you mean what was I doing in general, I was working. If you mean at that moment, the letter arrived while I was at work. I went to the movies that evening with a friend and got the good news at about 11:00 P.M. when I came home.

15. How are you paying for Harvard Law School? Parents? Loans? Savings? Work?

Loans, loans, loans! (A tiny amount of savings also, and I will probably work in a firm my second summer to help defray the costs.)

16. What do you plan to do in the immediate years following Law School graduation? What are your long-term career goals?

Some type of public-interest job, although I'm not sure exactly what. Long-term, ideally I'd like to do impact litigation, maybe in civil rights or women's rights, but I may change my mind way before I get to the long term.

Profile

Name Withheld
Harvard Law School class: 1997
UndergradFuate institution: University of Kentucky
Undergraduate GPA listed by category—3.75+, 3.50–3.74, 3.25–3.49, 3.00–3.24, below 3.00: 3.75+
Graduate institution and GPA, if applicable: Princeton University

LSAT Score listed by percentile—99–95, 94–90, 89–85, 84–80, 79–75, 74–70, 69–65, below 64: 99–95

Hometown and high school: Bowling Green, KY; Warren Central High School

Types of recommenders, i.e., professors or employers: Professor and employer

Race, sex, and class: White, male, lower-middle

Major undergraduate activities: Literary Magazine; Amnesty International; Humanities Fellowship; junior year spent abroad

Major scholastic or academic honors: Otis A. Singletary Scholar; Phi Beta Kappa; Gaines Fellowship in the Humanities; UK French Department Honors

Work experience (including summer) prior to HLS: Legal assistant, Sullivan & Cromwell, from 5/26/92 to 8/26/94; Summer assistant, Princeton Library, summer 1991; Summer assistant, UK Library, summer 1989; other summer jobs in college and high school.

Parents' occupations: Father—Factory worker, Mother—Public school teacher

Legacy factor: N/A

Questionnaire

1. When and why did you apply to Harvard Law School? Was your application completed early, late, or in the middle of the rolling admissions process?

I applied to HLS on December 3, 1993. My application was completed by mid-January 1994. I applied to HLS because I believed that it was one of the most preeminent law schools in the country, that the name recognition would help secure a job after law school and that I would enjoy living in Cambridge/Boston for three years.

2. How would you describe the undergraduate institution that you attended? Does it have a strong reputation and a solid track record of sending lots of its graduates to Harvard Law School?

I attended the University of Kentucky and found that I received an excellent education. I was fortunate in that I majored in French and that few students at UK did so, insuring that all of my classes were small and that I received much individualized attention. I also participated in the UK honors program which also guaranteed small classes, full of truly interesting students. I must add that most students at UK do not receive the same quality of education that I received, then again neither do they search for such an experience. I believe that I am the only student in the HLS class of 1997 to have graduated from UK. I assume that in any year there are no more than two UK students to attend HLS, so I would assume that UK does not have a solid track record in sending lots of its graduates to HLS.

3. Did you think, prior to being accepted, that you had a decent chance of being admitted to Harvard Law School?

Yes, after I had applied but before I had been accepted I thought that I had a very good chance of being accepted to HLS. My LSAT scores and undergraduate GPA were well within the norms for recent HLS admittees; moreover, I had taken time off from school to work in the legal field and I felt that this experience would make my application stronger.

4. Did you take any time off prior to applying or matriculating at HLS? If so, why did you take time off and what did you do?

After graduating from UK I went directly to graduate school at Princeton. After earning a master's degree, I went to work at a law firm in New York, where I worked for over two years.

5. What were your strongest assets when applying to Harvard Law School? Grades? LSAT score? Extracurriculars? Personal statement? Recommendations? Family connections? Personal background? Work experience?

I would say that my strongest assets were my grades and LSAT scores, combined with my personal statement and work experience. I was a highly qualified candidate who had done quite a lot after finishing college and that probably made me stand out from the crowd of college seniors that apply.

6. What type of courses did you take as an undergraduate to prepare yourself for Harvard Law School?

I did not plan during my undergraduate years to go to law school, so none of the courses I took were strictly preparation for HLS. The focus of my undergraduate education was the broad study of the humanities, in particular literature, languages, philosophy and history, and I believe that this course of study prepared me well for any later educational undertaking, including the study of law at HLS.

7. What was your LSAT score(s)? How did you prepare for the test? If you took an LSAT prep course, which one, and did it help?

I scored a 169 on the LSAT, which was in the 98th percentile. I did not take a prep course, but I did study on my own for about three weeks prior to the test.

8. *How long did you spend on your personal statement? What did you write about and how did you decide on the topic? Did anyone help you with your statement? If so, who?*

I wrote numerous personal statements, starting several months before I applied to HLS. After comparing the various drafts and different approaches I selected one for several friends to read. They made great suggestions which I incorporated into the draft. I then set it aside for a while, coming back a few weeks later to read it again and make a few minor changes. I ended up writing about my decision to enter and then leave graduate school, about changing careers, about my law firm work, and generally about my background.

9. *Who wrote your recommendations for Harvard Law School and how did you choose them? How much notice did you give your recommenders and when were the recommendations completed?*

I asked my graduate school adviser and my immediate supervisor at work to write letters of recommendation. I chose them because I felt that they knew me better than anyone else except my family and close friends. I gave them each about six weeks' time to complete the letters; they returned them to me within a month, leaving two full weeks before I mailed my application.

10. *What type of extracurricular activities did you participate in during your undergraduate years that you feel were beneficial to your being admitted to Harvard Law School, and why?*

I really can't say that some activities were more beneficial than others. I believe that the selection committee probably is looking for participation and leadership in whatever activities a student was involved in, regardless of what type of activity it was.

11. *Do you feel that your race, sex, or class played a role in the admissions process? If so, explain.*

Being a white male does not make one stand out in the HLS application pool; on the other hand it probably does not hurt one's chances either. I did write about my background, coming from a lower-middle-class family in Kentucky; I believe that since few applicants share this background, the class issue may have helped my application. I am also a gay man, and I did not disclose this fact on my application because at the time I feared that it would only hurt my chances of admission; however, I now believe that this fact would probably have improved my chances. The actual class of 1997 seems fairly heterogeneous and I would assume that the admis-

sions committee attempted to diversify it as much as possible, so that someone who was "out" on her application would see her chances of admission
increase. With that said, most of the gay and lesbian students that I have
met at HLS were not "out" on their application.

**12. Do you think that your political ideology played a role in the admis-
sions process? If so, explain.**

I do not believe that one's particular political ideology plays a role in
the admissions process; however, not having an ideology or political bent
at all will probably seem odd to the admissions committee. Many law students have been active in campus, local, or national politics, and wearing
one's politics on one's sleeve is common. I don't think the admissions
process would penalize one for having strong political convictions; in fact
it would probably reward such convictions whether on the left or the right.

**13. Did you see the Harvard Law School campus prior to applying or being
admitted? If so, what arrangements did you make for the visit, what were
your initial impressions, and have your impressions changed very much?
If you didn't visit the campus prior to being accepted, why not?**

I did not visit the campus prior to admission to HLS. I would have
liked to have seen Harvard but I was working and could not afford the time
nor the expense.

**14. When did you receive your letter of acceptance from the Dean of
Admissions and what were you doing?**

I received my letter of acceptance around May 13, 1994, and I had
been working that day.

**15. How are you paying for Harvard Law School? Parents? Loans? Sav-
ings? Work?**

I am paying for HLS by taking out a large amount of loans. My parents are not in a position to help with much of the expense and I do not
have any substantial savings.

**16. What do you plan to do in the immediate years following Law School
graduation? What are your long-term career goals?**

Immediately after law school I plan on working in a law firm in
New York. Depending upon my quality of life and how much I enjoy
the work, I may continue to do firm work or I may look for a job in the
public-interest sector.

Profile

Name Withheld
Harvard Law School class: 1996
Undergraduate institution: Harvard College (graduated 1971)
**Undergraduate GPA listed by category—3.75+, 3.50–3.74,
   3.25–3.49, 3.00–3.24, below 3.00:** 3.50–3.74
Graduate institution and GPA, if applicable: University of North
   Carolina at Chapel Hill (Master of Regional Planning). No GPA
   available (we were on a "high pass–low pass" system).
**LSAT Score listed by percentile—99–95, 94–90, 89–85, 84–80,
   79–75, 74–70, 69–65, below 64:** 99–95
Hometown and high school: Worcester, MA; North High School
Types of recommenders, i.e., professors or employers: One was a
   college instructor (who is now a college president), the other a
   town selectman who knew me well from town government and
   community activities.
Race, sex, and class: White, male, middle
Major undergraduate activities: College radio station. See other
   questions for information on my post-college activities.
Major scholastic or academic honors: Graduated college *magna
   cum laude*
Work experience (including summer) prior to HLS: After graduating
   from college, I researched and wrote a biography of Buddy Holly,
   which was first published in 1975 and issued in revised editions in
   1979 and 1987. I worked as a regional planner (1975–78), and
   operated a family-owned bookstore (1979–94).
Parents' occupations: My father had his own business, a plastics
   manufacturing company. My mother had been a nurse before
   marriage; after raising six children, she opened the bookstore that
   she and I operated until 1994.
Legacy factor: N/A

Questionnaire

*1. When and why did you apply to Harvard Law School? Was your appli-
cation completed early, late, or in the middle of the rolling admissions
process?*

   I applied fairly late—not until mid-January. I did not initially plan to
apply to Harvard Law School; I was applying instead to other schools in

the Boston area (where I already lived). I didn't think I could get into Harvard, and I didn't think I wanted to go, anyway; my undergraduate experience at Harvard had been unpleasant, and any law school guides I read made it sound like Harvard Law School would be more of the same. But after getting my (high) LSAT score in November, and after talking to friends who were lawyers, I decided to apply, because the advice was always that going to the best possible school was crucial for getting a job—and that Harvard was decidedly above Boston College or Boston University in that regard. Even after being admitted, I did not decide to accept until after attending the Admitted Students Day in March.

2. How would you describe the undergraduate institution that you attended? Does it have a strong reputation and a solid track record of sending lots of its graduates to Harvard Law School?

Well, it *was* Harvard. Actually, at the time I attended twenty-five years ago, the perception among Harvard undergraduates was that the Law School did *not* favor Harvard College grads. (My best friends in college went straight to law school, and none of them got admitted to Harvard Law School.) I don't know if that was actually true, then or now.

3. Did you think, prior to being accepted, that you had a decent chance of being admitted to Harvard Law School?

Before I took the LSAT, no. I had this image that everyone at Harvard Law School was beyond me intellectually, and I thought Harvard might not be receptive to older students. But after I did well on the LSAT and figured out my undergraduate GPA (something I had never had reason to do before), I realized that I was in the ballpark. I guess I thought, when I applied, that my chances were about 50–50.

4. Did you take any time off prior to applying or matriculating at HLS? If so, why did you take time off and what did you do?

As explained in the profile questions, I had been working for many years—indeed, up to the day before 1L orientation. (In fact, we did not close our store until February of my 1L year, so I was still working weekends at my store, even *after* I got here.)

5. What were your strongest assets when applying to Harvard Law School? Grades? LSAT score? Extracurriculars? Personal statement? Recommendations? Family connections? Personal background? Work experience?

My grades and LSAT score presumably put me in the same league with a lot of other applicants, and at least ensured that my application would be taken seriously. I think that my having written a book (and an influential one at that, with a movie and TV documentaries based on it) established my research and writing skills. I had been very involved in my community in town government (the town budget committee) and in civic organizations (youth-sports coaching) and held leadership roles in those activities; all of this was in unpaid positions. I think that that sort of civic-mindedness was a factor. I like to think that my personal statement was well written and displayed a thoughtfulness about my objectives, and I hope it indicated that I could bring a lot of real-world experience to a law school classroom that younger students could not.

6. What type of courses did you take as an undergraduate to prepare yourself for Harvard Law School?

None, since I didn't plan on going to law school when I was an undergraduate. But in retrospect: I was a history major, and that was certainly good preparation. My graduate degree in regional planning gave me a lot of training in economic analysis and systems of government regulation. My work experiences as a planner, a writer, and a business owner also were preparation for law school.

7. What was your LSAT score(s)? How did you prepare for the test? If you took an LSAT prep course, which one, and did it help?

I got 172. I did not take any prep course. I prepared for it by reading the commercially-published exam guides (*Princeton Review* was the most helpful, but I looked at ARCO and *Barron's*, too) and taking some of the practice tests in them, focusing on the mathematical games part of the LSAT (I didn't expect to have much problem with the verbal sections). I might have spent twenty or thirty hours all told studying during the month before the exam, which I took in October. I didn't have a lot of free time to do this, and I never had the time to sit down and take an entire practice exam from start to finish.

8. How long did you spend on your personal statement? What did you write about and how did you decide on the topic? Did anyone help you with your statement? If so, who?

How long? I don't really remember; I would guess about ten hours. I used the same one, with just some variations, for the different schools to which I applied. In my case, it was obvious that I needed to use the statement to highlight my work experiences and achievements, and to explain how that all contributed to my preparation for, and my interest in, studying law. Nobody helped me with the statement.

9. Who wrote your recommendations for Harvard Law School and how did you choose them? How much notice did you give your recommenders and when were the recommendations completed?

Having been out of school so long, this was a concern of mine. The few professors and instructors who knew me from back then are scattered or dead. But I tracked down one who remembered me and who, it turned out, is now president of a prestigious college, so *that* didn't hurt. For my second recommendation, I decided to get a non-academic reference who could corroborate my civic involvement: a town selectman who has known me for many years as a friend and colleague. I had given them recommendations to do for other law schools earlier in the fall, so even though I decided to apply to Harvard around the end of November, they were able to draw on their earlier letters to produce a recommendation for Harvard pretty quickly.

10. What type of extracurricular activities did you participate in during your undergraduate years that you feel were beneficial to your being admitted to Harvard Law School, and why?

I didn't do much as an undergraduate except study; I was active on the campus radio station, but I don't think that would have mattered much to the law school. My activities since entering the "real world" described in earlier questions were certainly important to my admission.

11. Do you feel that your race, sex, or class played a role in the admissions process? If so, explain.

No, unless it hurt. But my age and work background did present different elements of diversity, and I certainly tried in my application to encourage the law school to think of me as adding diversity to the class.

12. Do you think that your political ideology played a role in the admissions process? If so, explain.

No—nothing on my application would have revealed it. My town government is nonpartisan, so even my civic activities did not indicate any political bent.

13. Did you see the Harvard Law School campus prior to applying or being admitted? If so, what arrangements did you make for the visit, what were your initial impressions, and have your impressions changed very much? If you didn't visit the campus prior to being accepted, why not?

Not before applying or being admitted—but I did visit on Admitted Students Day, and that was crucial to my decision to come, as it gave me a chance to talk to the admissions staff, visit a class, and talk with some current students who were also older. All of this helped me overcome my qualms about coming here: my fears that the student body would be cold, arrogant, and overly competitive, the administration would be distant and unsupportive, and the faculty would be disdainful of students and uncommitted to teaching (all of which was pretty much true of my undergraduate experience at Harvard). I was also concerned about the potential for political disruption, in the wake of the *Law Review* mess and the Derrick Bell controversy; having been at Harvard during the campus uprisings of the 1960s, I had no desire to go through such a thing again. Everyone I met on my visit was friendly and well adjusted, and I came away feeling that I would be challenged intellectually at Harvard in a way that I would not be at other Boston schools. My impressions haven't really changed since I got here. I have found most of the students to be friendly and supportive of each other, and I have found the age difference to be less of an isolating factor than I expected. My professors have been quite approachable. There are administrative problems here, but I think they arise more from inefficiencies or passivity than from any disregard for the students.

14. When did you receive your letter of acceptance from the Dean of Admissions and what were you doing?

I heard in mid-March. I don't know what you mean by what was I doing—I was, as mentioned, working, if that's what you mean.

15. How are you paying for Harvard Law School? Parents? Loans? Savings? Work?

I am essentially paying for law school out of the money I have saved up during my adult life. I have chosen to take out some loans rather than liquidate all my assets, but that doesn't change the fact that I will be paying for it all myself.

16. What do you plan to do in the immediate years following Law School graduation? What are your long-term career goals?

I may do a judicial clerkship for my first year out. Then, I plan to work for a small-to-medium firm in New England, probably in one of the smaller cities rather than Boston. I would like to work with clients who are small-business people and private individuals; I haven't focused on any specialty yet. I would hope to stay with one firm for a long time: one aspect of being older is that changing jobs is both less appealing and less feasible, since few firms will be interested in hiring fifty-year-old attorneys, so it is important to stick with whomever I start with. If I were to leave, it would be to work on my own. Down the road, I would be interested in being a judge if that possibility arose, and in teaching part-time while still being in legal practice.

Profile

Name Withheld
Harvard Law School class: 1997
Undergraduate institution: Lafayette College
Undergraduate GPA listed by category—3.75+, 3.50–3.74, 3.25–3.49, 3.00–3.24, below 3.00: 3.75+
Graduate institution and GPA, if applicable: N/A
LSAT Score listed by percentile—99–95, 94–90, 89–85, 84–80, 79–75, 74–70, 69–65, below 64: 99–95
Hometown and high school: Staten Island, NY; Susan E. Wagner High School
Types of recommenders, i.e., professors or employers: Professors
Race, sex, and class: Caucasian, female, middle
Major undergraduate activities: Varsity fencing team; DJ/program director of college radio station; Geology Club
Major scholastic or academic honors: Phi Beta Kappa, Phi Alpha Theta (history honor society), Dean's List every semester, two gold medals and two silver medals for being an outstanding student athlete, graduated *magna cum laude*
Work experience (including summer) prior to HLS: Internship at Richmond County DA's Office for three summers prior to law school, camp counselor for the three summers before that.
Parents' occupations: Father—Pharmacist, Mother—Homemaker
Legacy factor: N/A

Questionnaire

1. When and why did you apply to Harvard Law School? Was your application completed early, late, or in the middle of the rolling admissions process?

I applied to HLS in October of my senior year of college (1993) because I had always wanted to go to law school from when I was very young. When I was really little, I used to say there was a seat at HLS with my name on it. In college, I knew that the only way I'd get a job was to go to a good law school and I figured with my grades and LSAT scores I could apply to Harvard without being laughed at—so it was worth a shot! I guess I applied fairly early in the admissions process.

2. How would you describe the undergraduate institution that you attended? Does it have a strong reputation and a solid track record of sending lots of its graduates to Harvard Law School?

I attended a small, private, liberal arts college. I received an excellent education and all of my classes were really small so I received lots of personal attention. The atmosphere was also really laid back. I think my school has a fairly solid reputation, although it isn't well known throughout the country. It doesn't have a strong record of sending people to HLS as far as I know. I'm the first person in fifteen years to come here from my college.

3. Did you think, prior to being accepted, that you had a decent chance of being admitted to Harvard Law School?

I knew I had at least a small chance, but I really had no idea that I really was going to get in. Lots of people told me there was no way I would not get in, but I didn't believe them. I was advised to apply to only the top three schools in the country, but I instead applied to the top seventeen!

4. Did you take any time off prior to applying or matriculating at HLS? If so, why did you take time off and what did you do?

No.

5. What were your strongest assets when applying to Harvard Law School? Grades? LSAT score? Extracurriculars? Personal statement? Recommendations? Family connections? Personal background? Work experience?

My LSAT and GPA were definitely strong, but I think they were absolutely necessary coming from the small, not-so-well-known college I was coming from. I think it was my undergraduate major (geology/history) which was unique as well as my extracurriculars which were fairly unique (varsity fencing, DJ at the school radio station) which really completed the whole package.

6. What type of courses did you take as an undergraduate to prepare yourself for Harvard Law School?

I didn't take anything to prepare me for Harvard purposely. As a history major I, of course, had a lot of writing to do and essay exams. But the big surprise is that being a geology major helped a lot because, though I am an organized person in general, it helped me to be more organized and methodical in my thinking. More importantly, I didn't just memorize facts, I learned how to apply what I knew, which is really helpful for exams here.

7. What was your LSAT score(s)? How did you prepare for the test? If you took an LSAT prep course, which one, and did it help?

I got a 170 (98th percentile). I took Kaplan and I got a lot out of it, but not everyone does. They have an amazing amount of resources and they don't teach gimmicky tricks like Princeton Review does. I used every resource they had because the best way to prepare for the LSAT is to practice as many questions as you can get your hands on. I did this all on my own using Kaplan's resources, but they have more resources than I ever could have gotten by myself. You have to be very self-motivated to take Kaplan, but if you are, it is clearly the course to take.

8. How long did you spend on your personal statement? What did you write about and how did you decide on the topic? Did anyone help you with your statement? If so, who?

I spent about a month or so on my personal statement. I had an advisor, who helps a lot of people with personal statements, helping me because I have a really hard time thinking of things about myself that might be interesting. We brainstormed together and she proofread my various drafts to make suggestions. For a topic, we just brainstormed about things in my life that show my determination and perseverance and tied that together with what I want to do in the future.

9. Who wrote your recommendations for Harvard Law School and how did you choose them? How much notice did you give your recommenders and when were the recommendations completed?

I had three geology professors writing my recommendations. This is because, between my two majors, I definitely spent the bulk of my time in the geology department. It was a very small department, so I knew all of the professors really well and felt that they would be the best people to write for me. Three out of four of them ended up writing for me. I asked them at the end of August when I returned to school for my senior year and gave them a deadline of the beginning of October. They were pretty much on time with that, maybe a week or so late.

10. What type of extracurricular activities did you participate in during your undergraduate years that you feel were beneficial to your being admitted to Harvard Law School, and why?

I think being on the varsity fencing team and winning a varsity letter was important because it shows I have a talent outside of the classroom. Also, it is a somewhat unique sport, and my team was the only co-ed team in the division, so I fenced only men, which I think shows my love of a challenge. It also shows I can balance my time. I also think that being a DJ at the radio station, as well as program director, shows that I have leadership qualities and am outgoing. But mostly I just did those things because they were fun and I think they made me a more well-rounded, interesting person.

11. Do you feel that your race, sex, or class played a role in the admissions process? If so, explain.

The only reason that I might think that my sex made a difference is because I know of two men who applied to HLS from my college, one the year before I did, and one the same year as I did, and both had excellent grades and LSATS, but neither were accepted. But it may not be gender that did it. It may be that I was a science major and I had more interesting extracurriculars, not just your run-of-the-mill fraternity president.

12. Do you think that your political ideology played a role in the admissions process? If so, explain.

Probably not. I am a middle-of-the-road Republican, but I don't think HLS could tell what my political ideology is. Maybe they think I'm a liberal because I want to do environmental law. I don't know. They probably do like to accept people with a desire to do public interest, but I don't think that tells a whole lot about political ideology.

13. Did you see the Harvard Law School campus prior to applying or being admitted? If so, what arrangements did you make for the visit, what were your initial impressions, and have your impressions changed very much? If you didn't visit the campus prior to being accepted, why not?

I didn't visit prior to being accepted because I didn't know if I was going to be accepted. I figured I'd visit if I was accepted.

14. When did you receive your letter of acceptance from the Dean of Admissions and what were you doing?

I received the letter toward the end of January. At the time I was driving up to Boston with my cousin to move her out of her apartment and when we stopped for food in Connecticut, I called home to let my mom know where we were. She had opened the letter already and almost didn't tell me because my aunt told her that if I knew I wouldn't be able to concentrate on my driving. But she told me anyway and I didn't get into a car accident, because it didn't sink in until I got home and saw the letter myself. I wish I got to open it myself because it would have been more exciting.

15. How are you paying for Harvard Law School? Parents? Loans? Savings? Work?

Parents and loans.

16. What do you plan to do in the immediate years following Law School graduation? What are your long-term career goals?

I'm not sure. Either I'll work for a law firm doing environmental law or trusts and estates, or I'll work for a consulting firm, or I'll work at a federal agency. Long-term, I will hopefully be doing something truly for public interest and possibly environmental work.

Profile

Name: R. Jordan Hall
Harvard Law School class: Class of 1997
Undergraduate institution: Texas A&M University
Undergraduate GPA listed by category—3.75+, 3.50–3.74, 3.25–3.49, 3.00–3.24, below 3.00: 3.75+
Graduate institution and GPA, if applicable: N/A
LSAT Score listed by percentile—99–95, 94–90, 89–85, 84–80, 79–75, 74–70, 69–65, below 64: 99–95
Hometown and high school: San Antonio, TX; John Marshall High School
Types of recommenders, i.e., professors or employers: Two professors
Race, sex, and class: White, male, upper-middle
Major undergraduate activities: None
Major scholastic or academic honors: Honors Fellowship, *summa cum laude*, various other minor related things (Dean's List, etc.)
Work experience (including summer) prior to HLS: Video store clerk; Duke University Talent Identification Program resident advisor.
Parents' occupations: Father—Airline pilot, Mother—Psychologist at a Catholic school
Legacy factor: N/A

Questionnaire

1. When and why did you apply to Harvard Law School? Was your application completed early, late, or in the middle of the rolling admissions process?

I applied late in the process, but after my third year at school. I was trying to decide between grad school and law school and since I could graduate in three years, I went ahead and applied to Harvard and Yale law schools on a lark in order to find out what the admissions process was like (in preparation for the next year). When I was accepted, I came to visit, decided that I liked the spirit of Harvard better than Yale (and the smell for that matter) and deferred for one year.

2. How would you describe the undergraduate institution that you attended? Does it have a strong reputation and a solid track record of sending lots of its graduates to Harvard Law School?

A&M is primarily an agricultural and mechanical (e.g., engineering) university. It is a large (40K+ students) state university. It looks like we have sent about one student to HLS per year for the last few years, but not as many in the past. We had two when I was accepted and then two more the next year as well.

3. Did you think, prior to being accepted, that you had a decent chance of being admitted to Harvard Law School?

No, I did not.

4. Did you take any time off prior to applying or matriculating at HLS? If so, why did you take time off and what did you do?

I deferred for one year. I stayed at A&M to complete an Honors Fellowship in philosophy and to hang out with my fiancée. At that point she still had two years left in undergrad and we didn't want to spend that much time apart.

5. What were your strongest assets when applying to Harvard Law School? Grades? LSAT score? Extracurriculars? Personal statement? Recommendations? Family connections? Personal background? Work experience?

My guess is that LSAT, grades, recommendations, and personal statement in that order were most critical to my acceptance. I highly doubt that my background and work experience had any effect, and I have no connections.

6. What type of courses did you take as an undergraduate to prepare yourself for Harvard Law School?

I took every philosophy course that was available. I did not do so to prepare myself for HLS and indeed it does not seem to have had that effect. Short of that, I did not do anything to prepare myself for law school.

7. What was your LSAT score(s)? How did you prepare for the test? If you took an LSAT prep course, which one, and did it help?

176. I did not prepare for the test with the exception of a Kaplan thirty-question pre-test to see what the thing was like.

8. How long did you spend on your personal statement? What did you write about and how did you decide on the topic? Did anyone help you with your statement? If so, who?

I spent about one week on the personal statement.

9. Who wrote your recommendations for Harvard Law School and how did you choose them? How much notice did you give your recommenders and when were the recommendations completed?

I asked Professors John McDermott and Scott Austin in the philosophy department to write my recommendations. Scott was my fellowship advisor and McDermott has national recognition and volunteered to write me a recommendation. I gave them both several months' notice and the recommendations were completed at least two weeks before the deadline.

10. What type of extracurricular activities did you participate in during your undergraduate years that you feel were beneficial to your being admitted to Harvard Law School, and why?

I don't think that any of my extracurricular activities were helpful in any way.

11. Do you feel that your race, sex, or class played a role in the admissions process? If so, explain.

No.

12. Do you think that your political ideology played a role in the admissions process? If so, explain.

There is that possibility. However, I have yet to discover even a single faculty member who shares my politics. Nonetheless, I might be part of a Crit. [Critical Legal Studies] quota.

13. *Did you see the Harvard Law School campus prior to applying or being admitted? If so, what arrangements did you make for the visit, what were your initial impressions, and have your impressions changed very much? If you didn't visit the campus prior to being accepted, why not?*

No, I visited after being admitted. I came up here in the early winter to check out HLS and Yale. I was wowed by the history of Harvard and by its potential. I have come to discover that Harvard lacks the heart and spirit I had attributed to it. I haven't given up hope quite yet though and still sometimes feel the ghosts of Christmas past.

I didn't visit campus prior to being accepted because it was too expensive and I had no confidence that I would be accepted at all.

14. *When did you receive your letter of acceptance from the Dean of Admissions and what were you doing?*

I got my letter in late February. I think it was a Saturday, and I was getting ready to enjoy a beautiful spring day with a little basketball when the mail came.

15. *How are you paying for Harvard Law School? Parents? Loans? Savings? Work?*

I am paying for HLS in equal parts parents, loans, savings, and work. If I am lucky, my loans will be no greater than 20K when I get out of here.

16. *What do you plan to do in the immediate years following Law School graduation? What are your long-term career goals?*

I have no idea whatsoever. I could make one up, but that would be dishonest. Tentatively, I can affirm that a firm job is out of the question. Academia is a possibility, as is environmental public interest. Or maybe I will not practice but secondarily use my J.D. and go into business for myself.

Profile

Name Withheld
Harvard Law School class: 1997
Undergraduate institution: University of Massachusetts at Amherst
**Undergraduate GPA listed by category—3.75+, 3.50–3.74,
      3.25–3.49, 3.00–3.24, below 3.00:** 3.75+
Graduate institution and GPA, if applicable: University of Texas at
      Austin, 3.50–3.74

LSAT Score listed by percentile—99–95, 94–90, 89–85, 84–80, 79–75, 74–70, 69–65, below 64: 99–95
Hometown and high school: Amherst, MA; Amherst Regional High School
Types of recommenders, i.e., professors or employers: Professors
Race, sex, and class: White (Jewish), female, middle
Major undergraduate activities: Founded and ran campus feminist organization
Major scholastic or academic honors: Phi Beta Kappa, *summa cum laude*
Work experience (including summer) prior to HLS: Secretarial, budgeting, mediation, political activism.
Parents' occupations: Father—Professor (retired), Mother—Professor, physical therapist
Legacy factor: N/A

Questionnaire

1. When and why did you apply to Harvard Law School? Was your application completed early, late, or in the middle of the rolling admissions process?

I sent in my application in the middle of November. I thought I had a reasonable chance (30 percent) of getting in, so I figured why not aim for the top? Also, I wanted to be back in Massachusetts after living in Texas.

2. How would you describe the undergraduate institution that you attended? Does it have a strong reputation and a solid track record of sending lots of its graduates to Harvard Law School?

UMass is a decent state school which has had a lot of funding problems in the last ten years or so. Judging by the fact that I am the only person in my class from UMass/Amherst, I do not think it has a reputation for sending people to HLS. UMass generally has a good reputation outside the state and an outstanding reputation for certain departments (linguistics, polymer chemistry), but inside Massachusetts, many people don't think too highly of the state school. It's a shame, because I think state schools are a wonderful resource and UMass could improve immensely if only it were better funded.

3. Did you think, prior to being accepted, that you had a decent chance of being admitted to Harvard Law School?

As I said before, about 30 percent. That's enough of a chance to spend the money applying.

4. Did you take any time off prior to applying or matriculating at HLS? If so, why did you take time off and what did you do?

I spent four years in Texas, getting my master's in linguistics for two years and then working as a secretary for two years. During that time, I did a lot of volunteer work as well, with Planned Parenthood and a housing co-op.

5. What were your strongest assets when applying to Harvard Law School? Grades? LSAT score? Extracurriculars? Personal statement? Recommendations? Family connections? Personal background? Work experience?

My LSAT scores and undergrad grades were quite high. I also graduated from college in three years, which might have made an impression. One of my recommendations was good—the other was very watery. Some of my volunteer work and extracurricular activities might have helped, although I don't think my paid work experience was anything special. I do think that having a master's degree made me more attractive as a candidate. I also think that being a Texas resident helped, even though I am originally from Massachusetts. Finally, I like to think that my personal statement was original and helpful in getting me accepted.

6. What type of courses did you take as an undergraduate to prepare yourself for Harvard Law School?

As an undergraduate, I had no idea that I would be going to law school at all. I took barely more than the requirements of my major (linguistics and philosophy/logic), the general education requirements, and requirements for my minor (Latin). The linguistics, logic, and Latin have all helped *a lot* in law school.

7. What was your LSAT score(s)? How did you prepare for the test? If you took an LSAT prep course, which one, and did it help?

I scored 170 (98th percentile) on the LSAT. I did not take a course, but bought two books, one general and one on logic games. I also ordered six back tests and took one every other weekend until the test, under approximate test conditions. I had somebody else grade the tests. I think this slow, persistent method of preparation was really helpful. I feel much better about my performance on the LSAT than on the GRE, which I took twice and for which I took a prep course.

The day of the test, I rented a car to drive to the test site, played some fun music on the radio, arrived early, and ate a sandwich before the test. All of this calmed me down.

8. *How long did you spend on your personal statement? What did you write about and how did you decide on the topic? Did anyone help you with your statement? If so, who?*

I spent about a month on my personal statement. I showed it to a number of friends (some grad students, some undergrads), and to one instructor. I also showed it to my parents and sisters. I disregarded a lot of the advice from everyone except one friend and the instructor, but I'm still glad I got the feedback.

The personal statement was about the role of hearing people in the deaf community and the education crisis facing deaf children in this country. I picked this topic because it interests me, it is important, and I thought it would make me stand out from the other applicants.

9. *Who wrote your recommendations for Harvard Law School and how did you choose them? How much notice did you give your recommenders and when were the recommendations completed?*

I asked two recommenders, my graduate advisor and my undergraduate advisor, in the spring ('93) before I took the LSAT. I asked them to send me the recommendations by October, which they did. I chose these two people because I thought they would be able to give the best feedback on each major section of my academic life.

10. *What type of extracurricular activities did you participate in during your undergraduate years that you feel were beneficial to your being admitted to Harvard Law School, and why?*

I founded the Progressive Organization for Women's Equal Rights (POWER) and then acted as co-president and treasurer in my last year at UMass. This position gave me some wonderful experience in public speaking, writing, fundraising, and dealing with bureaucracy (but not spelling— sorry). I was a recipient of the Alumni Association's Senior Leadership Award, which I think was helpful on my application.

I also think that the volunteer work I did during and after graduate school, with Planned Parenthood and the housing co-op, was helpful on my application.

11. *Do you feel that your race, sex, or class played a role in the admissions process? If so, explain.*

Being female might have given me an edge, especially because HLS is not yet 50/50 as far as sex ratio among students. I don't think my race or class played any part in the decision. Again, there might have been a regional diversity preference for "someone from Texas," which I am not, although I might have appeared to be. Then again, HLS does seem to have a lot of students from Texas, so maybe that didn't help.

12. Do you think that your political ideology played a role in the admissions process? If so, explain.

No.

13. Did you see the Harvard Law School campus prior to applying or being admitted? If so, what arrangements did you make for the visit, what were your initial impressions, and have your impressions changed very much? If you didn't visit the campus prior to being accepted, why not?

I didn't visit the campus because I was living in Texas at the time and could not afford a trip up just to visit a school that might possibly accept me.

14. When did you receive your letter of acceptance from the Dean of Admissions and what were you doing?

I was working as a secretary when I received my acceptance letter. The letter was dated 1/14/94 and I must have gotten it about a week later.

15. How are you paying for Harvard Law School? Parents? Loans? Savings? Work?

I am borrowing every penny.

16. What do you plan to do in the immediate years following Law School graduation? What are your long-term career goals?

I will probably go into legal aid right after graduation. I see myself with a career in legal aid, government, or as counsel to a political group (such as Planned Parenthood, etc.).

Profile

Name Withheld
Harvard Law School class: 1997
Undergraduate institution: Yale
Undergraduate GPA listed by category—3.75+, 3.50–3.74, 3.25–3.49, 3.00–3.24, below 3.00: 3.25–3.49
Graduate institution and GPA, if applicable: N/A

Lsat Score listed by percentile—99–95, 94–90, 89–85, 84–80, 79–75, 74–70, 69–65, below 64: 99–95

Hometown and high school: Washington, D.C.; Sidwell Friends

Types of recommenders, i.e., professors or employers: Supervisor at Department of Energy; dean of Residential College at Yale; professor at Yale

Race, sex, and class: Black/Latina, female, middle

Major undergraduate activities: Varsity track; freshperson counselor; residential college council; gospel choir

Major scholastic or academic honors: Nothing major

Work experience (including summer) prior to HLS: Two years at Department of Energy's Office of Hearings and Appeals as an Exceptions Analyst.

Parents' occupations: Father—Mailman, Mother—Housekeeper

Legacy factor: N/A

Questionnaire

1. When and why did you apply to Harvard Law School? Was your application completed early, late, or in the middle of the rolling admissions process?

I wasn't sure what type of law I wanted to practice—I was torn between becoming a public interest–type advocate (I'm interested in child and poverty issues) and making a lot of money. I knew that, regardless of what I chose to do, a law degree from a top school would be key.

I applied in late October/early November of 1993.

2. How would you describe the undergraduate institution that you attended? Does it have a strong reputation and a solid track record of sending lots of its graduates to Harvard Law School?

I graduated from Yale. Great reputation, and many of its graduates are at Harvard Law.

3. Did you think, prior to being accepted, that you had a decent chance of being admitted to Harvard Law School?

I thought that I had a chance—not a good chance, but I didn't think that it was completely out of reach.

4. Did you take any time off prior to applying or matriculating at HLS?

If so, why did you take time off and what did you do?

Yes—two years. I worked in D.C. at the Department of Energy.

5. What were your strongest assets when applying to Harvard Law School? Grades? LSAT score? Extracurriculars? Personal statement? Recommendations? Family connections? Personal background? Work experience?

My strongest assets, I think, were my extracurriculars, personal background, personal statement, and LSAT. I did some work with the Black Student Fund in D.C. after graduation and co-founded an alumni organization (they help African-American families in D.C. send their kids to private schools). I think that this and other volunteer work that I did made a big difference.

6. What type of courses did you take as an undergraduate to prepare yourself for Harvard Law School?

I took no courses with the intention that they'd prepare me for law school. I took one course, philosophy of law, because I found the subject interesting. I can't say that it prepared me for the likes of Professor Rosenberg.

7. What was your LSAT score(s)? How did you prepare for the test? If you took an LSAT prep course, which one, and did it help?

169. I bought as many study guides as possible, and ordered all the materials offered by the LSAT people. *The Princeton Review* study guide was far and away the most helpful of all the books I used in terms of suggesting test-taking strategies. Taking old exams (purchased through the company) under time-pressure was also key.

8. How long did you spend on your personal statement? What did you write about and how did you decide on the topic? Did anyone help you with your statement? If so, who?

I spent a couple of weeks on my statement. I wrote about my personal background—how I was affected by living in a lower–income neighborhood (we were poorer then) while attending schools with wealthier classmates. I also wrote about the responsibility I feel I have to do something to better the community from which I came.

I'm not sure how I decided on the topic. I'd been thinking about the statement for weeks, if not months, before I actually sat down to write. I thought about my goals in life, one of which is to provide children of lower-income families greater opportunities through education. I've always believed in community service and feel a duty to serve; I think this stems from the knowledge that, had certain individuals and groups not intervened on *my* behalf, I might have languished in D.C. public schools. I might not have attended Sidwell, and my teachers might not have encouraged me to apply to Yale. These issues seemed to me to be primary forces in my life. So I wrote about them.

9. Who wrote your recommendations for Harvard Law School and how did you choose them? How much notice did you give your recommenders and when were the recommendations completed?

I asked my three recommenders in late August to write my recommendations, which I wanted by October. Two of the three, the Dean of my residential college at Yale and my supervisor at the Department of Energy, wrote the letters right away. The professor from Yale did not complete the letter until mid- to late October.

10. What type of extracurricular activities did you participate in during your undergraduate years that you feel were beneficial to your being admitted to Harvard Law School, and why?

I was a hurdler on the varsity women's track team; I was active in several community-service organizations; I think that becoming a freshperson counselor was the most beneficial "activity" I participated in (in terms of law school).

11. Do you feel that your race, sex, or class played a role in the admissions process? If so, explain.

Yes. I think that being half-Latina and half-black helped (although I self-identified as black). However, I think that being from a lower-middle-class background played at least as large a role.

12. Do you think that your political ideology played a role in the admissions process? If so, explain.

No, I don't think so. I don't think that my political ideology really came out in my application.

13. Did you see the Harvard Law School campus prior to applying or being admitted? If so, what arrangements did you make for the visit, what were your initial impressions, and have your impressions changed very much? If you didn't visit the campus prior to being accepted, why not?

Yes. I visited in the spring (April). I stayed with a friend of a friend from the Department of Energy. Since I came on a weekend which was both the New Admits Weekend and the weekend of the BLSA Spring Conference, my impression was that Harvard was an amazingly active, heady place. My initial impressions have changed slightly. I've found that, like the weekend I visited, the administrators at Harvard are involved and helpful (this may have a lot to do with the fact that I'm now a member of the Administrative Board so I interact with them more than most). Although the school is less hectic and active than it was that weekend, other students are constantly arranging panels and sessions designed to ease the stress and confusion of the first year.

14. When did you receive your letter of acceptance from the Dean of Admissions and what were you doing?

I received my letter in January. I was visiting a friend in New York and my parents opened it (without my permission! But they said it was a big envelope so they'd known I'd gotten in). They called me on the telephone and told me. I couldn't really celebrate, because I felt a little uncomfortable around my friend and her husband. But I think that my parents celebrated enough for all of us.

15. How are you paying for Harvard Law School? Parents? Loans? Savings? Work?

Loans.

16. What do you plan to do in the immediate years following Law School graduation? What are your long-term career goals?

I think I'll work in a firm for three or four years. Eventually, I'd like to do criminal work. I'd love to be a judge someday.

Profile

Name: Matthew T. Henshon
Harvard Law School class: 1995
Undergraduate institution: Princeton
Undergraduate GPA listed by category—3.75+, 3.50–3.74, 3.25–3.49, 3.00–3.24, below 3.00: 3.50–3.74
Graduate institution and GPA, if applicable: N/A
LSAT Score listed by percentile—99–95, 94–90, 89–85, 84–80, 79–75, 74–70, 69–65, below 64: 99–95
Hometown and high school: Wilbraham, MA; Minnechaug Regional High School; Loomis Chaffee, Windsor, CT

Types of recommenders, i.e., professors or employers: Professors
and employers

Race, sex, and class: White, male, middle

Major undergraduate activities: Basketball, writing column for
alumni magazine, coaching youth basketball

Major scholastic or academic honors: Graduated with honors

Work experience (including summer) prior to HLS: Worked at
Independent Sector, a "trade group" for nonprofits and charities in
Washington, D.C., 1991–92; Worked for Pearson Construction,
general contracting firm in West Springfield, MA, in various
capacities from day laborer to financial analyst, summers 1990,
1989, 1988, 1987; Worked as English teacher and basketball coach
in Morelos, Mexico, summer 1989; Worked as counselor/coach at
Five-Star Basketball Camps in Pennsylvania and Virginia, various
weeks in summers 1990, 1989, 1988; Worked as intern in
Edward P. Boland (D-MA) Congressional Office, Washington, D.C.,
summer 1988.

Parents' occupations: Father—General contractor, Mother—College
administrator

Legacy factor: N/A

Questionnaire

1. When and why did you apply to Harvard Law School? Was your application completed early, late, or in the middle of the rolling admissions process?

I finished my application in late October/early November 1991, which I thought was early in the rolling process. I clearly felt that my chances of admission would be enhanced by applying as early as possible in the cycle.

2. How would you describe the undergraduate institution that you attended? Does it have a strong reputation and a solid track record of sending lots of its graduates to Harvard Law School?

Princeton . . . strong record, etc.

3. Did you think, prior to being accepted, that you had a decent chance of being admitted to Harvard Law School?

I figured I was on the bubble—depending on when I applied (in the rolling admissions process).

4. Did you take any time off prior to applying or matriculating at HLS? If so, why did you take time off and what did you do?

I worked for a year down in Washington, D.C. I decided to do this primarily because I was sort of burned out after senior year (between writing a thesis, playing basketball almost year-round for four years, etc.) and wanted a break from school—knowing that I would be going back to school right away. I worked at a "trade group" for nonprofits and charities, called Independent Sector.

5. What were your strongest assets when applying to Harvard Law School? Grades? LSAT score? Extracurriculars? Personal statement? Recommendations? Family connections? Personal background? Work experience?

More than most people, I don't feel that I was outstanding in any one area—even in standardized testing (LSAT) because the old scoring system had been eroded by the time I was applying (and in fact replaced by a tougher system). So I think it was more the sum of parts rather than any one area.

6. What type of courses did you take as an undergraduate to prepare yourself for Harvard Law School?

I took two specific law classes: civil liberties (a summary of the Bill of Rights) and writing about law (a writing class taught by an HLS grad.) However, although they were legal courses, they weren't nearly the same thing as HLS classes. Nevertheless, both gave me some sense of what the law was all about.

7. What was your LSAT score(s)? How did you prepare for the test? If you took an LSAT prep course, which one, and did it help?

I took the old LSAT, and received a 47 (on a scale of 48). I had taken the Kaplan test-prep course, and it probably helped me more in confidence and comfort level with the test than in any substantive way.

8. How long did you spend on your personal statement? What did you write about and how did you decide on the topic? Did anyone help you with your statement? If so, who?

I spent a great deal of time with my statement because I wanted to use it to draw together information that wouldn't necessarily stand out in other parts of my application. Additionally, I figured that it would be significantly different than a lot of applications because I didn't write about the law very much—hardly at all. However, I wanted to talk in particular about the (serious) time commitment of playing a varsity sport at a Division I school (even if it was the Ivy League!).

I faxed several copies to my father for his reactions and comments during the writing process (and my mother also saw it in various stages).

9. Who wrote your recommendations for Harvard Law School and how did you choose them? How much notice did you give your recommenders and when were the recommendations completed?

The recommenders that I chose were primarily professors that I had in college, but I specifically chose those with whom I had a personal relationship—even if the grades I received in the class were not "the highest." I don't really remember the specifics of the recommendations, but I would imagine I gave about four to six weeks notice, and the recs were turned in on time, as far as I know!

10. What type of extracurricular activities did you participate in during your undergraduate years that you feel were beneficial to your being admitted to Harvard Law School, and why?

Playing a sport at a Division I school requires a serious time commitment, and I was prevented from getting involved with a lot of other activities. As a result, I had to pick and choose my other activities and did a lot of writing (for various magazines on campus). I don't know that either of these helped me to gain admission, but I don't think that they hurt, either.

11. Do you feel that your race, sex, or class played a role in the admissions process? If so, explain.

No. White male.

12. Do you think that your political ideology played a role in the admissions process? If so, explain.

No. I didn't try to get into political rhetoric or ideology, other than a contextual reference to Anita Hill in my personal statement.

13. Did you see the Harvard Law School campus prior to applying or being admitted? If so, what arrangements did you make for the visit, what were your initial impressions, and have your impressions changed very much? If you didn't visit the campus prior to being accepted, why not?

No. I had been around the area (Harvard Yard) and have never felt that going to a school gives you much more than a sense of where the buildings are.

14. When did you receive your letter of acceptance from the Dean of Admissions and what were you doing?

I was working in Washington, D.C., and living over the bridge in Arlington, Virginia, when I applied to HLS. I was actually visiting my girlfriend (who was still at Princeton), and one of my roommates called down with the news. [I assume you want that level of specificity!]

15. How are you paying for Harvard Law School? Parents? Loans? Savings? Work?
Combination of savings and parents.

16. What do you plan to do in the immediate years following Law School graduation? What are your long-term career goals?
Immediately, I will be working for a medium-sized law firm in Boston (Hill & Barlow). In the long-term, my plans include public service in various forms and continued work in the private sector.

Profile

Name Withheld
Harvard Law School class: 1997
Undergraduate institution: Duke University
Undergraduate GPA listed by category—3.75+, 3.50–3.74, 3.25–3.49, 3.00–3.24, below 3.00: 3.50–3.74
Graduate institution and GPA, if applicable: N/A
LSAT Score listed by percentile—99–95, 94–90, 89–85, 84–80, 79–75, 74–70, 69–65, below 64: 99–95
Hometown and high school: College Park, GA; Woodward Academy
Types of recommenders, i.e., professors or employers: Professors
Race, sex, and class: African American, female, middle
Major undergraduate activities: Undergraduate Admissions Office tour guide, sorority officer, dance program, part-time jobs
Major scholastic or academic honors: National Merit Scholar, IBM Thomas J. Watson Scholarship, Reginaldo Howard Memorial Scholarship (from Duke), Departmental Research Grant, Dean's List with Distinction, *cum laude*
Work experience (including summer) prior to HLS: Two summers ('90 and '91) at IBM as intern, part-time jobs during college (waitress, book store clerk, student assistant for Duke Annual Fund), summer with USPublic Interest Research Group (PIRG) as field manager.

Parents' occupations: Father—Locomotive engineer, Stepmother—
    Semi-retired/housewife (retired from IBM), Mother (deceased)—
    Registered nurse
Legacy factor: N/A

Questionnaire

1. When and why did you apply to Harvard Law School? Was your application completed early, late, or in the middle of the rolling admissions process?

I applied in late January/early February, which was late in the rolling admissions process. I decided to apply after I talked with Duke's pre-law advisor; he encouraged me to apply to the top five schools because he thought I had an excellent shot of getting in. I, on the other hand, thought I was taking a gamble but decided to apply to Harvard, Yale, and Columbia just to see if I would get in.

2. How would you describe the undergraduate institution that you attended? Does it have a strong reputation and a solid track record of sending lots of its graduates to Harvard Law School?

Duke has an amazingly solid track record with HLS. Each year, we send about fifteen to twenty students to the law school. Duke is a top-ten national university. I think most people are familiar enough with the school that it doesn't need much more introduction.

3. Did you think, prior to being accepted, that you had a decent chance of being admitted to Harvard Law School?

I thought Harvard only admitted people with 4.0 GPA/180 LSAT. So, not having those numbers, I didn't think I had a great shot of being admitted initially (despite my adviser's confidence). Then, after applying so late in the process, I was sure that I would probably be wait-listed, if not rejected.

4. Did you take any time off prior to applying or matriculating at HLS? If so, why did you take time off and what did you do?

No.

5. What were your strongest assets when applying to Harvard Law School? Grades? LSAT score? Extracurriculars? Personal statement? Recommendations? Family connections? Personal background? Work experience?

I think my strongest assets were my recommendations, personal statement, and my personal background. My recommendations came from two professors who knew me rather intimately. I had known one since I visited Duke as a prospective freshman and had taken several classes with her including one very small seminar (six people). I had met her son, had dinner with her on a few occasions, and communicated with her during my semester abroad; she was also my pre-major adviser. The other professor was the director of my study-abroad program and was actually a Cornell professor. I took the class that he taught in France and spent a lot of time with him outside of class (as was the nature of the program—we had several weekend excursions and he hosted dinners at his house). I think my recommenders were able to give very detailed and genuine recommendations, and I had done very good and very difficult work in their classes (both advanced French classes). My personal statement was also very open and frank, sort of a candid look at my experience in France and my reactions to it. As for my background, I think the semester abroad, coupled with a summer of research in France, was somewhat impressive. I think writing a thesis probably helped out. I also think that my performance is a bit more remarkable in light of the fact that neither of my parents has a four-year degree and that my mother died when I was still very young (eleven years old). I don't think of myself as the "hard luck kid," but some people might see my background and think of me that way.

6. What type of courses did you take as an undergraduate to prepare yourself for Harvard Law School?

I took a few political science classes on international law and international security. I also took two cultural anthropology classes that were being taught by UNC law professor John Conley (law in complex societies, and anthropology of law). I think most of my classes prepared me for law school indirectly because they involved a lot of comparative and analytical thinking.

7. What was your LSAT score(s)? How did you prepare for the test? If you took an LSAT prep course, which one, and did it help?

I scored a 168. I just did a few practice questions in the Barron's and did one "self-timed" exam.

8. How long did you spend on your personal statement? What did you write about and how did you decide on the topic? Did anyone help you with your statement? If so, who?

I wrote and revised my personal statement over the course of a week or two weeks. I wrote about my experience in France and the fears I had before going there that I, as a black person, would not fit in to the society. I chose the topic because going to France and finding out that everyone in the world is not color prejudiced (in France, their prejudices are more culturally based) had a profound effect on my life. I wondered why I felt more at ease in a foreign country than I did in my own. I also realized that France is not utopia because there are people there who feel just as ill at ease as I sometimes do here in the United States simply because they have a different religion.

9. *Who wrote your recommendations for Harvard Law School and how did you choose them? How much notice did you give your recommenders and when were the recommendations completed?*

My recommenders were both French professors, Michele Longino of the Duke romance studies department and Jacques Bereaud of the Cornell romance languages department. I chose them because they were the two professors to whom I felt the closest, because I had done excellent (their word) work in their classes, and because I knew they both thought very highly of me. I gave them about a month to a month-and-a-half notice (neither of them was at Duke so I had to mail them the recommendations). I think they completed the recommendations in early January or late December.

The pre-law office at Duke coordinated all of the recommendations and sent them to the appropriate schools once we submitted the forms.

10. *What type of extracurricular activities did you participate in during your undergraduate years that you feel were beneficial to your being admitted to Harvard Law School, and why?*

I don't really think any of my extracurriculars were extraordinary.

11. *Do you feel that your race, sex, or class played a role in the admissions process? If so, explain.*

I honestly don't know if my race or sex played a role in admissions.

12. *Do you think that your political ideology played a role in the admissions process? If so, explain.* .

I don't really think it did since I did not make it explicit in my applications and it's not really obvious from any of my activities.

13. *Did you see the Harvard Law School campus prior to applying or being admitted? If so, what arrangements did you make for the visit, what were your initial impressions, and have your impressions changed very much? If you didn't visit the campus prior to being accepted, why not?*

I did not see the campus prior to coming to Harvard because I did not have the time or the money to arrange a visit. I was not really interested in attending the school until after I was admitted. So, prior to admission, I never made the effort to come up and visit the school.

14. When did you receive your letter of acceptance from the Dean of Admissions and what were you doing?

I received my letter of admission at the very end of March (the 29th or 30th). I was actually on my way to Duke Law School for its annual Black Admitted Students' Weekend and stopped off to check my mailbox on the way.

15. How are you paying for Harvard Law School? Parents? Loans? Savings? Work?

Loans, summer work, and more loans.

16. What do you plan to do in the immediate years following Law School graduation? What are your long-term career goals?

I would like to work for an international organization or a firm that does international work. Long-term, I would like to work in the State Department (depending on the administration) or in public international law somewhere else.

Profile

Name Withheld
Harvard Law School class: 1995
Undergraduate institution: Yale University
Undergraduate GPA listed by category—3.75+, 3.50–3.74, 3.25–3.49, 3.00–3.24, below 3.00: 3.50–3.74
Graduate institution and GPA, if applicable: N/A
LSAT Score listed by percentile—99–95, 94–90, 89–85, 84–80, 79–75, 74–70, 69–65, below 64: 89–85
Hometown and high school: Port Arthur, TX; Thomas Jefferson High School
Types of recommenders, i.e., professors or employers: Professors, employer, professor at other school whom I had worked with on a major research project
Race, sex, and class: Mexican American, female, middle
Major undergraduate activities: *Yale Daily News*, reporter, community

service beat reporter, city editor and managing board; Phoenix
Film Society, director/manager for on-campus film screening
company; Pi Beta Phi Sorority, philanthropy chair, historian;
Compas Latino Journal, one of the founders and editors of a
bilingual literary journal; intramural sports: volleyball, softball,
billiards, racquetball, football, bowling; Mexican-American
Women's Forum/MECHA; helped organize 25th anniversary
conference celebrating the first Mexican American graduation from
Yale; Interfraternity Service Council

Major scholastic or academic honors: Distinction in the American
studies major; Texaco Academic Scholarship; VFW Voice of America
Scholarship; Father P. Fernandez Our Lady of Guadalupe
Scholarship; Outstanding Young Woman of America 1991; Ford
Mellon Minority Summer Research Fellowship; Poetry in a
Residential College Freshman Program

Work experience (including summer) prior to HLS: Office assistant,
Yale Medical School, 9/88–12/88; Child Study Center Survey Team,
1/89–5/89; Affordable Maintenance and Repair, receptionist and
dispatcher, summer 1989; Yale Office of Public Affairs/Weekly
Bulletin and Calendar, editorial assistant, 9/89–5/92; UCLA Power of
Place research assistant, summer 1990; Dow Jones, Inc.,
businesswire/ticker, editorial assistant, copy editor, intern,
5/91–8/91; Capital Cities/ABC, Inc. Legal Department, intern,
summer 1992.

Parents' occupations: Mother—Housewife, Father—Territory
manager/sales representative

Legacy factor: N/A

Questionnaire

*1. When and why did you apply to Harvard Law School? Was your appli-
cation completed early, late, or in the middle of the rolling admissions
process?*

I applied the end of January/early February. *Late.*

*2. How would you describe the undergraduate institution that you
attended? Does it have a strong reputation and a solid track record of
sending lots of its graduates to Harvard Law School?*

Yale. It is better than Harvard undergrad. I guess I would say it's a
strong institution.

Yep, it tends to send a lot of people here to school.

3. Did you think, prior to being accepted, that you had a decent chance of being admitted to Harvard Law School?

I guess so, cuz otherwise I wouldn't have applied. I only applied to four schools—Harvard, Yale, Columbia, and UCLA. I also applied to grad school in American history/studies at Harvard and Yale.

4. Did you take any time off prior to applying or matriculating at HLS? If so, why did you take time off and what did you do?

Nope.

5. What were your strongest assets when applying to Harvard Law School? Grades? LSAT score? Extracurriculars? Personal statement? Recommendations? Family connections? Personal background? Work experience?

Extracurriculars, recommendations, and personal background. I was involved in a lot of activities and there tends to be a lot of *Yale Daily News* (YDN) editors who proceed to Harvard. I think it goes back to the old days when the YDN was a stuffy, elitist, well-respected publication (oldest college daily attitude) that fed into the top law schools and newspapers. My recs were really strong because I had also set up good relationships with a number of my professors, as well as my editor/boss at the Yale Office of Public Affairs—she had known me for a while and knew my writing and editing skills.

Personal background: because there aren't many people from my area who proceed to Yale and certainly it is extremely rare that they go on to HLS. My old high-school advanced-placement English teacher told me when I went to Yale that it had been ten to fifteen years since she remembered someone going there and when I got to HLS, she couldn't remember the last time someone had gotten into Harvard. I can happily say that there were two undergrads from my high school when I arrived at Harvard. The high school was pretty good—just fed a lot into local schools and the military academies. I'm happy to say that we've been pretty successful. A woman who graduated the year after me is now a Rhodes Scholar. So while we did not go to big schools, we were definitely given a decent education.

6. What type of courses did you take as an undergraduate to prepare yourself for Harvard Law School?

Not much. I took some poli sci classes, including constitutional law and civil liberties/rights but I wasn't really thinking about law school so seriously that I was preparing for it. I took mostly American history and literature courses, then lots of film classes. My concentration was in history (within the American studies major) but I did have a secondary interest in film studies.

7. What was your LSAT score(s)? How did you prepare for the test? If you took an LSAT prep course, which one, and did it help?

I think it was in the 88–90 percentile range. I didn't prepare for the test. I opened the free book that you get with the registration packet the night before the exam, probably around 10 or 11 and read it over for a couple of hours. I was also sick with the flu at the time, studying for finals and working on this project for a graduate school class I was taking, so I didn't really worry too much about the LSAT and the like. I was more concerned with what was going on around me.

8. How long did you spend on your personal statement? What did you write about and how did you decide on the topic? Did anyone help you with your statement? If so, who?

Maybe a couple of hours . . . [on] one statement about the intellectual topic or whatever, since I had been working on the project I mentioned in question 8. I thought I would incorporate that into the topic since it was on my mind and since I had, if I remember correctly, had lunch that day with my partner about the project and we had been reflecting about the class.

The other topic—well I always have felt this allegiance to my hometown and the area I grew up in so it seemed appropriate.

No one helped me with the statement. I don't remember if I let my roommate read over it or anything.

9. Who wrote your recommendations for Harvard Law School and how did you choose them? How much notice did you give your recommenders and when were the recommendations completed?

Professors wrote my recs, including a professor at UCLA (whom I had been working with on a research project and had helped find information for his book), my advisor for my senior thesis, a graduate school professor (architecture/American studies), and my employer at the Yale Office of Public Affairs.

I gave them an adequate amount of time; I think I told them in September or October. Yale's system is cool—they send recs ("general") to our college dean's office (somewhat like the Harvard houses) and the dean then distributes them to each school you apply to when you send in a request for them to be sent.

10. *What type of extracurricular activities did you participate in during your undergraduate years that you feel were beneficial to your being admitted to Harvard Law School, and why?*

Yale Daily News—see questions above.

Pi Phi—reinforced confidence in myself—more personal than actual application aid.

11. *Do you feel that your race, sex, or class played a role in the admissions process? If so, explain.*

No, but I have heard so much from others about it that I do wonder sometimes.

12. *Do you think that your political ideology played a role in the admissions process? If so, explain.*

No, because I don't have a particular political ideology. I have developed a great deal over the past few years and have moved from being conservative to liberal to moderate.

13. *Did you see the Harvard Law School campus prior to applying or being admitted? If so, what arrangements did you make for the visit, what were your initial impressions, and have your impressions changed very much? If you didn't visit the campus prior to being accepted, why not?*

Not exactly, I had been to HLS before but only passing by with friends and such. Never really here at the school itself.

14. *When did you receive your letter of acceptance from the Dean of Admissions and what were you doing?*

I received it the last week in August. I was working for Cap Cities/ABC, finishing up my internship and had begun preparation for orientation at Columbia Law.

15. *How are you paying for Harvard Law School? Parents? Loans? Savings? Work?*

Loans, summer earnings, grants.

16. *What do you plan to do in the immediate years following Law School graduation? What are your long-term career goals?*

Working for a Washington, D.C., law firm, Crowell & Moring. Planning to do that for a few years, then settling down to have a family and preparing for the next stage of my life. I am hoping to enter the political arena—possibly by the time that I am thirty to thirty-two—running for Congress is currently a consideration.

Profile

Name Withheld
Harvard Law School class: 1997
Undergraduate institution: University of Miami
Undergraduate GPA listed by category—3.75+, 3.50–3.74, 3.25–3.49, 3.00–3.24, below 3.00: 3.75+
Graduate institution and GPA, if applicable: Yokohama National University, Yokohama, Japan; GPA N/A
LSAT Score listed by percentile—99–95, 94–90, 89–85, 84–80, 79–75, 74–70, 69–65, below 64: 99–95
Hometown and high school: Miami, FL; Miami Sunset Senior High School
Types of recommenders, i.e., professors or employers: Former employer, graduate professor
Race, sex, and class: White, male, upper-middle
Major undergraduate activities: Unitarian Universalist Young Adults Fellowship (religious organization), environmental action organization, College Democrats, Alumni Association Student Liaison, work (worked 20–30 hours per week throughout undergraduate years)
Major scholastic or academic honors: Phi Beta Kappa, *magna cum laude*, Dean's List (all four years), Honors and Privileged Studies degree (university honors program), General University Honors
Work experience (including summer) prior to HLS: Two-and-a-half years at a large law firm in Miami (during college), one year as an optical lab assistant (first year of college), Princeton Review (SAT test prep) part-time 3rd and 4th years.
Parents' occupations: School psychologists (both)
Legacy factor: N/A

Questionnaire

1. When and why did you apply to Harvard Law School? Was your application completed early, late, or in the middle of the rolling admissions process?

I applied to Harvard because I thought it was the number one or two law school in the country. I wanted a large law school experience, at a school with great resources. The "gilt-edged diploma" factor probably also had something to do with it. My application was probably fairly late in the admissions process; there were complications because I applied from overseas.

2. How would you describe the undergraduate institution that you attended? Does it have a strong reputation and a solid track record of sending lots of its graduates to Harvard Law School?

My undergraduate institution is not particularly known for its academic prowess. It is a decent school, perhaps one of the best in Florida, but certainly not highly competitive. My school does not send a vast number to Harvard Law each year: maybe two or three at most per year.

3. Did you think, prior to being accepted, that you had a decent chance of being admitted to Harvard Law School?

I thought I had a decent chance; if I didn't, I wouldn't have spent the money on the application fee. I had good grades, a few good honors, great LSAT scores, work experience, and I took two years off to live and study overseas in an Asian country. I thought I looked pretty good on paper, and my background would allow me to stand out a little from the rest of the pack. I was by no means confident that I would be accepted, but I thought I had decent chances.

4. Did you take any time off prior to applying or matriculating at HLS? If so, why did you take time off and what did you do?

I spent two years living and studying in Japan. I had a full-tuition and living-expenses scholarship from Rotary Foundation, so the decision to take time off was easy. I did an intensive language program and then went to law school for a couple semesters there.

5. What were your strongest assets when applying to Harvard Law School? Grades? LSAT score? Extracurriculars? Personal statement? Recommendations? Family connections? Personal background? Work experience?

I think my strongest assets when applying were my LSATS, my grades and Phi Beta Kappa, and my personal background (my Japanese background). My work experience may have been something of a factor.

6. What type of courses did you take as an undergraduate to prepare yourself for Harvard Law School?

I double-majored in English (literature) and political science, so I guess I was pretty much pre-law. I've always been interested in languages and international law, so I minored in foreign languages and international studies.

7. What was your LSAT score(s)? How did you prepare for the test? If you took an LSAT prep course, which one, and did it help?

My LSAT score was 173, which was 99th percentile. I took the Princeton Review prep course (because I worked for them and they let me register for free). I think the prep course really helped; my score was something like 155 before I took the class.

8. How long did you spend on your personal statement? What did you write about and how did you decide on the topic? Did anyone help you with your statement? If so, who?

I agonized about what to write for my personal statement for months. I probably started over again five or six times. But when I actually figured out what to write, I wrote and revised the whole thing in about three days. I had a friend read it over and comment on it for me, but I was overseas, so I didn't have the benefit of a pre-law counselor.

9. Who wrote your recommendations for Harvard Law School and how did you choose them? How much notice did you give your recommenders and when were the recommendations completed?

A lawyer from the firm where I previously worked as a paralegal wrote one recommendation, and my supervisor for my studies in Japan wrote the other. I chose them because I knew they'd write stellar recommendations for me; I knew I could basically tell the Japanese professor what to write because he was unfamiliar with the American recommendation process, which is quite different from Japan. He was also the only academic figure I was really in contact with at that point (I had graduated, in Miami, almost two years before that). I gave them both about three months notice or so.

10. What type of extracurricular activities did you participate in during your undergraduate years that you feel were beneficial to your being admitted to Harvard Law School, and why?

I didn't do a lot of extracurriculars because I worked so much. I was involved with the young adults' group at my church, the environmental organization, the college Democrats, and I had a few other low-key commitments, but my extracurriculars were definitely not my strongest point.

11. Do you feel that your race, sex, or class played a role in the admissions process? If so, explain.

I'm sure my race and sex played a role in the process; I think if I were a person of color or a woman, I would have had to excel even more to "earn" my place in the class. At least that's the impression I get from the students of color I've spoken to about their achievements before coming here. I do not think the process is color- or gender-blind, as the administration would have us think. Somewhere in the back of the reviewer's minds is the fear that they are creating a disproportionately "colored" student body. My class was probably not much of a factor because I've never had any relatives attend Harvard, and my education was financed by academic scholarships, all factors that would have come out on the application. My studies in Japan were paid for by a wealthy scholarship organization. I think I looked somewhere between lower-middle class and the high range of upper-middle class; other than that, the application probably didn't give them specific clues as to my social or economic class.

12. Do you think that your political ideology played a role in the admissions process? If so, explain.

Probably not; my application was fairly non-political. One might have inferred that I am somewhat liberal by my membership in a Unitarian Universalist congregation and my involvement with the college Democrats, but those would have been the only clues, and not very radical ones at that. My personal statement was silent on politics.

13. Did you see the Harvard Law School campus prior to applying or being admitted? If so, what arrangements did you make for the visit, what were your initial impressions, and have your impressions changed very much? If you didn't visit the campus prior to being accepted, why not?

I didn't come to Harvard before September because I was overseas. I wanted to come over the summer, but I was working. So I had no initial impressions aside from popular images of HLS.

14. When did you receive your letter of acceptance from the Dean of Admissions and what were you doing?

I got the acceptance letter in the middle of May—I may have been on the wait-list without knowing it because it came so late. (My application got screwed up because I was overseas; a number of miscommunications and unreliable mail mishaps delayed the process.) I had already planned to matriculate at Columbia Law School, so the Harvard letter came as a surprise. I was working as a paralegal in Miami at the time.

15. How are you paying for Harvard Law School? Parents? Loans? Savings? Work?

My parents give me a couple thousand dollars a year; the rest is all in loans, both Stafford and MEFA. I hope to make a little money this summer and next to offset my borrowing.

16. What do you plan to do in the immediate years following Law School graduation? What are your long-term career goals?

I think I want to work for a firm my first few years out of law school in order to pay off my loans (probably upwards of $90,000 for all three years!). If I can swing it, I might like to work in the State Department's Legal Advisor's Office or the Office of the Trade Representative for a while and then maybe go into private practice. Otherwise, I'll probably try to find a good, liberal firm and work there for a while, trying different kinds of law and making a career for myself.

Profile

Name Withheld
Harvard Law School class: 1997
Undergraduate institution: Georgetown University
Undergraduate GPA listed by category—3.75+, 3.50–3.74,
    3.25–3.49, 3.00–3.24, below 3.00: 3.50–3.74
Graduate institution and GPA, if applicable: Yale University, M.A.,
    political science, GPA N/A
LSAT Score listed by percentile—99–95, 94–90, 89–85, 84–80,
    79–75, 74–70, 69–65, below 64: 99–95 (2nd time), 94–90 (1st)
Hometown and high school: San Jose, CA; Bellarmine College
    Preparatory
Types of recommenders, i.e., professors or employers: Two
    professors, one employer
Race, sex, and class: White, male, middle
Major undergraduate activities: Newspaper, some campus politics,
    some national politics
Major scholastic or academic honors: Graduated Georgetown *magna
    cum laude*, Phi Beta Kappa, Pi Sigma Alpha (political science honor
    society), completed undergraduate honors program in Government
    (including thesis), Yale University Fellowship Recipient
Work experience (including summer) prior to HLS: Special
    Assistant, U.S. Department of Education, 1993–94; Policy Analyst,
    White House Domestic Policy Council, 1993; Policy Analyst,
    Clinton/Gore Campaign, 1992; Test programmer, IntelliGenetics,
    Inc., summers 1988, 1989, 1991; Intern, U.S. Rep. Don Edwards,
    summer 1990.
Parents' occupations: Father—Trained (Ph.D.) biochemist, but has

been business executive in scientific instrument companies for 20 years, Mother—Laboratory research technician

Legacy factor: N/A

Questionnaire

1. When and why did you apply to Harvard Law School? Was your application completed early, late, or in the middle of the rolling admissions process?

I had decided some time ago that law school was probably something that I would want to do, though I wasn't sure exactly when would be a good time. The desire to go to law school came mainly from a need to understand social and political structures, with law being one of the chief ideas that undergirds the distribution of political power in the United States.

Like many of my college classmates, I applied right out of school, but unlike many of them also put in applications at graduate schools. These applications were filed pretty late in the process, as I was fairly ambivalent about what exactly to do with my life. With some acceptances from law schools (but not Harvard) and some from graduate schools, I decided that Yale's political science department would be the best place to continue my education because of the presence of Roger Smith, whom I continue to believe is one of the most intelligent commentators on the relation between law and political theory.

Going to graduate school right from Georgetown turned out to be somewhat of a mistake. At the end of the first year, I felt quite burned out, even though it had been a fairly productive time for me. Through the late fall of 1991 and early spring of 1992, I had become more and more involved with the Clinton campaign, and decided that campaigning in the real political world would be more productive than going on to finish the class requirements for the Ph.D.

After part of a year off, I thought about returning to school, though I was more thinking about setting things up for the following year, especially if the election worked out well. I filed applications in the fall of 1992, and was accepted at a few schools, and wait-listed by Harvard. In the end, I decided that I would be better off waiting another year and applying again than reserving a place at any of the other schools.

In early fall of 1993, I filed a small number of applications, and was accepted by Harvard in early January.

2. How would you describe the undergraduate institution that you attended? Does it have a strong reputation and a solid track record of sending lots of its graduates to Harvard Law School?

When I applied, Georgetown was still building its reputation as the type of place that sends lots of people to Harvard. Over the past few years, especially judging from the large number of Georgetown grads in my class, that reputation has solidified.

3. Did you think, prior to being accepted, that you had a decent chance of being admitted to Harvard Law School?

I thought initially that there was somewhat of a chance, but without any real experience to make me stand out, it seemed like a bit of a longshot. With the national political experience I built, and a graduate degree, my chances were much better.

4. Did you take any time off prior to applying or matriculating at HLS? If so, why did you take time off and what did you do?

See question 1.

5. What were your strongest assets when applying to Harvard Law School? Grades? LSAT score? Extracurriculars? Personal statement? Recommendations? Family connections? Personal background? Work experience?

My strongest asset after I left school was my political experience. Among the other factors, I had lined up strong recommenders: Roger Smith, my graduate school advisor; Bob Gordon, who teaches law at Stanford and whom I had for a class at Yale; and Bill Galston, my boss at the White House, who is both a very eminent political philosopher and someone who does practical political work as well. With my better score on the LSAT in 1993, I removed what might have been some worries on the part of the admissions committee. Grades from undergraduate put me pretty firmly in the middle of the accepted pack, and my graduate school grades were very good. The personal statement that I put together captures pretty well what I want to accomplish here (and was helpful for me in getting it down on paper). There were no family connections.

6. What type of courses did you take as an undergraduate to prepare yourself for Harvard Law School?

I had a number of law/political theory courses, as a double-major in government and philosophy. Particularly helpful were courses like philosophy of law, and ethics and public policy. These made me comfortable with the combination ethics/social policy discussions that pervade law school classrooms.

7. What was your LSAT score(s)? How did you prepare for the test? If you took an LSAT prep course, which one, and did it help?

The first time I took the test, I took the *Princeton Review* and ended up doing worse on the actual test than I had ever done on any practice exam. This could have been due to a bad testing day, but needless to say, I wasn't very enamored of the prep program.

The second time around, I did some practice exams on my own, and ended up doing substantially better.

8. How long did you spend on your personal statement? What did you write about and how did you decide on the topic? Did anyone help you with your statement? If so, who?

I spent a fair amount of time on the statement, for my own personal reasons as well as for the school, because I wanted to try to capture what I felt about where my life was going. I believed from the beginning that a personal statement needed to take such an approach if it was to be persuasive.

I ran it by some of my closest friends, and was most helped by my then-girlfriend, and now-wife, Cynthia.

9. Who wrote your recommendations for Harvard Law School and how did you choose them? How much notice did you give your recommenders and when were the recommendations completed?

See question 5 for basic background.

In general, I gave the recommenders plenty of time, handing out the forms almost as soon as I got them. I then followed up to make sure that the process was moving along. The result was that the recommendations were in shortly after I filed my completed application.

10. What type of extracurricular activities did you participate in during your undergraduate years that you feel were beneficial to your being admitted to Harvard Law School, and why?

My time on the school newspaper was probably somewhat helpful, and definitely helped me in learning more about people, but the most helpful activities happened in the time I spent away from school working in politics.

11. Do you feel that your race, sex, or class played a role in the admissions process? If so, explain.

Not really.

12. Do you think that your political ideology played a role in the admissions process? If so, explain.

I was much more comfortable applying coming out of a Democratic Administration than I would have been had I worked for George Bush. As I worked on my personal statement, I did not have much of a worry that any of my ideas would be seen as strange or radical, though I did wonder if my belief that we should pay lots more attention to Madison and Jefferson—though not at all in the way that conservative thinkers do—would go over well.

13. Did you see the Harvard Law School campus prior to applying or being admitted? If so, what arrangements did you make for the visit, what were your initial impressions, and have your impressions changed very much? If you didn't visit the campus prior to being accepted, why not?

For me, the campus visit was key. I had substantial worries about Harvard being a place that attracted smart people who were also quite arrogant. I had called ahead to figure out when tours would be, but hadn't really done anything else.

My impression was totally altered by a wonderful, down-to-earth tour guide. Cynthia and I came up together, as by this point she had decided that Boston wouldn't be such a bad place to move, and were very pleasantly surprised. Her law-school experience (she graduated from Georgetown Law in May 1994) had been full of unpleasant people, and we both feared that there would be even more of them here. We spent almost an hour after the tour talking to the guide about the ins and outs of the school, and how most people weren't that bad.

I am quite happy to say that none of my fears have been borne out. I've heard some horror stories from other sections, but can honestly say that there is not one person in my section I find unbearable.

14. When did you receive your letter of acceptance from the Dean of Admissions and what were you doing?

I had just returned from a trip to Los Angeles in late January 1994 and was greeted by Cynthia at Dulles Airport with the acceptance. My housemates had recognized the meaning of a big envelope and called her so she could surprise me with it when I got off the plane.

15. *How are you paying for Harvard Law School? Parents? Loans? Savings? Work?*

Primarily loans, with most living expenses covered by my wife's job.

16. *What do you plan to do in the immediate years following Law School graduation? What are your long-term career goals?*

I expect to take a firm job in California for at least a few years after graduation, while maintaining substantial political involvement. Another possible option is government-attorney work, but that will, in part, depend on the 1996 election. At this point, I'm still not sure where I'll end up, but possible options are teaching law, full-time government work, and political office.

Profile

Name Withheld
Harvard Law School class: 1997
Undergraduate institution: Amherst College
Undergraduate GPA listed by category—3.75+, 3.50–3.74, 3.25–3.49, 3.00–3.24, below 3.00: 3.25–3.49
Graduate institution and GPA, if applicable: N/A
LSAT Score listed by percentile—99–95, 94–90, 89–85, 84–80, 79–75, 74–70, 69–65, below 64: 89–85
Hometown and high school: Woodcliff Lake, NJ; Lycée Francais de New York, NY
Types of recommenders, i.e., professors or employers: Two professors, my class dean (Dean Moss) and one summer employer
Race, sex, and class: Haitian American, female, middle
Major undergraduate activities: Women's rugby, tutoring for Hispanic elementary school students, vice president French House
Major scholastic or academic honors: *cum laude*
Work experience (including summer) prior to HLS: I worked for two summers in a doctor's office. I spent one summer doing an internship at the Center for Human Rights of the United Nations at Geneva. The summer before I came here, I worked as a cook in a gourmet food shop in Hilton Head, SC. At Amherst, I was a French tutor for the Dean of Students' Tutorial Program. I also worked at various different times for Amherst College Catering, the Library, and Security.

Parents' occupations: My father is a surgeon. My mother originally worked as a laboratory technician. She now manages and does the accounting for my father's practice.

Legacy factor: N/A

Questionnaire

1. When and why did you apply to Harvard Law School? Was your application completed early, late, or in the middle of the rolling admissions process?

I applied to HLS in the fall of my senior year at Amherst. I applied not so much because I thought that I had great chances of getting in or because I had done much research on the school and knew that this was the place that I wanted to be, but more because I figured that it couldn't hurt to try. If I didn't apply, I would never know whether I would have gotten in or not.

Because I was writing a thesis and the rough draft was due in January, I put off my applications until late January. If I remember correctly, my HLS application was probably sent a day or two short of the deadline.

2. How would you describe the undergraduate institution that you attended? Does it have a strong reputation and a solid track record of sending lots of its graduates to Harvard Law School?

I definitely think that Amherst College has a very strong reputation and is considered within the top three of the small liberal arts colleges. In terms of sending a lot of graduates to Harvard, I'm not sure what the trend was before I got here but from the number of Amherst students here now, I would say that Amherst is well represented in comparison to other small colleges.

3. Did you think, prior to being accepted, that you had a decent chance of being admitted to Harvard Law School?

When I first applied, I really didn't know what to expect. I remember speaking to you [the author] at a law school forum that Amherst hosted and your telling me that the admissions people really do their best to put together a well-rounded class and that lower-than-average "numbers" did not necessarily automatically exclude applicants. I think that, by my senior year, I had heard so many "fluke" stories of people getting into places that they did not expect or of very strong applicants getting turned down that I honestly felt that you just never can tell.

As I started getting positive responses from other schools, my confidence did rise and I started to think that Harvard might not be such a long-shot after all. (I was accepted at Duke, Georgetown, NYU, Boston College, University of Michigan, and Columbia, and turned down from Yale.)

4. Did you take any time off prior to applying or matriculating at HLS? If so, why did you take time off and what did you do?

No.

5. What were your strongest assets when applying to Harvard Law School? Grades? LSAT score? Extracurriculars? Personal statement? Recommendations? Family connections? Personal background? Work experience?

I definitely do not think that it was my grades or my LSAT scores that put me over the top! I had a B+ average from a good school and decent LSAT scores (160 and 162), but then so does everybody else who applies to HLS. In terms of extracurricular activities, I think that a woman who plays rugby (as opposed to field hockey, lacrosse, soccer, or basketball, which are more common) might spark a bit of interest. I had no family connections whatsoever.

I ended up writing two personal statements. I had written two because some schools wanted two and then just sent both to Harvard, even though I think that they only asked for one. The longer statement was a "why law school" type. I wrote about my interest in international relations. This might have been a little different from some of the other statements that the admissions office received. The second one was about the race boxes that they ask you to check. I said that they should leave a blank space and let everyone describe themselves as they saw fit because "a check in a box" does not do justice to the ethnic minorities who apply. I think that this essay was a little out of the ordinary and might have caught the admission committee's eye.

My letters of recommendation from my professors were good. I ended up reading them and remember thinking that they had definitely written positive things but nothing extraordinary. Dean Moss wrote a great letter even though she did not necessarily know me as well as it came out in the letter.

I think that what really stuck out in my application was the internship at the United Nations. They wrote a very impressive letter for me detailing all that I had done during the ten weeks that I was there and recommending me highly for any academic, legal, or professional endeavor.

6. What type of courses did you take as an undergraduate to prepare yourself for Harvard Law School?

I didn't take anything to really "prepare" myself for HLS. I was a political science major and some people see that as a kind of pre-law (although I don't necessarily see the connection). I took one LJST [Law, Jurisprudence, and Social Thought] class with Professor Sarat on the social organization of the law and thus had some experience at reading cases. My main focus in terms of choosing classes was to take a wide variety of different classes (poli-sci, economics, psychology, biology, languages, English, history, etc.) and I think that I achieved that.

7. What was your LSAT score(s)? How did you prepare for the test? If you took an LSAT prep course, which one, and did it help?

I got a 162 the first time that I took the exam and a 160 the second time. I did not take a prep course (I thought that $750 was an outrageous price). I just bought one of those LSAT prep books and did a few exercises to familiarize myself with the types of questions.

8. How long did you spend on your personal statement? What did you write about and how did you decide on the topic? Did anyone help you with your statement? If so, who?

By the time that I got around to my personal statement (post-thesis rough draft), I did not have much time to agonize over it. I think that I spent three to five days writing and then editing here and there. For the topics, see question 5. I chose the international-relations topic because it explains a lot about me and my "international background": that my mother is Haitian-born, that I lived for four years (from three months to four) in France where my father went to medical school, that I went to a French school in New York from kindergarten to graduation, that I had spent my junior year abroad in Spain, that I had worked at the United Nations, that I was interested in languages and travel. The second one was just something that I had been thinking about as I was filling out applications and that I had thought about when I did my college applications. After I wrote my essays, I took them to the writing counselor at Amherst, Susan Snively. She looked them over, added a comma here and there and that was it.

9. Who wrote your recommendations for Harvard Law School and how did you choose them? How much notice did you give your recommenders and when were the recommendations completed?

My thesis advisor, Professor Ronald Tiersky, was one of my recommenders. Since I was abroad junior year and had been in larger classes freshman and sophomore year, I did not really know any of my other professors well enough for them to write recommendations. Since I met with

Professor Tiersky every week and discussed with him what I had been researching or writing, I figured that he would be in a position to do a good job even though I had never interacted with him in a classroom setting. My other recommender was Professor Beth Yarbrough from the economics department. I had had her for an advanced economics class in the fall of my senior year and had done well. I asked her because I was a bit desperate.

I gave the recommendations to the two professors on pretty short notice. I remember that I wanted to give them the recommendation with my personal statement so that they could get an idea of why I wanted to go to law school. Since I didn't get my statement done until pretty late, I didn't get the forms to them until maybe one week before the first deadlines. They were very understanding about the whole thing and did them pretty much immediately.

10. What type of extracurricular activities did you participate in during your undergraduate years that you feel were beneficial to your being admitted to Harvard Law School, and why?

As I said before, I think that playing rugby was a bit of a spin on what people usually do, especially for a woman. The other activities, tutoring or being vice president of the French House, probably did not stick out because I think that everyone who applies here does those types of things.

11. Do you feel that your race, sex, or class played a role in the admissions process? If so, explain.

I definitely think that being a minority helped my admission. I was probably a borderline case and that might have put me over the edge.

12. Do you think that your political ideology played a role in the admissions process? If so, explain.

No, not at all. I don't think that it came out in my application in any way.

13. Did you see the Harvard Law School campus prior to applying or being admitted? If so, what arrangements did you make for the visit, what were your initial impressions, and have your impressions changed very much? If you didn't visit the campus prior to being accepted, why not?

I didn't visit the campus prior to applying or being accepted. I had visited the undergrad campus when I applied to college so I had a general idea of what it looked like. I also didn't really have time to visit in the fall.

I felt that visiting before being accepted was pointless in that there was no reason to get excited about a place until you knew whether you could go or not.

14. *When did you receive your letter of acceptance from the Dean of Admissions and what were you doing?*

I received my letter of acceptance very late, at the end of June. I was actually all set and ready to go to Columbia and had sent them my deposit already. When I got the news, I was in Hilton Head and had honestly completely forgotten about it. I had called Harvard before I left and they told me that they were still deliberating. I wasn't going to worry about it all summer (although the thought did cross my mind that if they were still deliberating, it meant that there was a remote possibility) and by the end of June, I just figured that they had forgotten to send the rejection letter.

When I got news of the acceptance, I had mixed feelings. I really had my heart set on being in New York for various personal reasons (family nearby, boyfriend and college friends in Manhattan). I ended up flying to visit the two schools a week later. I never got to Columbia. The people in the Admissions Office went out of their way to accommodate me here and I even met with Dean Joyce Curll. I expected people to have the attitude of "this is Harvard and we don't need to sell you on the school," but they were very welcoming. (The people at Columbia were rude over the phone and not very inviting at all.) I gave Harvard my acceptance deposit and cancelled the trip to Columbia.

15. *How are you paying for Harvard Law School? Parents? Loans? Savings? Work?*

I am paying for HLS entirely through loans. I have both Staffords and a MEFA loan to supplement them.

16. *What do you plan to do in the immediate years following Law School graduation? What are your long-term career goals?*

I will probably "do the firm thing" for a few years to pay off my loans rapidly. After that I will probably want to take some time off from work to have a family. When I go back to work, I want to make the switch to public interest. I'm not sure yet what area of public interest work I want to do but that type of work is definitely my long-term goal. (The whole international law idea is on the back burner for now . . . it's going to take a while to get over the incredibly boring international law class that I am suffering through this semester!)

Profile

Name: Sam Liccardo
Harvard Law School class: 1996
Undergraduate institution: Georgetown University
**Undergraduate GPA listed by category—3.75+, 3.50–3.74,
    3.25–3.49, 3.00–3.24, below 3.00:** 3.75+
Graduate institution and GPA, if applicable: John F. Kennedy School
    of Government, 3.75+
**LSAT Score listed by percentile—99–95, 94–90, 89–85, 84–80,
    79–75, 74–70, 69–65, below 64:** 99–95
Hometown and high school: Saratoga, CA; Bellarmine College
    Preparatory
Types of recommenders, i.e., professors or employers: One
    lawyer, for whom I worked the year after graduation, one
    professor/Jesuit priest
Race, sex, and class: White, male, upper
Major undergraduate activities: Captain, heavyweight crew;
    coordinator, One-to-One tutoring program, D.C. Schools Project;
    tutor, D.C. Schools Project and Big Buddy program; intern,
    Congressman Norman Y. Mineta (D-CA); counselor, Ascent
    Employment Program; teacher and coach, Umandagu Lescuelana
    Program; other small junk
Major scholastic or academic honors: *magna cum laude*; Phi Beta
    Kappa; Alpha Sigma Nu; honors government program; honors
    English program; finalist, Rhodes Scholarship Competition, state
    of California
Work experience (including summer) prior to HLS: In the summers,
    I had done some work for a maintenance company and lifeguarding
    in California for a couple years in college. Eventually, I started
    working for my dad's firm, doing research of a non-legal nature,
    until a couple of the attorneys showed me how to do legal research.
    For the year after graduation, I did both legal and non-legal
    research.
Parents' occupations: Father—Lawyer, Mother—Homemaker, was a
    nurse for a while
Legacy factor: N/A

Questionnaire

1. When and why did you apply to Harvard Law School? Was your application completed early, late, or in the middle of the rolling admissions process?

Early to mid-December

2. How would you describe the undergraduate institution that you attended? Does it have a strong reputation and a solid track record of sending lots of its graduates to Harvard Law School?

Out of my class, about eight or nine of us made it here. The institution is somewhere in the middle–bottom of the top twenty-five in most surveys, but very strong in my major (government/international relations).

3. Did you think, prior to being accepted, that you had a decent chance of being admitted to Harvard Law School?

Yes. I heard from Yale before I heard from Harvard, and since Yale took me, I figured Harvard probably would, too.

4. Did you take any time off prior to applying or matriculating at HLS? If so, why did you take time off and what did you do?

Yes. I had planned to go to Mexico to teach in a program in Cuernavaca, but I had contracted a parasite from my previous summer's work in Belize. I was sick for much of my senior year and for about nine months after graduation, and during that time, I stayed at home and worked part-time for my dad, waiting for my health to improve. Eventually I found a doctor who could cure me, and I then switched to working full-time, as well as teaching English at nights in a homeless immigrant family shelter in Santa Clara, and I also worked on a congressional campaign.

5. What were your strongest assets when applying to Harvard Law School? Grades? LSAT score? Extracurriculars? Personal statement? Recommendations? Family connections? Personal background? Work experience?

Probably the extracurriculars and grades.

6. What type of courses did you take as an undergraduate to prepare yourself for Harvard Law School?

I didn't really have any intention to "prepare" for law school. I felt as though college was for learning, and I'd leave preparation for professional school. My classes overwhelmingly fit into one of five categories: government (especially international relations), economics, Spanish, theology/philosophy, and English literature.

7. What was your LSAT score(s)? How did you prepare for the test? If you took an LSAT prep course, which one, and did it help?

As I recall, I think I had a 172 or so (that's on a 180 scale, I believe). I took an LSAT prep course for a week—I'm not sure which one—but I thought it was a waste, so I bailed and got a partial refund.

8. How long did you spend on your personal statement? What did you write about and how did you decide on the topic? Did anyone help you with your statement? If so, who?

I wrote it for my Rhodes Scholarship application, and modified it thereafter—it took somewhere around 5 hours, I would guess. I wrote about hope, and experiences in my life that I thought had something to do with my convictions about being hopeful. I got a Jesuit friend of mine to offer some critiques, but it didn't get changed much.

9. Who wrote your recommendations for Harvard Law School and how did you choose them? How much notice did you give your recommenders and when were the recommendations completed?

I don't remember the specifics too well, but the same Jesuit friend of mine (whom I had as a professor in my junior year) had already written me a letter for other purposes, so he just fired off a copy with a couple weeks' notice.

I also got a letter from a lawyer I worked for that summer, and I gave him about a month's notice. I have no idea when they completed the letters.

10. What type of extracurricular activities did you participate in during your undergraduate years that you feel were beneficial to your being admitted to Harvard Law School, and why?

The three that I mentioned were all beneficial, I believe. Being a captain of a forty-member crew and a coordinator of a tutoring program show some familiarity with positions of responsibility and leadership, and I suppose that's important. Tutoring inner-city children shows some concern for others in the local community, and I imagine that the Law School doesn't want only a bunch of self-serving folks around. For those familiar with crew, it is a sport that requires a lot of determination and discipline, and that seems like a plus.

11. *Do you feel that your race, sex, or class played a role in the admissions process? If so, explain.*

Race and sex: No. Being a white male, it might have hurt my chances some, but I don't think I've ever suffered any real disadvantage for being a white male.

Class: Absolutely yes. Regardless of what people say about diversity at Harvard, the students are overwhelmingly (like me) of upper- and upper-middle-class stock. That is true for a variety of reasons: one's family's wealth is correlated with the quality of one's primary and secondary schooling, the education of one's parents, the access to computers and other educational resources, etc.

12. *Do you think that your political ideology played a role in the admissions process? If so, explain.*

Maybe. I'm a liberal, and that probably shows in my activities and in my personal statement. I'd guess Harvard is somewhat left of center, so there may be some amount of unconscious bias among the admissions folks.

13. *Did you see the Harvard Law School campus prior to applying or being admitted? If so, what arrangements did you make for the visit, what were your initial impressions, and have your impressions changed very much? If you didn't visit the campus prior to being accepted, why not?*

I didn't visit because I was broke and I didn't have the money to fly out. I was making enough money to cover rent and food and not much else, and I figured that I wasn't going to law school to enjoy a beautiful campus.

14. *When did you receive your letter of acceptance from the Dean of Admissions and what were you doing?*

I don't really remember. I know it was in January or early February (earlier than I expected), and I was probably looking at the heap of mail in my apartment, hoping that a Visa bill wasn't hiding somewhere in the pile.

15. *How are you paying for Harvard Law School? Parents? Loans? Savings? Work?*

My folks are footing the whole bill, thank God.

16. What do you plan to do in the immediate years following Law School graduation? What are your long-term career goals?

I got a clerkship with a U.S. District Court judge in San Francisco (William Orrick). After that, I dunno—I've still got another year before graduation, so there's time to decide. I'd like to do one of the two things that I'm doing this summer—financing and legal work related to affordable housing development, and working in a U.S. Attorney's Office (white collar crime or organized crime). I'd love to do one of those two things or both for a bunch of years, and maybe in a decade or two I'll run for public office. Another decade after that, I'll run for pope.

Profile

Name: David J. Markese
Harvard Law School class: 1996
Undergraduate institution: Southern California College
Undergraduate GPA listed by category—3.75+, 3.50–3.74, 3.25–3.49, 3.00–3.24, below 3.00: 3.75+
Graduate institution and GPA, if applicable: N/A
LSAT Score listed by percentile—99–95, 94–90, 89–85, 84–80, 79–75, 74–70, 69–65, below 64: 99–95
Hometown and high school: Keizer, OR; Woodlawn High School, Baton Rouge, LA
Types of recommenders, i.e., professors or employers: Undergraduate professors
Race, sex, and class: ¾ white, ¼ Asian; male; middle
Major undergraduate activities: Writing Center tutor; student newspaper staff writer; member school Constitutional Review Committee; member International Students group; intramural sports; English and U.S. Government tutor; school group involved in inner-city Los Angeles Saturday School program; Spring Break Mexico outreach as member of Tae kwon do team
Major scholastic or academic honors: Dean's List; President's List; Social Science Student of the Year, 1991–92
Work experience (including summer) prior to HLS: French translator; Temporary agency (office work); Retail sales; Fast food, kitchen; Janitorial service; Car washer; Dry cleaner; Painter; Mail room assistant; Tutor.

Parents' occupations: Father—Pastor, Mother—Church staff
Legacy factor: N/A

Questionnaire

1. When and why did you apply to Harvard Law School? Was your application completed early, late, or in the middle of the rolling admissions process?

I was originally planning on attending either Willamette School of Law (Salem, Oregon) or the University of Washington Law School. When I got my LSAT score back in January, I decided to aim a little higher. Consequently, I applied very late—just under the extended deadline of Feb. 15.

2. How would you describe the undergraduate institution that you attended? Does it have a strong reputation and a solid track record of sending lots of its graduates to Harvard Law School?

It is a four-year liberal arts college affiliated with the Assemblies of God Church. There is a strong Christian emphasis, including several religion requirements in every degree program. It is very small: the total student body was about 900 when I graduated in 1992. It is very regional—most students are California residents. It has a strong reputation among Christian colleges, but is mostly unknown outside that circle. The school began as a bible college in 1920, and became an accredited liberal arts school in the 1950s. I am the only graduate to ever attend HLS. However, a woman several years ago went to Yale Law School.

3. Did you think, prior to being accepted, that you had a decent chance of being admitted to Harvard Law School?

Once I applied, I was very confident I would be admitted.

4. Did you take any time off prior to applying or matriculating at HLS? If so, why did you take time off and what did you do?

I took one year off, mainly because I put off taking the LSAT too long. I went home to Oregon and worked odd jobs, mainly with a temporary agency.

5. What were your strongest assets when applying to Harvard Law School? Grades? LSAT score? Extracurriculars? Personal statement? Recommen-

dations? Family connections? Personal background? Work experience?

My strongest assets were my grades and LSAT, as well as my diverse personal background. I have no family connections, my recommenders are unknown here, and my extracurriculars are very run-of-the-mill. My work experience is minimal, except my job as a French TV translator, which might have been considered as interesting and different.

6. What type of courses did you take as an undergraduate to prepare yourself for Harvard Law School?

The only course I took with an eye on law school was a business law course. The rest of my courses were history and political science courses.

7. What was your LSAT score(s)? How did you prepare for the test? If you took an LSAT prep course, which one, and did it help?

My LSAT score was 176 out of 180. I prepared by taking practice tests provided by LSAS and one commercial publication. I didn't take any courses.

8. How long did you spend on your personal statement? What did you write about and how did you decide on the topic? Did anyone help you with your statement? If so, who?

I spent maybe a couple of hours on it. I wrote about my international background mostly. I wanted to talk about anything that would set me apart from others—something to contribute to "diversity" at HLS. An attorney friend of mine read through it after I wrote it, but I made no changes at that time.

9. Who wrote your recommendations for Harvard Law School and how did you choose them? How much notice did you give your recommenders and when were the recommendations completed?

Three of my professors from college wrote them: one history professor, one political science professor, and one anthropology professor. I chose the first two because I knew them the best and they knew me very well. I chose the last one because he knew me somewhat, and also because he is developing a reputation in academic circles as an authority on AIDS and AIDS-related issues, predominantly anthropological. (No one else at the school has any sort of reputation outside the area.) Since I applied very late, I gave my recommenders very little notice, and they completed them at the last minute.

10. What type of extracurricular activities did you participate in during your undergraduate years that you feel were beneficial to your being admitted to Harvard Law School, and why?

Activities such as school newspaper staff writer and Writing Center tutor may have helped to establish my writing ability; activities such as the Mexico outreach and the inner-city Saturday School might have helped round me out and show a humanitarian side to me; being a member of the Constitutional Review Committee might have helped, since it is somewhat law-related (though it probably didn't have that great an impact on the admissions committee).

11. *Do you feel that your race, sex, or class played a role in the admissions process? If so, explain.*

Since I am a middle-class white male, my race, sex, and class were, if anything, a detriment to me, if in fact the school looks for diversity in admittees.

12. *Do you think that your political ideology played a role in the admissions process? If so, explain.*

I didn't write anything about my political ideology in my personal statement or in my essay. I don't imagine it came out anywhere else. However, if it did, since I am somewhat conservative (and a born-again Christian, at that), I think my political ideology may actually have been a plus, again looking to diversity (if one believes that more Harvard Law students characterize themselves as liberal as opposed to conservative, which I believe they do, though many disagree).

13. *Did you see the Harvard Law School campus prior to applying or being admitted? If so, what arrangements did you make for the visit, what were your initial impressions, and have your impressions changed very much? If you didn't visit the campus prior to being accepted, why not?*

I didn't visit the campus. For one, it would have been expensive for me, since I live on the West Coast. In addition, I knew the campus and location would play no role whatsoever in my decision.

14. *When did you receive your letter of acceptance from the Dean of Admissions and what were you doing?*

I was accepted in the middle of April 1993. I was working in the mailroom at the Oregon Department of Education, and washing cars part-time at a local car dealership.

15. *How are you paying for Harvard Law School? Parents? Loans? Savings? Work?*

I am taking out loans.

16. *What do you plan to do in the immediate years following Law School graduation? What are your long-term career goals?*

I am hoping to work for a small law firm in Atlanta; if not, a small law firm in Orlando. If I don't get offers from either of them after this summer, I may try to work for another firm, or I may follow my original plan and try to get a government job in D.C. I'm not sure what will happen in the long-term. If I go to a firm, I may stay for a long time, or I may end up in government. I would also like to do some writing eventually. There is a chance I could end up with some private special interest group representing religious freedom-type claims, but I don't really see that now.

Profile

Name: Robert A. McCarter
Harvard Law School class: 1997
Undergraduate institution: Boston College
Undergraduate GPA listed by category—3.75+, 3.50–3.74,
    3.25–3.49, 3.00–3.24, below 3.00: 3.75+
Graduate institution and GPA, if applicable: N/A
LSAT Score listed by percentile—99–95, 94–90, 89–85, 84–80,
    79–75, 74–70, 69–65, below 64: 94–90
Hometown and high school: Waldorf, MD; Thomas Stone High School
Types of recommenders, i.e., professors or employers: Professors
    and employers
Race, sex, and class: White, male, middle
Major undergraduate activities: Intramural sports
Major scholastic or academic honors: Top-ranked student in class of
    1994, Phi Beta Kappa, Golden Key National Honor Society, Alpha
    Sigma Nu National Jesuit Honor Society, Dean's Scholar, Dean's List
Work experience (including summer) prior to HLS: Miller &
    Webster, P.A. (law firm); Marylanders for Miller (political
    campaign); Hoyer for Congress Committee (political campaign);
    U.S. House of Representatives, Committee on Ways and Means.
Parents' occupations: Father—Imports and sells wicker baskets,
    Mother—Office manager of small accounting business
Legacy factor: N/A

Questionnaire

1. When and why did you apply to Harvard Law School? Was your application completed early, late, or in the middle of the rolling admissions process?

I applied to Harvard Law School in November 1993, which was at the beginning of the admissions process. I chose Harvard over other law schools because I felt that Harvard's national reputation would allow me to get one of the best legal educations available and go back home to work, even though I did not go to law school in Maryland.

2. How would you describe the undergraduate institution that you attended? Does it have a strong reputation and a solid track record of sending lots of its graduates to Harvard Law School?

Boston College is consistently within the top thirty to fifty schools in rankings of colleges. My understanding is that it's pretty common for three or four students to be admitted from B.C. into Harvard Law School each year.

3. Did you think, prior to being accepted, that you had a decent chance of being admitted to Harvard Law School?

I was always confident that I would get into Harvard Law School, knowing the track record of Boston College and the median LSAT scores and GPAs of Harvard's students.

4. Did you take any time off prior to applying or matriculating at HLS? If so, why did you take time off and what did you do?

I went straight from college to law school.

5. What were your strongest assets when applying to Harvard Law School? Grades? LSAT score? Extracurriculars? Personal statement? Recommendations? Family connections? Personal background? Work experience?

I feel that my grades and my personal background were my strongest assets when applying to Harvard Law School. Prominently displayed on my resume was my class rank and GPA, since I wanted to stress the aspect of my academic career that was more unique than others. While these were highly visible on my application, my personal background was not. However, I am confident that, in reading my application, the admissions committee noticed that I am a product of public schools in a part of Maryland that has not sent many, if any, students to Harvard Law School.

6. What type of courses did you take as an undergraduate to prepare yourself for Harvard Law School?

I took a lot of political science, philosophy, and history classes in college, not so much to prepare me for Harvard Law School, but to learn some things that I thought would make me a more knowledgeable and well-rounded person.

7. What was your LSAT score(s)? How did you prepare for the test? If you took an LSAT prep course, which one, and did it help?

My LSAT score was 165. I prepared for the test by ordering and taking seven or eight practice tests on weekends or after work during the end of spring in my junior year of college. An LSAT prep course was too expensive, but probably would have improved my test-taking ability.

8. How long did you spend on your personal statement? What did you write about and how did you decide on the topic? Did anyone help you with your statement? If so, who?

I spent a few hours a day unable to come up with a topic to write on that would explain me without being too standard. Finally, after moving from the kitchen table into my room, I started to look around, tired of racking my brain for a topic. All of a sudden, I came up with the idea to describe my room as a means to describe me— where I have come from, my interests, my values, and my dreams. The only help I got was from my family, who patiently listened to it, particularly my sister, who made me read it over the phone to her friends.

9. Who wrote your recommendations for Harvard Law School and how did you choose them? How much notice did you give your recommenders and when were the recommendations completed?

I had a political science professor whom I had had for two classes the previous year and the president of the Maryland State Senate for whom I had worked the previous summer write letters of recommendation for me. I chose them because they knew me well, were respected by me, and would be respected by the admissions committee. I gave them the recommendation forms in September and they returned the forms to me in November.

10. What type of extracurricular activities did you participate in during your undergraduate years that you feel were beneficial to your being admitted to Harvard Law School, and why?

My major undergraduate activities were intramural sports. They may have been beneficial in the sense that they may show that I am well-rounded.

11. Do you feel that your race, sex, or class played a role in the admissions process? If so, explain.

I do not think that my race, sex, or class made it harder or easier for me to get into Harvard Law School.

12. Do you think that your political ideology played a role in the admissions process? If so, explain.

I do not know if my political ideology played a role in my admission.

13. Did you see the Harvard Law School campus prior to applying or being admitted? If so, what arrangements did you make for the visit, what were your initial impressions, and have your impressions changed very much? If you didn't visit the campus prior to being accepted, why not?

I never visited the campus prior to being accepted even though I was only a few miles away, since it was just as easy to wait until I was admitted. In addition, the specter of getting a parking ticket, which became real on one visit, scared me.

14. When did you receive your letter of acceptance from the Dean of Admissions and what were you doing?

I got my letter of admission in February while checking my mail on the way to class. After getting over the initial shock, I ran to a pay phone and called my mom.

15. How are you paying for Harvard Law School? Parents? Loans? Savings? Work?

I am paying for law school by myself through loans and summer earnings.

16. What do you plan to do in the immediate years following Law School graduation? What are your long-term career goals?

Immediately after graduation I plan on working either as a lawyer in a private firm or as a prosecutor in the state's attorney's office in my county. After that I would like to go into public service and help keep my community a nice place to live.

Profile

Name: Erin McPherson
Harvard Law School class: 1995
Undergraduate institution: Middlebury College
Undergraduate GPA listed by category—3.75+, 3.50–3.74, 3.25–3.49, 3.00–3.24, below 3.00: 3.75+
Graduate institution and GPA, if applicable: N/A
LSAT Score listed by percentile—99–95, 94–90, 89–85, 84–80, 79–75, 74–70, 69–65, below 64: 99–95
Hometown and high school: Aspen, CO; Aspen High School
Types of recommenders, i.e., professors or employers: Two English professors—one was my thesis advisor, one sociology professor (my minor)
Race, sex, and class: White, female, upper-middle
Major undergraduate activities: Theater, campus newspaper, editor of the campus literary magazine, volunteer work teaching children's theater
Major scholastic or academic honors: Phi Beta Kappa, high honors in my major (English), *magna cum laude*, Henry Prickett Prize for English Literature, awarded to outstanding senior in English
Work experience (including summer) prior to HLS: During college, I worked for the Aspen Resort Association (like a chamber of commerce, reservations place). When I got out of Middlebury, I moved home and painted houses, waited tables. Then I traveled for a year and returned to Aspen. The second year, I worked for my mom at her ski mountain restaurant, *Cafe Suzanne*, until the season ended. My final job before starting law school was at the Aspen Institute, a nonprofit "think-tank" organization that holds conferences on business, law, communication, etc., throughout the summer in Aspen.
Parents' occupations: My mom is the owner/operator of a restaurant, located on Snowmass Ski Mountain outside of Aspen, Colorado. My dad sells general real estate and does some property development.
Legacy factor: N/A

Questionnaire

1. When and why did you apply to Harvard Law School? Was your application completed early, late, or in the middle of the rolling admissions process?

I applied to Harvard after I had spent a year out of college. I wasn't very concerned about "my future" right out of school—I only knew that I wanted to 1) travel for a long time, and 2) continue with some kind of graduate program. I had thought about law school during undergrad—to the point where I took the LSAT my senior year, figuring that I was in the studying mode, and in case I wanted to use it later. When my friend and I left in October 1990, with around-the-world tickets and backpacks, I was still uncertain about law school.

I hoped the trip would clarify my desires (and in my personal statement, I certainly made it seem that way!), but in all honesty, I really was unsure about it all the way through the application process. I applied to five law schools and five to six graduate programs in English literature (for a Ph.D. program). Although I talked to some of my parents' friends who were attorneys (most of them disenchanted) and I read the usual law-applicant staples (*One L, The Top Ten Law Schools,* etc.) I don't think I had an idea about what learning or practicing law would be like.

Anyhow, in true form, I FedExed™ my applications on the February 2 deadline. Harvard was the last school to respond to me, the last week of the ski season, in April. Although I'd even written a check out to Stanford, I couldn't "just say no" to the big H.

2. How would you describe the undergraduate institution that you attended? Does it have a strong reputation and a solid track record of sending lots of its graduates to Harvard Law School?

I think Middlebury is regarded as a very decent small liberal arts college in New England. Although their academic reputation improved while I was there, and continues to improve, they are still "a notch below" the Amherst/Williams/Ivies track. In other words, Midd was full of prep-schoolers who didn't get into Harvard, Yale, Amherst, etc.—good students, athletic, "well-rounded." (I'm being a bit of a cynic—and I loved Midd—but I think this is accurate). Anyhow, I think that HLS likes to take a qualified student each year from Midd; when I got here, there was one 3L, and now there is myself, a 2L, and a 1L. I'm the token 1995'er.

3. Did you think, prior to being accepted, that you had a decent chance of being admitted to Harvard Law School?

Unlike a lot of friends here, who have told me that they didn't feel sure at all, I focused my applications on schools that accepted students in my range: Michigan, Cornell, Georgetown, Harvard, and Stanford. (I left Yale out because I didn't think I could get in there!) When I heard yes from the other four, I was more certain that HLS might take me, especially because they have a larger class.

4. Did you take any time off prior to applying or matriculating at HLS? If so, why did you take time off and what did you do?

As I've mentioned, I took two years off before starting law school (meaning that I applied in the beginning of my second year off). I spent the first year (eleven months) backpacking around the world with a friend. We started in the Pacific, New Zealand, Australia, Asia, and finally Eurailed around Europe. It was amazing and well worth the uncertainty and poverty. Broke and clueless, I spent the second year living off the generosity of my folks, working for my mom, skiing a lot, and pondering on my future.

The one thing I was certain of when I graduated from college was that I wanted to take time off and travel. I believed strongly that my life would begin gathering too much momentum, and too many contingencies, to take such a trip that easily again. (I already feel justified, what with my loans, and my job, and my clerkship, and my future apartment, and multitudinous belongings, etc., etc.) I was fortunate to have a jobless and malleable friend that I could convince to join me, and a supportive family. Extending my youth, my freedom, and my lack of commitments was a priority for me then—although I will admit that the trip started to feel incredibly self-serving much of the time (aside from working in youth hostels, we were simply "being" wherever we were). When I returned, I was definitely ready to become part of a community again, and find stability and productivity.

5. What were your strongest assets when applying to Harvard Law School? Grades? LSAT score? Extracurriculars? Personal statement? Recommendations? Family connections? Personal background? Work experience?

On this count, I think what got me in here were my numbers. I had high undergrad grades, and a 97th percentile LSAT. When you figure that most everyone who applied (and who got in) had those same stats, I think it was a combination of things. I think it helped that I took the time off, in what I would call the "life experience" category. (At least it separated me somewhat from the hundreds of other college students with good numbers.) I had two incredible recommenders—my thesis adviser wrote me a great rec.

My dad's cynical theory is that I got in because we didn't check the financial-aid box—good one, Dad, considering he's never even seen my loan applications or sent in his financial stats. Parents will be parents . . .

6. *What type of courses did you take as an undergraduate to prepare yourself for Harvard Law School?*

"Prepare myself" was not in my vocabulary! Middlebury had a loosely structured pre-law program—mostly political science classes. I thought I might want to major in poli-sci—but one visit to an introductory Socratic-method poli-sci class and that idea was dropped. I really bought into the "learning for its own sake" philosophy and took the courses that I was interested in. I loved English literature and didn't have a thought of whether I wanted to continue in it or not.

7. *What was your* LSAT *score(s)? How did you prepare for the test? If you took an* LSAT *prep course, which one, and did it help?*

My score was a 44 out of 48, I think (old scoring system). I took a Kaplan that was offered at the college. The course was usually cancelled—I think it had two real meetings, but the materials and practice tests definitely helped prepare me for the test. I think the most important thing Kaplan did was familiarize me with the format, and remind me that being thorough and well-thought-out is less important than being efficient and going for the right answer (not the best answer)—this logic also would have helped in law school—bummer I forgot and reverted to my earnest mode!

8. *How long did you spend on your personal statement? What did you write about and how did you decide on the topic? Did anyone help you with your statement? If so, who?*

I couldn't tell you how long I spent—I would go to the Colorado Mountain College campus in Aspen and borrow their computer. Probably a few afternoons work for a week or so. I knew I wanted to write about my trip, but I was worried about justifying it and connecting it to law school (almost as if I needed to do those things for myself). I had applied for a Luce Scholarship to go to Asia for a year that fall, and made it to the finals—but they had told me I lacked a definite focus. Reading my statement now, I can see how that experience also influenced my tone of "purposefulness." No one read it or helped.

9. *Who wrote your recommendations for Harvard Law School and how did you choose them? How much notice did you give your recommenders and when were the recommendations completed?*

I chose my two English professors: my senior thesis advisor, whom

I knew very well, and one of the readers of my thesis, an assistant professor who had really liked my work in her classes. I then chose a sociology professor, from whom I had taken three courses (two of them small seminars); he was also a friend. The distinguishing factor is that all of these recommenders not only knew me academically, but personally as well. I had all of them write a general recommendation before I left Middlebury, so their memories and impressions would be fresh. They were on file at the college career center.

10. What type of extracurricular activities did you participate in during your undergraduate years that you feel were beneficial to your being admitted to Harvard Law School, and why?

My activities were all fairly centered around writing and theater, so I don't think being a Renaissance woman was a factor. I think my steady involvement in college theater productions showed consistency in my commitment level, as did my involvement with the newspaper. Editing the literary magazine probably showed that I could handle things in an administrative/leadership way. My teaching work, which was only senior year, would have showed leadership as well. I can't say there is any one thing I can remember being a standout, though.

11. Do you feel that your race, sex, or class played a role in the admissions process? If so, explain.

It could have helped to be "Erin McPherson" instead of "Eric McPherson," considering that the law school is striving for a balanced gender ratio. I think women were the majority in this year's pool of applicants, so it may not be such a boon anymore.

12. Do you think that your political ideology played a role in the admissions process? If so, explain.

No, unless being *apolitical* was a bad thing. It was all so much drivel to me—I cared more about bringing people beauty through art and literature than making them Democrats, Republicans, Marxists, Conservatives, etc.

13. Did you see the Harvard Law School campus prior to applying or being admitted? If so, what arrangements did you make for the visit, what were your initial impressions, and have your impressions changed very much? If you didn't visit the campus prior to being accepted, why not?

I was going to say that I didn't visit, and then I remembered—I picked my application up in Pound, on a visit to my college friends in Boston. We all went directly from the T through Harvard yard, fumbled awkwardly with our campus maps, located Pound, asked someone in a suit where to go (it was interview season, but I remember thinking "Do they wear *that* to classes?"). I remember surreptitiously grabbing a red-bound application packet from the enormous pile on the third floor—and feeling like buzzers would go off, or that a woman behind the counter (probably Paula Garvin) would try to stop me unless I showed an ID and transcript. Not one to dally, we were out of there in about ten seconds. My impressions: "Jeez, this building is kind of ugly," and "this doesn't look like the rest of Harvard." Also: "I *do not* belong here—massive intimidation." Although my aesthetic impressions haven't changed, I am (finally) less intimidated to be here.

After being admitted, it was just too far to come for an "official" visit, and I was admitted after Admitted Students Day, so I went for the myth and the grandeur and sent in my check without knowing much at all.

14. When did you receive your letter of acceptance from the Dean of Admissions and what were you doing?

This is the "where were you when . . ." question, and everyone always remembers, which is great!!

As I said earlier, I received the Harvard acceptance after all my other schools had responded. I had decided not to go for a Ph.D. program (UVA was the school I had there), much on the advice of my English professors, who were rather unanimously cynical at the time about a career in academia. So I was ready to respond to Stanford, but I was waiting to see if Harvard would accept me.

It was the last weekend of the ski season in Crested Butte (first or second weekend in April), where the town of Crested Butte opens up the mountain for free. My ex-boyfriend and I had gone to ski for the weekend, and when he drove into our driveway Monday to drop me off, my Mom walked slowly out of the house in her bathrobe, holding the large-size manilla envelope in her hand. She didn't say a word—just handed it to me—and I knew from the size of the envelope that I had been accepted. After opening it and reading the first lines two or three times to make sure, I was ecstatic, and I knew I'd have a hard choice (I'd already cognitively decided on Stanford—this opened Pandora's box.) My ex and I then proceeded to get into a two-hour fight about the fact that "I would go to Harvard and become a snob" and "get an attitude and leave him and etc."—now *that* was some advice I should have taken—sooner rather than later!!!

15. How are you paying for Harvard Law School? Parents? Loans? Savings? Work?

Parents and loans. For some strange reason, those giant summer paychecks disappear rather rapidly.

16. What do you plan to do in the immediate years following Law School graduation? What are your long-term career goals?

I have accepted an offer at a small firm in San Francisco—I interviewed there as a 3L, so it's a bit of a mystery. I have also accepted a clerkship with a Federal District Court Judge in L.A., which starts in the spring of 1997. This would be my ideal exit from the firm, unless I really enjoy it and want to return. Like many of my peers, I don't see myself having a career at a firm. I might like to go into government lawyering (say, for the District Attorney or U.S. Attorney). I also am interested in possibly working for a nonprofit organization, like the Aspen Institute, where I could be more closely involved with art or literature. (i.e., administrative work, which would be non-litigatory, where ironically, most of my experience will lie). These plans are about as firm as they were when I entered law school.

Profile

Name: Christopher Messina
Harvard Law School class: 1997
Undergraduate institution: Notre Dame
Undergraduate GPA listed by category—3.75+, 3.50–3.74, 3.25–3.49, 3.00–3.24, below 3.00: 3.75+
Graduate institution and GPA, if applicable: N/A
LSAT Score listed by percentile—99–95, 94–90, 89–85, 84–80, 79–75, 74–70, 69–65, below 64: 99–95
Hometown and high school: Redding, CT; Fairfield Preparatory
Types of recommenders, i.e., professors or employers: Employers
Race, sex, and class: White, male, middle
Major undergraduate activities: Italian Society; interhall hockey, baseball, lacrosse; spent one year studying in Rome; Beta Gamma Sigma; Beta Alpha Psi; Accounting Club
Major scholastic or academic honors: Highest Honors; Beta Gamma Sigma; Beta Alpha Psi; Deloitte & Touche Accounting Award; Becker CPA Review Scholarship
Work experience (including summer) prior to HLS: KPMG Peat Marwick, Supervising Senior Tax Specialist, three years; Arthur Andersen, tax intern, summer; MCA & Co., P.C., tax intern, summer.

Parents' occupations: Father—cpa, Mother—Social worker
Legacy factor: N/A

Questionnaire

1. When and why did you apply to Harvard Law School? Was your application completed early, late, or in the middle of the rolling admissions process?

I applied in the end of January, late in the application process. I think I had to FedEx™ it in to meet the deadline. I applied to hls because it was considered one of the top law schools in the country and it offered some interesting tax classes.

2. How would you describe the undergraduate institution that you attended? Does it have a strong reputation and a solid track record of sending lots of its graduates to Harvard Law School?

Notre Dame is a small-to-medium (8,000 students) liberal arts university with highly regarded accounting, engineering, theology, and chemistry departments. Its student body is predominantly Catholic and white. Notre Dame has students from all over the country with the majority being from the midwest and northeast.

3. Did you think, prior to being accepted, that you had a decent chance of being admitted to Harvard Law School?

Yes, I thought I had a decent chance.

4. Did you take any time off prior to applying or matriculating at HLS? If so, why did you take time off and what did you do?

I took three years off from school. I worked at a big-six accounting firm in Chicago for the full three years. I didn't plan on going to law school when I graduated college so I didn't make a conscious effort to "take time off" before law school. I only decided to go to law school after I realized that I would rather do what a tax lawyer does than what a tax accountant does. My original plan was to just be a cpa.

5. What were your strongest assets when applying to Harvard Law School? Grades? Lsat score? Extracurriculars? Personal statement? Recommendations? Family connections? Personal background? Work experience?

Probably grades, lsat score, cpa accreditation, and work experience. I don't think any of the rest would have gotten me where I wanted to go.

6. What type of courses did you take as an undergraduate to prepare yourself for Harvard Law School?

I didn't take any courses in college that specifically prepared me for HLS. But I think my accounting, business law, and finance classes (what I remember from them) have been helpful thus far.

7. What was your LSAT score(s)? How did you prepare for the test? If you took an LSAT prep course, which one, and did it help?

171. I bought one of those "How to take the LSAT" books, but I don't remember which one. I read through that and did their practice tests. I also did the practice tests sent to me by LSDAS.

8. How long did you spend on your personal statement? What did you write about and how did you decide on the topic? Did anyone help you with your statement? If so, who?

Two to two and one-half hours. I wrote about my year studying abroad and how it affected my life. I chose that topic because I consider that year the most exciting year of my life and I feel that I am a better person because of it. I also wrote about the passing of the CPA exam and how that was an example of my abilities. I thought that might show I had the aptitude to succeed in law school. Nobody helped me with my statement.

9. Who wrote your recommendations for Harvard Law School and how did you choose them? How much notice did you give your recommenders and when were the recommendations completed?

A partner and a senior manager at my office. I chose them because they were the two people with whom I worked the most closely while at Peat Marwick. I gave them about three weeks' notice and the recommendations were completed about three weeks after I gave them to the recommenders. I probably would have received them sooner but it was right around the Christmas holiday and they had other things going on.

10. What type of extracurricular activities did you participate in during your undergraduate years that you feel were beneficial to your being admitted to Harvard Law School, and why?

Italian Society. I was the president of the society, so this may have been a demonstration that I had leadership ability. Involvement in inter-hall athletics and the Rome program may have shown that I had interests outside of the classroom.

11. Do you feel that your race, sex, or class played a role in the admissions process? If so, explain.

No, not at all.

12. Do you think that your political ideology played a role in the admissions process? If so, explain.

No, not at all.

13. Did you see the Harvard Law School campus prior to applying or being admitted? If so, what arrangements did you make for the visit, what were your initial impressions, and have your impressions changed very much? If you didn't visit the campus prior to being accepted, why not?

I did not see HLS campus prior to applying, being accepted, or accepting at HLS. I was working in Chicago and I did not have time to come out and look at the school.

14. When did you receive your letter of acceptance from the Dean of Admissions and what were you doing?

Sometime in the first few days of April. I had just come home from work and I was cooking dinner.

15. How are you paying for Harvard Law School? Parents? Loans? Savings? Work?

The first year was all loans. The next two years may be about 90 percent loans and the rest savings based on how much I make during the summers.

16. What do you plan to do in the immediate years following Law School graduation? What are your long-term career goals?

Work for a law firm with a strong tax department, probably in Chicago. For the long-term I hope to either make partner at a firm or start my own firm and run that for a while. Then retire while I'm still young enough to enjoy it.

Profile

Name: Kevin D. Mohr
Harvard Law School class: 1997
Undergraduate institution: Ohio University
Undergraduate GPA listed by category—3.75+, 3.50–3.74, 3.25–3.49, 3.00–3.24, below 3.00: 3.75+
Graduate institution and GPA, if applicable: N/A

LSAT **Score listed by percentile—99–95, 94–90, 89–85, 84–80,**
    79–75, 74–70, 69–65, below 64: 99–95
Hometown and high school: Fairborn, OH; Fairborn High School
Types of recommenders, i.e., professors or employers: Professors
Race, sex, and class: White, male, middle
Major undergraduate activities: Residence Hall Council, vice
    president, president; Council of Presidents, advisory group;
    Ultimate Frisbee, player and treasurer
Major scholastic or academic honors: Phi Kappa Phi graduate fellow,
    Ohio University Outstanding Graduate in Political Science,
    National Merit Scholar
Work experience (including summer) prior to HLS: Research
    assistant for a professor at Ohio University, several minimum wage
    jobs (movie theater, department store, UPS)
Parents' occupations: Currently retired. Formerly, father was in U.S.
    Civil Service (manpower analyst for U.S. Air Force) and mother
    was a bank clerk.
Legacy factor: N/A

Questionnaire

1. When and why did you apply to Harvard Law School? Was your application completed early, late, or in the middle of the rolling admissions process?

I applied to HLS in early January of my last year in college. I applied because I knew I wanted to go to law school, my grades and LSAT scores were very good, and I wanted to at least try to get into the best law school. HLS is the best law school.

2. How would you describe the undergraduate institution that you attended? Does it have a strong reputation and a solid track record of sending lots of its graduates to Harvard Law School?

Ohio University is a medium-sized state university (18,000 undergrads). It has a good reputation among public universities, but not a great national reputation. (However, the Honors Tutorial College I attended within the University does have a stronger national reputation). As far as I know, I am the first Ohio U. graduate to attend HLS. (Most likely not true, but that's indicative of its track record for sending grads to HLS.)

3. Did you think, prior to being accepted, that you had a decent chance of being admitted to Harvard Law School?

I thought I had a good chance of being accepted because my grades and LSAT scores were good enough to get my application a second look. Beyond that, I believed getting into HLS was a crap shoot at best.

4. Did you take any time off prior to applying or matriculating at HLS? If so, why did you take time off and what did you do?
No time off.

5. What were your strongest assets when applying to Harvard Law School? Grades? LSAT score? Extracurriculars? Personal statement? Recommendations? Family connections? Personal background? Work experience?
My strongest asset was my LSAT score, because it was high and nationally controlled. My grades were very high, but were less valuable because of the university I attended. My exracurriculars were not strong, but my recommendations were valuable, because I developed several close relationships with faculty (including two deans) at OU through the tutorials I took in the Honors Tutorial College (HTC). The tutorials were one-on-one classes.

6. What type of courses did you take as an undergraduate to prepare yourself for Harvard Law School?
I took almost all liberal arts courses. HTC waived all math and science graduation requirements, so I took many political science, history, and English courses. In addition, the tutorials prepared me best for HLS, because the rigorous one-on-one classes simulated the pressure of Socratic learning fairly well.

7. What was your LSAT score(s)? How did you prepare for the test? If you took an LSAT prep course, which one, and did it help?
171. I took practice tests on my own for about a week prior to the test, and I took no prep courses.

8. How long did you spend on your personal statement? What did you write about and how did you decide on the topic? Did anyone help you with your statement? If so, who?
About four hours, to the best of my memory. I wrote a general statement about why I wanted to be a lawyer and why I thought I belonged in law school. I then adapted that statement to the particular questions raised by each law school I applied to. I don't remember exactly what HLS asked, but I'm sure my statement is to some degree tailored to that question.

9. Who wrote your recommendations for Harvard Law School and how

*did you choose them? How much notice did you give your recommenders
and when were the recommendations completed?*

All three recommenders were faculty in the department of political
science at OU. One was my mentor, whom I had worked closely with as a
research assistant the summer before. The other two were professors who
had taken dean jobs with the college of arts and sciences and the University
College. I had done tutorials with them, so they knew me well. Since
I knew any professor would write good things (don't they always?), I
chose all three based on how well they knew me and, of course, on the
significance of their titles. As I recall, I gave each about a month.

**10. What type of extracurricular activities did you participate in during
your undergraduate years that you feel were beneficial to your being
admitted to Harvard Law School, and why?**

None of my extracurriculars were all that significant. I did a lot for
the residence hall council, and I played on the Ultimate Frisbee team. Perhaps
they showed that I was a well-rounded individual, but beyond that
my extras were probably not that helpful.

**11. Do you feel that your race, sex, or class played a role in the admissions
process? If so, explain.**

If anything, my race and sex cut against me simply because of the
demographic breakdown. However, my class, geographic region, and the
fact that I went to a state school might have helped me. I have no clue.

**12. Do you think that your political ideology played a role in the admissions
process? If so, explain.**

I don't think ideology played a role at all. I can think of no way the
committee would have even known my ideology.

**13. Did you see the Harvard Law School campus prior to applying or being
admitted? If so, what arrangements did you make for the visit, what were
your initial impressions, and have your impressions changed very much?
If you didn't visit the campus prior to being accepted, why not?**

I didn't visit because it wasn't worth the money to visit. I was able to
confidently select HLS over my other options, based on its reputation and
my visit after admission (at prospective students' day).

**14. When did you receive your letter of acceptance from the Dean of
Admissions and what were you doing?**

I found the letter in the mail upon return to my apartment after spring break (late March). I remember it clearly because none of my friends had returned from break yet, so I couldn't find anyone to tell in my moment of excitement.

15. How are you paying for Harvard Law School? Parents? Loans? Savings? Work?

This year I have a $7,000 fellowship from Phi Kappa Phi, and my parents are contributing about $3,000. The rest comes from loans. In the future, without the fellowship, the money will come from loans and summer employment.

16. What do you plan to do in the immediate years following Law School graduation? What are your long-term career goals?

I hope to do a clerkship immediately after law school. After that, I'll likely enter the firm world to pay off my loans and gather experience as a litigator. Eventually, I hope to teach, either at law school or college level (which unfortunately would require more education.)

Profile

Name: Timothy E. Moran
Harvard Law School class: 1997
Undergraduate institution: Amherst College
Undergraduate GPA listed by category—3.75+, 3.50–3.74, 3.25–3.49, 3.00–3.24, below 3.00: 3.50–3.74
Graduate institution and GPA, if applicable: N/A
LSAT Score listed by percentile—99–95, 94–90, 89–85, 84–80, 79–75, 74–70, 69–65, below 64: 99–95
Hometown and high school: Milford, CT; Fairfield College Preparatory
Types of recommenders, i.e., professors or employers: Two professors
Race, sex, and class: White, male, middle
Major undergraduate activities: Amherst College Rugby Football Club, Chi Psi Fraternity, Decisional training instructor (counselor at Hampshire County House of Corrections), Amherst College Gospel Choir
Major scholastic or academic honors: *cum laude*

Work experience (including summer) prior to HLS: Five summers
waiting tables at various restaurants (1989–1993) and three
summers as a Special Deputy Sheriff in New Haven County
(1992–1994), basically a bailiff.
Parents' occupations: Mother—Kindergarten teacher, homemaker,
Father—Lawyer, Connecticut Superior Court judge
Legacy factor: N/A

Questionnaire

1. When and why did you apply to Harvard Law School? Was your application completed early, late, or in the middle of the rolling admissions process?

I got my application in late in the admissions process, close to the deadline. I think it was the end of December.

I applied during my senior year of college, with the intention of accepting and deferring the best school that accepted me (Harvard later refused my deferral application). I applied to Harvard because I thought it was the best school at which I had a shot.

2. How would you describe the undergraduate institution that you attended? Does it have a strong reputation and a solid track record of sending lots of its graduates to Harvard Law School?

Amherst College has an excellent academic reputation and, considering its size, sends a good number of its graduates to HLS— some of those becoming more illustrious HLS students than others. Amherst, in my opinion, is stronger academically than all but the very best of the Ivy League (Harvard, Princeton, and Yale), and competes well with even these schools. I suppose, as a small liberal arts school, it may give the impression of being a little less focused on hard academics or law school, but I haven't found this to be the case.

3. Did you think, prior to being accepted, that you had a decent chance of being admitted to Harvard Law School?

I felt I had, at best, a decent chance—that my numbers were good enough at least to have me considered—but I didn't expect to get in. It came as a surprise that I did, especially considering that my neighbor at Amherst, who had almost identical numbers and applied much earlier, was outright rejected. I thought my qualifications put me in a very large pool from which the Admissions Committee could choose seemingly at random.

4. Did you take any time off prior to applying or matriculating at HLS? If so, why did you take time off and what did you do?

I asked to take time off so that I could work and travel in Europe. My request was a little late, and I guess deemed too frivolous, so it was denied. I decided that reapplying was tempting fate a little too far.

5. What were your strongest assets when applying to Harvard Law School? Grades? LSAT score? Extracurriculars? Personal statement? Recommendations? Family connections? Personal background? Work experience?

I think my strongest assets at least initially were first my LSAT score (99th percentile) and then my grades in light of my undergrad school (Amherst). I think they were good enough to get me in the door, so to speak. After that, I would guess that my involvement in the legal world through working as a sheriff and counselling in prison displayed some sort of concrete dedication and interest to the legal profession. Finally, I don't suppose my recommendations hurt me at all.

6. What type of courses did you take as an undergraduate to prepare yourself for Harvard Law School?

I was pretty sure that I would attend law school so I didn't worry too much about courses to see what it would be like. Furthermore, Amherst doesn't have, nor does it encourage, pre-law-type pursuits. I approached college as an opportunity to indulge my intellectual curiosity before I would concentrate on learning a trade in law school. So I tried to take at least something in a lot of areas, except science which I avoid unless it's of the softest variety. More than half of my courses, though, were in either of my two majors: political science and classics. Many of these classes were of the tutorial or lecture variety. Finally, I wrote a thesis in poli sci my senior year.

7. What was your LSAT score(s)? How did you prepare for the test? If you took an LSAT prep course, which one, and did it help?

My score was a 173, which was the 99th percentile. I took Kaplan the summer before I took the exam, and I used their test prep center in Amherst six or seven times during the fall before the test. I felt that Kaplan helped, if only because it got me to do the prep. The most important thing for me was having taken the test six or seven times before the real one.

8. *How long did you spend on your personal statement? What did you write about and how did you decide on the topic? Did anyone help you with your statement? If so, who?*

I spent a pretty long time on my personal statement—a couple of weekends, only because I couldn't choose between three or four possible themes. I think I combined two and once I knew what I was going to say, it wasn't too hard. I remember thinking that it would have to be pretty good to distinguish me; I also wanted it to dovetail with and highlight my extracurricular activities. The theme was basically that I would make a good lawyer because I really wanted to be a lawyer, that I wasn't going to law school for lack of something better to do. I was trying to put myself in contrast to many of the high-powered academic types that Harvard sees.

I had some help with my personal statement from my girlfriend and my roommate, but not from any professors or counselors.

9. *Who wrote your recommendations for Harvard Law School and how did you choose them? How much notice did you give your recommenders and when were the recommendations completed?*

Hadley Arkes, my poli sci and thesis advisor, and Holly Montague, my advisor in classics, wrote my recommendations. I chose them because they were the professors that knew me and my work best. I didn't give them too much notice because I was late—probably three weeks. I don't know when they were done because I directed them to mail the recommendations to my schools directly in order to give them more time.

10. *What type of extracurricular activities did you participate in during your undergraduate years that you feel were beneficial to your being admitted to Harvard Law School, and why?*

I volunteered as a Decisional Training instructor, in which I entered Hampshire County House of Corrections to counsel and teach inmates there one-on-one in decision and planning skills. I think this activity, along with my summer job as a sheriff (basically a bailiff), displayed an interest in the law that went beyond the classroom and was practical. I think they also demonstrated a dedication to, and experience with, the law as a profession.

My other activities revealed me to be, I hope, a well-rounded, solid sort of person, but I don't believe they did too much to distinguish me.

11. *Do you feel that your race, sex, or class played a role in the admissions process? If so, explain.*

I don't think any of these factors played a role in my admission. In all respects, I am comfortably in the majority. If anything, these factors may have made me a somewhat less desirable candidate for not adding too much to the diversity of the school, unless it's as someone who falls so squarely in the middle that he's exceptional.

12. Do you think that your political ideology played a role in the admissions process? If so, explain.

Not really; again I'm as in the middle as a person can get. My views tend to run conservatively, but I was not active at all in promoting them in college, so I don't see how they would be known to the admissions committee or how they would play a role even if my views were known.

13. Did you see the Harvard Law School campus prior to applying or being admitted? If so, what arrangements did you make for the visit, what were your initial impressions, and have your impressions changed very much? If you didn't visit the campus prior to being accepted, why not?

I did come to the prospective-student open-house on April 14. (I think it was then; I remember it was the same day that my thesis was due so I had to take an extension so that I could come.) It was important to me to see the school because I was having a hard time choosing between here and Chicago, which I had heard was "friendlier." I remember having a mixed impression: I knew that HLS wasn't nearly as bad as the books and movies make it seem, but at the same time I suspected that it was probably a little worse than people said. Also, while I found many things I liked, there were also a number of things I didn't like. I've found that my impression was a little more negative than necessary, but basically on track.

14. When did you receive your letter of acceptance from the Dean of Admissions and what were you doing?

I got my letter during spring break at Amherst (sometime in March). I had come back early to work on my thesis, which was behind schedule. After getting in, I found it much harder to work on my thesis and I fell further behind.

15. How are you paying for Harvard Law School? Parents? Loans? Savings? Work?

I'm getting help from my parents and contributing what I can.

16. What do you plan to do in the immediate years following Law School graduation? What are your long-term career goals?

I'm not too sure yet, but I do plan on clerking for a year after graduation. Then, I'm thinking I'd like to work for a firm for at least a few years, but public interest work is also very interesting to me. Longer term, I've considered the U.S. Attorney's Office.

Profile

Name: Robert Musslewhite
Harvard Law School class: 1996
Undergraduate institution: Princeton University
Undergraduate GPA listed by category—3.75+, 3.50–3.74, 3.25–3.49, 3.00–3.24, below 3.00: 3.75+
Graduate institution and GPA, if applicable: N/A
LSAT Score listed by percentile—99–95, 94–90, 89–85, 84–80, 79–75, 74–70, 69–65, below 64: 99–95
Hometown and high school: Dallas, TX; St. Mark's School of Texas
Types of recommenders, i.e., professors or employers: Professors
Race, sex, and class: White, male, upper-middle
Major undergraduate activities: Varsity swimming, teaching assistant, hanging out with friends
Major scholastic or academic honors: Charles Caldwell graduate scholarship (for athletic and academic achievement); *cum laude*; Rhodes scholarship state finalist
Work experience prior to HLS: Summers: taught swimming lessons in Dallas, TX.
Parents' occupations: Father—Attorney, Mother—Flight attendant
Legacy factor: N/A

Questionnaire:

1. When and why did you apply to Harvard Law School? Was your application completed early, late, or in the middle of the rolling admissions process?

I applied to Harvard during November 1992 (five months after graduating from college); while I was not certain that I wanted to go to law school the next year, it was a possible option, so I applied just in case. I think that deep down I wanted to go to the University of Texas (much less expensive, closer to home, better weather), but I applied to Harvard and Stanford as well, thinking I probably wouldn't be admitted to either. My application was submitted before rolling admissions began (or at least before the "early" deadline).

2. How would you describe the undergraduate institution that you attended? Does it have a strong reputation and a solid track record of sending lots of its graduates to Harvard Law School?

I attended Princeton University, which sends many of its graduates here.

3. Did you think, prior to being accepted, that you had a decent chance of being admitted to Harvard Law School?

I did not think that I would be admitted to Harvard; it seemed to me that everyone I knew who had been admitted had much stronger academic records. In fact, I was not admitted to Stanford.

4. Did you take any time off prior to applying or matriculating at HLS? If so, why did you take time off and what did you do?

I took one year off before coming to Harvard. Not knowing what I wanted to do after college, I decided to spend a year either working at a ski area or at a Club Med or similar resort, having fun while deciding what to do the following year. I had swum competitively since I was six years old, and in college that meant no skiing, which is something I love to do. So I eventually settled on living in Colorado with two high-school friends. Knowing what I know now, I should have taken more time off before coming to law school—there probably will never be a chance for me to have the freedom to go anywhere and do anything for such a long period of time again.

During the summer after graduation, I taught swimming lessons (which I had done for two previous summers) and then travelled through Europe for five weeks.

In September, I returned to Princeton to take the LSAT course and then the October LSAT. After the test, I prepared my law school applications and worked on my resumé in Dallas, then moved out to Crested Butte, Colorado, where I spent the ski season working as an auditor for the ski resort (a "good-sounding" job that really involved only counting money—but hey, it came with a season ski pass!). During the winter I applied for several management consulting jobs before I decided to attend law school (Texas, I thought).

After visiting both Texas and Harvard in the spring, I taught swimming lessons again in the summer and came here in the fall of 1993.

5. *What were your strongest assets when applying to Harvard Law School? Grades? LSAT score? Extracurriculars? Personal statement? Recommendations? Family connections? Personal background? Work experience?*

While my grades were good, I didn't think they were great compared to most applicants. I think the strengths of my application were: my swimming (I was co-captain in 1991–92 and an NCAA Champion and All-American in the 200-yard medley relay in 1989; we practiced over 20 hours per week), my independent work (though Princeton requires two junior papers and a senior thesis, I still think being able to discuss such work on the application helped), my courses (pretty hard-core analytic economics courses), my LSAT score, and the personal statement. Also, I think my recommenders spent a good deal of time on their letters and wrote very thoughtful and good letters.

I wouldn't have thought that swimming would have helped (in fact, the career services office at Princeton had told me that it wouldn't matter in a law school application, while it might in a business school application), but there is a reason why I think it did. The article in the Record about our class began by saying something like "a Rhodes scholar, a peace corps volunteer, a champion swimmer . . . Those are some of the people in the 1L class." So I guess the admissions office gave the information to the writer—it must have helped my application for them to have remembered it like that. To be honest, my first reaction was that there must be another swimmer in our class!

6. *What types of courses did you take as an undergraduate to prepare yourself for Harvard Law School?*

I did not think I was going to law school at that time, so none, really. In retrospect, I think that my economics classes were helpful (I was an econ major); I took lots of mathematical and quantitative courses.

7. *What was your LSAT score(s)? How did you prepare for the test? If you took an LSAT prep course, which one, and did it help?*

I think it was 173. I took the Princeton Review course to prepare for it, and I think it helped a bit but mostly because it forced me to practice beforehand.

8. *How long did you spend on your personal statement? What did you write about and how did you decide on the topic? Did anyone help you with your statement? If so, who?*

I spent quite a bit of time on the personal statement—it took several days to write and I edited it for about two weeks. I wrote about what parts of my life were important to me, why they influenced my life, and how law school would fit in with everything I had done and with what I wanted to do afterwards. It was the typical personal statement—an attempt to write something meaningful about yourself while making sure the admissions committee knows about some of your accomplishments that don't come out in other parts of the application.

My father and mother read the essay and offered some advice.

9. Who wrote your recommendations for Harvard Law School and how did you choose them? How much notice did you give your recommenders and when were the recommendations completed?

I had several people write recommendations, and I had the career services office at Princeton tip me off as to which two letters would be most helpful. My high-school headmaster, my college swim coach, and three professors wrote letters; I ended up choosing two professors' recs: Uwe Reinhardt (I took his accounting class and then worked as his teaching assistant in the course for the next two years) and Phil Levine (an economics grad student and now an assistant professor at Wellesley; my advisor for both of my junior papers and an instructor in one of my basic economics courses). I gave them plenty of time to write the letters.

10. What type of extracurricular activities did you participate in during your undergraduate years that you feel were beneficial to your being admitted to Harvard Law School, and why?

See number 5. Also, I worked as a teaching assistant (see number 10).

11. Do you feel that race, sex, or class played a role in the admissions process? If so, explain.

I thought that my race and sex would actually work against me in being admitted to Harvard—alums had told me that, and several people I knew who had outstanding academic records but who were white males were not admitted.

12. Do you think that your political ideology played a role in the admissions process? If so, explain.

No.

13. Did you see the Harvard Law School campus prior to applying or being admitted? If so, what arrangements did you make for the visit, what were

*your initial impressions, and have your impressions changed very much?
If you didn't visit the campus prior to being accepted, why not?*

Yes—I knew Matt Henshon from college, and I had lunch with him in the fall and went to a class. Then, after I was admitted, I visited him in the spring and went to a couple of classes. While the visit in the fall made me want to apply, the spring visit left me absolutely certain that I was going to the University of Texas. It was the end of April, but it was cold and rainy, and everyone was starting to get stressed about exams. I thought there was no way I would come here.

14. When did you receive your letter of acceptance from the Dean of Admissions and what were you doing?

I got the letter while I was in Colorado in mid- or late February.

15. How are you paying for Harvard Law School? Parents? Loans? Savings? Work?

My father pays $12,000 a year. I borrow $8,500 a year and, so far, I've paid the rest out of savings and summer money (with the exception of borrowing $7,500 from my grandfather this spring, which I will repay this summer). I also work for a professor (not that it brings in much cash, but it helps).

16. What do you plan to do in the immediate years following Law School graduation? What are your long-term career goals?

I will clerk for a district court judge in Dallas for one year before working at either a law firm or management consulting firm. Long-term I am still very undecided.

Profile

Name Withheld
Harvard Law School class: 1995
Undergraduate institution: Duke University
**Undergraduate GPA listed by category—3.75+, 3.50–3.74,
    3.25–3.49, 3.00–3.24, below 3.00:** 3.50–3.74
Graduate institution and GPA, if applicable: N/A
**LSAT Score listed by percentile—99–95, 94–90, 89–85, 84–80,
    79–75, 74–70, 69–65, below 64:** 99–95

Hometown and high school: Chadds Ford, PA; Unionville High School

Types of recommenders, i.e., professors or employers: Three recommenders, all Duke professors. One was a professor I had worked for as a teaching assistant. Another was an assistant dean who I had as a professor but also advised pre-law students.

Race, sex, and class: White, female, upper

Major undergraduate activities: Undergraduate Judicial Board; Public Policy Majors Union Board of Directors; Kappa Alpha Theta (various offices); University Church Choir; Freshman Advisory Counselor; Duke tour guide; Dukes and Duchesses (university student representatives)

Major scholastic or academic honors: Phi Beta Kappa; *magna cum laude*

Work experience (including summer) prior to HLS: Senate Judiciary Committee, Staff Assistant, 1991–92; U.S. State Department, U.S. Embassy, Canada, Student Intern, summer 1990; Computer consultant to business consulting firm, summer 1989; Temporary secretary for DuPont Company, Summer 1988; Public Policy Studies intro course, teaching assistant; Student manager in on-campus restaurant, during school.

Parents' occupations: Father—Chemical engineer, Mother—Elementary schoolteacher

Legacy factor: N/A

Questionnaire

1. When and why did you apply to Harvard Law School? Was your application completed early, late, or in the middle of the rolling admissions process?

I applied to HLS on the advice of the pre-law dean who gave me a list of schools. I was not planning to apply to HLS because I didn't consider myself having a chance to get in. My application was completed in November of the year I applied (very early in the process). I was applying the year after I graduated from Duke, after I was already working.

2. How would you describe the undergraduate institution that you attended? Does it have a strong reputation and a solid track record of sending lots of its graduates to Harvard Law School?

My undergraduate institution has a strong national reputation for academics and a strong record of sending several students a year to HLS.

3. Did you think, prior to being accepted, that you had a decent chance of being admitted to Harvard Law School?

No, as mentioned above, I didn't even think my chance was worth the price of the application fee. I applied on the advice of one of my recommenders, but was relatively certain that I would be going to a different school.

4. Did you take any time off prior to applying or matriculating at HLS? If so, why did you take time off and what did you do?

Yes, I took off one year. I worked in Washington for the Senate Judiciary Committee (majority staff). I took a year off because I didn't decide I wanted to go to law school until my senior year and thus couldn't take the LSAT in time to apply that year. I probably would've taken a year off anyway because I didn't think it was wise to go on.

5. What were your strongest assets when applying to Harvard Law School? Grades? LSAT score? Extracurriculars? Personal statement? Recommendations? Family connections? Personal background? Work experience?

Generally, I looked at it this way. My grades and LSAT scores were solid but not the top of the class. My extracurriculars were also okay but nothing startling. The strongest aspect of my application was probably my recommendations and my work experience, but again, probably not the most amazing thing the admissions committee had ever seen. Thus, I figured I would get into the "not in but not out" category and so my personal statement would have to push me over the top. I worked hard on my personal statements and felt good about them.

6. What type of courses did you take as an undergraduate to prepare yourself for Harvard Law School?

I wasn't planning to go to Law School, so none. However, in retrospect I feel I had taken classes that helped a lot. I was a double-major in public policy studies and economics, and both disciplines have helped me a lot in law school.

7. What was your LSAT score(s)? How did you prepare for the test? If you took an LSAT prep course, which one, and did it help?

I got a 46 out of 48, which was in a high percentile for that particular test. I took Kaplan but I thought it was a huge waste of my time and money and I told everyone I knew just to buy prep books and do practice tests themselves.

8. How long did you spend on your personal statement? What did you write about and how did you decide on the topic? Did anyone help you with your statement? If so, who?

I spent a *long* time on my personal statements (both of them). HLS was my number one choice and so I wrote the essays with HLS in mind and then used them for other schools. I wrote about four different full statements, some with broader focuses and some with more narrow focuses, so I could see which one worked best. I had only a few people read my essays: my parents, one close friend, and our pre-law dean. Mostly I had them help me decide which of the statements to use, rather than any specific editorial comments—I did most of the rewriting/editing myself.

9. Who wrote your recommendations for Harvard Law School and how did you choose them? How much notice did you give your recommenders and when were the recommendations completed?

I had three professors. One was a professor whom I had had for class and then later worked for as a teaching assistant. The second was the pre-law dean, who had to write recommendations for all students applying to law school, but whom I had also had for class. The third was a professor I had had for several classes and had done several large writing assignments for. I chose this group because I thought they had a wide variety of perspectives on my working abilities and they all knew me well through out-of-class interaction. Although I was working at the time I applied, and working for HLS grads, I didn't get recommendations from them because I hadn't been working there long and I didn't know them very well. I also knew the professors would get them done and I wouldn't have to stress about not having my application complete.

10. What type of extracurricular activities did you participate in during your undergraduate years that you feel were beneficial to your being admitted to Harvard Law School, and why?

Probably the most important was the Undergraduate Judicial Board, which was a group of students that heard and decided student violations of the university rules — the relevancy for law school is pretty obvious. I think my employment history was probably much more persuasive.

11. Do you feel that your race, sex, or class played a role in the admissions process? If so, explain.

Being female probably helped me, given the low percentage of women in my class. Other than that, I doubt my race or class was an issue.

12. Do you think that your political ideology played a role in the admissions process? If so, explain.

I have no idea if that was an issue, although if it was, my ideology would probably have been pretty easy to figure out. I worked for a Democratic senator but had not been involved in any activist type groups or extracurriculars.

13. Did you see the Harvard Law School campus prior to applying or being admitted? If so, what arrangements did you make for the visit, what were your initial impressions, and have your impressions changed very much? If you didn't visit the campus prior to being accepted, why not?

I didn't visit before I applied. After I was accepted, I visited a friend from Duke who was a first-year at the time. I stayed with her in the dorm. When I visited, I was already pretty sure I would come, and I was actually apartment-hunting at the same time. I didn't labor much over the choice to come here. Harvard was Harvard and I wasn't about to turn it down.

14. When did you receive your letter of acceptance from the Dean of Admissions and what were you doing?

I received my letter in early February. I was working in Washington, D.C., at the time. I celebrated by going to watch North Carolina beat Duke in basketball—what you might call a bittersweet day.

15. How are you paying for Harvard Law School? Parents? Loans? Savings? Work?

All loans.

16. What do you plan to do in the immediate years following Law School graduation? What are your long-term career goals?

I am going to clerk and then go work for a law firm in Washington, D.C. Long-term I want to work in the government in Washington—either the SEC or the Hill.

Profile

Name Withheld
Harvard Law School class: 1995

Undergraduate institution: Yale

Undergraduate GPA listed by category—3.75+, 3.50–3.74, 3.25–3.49, 3.00–3.24, below 3.00: 3.50–3.74

Graduate institution and GPA, if applicable: N/A

LSAT Score listed by percentile—99–95, 94–90, 89–85, 84–80, 79–75, 74–70, 69–65, below 64: 94–90

Hometown and high school: Philadelphia, PA; Mount Saint Joseph Academy

Types of recommenders, i.e., professors or employers: Professor, residential college dean, and employer

Race, sex, and class: African American, female, middle

Major undergraduate activities: Black Student Alliance at Yale, Financial Aid Committee, tutor at Wilbur Cross High School

Major scholastic or academic honors: None

Work experience (including summer) prior to HLS: Paralegal, Howard Darby & Levin, NY, NY, 1991–92; Leadership development projects assistant, Prep for Prep, NY, NY, 1990–91; Paralegal assistant, Goldfein & Joseph, Philadelphia, PA; Summers in college.

Parents' occupations: Father—Manager of Computer Systems, Mother—Management analyst, both retired, U.S. Dept. of Defense

Legacy factor: N/A

Questionnaire:

1. When and why did you apply to Harvard Law School? Was your application completed early, late, or in the middle of the rolling admissions process?

I applied to HLS in 1991. I applied because I believed it to be one of the best law schools in the country with a strong reputation. Also after speaking with and working for attorneys in my summer and full-time jobs, I realized the importance of going to a top law school in order to have the best job and career opportunities. My application was completed three weeks before the deadline for regular admissions.

2. How would you describe the undergraduate institution that you attended? Does it have a strong reputation and a solid track record of sending lots of its graduates to Harvard Law School?

Yale was a strong liberal arts college with a high track record of sending students to law schools like Yale. I majored in political science so I had some limited knowledge of the legal system.

3. *Did you think, prior to being accepted, that you had a decent chance of being admitted to Harvard Law School?*

I was not sure how strong of a chance I had to be accepted. This was the case particularly because I applied so late. All of my other law school applications were completed by mid-December of 1991. Harvard was the last school I applied to because I had to write an extra essay which took some time to develop. I knew that with my work experience and my strong GPA that I stood a fairly decent chance of being accepted.

4. *Did you take any time off prior to applying or matriculating at* HLS? *If so, why did you take time off and what did you do?*

I took off two years before attending HLS. For the first ten months after college (August 1990 to June 1991) I worked with gifted minority students at an organization called Prep for Prep in New York City. My job included planning activities for the students and running a mentoring program for the students. After Prep I worked for a year as a paralegal at a small (thirty-person) law firm in New York. This gave me the opportunity to see what lawyers do and allowed me to speak with many attorneys about their profession.

I decided to take time off for several reasons. First, I was burnt out after college and really needed a break from the academic scene. Also, I was not sure that I wanted to go to law school and thought that I should work first in order to make up my mind. I also just wanted time to explore New York and to do new things with new people.

5. *What were your strongest assets when applying to Harvard Law School? Grades?* LSAT *score? Extracurriculars? Personal statement? Recommendations? Family connections? Personal background? Work experience?*

It's hard to say what were my strongest assets. In my mind going to Yale and graduating with a high GPA definitely helped. My LSAT scores were solid and I know that my recommendations were strong as well. The fact that I took off and worked in two very different jobs also made me a strong candidate. I had no family connections to HLS before applying.

6. *What type of courses did you take as an undergraduate to prepare yourself for Harvard Law School?*

I do not think that any of my courses really "prepared" me for HLS. I was a political science major, so those classes introduced me to political theory and government regulation, but I do not think they mirrored the kind of classes I took first year at HLS. I also took many classes about African and African-American culture, history, literature, and art.

7. *What was your* LSAT *score(s)? How did you prepare for the test? If you took an* LSAT *prep course, which one, and did it help?*

I received a 39 out of 48 on the LSAT. I took the Stanley Kaplan review course. I think it was helpful in the sense that it forced me to be disciplined about studying for the test and offered helpful suggestions on dealing with the different sections, especially the logic games section.

8. *How long did you spend on your personal statement? What did you write about and how did you decide on the topic? Did anyone help you with your statement? If so, who?*

It took me about two months to work on my personal statement. I wrote about my work for a professor at Yale who taught developmental psychology and child development. I basically talked about the research I did for him about child development and how I would like to work for children's rights one day. I decided on this topic because it was very interesting to me and because the work had such a strong impact on me at the time. A friend of mine read my first draft of the personal statement. I received no other help with it.

9. *Who wrote your recommendations for Harvard Law School and how did you choose them? How much notice did you give your recommenders and when were the recommendations completed?*

A professor and my residential college dean from Yale wrote two of my recommendations. I asked them because they were the two people who knew me the best while at college. Because we keep recommendations on file at Yale, I just called and had my recommendations sent to the various law schools. I also asked a lawyer I worked with to prepare a recommendation for me. I gave him one-and-a-half months' notice about the recommendation. They were all completed several weeks before I mailed my applications.

10. *What type of extracurricular activities did you participate in during your undergraduate years that you feel were beneficial to your being admitted to Harvard Law School, and why?*

I did a few community-service projects through the Black Student Alliance at Yale and I tutored at a high school in the New Haven area. I think that these activities were beneficial because the community outreach was consistent with my personal statement goals and because it demonstrated my desire to work with the community.

11. *Do you feel that your race, sex, or class played a role in the admissions process? If so, explain.*

I would like to think that my race and sex played a positive role in my admittance to HLS. I was qualified both in terms of the "numbers" and the undergraduate institution, and my race and sex could only enhance those qualifications by allowing me to contribute to a more diverse population at the law school.

12. Do you think that your political ideology played a role in the admissions process? If so, explain.

I do not think that my political ideology played a role because there was no way the admissions committee could determine it based on my personal statement or transcript.

13. Did you see the Harvard Law School campus prior to applying or being admitted? If so, what arrangements did you make for the visit, what were your initial impressions, and have your impressions changed very much? If you didn't visit the campus prior to being accepted, why not?

I visited Harvard during BLSA's Spring Conference weekend. They had a special program for newly admitted students. I stayed with a friend from New York who lived in Medford at the time. My first impression of HLS was that it was a very "academic" place where I could be focused and study hard. I thought the campus was nice, but smaller than I originally imagined. I also thought that Harvard Square was a nice place to shop and socialize. My initial impressions have changed in a limited way. I still think that I was able to be more focused here because of the atmosphere and because of the types of students who attend school here. Indeed this is a very "academically-oriented" place, which at times has been a bit intense. I really had no prior impressions of the students because I did not spend much time with them before coming here.

14. When did you receive your letter of acceptance from the Dean of Admissions and what were you doing?

I received my letter in early March 1992. I applied sometime around January 20, 1992. I received the letter in the mail during the week after I returned home from work.

15. How are you paying for Harvard Law School? Parents? Loans? Savings? Work?

I am primarily paying for HLS through loans. I was able to save a little bit of money in the summers and I also work for the Board of Student Advisors, which pays $4,000 for the school year. My parents are not helping me to pay for HLS.

16. What do you plan to do in the immediate years following Law School graduation? What are your long-term career goals?

After law school, I will be working in a large New York law firm as an associate. I plan to do that for three to four years and then pursue a career either in entertainment law or working for a foundation of some sort. In the long run I would like to work in a position where I can be involved with cultural programs or organizations. I also would like to pursue my interest in literature and the arts.

Profile

Name Withheld
Harvard Law School class: 1995
Undergraduate institution: Williams College
Undergraduate GPA listed by category—3.75+, 3.50–3.74, 3.25–3.49, 3.00–3.24, below 3.00: 3.50–3.74
Graduate institution and GPA, if applicable: N/A
LSAT Score listed by percentile—99–95, 94–90, 89–85, 84–80, 79–75, 74–70, 69–65, below 64: 99–95
Hometown and high school: Kirkwood, MO; Kirkwood High School
Types of recommenders, i.e., professors or employers: Professors at Williams College
Race, sex, and class: White, male, upper-middle
Major undergraduate activities: JV Soccer team, Williamstown Big Brother program, junior advisor (similar to RA or tutor in Harvard system), sportswriter on *Williams Record* newspaper
Major scholastic or academic honors: Presidential Scholar (1986), Robert C.L. Scott Prize for best history thesis (1990), Benedict Prize for best GPA in history department (1990), Phi Beta Kappa (1990)
Work experience (including summer) prior to HLS: Legal assistant, Bryan Cave, London 1991–92; Legal assistant, Testa, Hurwitz, & Thibeault, Boston 1990–91; Environmental Affairs Intern, Emerson Electric Company, St. Louis, summer 1989; Intern, Senator John Danforth, summer 1988; Asst. manager, Country Surf Pool, St. Louis, summer 1987; Lifeguard, Country Surf Pool, St. Louis, summer 1986; Lawnmowing, St. Louis, summers 1980–85.
Parents' occupations: Mother—Educator and nonprofit administrator, Father—Attorney, specializing in education law
Legacy factor: N/A

Questionnaire

1. When and why did you apply to Harvard Law School? Was your application completed early, late, or in the middle of the rolling admissions process?

I applied to HLS early November 1990 for a place in the class of 1994. I also applied to Boalt Hall (UC-Berkeley), Stanford, and Yale, and was ready to send out others at the last minute if these didn't work out. A few months of paralegal work had not dissuaded me from law school, and I thought I wanted to become a practicing lawyer or a government employee where a law degree would be useful.

At the time I applied, I did not have positive feelings toward Harvard, and was leaning toward the other schools I applied to because of better quality of life, etc. However, a few things happened to change my mind. First, HLS accepted me quite early, by the end of December 1990, while the other schools took much longer. Although I heard I was accepted at Boalt a few months later, as of May 1991 I was wait-listed at Yale, and had heard nothing from Stanford. Second, having a spouse (then fiancée) who I knew would be either working or doing graduate study made the city of Boston a very attractive choice. Lastly, I really enjoyed the Admitted Students' Day at HLS the spring of 1991.

After accepting my offer from HLS, I deferred for a year so that I could accompany my wife Jennifer in England for a year. She had an opportunity to do a year of graduate study at Oxford University. I thus became a member of the class of 1995.

2. How would you describe the undergraduate institution that you attended? Does it have a strong reputation and a solid track record of sending lots of its graduates to Harvard Law School?

Williams College is a small liberal arts college in far Western Massachusetts. It is very strong academically, especially in the sense that the class sizes are very small and the faculty places a premium on interaction with students. The college atmosphere also has a heavy emphasis on athletic participation (both intercollegiate and intramural), outdoor activities, and beer drinking. For a school its size (500 per graduating class), Williams sends a fair amount—about a half dozen—of graduates to HLS every year.

3. Did you think, prior to being accepted, that you had a decent chance of being admitted to Harvard Law School?

I thought I would be accepted at HLS. I had a very high LSAT score, and given the large class size admitted each year at HLS, I figured my good but not great college GPA would not pose a problem.

4. Did you take any time off prior to applying or matriculating at HLS? If so, why did you take time off and what did you do?

    I took one year off because I was tired of school and I wanted to be more certain that I wanted to go to graduate school. I deferred my admission for a second year because of my wife's opportunity to study at Oxford.

5. What were your strongest assets when applying to Harvard Law School? Grades? LSAT score? Extracurriculars? Personal statement? Recommendations? Family connections? Personal background? Work experience?

    My LSAT score, a 48, was my strongest asset in my HLS application. Also, although my overall undergraduate GPA of 3.7 was not stellar by HLS standards, to the extent they looked more closely at my work in the history department at Williams, such as my thesis and my faculty recommendations, that would have been a plus factor. I also think that the fact I was from Missouri may have helped if HLS was seeking more geographic diversity.

6. What type of courses did you take as an undergraduate to prepare yourself for Harvard Law School?

    I didn't specifically prepare for law school, but my courses at Williams turned out to be great preparation. Substantively, my history major and other humanities courses were a good background, and more pragmatically, the constant focus on writing at Williams and the fact that all exams were three-hour bluebook essay exams (just like at HLS) provided good practice.

7. What was your LSAT score(s)? How did you prepare for the test? If you took an LSAT prep course, which one, and did it help?

    My LSAT score was a 48. I did not take a course, but bought a prep book (I forget which one) and did about five to ten practice exams.

8. How long did you spend on your personal statement? What did you write about and how did you decide on the topic? Did anyone help you with your statement? If so, who?

    I spent a few weeks of on-and-off work composing my statement, which I used in various forms on all of my law school applications. I wrote a very introspective type of statement about some varied personal experiences which had influenced me in an almost spiritual way. Law school was part of the statement as more of an afterthought. My wife (then fiancée) was the only person who read and commented on it.

Ironically, reading it now after three years of law school, I realize that I would probably not write such a broadly introspective essay today. Sadly, I would probably write something "safer" and more instrumental, and consequently less original, about how a law degree would help me to accomplish some rather specific goals for myself and for society.

9. Who wrote your recommendations for Harvard Law School and how did you choose them? How much notice did you give your recommenders and when were the recommendations completed?

I had two Williams College history professors write my recommendations. Regina Kunzel was my thesis advisor, and Robert Dalzell was a leading professor I knew well. I think I gave them a month or two of notice, and they sent them in in plenty of time.

10. What type of extracurricular activities did you participate in during your undergraduate years that you feel were beneficial to your being admitted to Harvard Law School, and why?

I frankly doubt that HLS gives much of a look at what its applicants did extracurricularly as undergrads. Even if they did, I had a balanced and diverse set of activities but nothing that outstanding or unusual. I was a JV athlete for a few years, a junior advisor (like an RA), and participated in the Williamstown Big Brother program, among other things.

11. Do you feel that your race, sex, or class played a role in the admissions process? If so, explain.

No. Geographic background (Missouri) may have played some role.

12. Do you think that your political ideology played a role in the admissions process? If so, explain.

No.

13. Did you see the Harvard Law School campus prior to applying or being admitted? If so, what arrangements did you make for the visit, what were your initial impressions, and have your impressions changed very much? If you didn't visit the campus prior to being accepted, why not?

Yes. I attended an Admitted Students' Day for the class of 1994 in the spring of 1991. This made a positive impression on me, and increased my desire to attend HLS for a few reasons. First, I had only heard negative things about "aggressive and uptight" HLS students, and met a number of prospective classmates and current students on campus I liked very much. Ironically, because I deferred for a year I wasn't a member of that class after all. Second, I sat in on a very exciting mock criminal law class taught by Professor Charles Ogletree, which greatly increased my immediate interest in studying law.

14. When did you receive your letter of acceptance from the Dean of Admissions and what were you doing?

My letter of acceptance was waiting at my Medford, Massachusetts, apartment when my fiancée and I returned from Christmas vacation in St. Louis at the end of December in 1990. I was then working as a paralegal at a Boston firm.

15. How are you paying for Harvard Law School? Parents? Loans? Savings? Work?

My wife and I are together funding our graduate educations on our own. With this in mind, we have tried over the past five years to alternate, with one of us in school and the other working. When Jennifer completes her Ph.D. in health policy in 1998, we will have had eight consecutive years where one of us has been in school, and in only one of those, 1994–95, were we *both* in school. As a result, we have tried to cover living expenses with our salaries, and to rely on government loans to cover tuition each year.

16. What do you plan to do in the immediate years following Law School graduation? What are your long-term career goals?

Next year, I will work for a year at a Boston law firm, Ropes & Gray, and then in 1996–97 clerk for Judge Michael Boudin on the First Circuit Court of Appeals. I had originally been hired by then Chief Judge Stephen Breyer to work for him on the First Circuit, and there is a good chance I will be able to join him at his new post on the Supreme Court in 1997–98, although this is not certain at this time.

Longer term, I will likely spend part of my career at a private law firm, and would also love to work as a government lawyer (e.g., U.S. Attorney, Justice Department, public defender). I also consider a career in law teaching, although this is a route I remain a bit unsure about.

Profile

Name: Alexei M. Silverman
Harvard Law School class: 1996
Undergraduate institution: Rice University
**Undergraduate GPA listed by category—3.75+, 3.50–3.74,
    3.25–3.49, 3.00–3.24, below 3.00:** 3.75+
Graduate institution and GPA, if applicable: N/A
**LSAT Score listed by percentile—99–95, 94–90, 89–85, 84–80,
    79–75, 74–70, 69–65, below 64:** 99–95
Hometown and high school: Chicago, IL; Lincoln Park High School
    (inner-city public high school)
Types of recommenders, i.e., professors or employers: Professors
    and a professor/employer
Race, sex, and class: White, male and middle
Major undergraduate activities: Literary journals and advertising for
    college events
Major scholastic or academic honors: Phi Beta Kappa; *magna cum
    laude*; variety of academic scholarships
Work experience (including summer) prior to HLS: Opened own
    freelance decorative painting business; Worked in clothing and
    accessories portion of an Evanston, IL, bike store.
Parents' occupations: Father—Coordinator of Refugee Programs for
    the State of Illinois, Mother—Chief concierge at the Hotel
    Intercontinental–Chicago
Legacy factor: N/A

Questionnaire

1. When and why did you apply to Harvard Law School? Was your application completed early, late, or in the middle of the rolling admissions process?

I applied to HLS for the following reasons:

1) range of opportunities, e.g., clinical programs, journals, student activities, course offerings;

2) reputation and strength of faculty;

3) the international strength of Harvard's reputation;

4) advantage in the legal job market;

5) and the diversity of the student body.

2. How would you describe the undergraduate institution that you attended? Does it have a strong reputation and a solid track record of sending lots of its graduates to Harvard Law School?

I attended a small Southern, private institution with a growing national reputation. While I have never harbored any doubt about the excellence of the institution, I realize that its graduates are underrepresented at East Coast graduate schools and therefore its name does not precede it as the name of an East Coast institution might. I don't know what proportion of Rice grads who apply to HLS get in. But, I do know that every entering HLS class for the past few years seems to have three to five students from Rice. For a school that is attended only by some 2,200 undergrads—the majority who attend Texas graduate schools—I suppose that is a solid track record. Of course Rice is not one of the powerhouse schools that traditionally sends 20+ graduates to HLS.

3. Did you think, prior to being accepted, that you had a decent chance of being admitted to Harvard Law School?

I thought that based on my grades, LSAT scores, and range of intellectual interests that I had an outside chance at being admitted.

4. Did you take any time off prior to applying or matriculating at HLS? If so, why did you take time off and what did you do?

I took time off after graduation primarily to recuperate from a long four years and also to apply to law schools in a more relaxed fashion than would have been possible had I done so in my senior year at Rice. During my time off I pursued a range of hobbies of mine in a professional setting. I started a freelance decorative-painting business that sort of grew out of a clientele based on friends of my parents. I contracted to do decorative details, *faux marbre*, and other decorative techniques.

Once the business started to slow I supplemented my income by working at Turin Bicycle in Evanston, IL.

5. What were your strongest assets when applying to Harvard Law School? Grades? LSAT score? Extracurriculars? Personal statement? Recommendations? Family connections? Personal background? Work experience?

The law school admissions process continues to be somewhat mystifying to me. I know that my grades, and LSAT scores certainly were not negatives, but I don't really believe they were my chief assets. I think my personal background and the diversity of my pursuits were my chief assets. I wrote my personal statement about my year abroad in Italy and I think it adequately captured my character and commitment to intellectual pursuits. Compared to the more typical HLS applicant—if there is such a thing—my background might seem less conventionally geared to the study of law. I think I was able to turn the unconventional aspects of my prior pursuits into positives through my application and that this was my greatest asset of all in applying to HLS.

6. What type of courses did you take as an undergraduate to prepare yourself for Harvard Law School?

Because I didn't formally decide to apply to law school until I was a junior—when I was already committed to a double-major in English and art history with an Italian minor—I did not take courses specifically with the intent of preparing myself for HLS. My approach to my undergraduate education was simply to pursue academic interests that might prepare me for a range of different professional pursuits. My general goals were to refine skills in writing, research, and analysis.

7. What was your LSAT score(s)? How did you prepare for the test? If you took an LSAT prep course, which one, and did it help?

I forget my numerical score. My percentile rank was 97. My preparation for the test consisted of using several books on taking the LSAT to take practice exams. My main objectives were to become familiar with the format of the examination and to develop the right pace to optimize my score.

8. How long did you spend on your personal statement? What did you write about and how did you decide on the topic? Did anyone help you with your statement? If so, who?

I think I spent about two days maximum choosing topics and then developing a personal statement. I decided to write about my year abroad in Italy because the strangeness of the endeavor, and the personal demands it made of me seemed to parallel those that I expected I would face as a first-year law student. Part of my idea was to display that I had the character and fortitude to survive a year of academics in a foreign country; thus law school is exactly the type of challenge I was prepared to tackle.

9. Who wrote your recommendations for Harvard Law School and how did you choose them? How much notice did you give your recommenders and when were the recommendations completed?

One of my recommendations was written by an English professor I had taken two courses with in small classroom settings. He was the most acquainted with my writing and analytical skills. I gave him about a month's notice. My other recommendation was written by the director of Rice University's Sewell Art Gallery whom I had been a student of in a class on museum curation and whom I worked for throughout my senior year. Of my recommenders she had better insight into my social and interpersonal skills. The other recommendation was purely academic and written by Rice's pre-law advisor.

10. What type of extracurricular activities did you participate in during your undergraduate years that you feel were beneficial to your being admitted to Harvard Law School, and why?

I didn't pursue a wide range of undergraduate extracurriculars and thus I have a hard time believing any of them were beneficial to my being admitted. I think perhaps my extracurricular involvement with a literary journal demonstrated a valuable interest in writing and editing.

11. Do you feel that your race, sex, or class played a role in the admissions process? If so, explain.

No.

12. Do you think that your political ideology played a role in the admissions process? If so, explain.

No.

13. Did you see the Harvard Law School campus prior to applying or being admitted? If so, what arrangements did you make for the visit, what were your initial impressions, and have your impressions changed very much? If you didn't visit the campus prior to being accepted, why not?

My only visit to the campus was an informal visit in the middle of January 1993. I attended Dershowitz's criminal law class and was given a brief tour of the facilities by a Rice graduate, then a first year law student.

I was initially overwhelmed by the professor's command of the Socratic method, the range of insights, and the intricate analysis of the material. Now that I have been indoctrinated, the professors seem far less exciting and insightful and the Socratic method more an instrument of tedium (get to the point already), than an instrument of focused instruction. Overall, I still retain much of my initial admiration of the school and the way classes are conducted; it just seems far less awe-inspiring than it once did.

14. When did you receive your letter of acceptance from the Dean of Admissions and what were you doing?

I was having breakfast with my family on a Saturday, February 23, I believe, when I went to check the mail and saw the sizable packet that I knew could mean nothing else but admittance.

15. How are you paying for Harvard Law School? Parents? Loans? Savings? Work?

I am financing my education primarily with a battery of loans. When I decided to attend law school I resolved not to be daunted by the sizable cost of the education and to finance it in whatever fashion available.

16. What do you plan to do in the immediate years following Law School graduation? What are your long-term career goals?

I hope to clerk for a judge for a year or two then commence private litigation practice in a large Chicago law firm. I can say with no certainty that I will remain in a large firm for longer than it takes to be trained as a litigator. My long-term goals are to have attained a legal position I find demanding and intellectually satisfying, and to have the freedom to decide much of what I do in the legal workplace. Most of all I want to feel like I am making a contribution to something I find personally gratifying.

Profile

Name: Kristen J. Smith
Harvard Law School class: 1996
Undergraduate institution: Brigham Young University
Undergraduate GPA listed by category—3.75+, 3.50–3.74, 3.25–3.49, 3.00–3.24, below 3.00: 3.75+
Graduate institution and GPA, if applicable: N/A
LSAT Score listed by percentile—99–95, 94–90, 89–85, 84–80, 79–75, 74–70, 69–65, below 64: 99–95
Hometown and high school: Batesville, IN; Batesville High School
Types of recommenders, i.e., professors or employers: One professor, two university administrators
Race, sex, and class: White, female, upper
Major undergraduate activities: Student Government (student body vice president); University Honor Code Committee; New Student Orientation and Leadership Conference coordination
Major scholastic or academic honors: Trustee Scholar (4-year scholarship), Dean's List; Pi Sigma Alpha (political science honor

society); Omicron Delta Epsilon (economics honor society);
cum laude

Work experience (including summer) prior to HLS: Historian for
Hill-Rom Company; Research and development—Forethought
Corp.; Teaching assistant; Student assistant to Dean of Student Life;
Student activities coordinator.

Parents' occupations: Mother—Housewife, high-school English
teacher, Father—Senior executive vice president, Hillenbrand
Industries

Legacy factor: N/A

Questionnaire

1. When and why did you apply to Harvard Law School? Was your application completed early, late, or in the middle of the rolling admissions process?

My application went in around Christmas of 1992. I applied to Harvard because I'd decided I wanted to go to law school and it was one of the eleven schools I applied to. I had lived in the Boston area as a child when my father was at Harvard Business School and knew that I liked the area so I was interested in moving back east.

2. How would you describe the undergraduate institution that you attended? Does it have a strong reputation and a solid track record of sending lots of its graduates to Harvard Law School?

How would I describe it? *Wonderful!!!* It's a very student-oriented institution and very personal despite its large size (32,000 students). I don't know of its reputation and track record in terms of sending *lots* of students to HLS but BYU students have always done well here. I do know that the number of HLS students coming from BYU has increased every year (next year there should be eight arriving).

3. Did you think, prior to being accepted, that you had a decent chance of being admitted to Harvard Law School?

I was one of the most naive pre-law students ever and had no idea what law schools were looking for. Because of that I denied that I had a first choice among the schools I was applying to (everyone else was sure I was leaning toward Harvard). I think I insisted that I had no first choice so long that I convinced myself it didn't matter to me. When the acceptance came and my emotional reaction was much stronger than the reactions all the other acceptances had received, I knew I'd been deceiving myself and I was excited enough that I suppose I was surprised.

4. Did you take any time off prior to applying or matriculating at HLS? If so, why did you take time off and what did you do?

I graduated in August and was out here at the end of the month—no time off at all.

5. What were your strongest assets when applying to Harvard Law School? Grades? LSAT score? Extracurriculars? Personal statement? Recommendations? Family connections? Personal background? Work experience?

Not sure. My grades were strong but not amazing. My LSAT score was very high and I was more involved in my extracurriculars, in terms of student leadership and serving as a representative of the school, than I was in either of my two majors. Because of my heavy involvement in the university I had great recommendations. I don't think my family had any connections that got me into HLS. My personal statement, background, and work experience were solid but nothing incredibly outstanding.

6. What type of courses did you take as an undergraduate to prepare yourself for Harvard Law School?

I didn't know I'd be coming to Harvard Law School, nor did I really intend to go to law school when I began my majors. I didn't even start preparing for the LSAT until I went into the pre-law office in August to pick up the forms for the October test so that I could apply for school the next month (advance planning is not my forte). I suppose political science and economics sound fairly pre-law, but they were picked innocently.

7. What was your LSAT score(s)? How did you prepare for the test? If you took an LSAT prep course, which one, and did it help?

My LSAT score was 174. I didn't have a lot of time to prepare, but I did run through lots of past LSAT tests and used the preparation books that LSAT sells. I also signed up for Kaplan and attended their classes although I had very little time to use the lab facilities. I did use many of the Kaplan materials at home, however. I am not sure how much it helped, but as I look at it, it certainly didn't hurt.

8. How long did you spend on your personal statement? What did you write about and how did you decide on the topic? Did anyone help you with your statement? If so, who?

No one really helped me with it but I had a few friends read it for their initial impressions (I don't think I changed it at all after they read it). I probably spent one or two evenings on it and as for the topic, I just decided to be forthright and simple and tell them why I'd decided to pursue a degree in law and what my interests were in the future.

9. Who wrote your recommendations for Harvard Law School and how did you choose them? How much notice did you give your recommenders and when were the recommendations completed?

The dean of students wrote a letter for me—I had taken a class from her as a freshman, worked for her as a student assistant and a teaching assistant, and been mentored by her as a colleague and close friend in my student-leadership experiences.

The vice president of student life had headed several committees I sat on and I frequently interacted with him in the administration. He had years of experience in university administration among several schools and I had him write a letter.

The vice president of academics taught one of my economics classes and he wrote my faculty recommendation.

I don't remember how much notice I gave them—I probably asked for their help around Thanksgiving and I believe they each completed their letters within three weeks.

10. What type of extracurricular activities did you participate in during your undergraduate years that you feel were beneficial to your being admitted to Harvard Law School, and why?

Student government—it exposed me to a lot of different issues and people and enhanced my communication and leadership skills. My role on the Honor Code Advisory Committee was enlightening as I headed up the revision of the school's honor code which involved twenty years worth of research and data, much drafting and redrafting, and several focus groups. I think the entire process was as close to drafting legislation and regulations as one can get and it raised my curiosity as to how law is both a product and input of the values in a given society.

11. Do you feel that your race, sex, or class played a role in the admissions process? If so, explain.

No.

12. Do you think that your political ideology played a role in the admissions process? If so, explain.

No, unless they assumed that coming from BYU I would be one of the rare conservatives on the Harvard campus (which I am).

13. Did you see the Harvard Law School campus prior to applying or being admitted? If so, what arrangements did you make for the visit, what were your initial impressions, and have your impressions changed very much? If you didn't visit the campus prior to being accepted, why not?

I had seen the campus before on prior trips to Boston but toured the Law School specifically in April before coming. I took a tour offered through the dean of students' office. I was disappointed in the appearance of the campus (as it compares unfavorably to HBS, which I was more familiar with), but I was very relieved to find that the students I talked with were human beings who were fairly balanced and had lives outside the academic realm. I am still glad that that is true—I wouldn't fit in very well otherwise.

14. When did you receive your letter of acceptance from the Dean of Admissions and what were you doing?

I received it at the beginning of March and I was a senior at BYU at the time. What was I doing? Opening an envelope.

15. How are you paying for Harvard Law School? Parents? Loans? Savings? Work?

Parents and an educational trust set up by a grandmother.

16. What do you plan to do in the immediate years following Law School graduation? What are your long-term career goals?

I plan on either taking a clerkship for a year or working at Gibson, Dunn & Crutcher in Washington, D.C., for a few years. Long-term I am more interested, frankly, in raising a family than in pursuing the sixty-plus hour a week lifestyle of a law firm. Therefore, I plan on cutting back my practice of law and may even leave law to pursue a career that is less time-intensive. I have always planned on working within the educational sector eventually and would like to be associated with a university, teaching public policy courses and doing research and private consulting specifically targeted to challenges within the arena of public education.

Profile

Name Withheld
Harvard Law School class: 1996
Undergraduate institution: University of Southern California
**Undergraduate GPA listed by category—3.75+, 3.50–3.74,
   3.25–3.49, 3.00–3.24, below 3.00:** 3.75+
Graduate institution and GPA, if applicable: N/A
**LSAT Score listed by percentile—99–95, 94–90, 89–85, 84–80,
   79–75, 74–70, 69–65, below 64:** 94–90
Hometown and high school: Tuckahoe, New York
Types of recommenders, i.e., professors or employers: Professors
Race, sex, and class: Black, female, middle
Major undergraduate activities: Neighborhood Academic Initiative
   Program, volunteer teacher and tutor; Phi Alpha Delta Pre-Law
   Fraternity, membership chairperson; Joint Educational Project,
   tutor and volunteer teacher
Major scholastic or academic honors: Golden Key National Honor
   Society; Beta Gamma Sigma, business honor society
Work experience (including summer) prior to HLS: New York
   District Attorney's Office, summer intern; Other campus jobs
   during the school year.
Parents' occupations: Mother—Registered nurse, Father—Math
   professor
Legacy factor: N/A

Questionnaire

1. When and why did you apply to Harvard Law School? Was your application completed early, late, or in the middle of the rolling admissions process?

I applied in November and my application was completed early in the admissions process. I knew that I wanted to go to Harvard Law School before I graduated high school simply because I thought that it was the best law school.

2. How would you describe the undergraduate institution that you attended? Does it have a strong reputation and a solid track record of sending lots of its graduates to Harvard Law School?

Usc is also known as the University of Spoiled Children. It is located in Southern California, has (or had) a great football team and as a result is labeled a party school. I attended the business school at usc which is somewhat separate from the rest of the school. The business school has a national reputation and is academically challenging. Usc does not have a strong track record of sending lots of its graduates to HLS. In fact, I was discouraged from applying here because of the fact that usc is a West Coast school.

3. Did you think, prior to being accepted, that you had a decent chance of being admitted to Harvard Law School?

I think that I was overly optimistic—I always thought that I would be accepted to Harvard.

4. Did you take any time off prior to applying or matriculating at HLS? If so, why did you take time off and what did you do?

No.

5. What were your strongest assets when applying to Harvard Law School? Grades? LSAT score? Extracurriculars? Personal statement? Recommendations? Family connections? Personal background? Work experience?

I think that my strongest assets were my grades and extracurricular activities.

6. What type of courses did you take as an undergraduate to prepare yourself for Harvard Law School?

I didn't really take any classes to prepare myself for Harvard Law School. My undergraduate major was business administration with an emphasis in finance and economics but I did take real estate law and business law in connection with my studies.

7. What was your LSAT score(s)? How did you prepare for the test? If you took an LSAT prep course, which one, and did it help?

164. I took the Princeton Review and my scores improved by 9 points.

8. How long did you spend on your personal statement? What did you write about and how did you decide on the topic? Did anyone help you with your statement? If so, who?

I spent about a month thinking about and drafting my personal statement. I wrote about the various influences on my life and the fact that because of them I was able to decide early on that I wanted to be a lawyer. The topic was a natural one for me because it revealed my attitude toward the law when I was in junior high and high school up to the moment when I wrote the statement. I worked at the Freshman Writing Program for a brief period of time, and two professors in the program proofread my statement.

9. *Who wrote your recommendations for Harvard Law School and how did you choose them? How much notice did you give your recommenders and when were the recommendations completed?*

Recommenders: my marketing professor, communications professor, business law professor.

I chose my marketing professor because I received an A in his class. I had worked on a substantial project for his class that was well received by him as well as the class. I chose my communications professor because I received an A in her class and because the course required class presentations and student evaluations in which I excelled. I chose my business law professor because I received an A in the class and she rarely gave out As so I knew that she would be able to write a good recommendation. I also chose my business law professor because I thought that the fact that I took law classes during my undergraduate studies would support the idea that I have always wanted to go to law school and that I decided this long before my junior year in college.

10. *What type of extracurricular activities did you participate in during your undergraduate years that you feel were beneficial to your being admitted to Harvard Law School, and why?*

I think that all of the activities that I named earlier in this survey helped. Most of the activities involved teaching junior-high-school students and required strong communication skills as well as leadership ability.

11. *Do you feel that your race, sex, or class played a role in the admissions process? If so, explain.*

I think that both my race and sex played a role in the admissions process. I think that my record is strong but many people with strong records get rejected. Who really knows?

12. *Do you think that your political ideology played a role in the admissions process? If so, explain.*

No.

13. *Did you see the Harvard Law School campus prior to applying or being admitted? If so, what arrangements did you make for the visit, what were your initial impressions, and have your impressions changed very much? If you didn't visit the campus prior to being accepted, why not?*

I didn't visit the campus prior to being accepted because I was living in California and waited to visit Harvard after my acceptance.

14. *When did you receive your letter of acceptance from the Dean of Admissions and what were you doing?*

I received my letter of acceptance early February and at that time I was coming back to my apartment from one of my business classes.

15. *How are you paying for Harvard Law School? Parents? Loans? Savings? Work?*

Loans and my parents.

16. *What do you plan to do in the immediate years following Law School graduation? What are your long-term career goals?*

I plan to work in Washington, D.C., at Jones Day.

Profile

Name: Joseph Stuligross
Harvard Law School class: 1997
Undergraduate institution: College of Wooster
**Undergraduate GPA listed by category—3.75+, 3.50–3.74,
    3.25–3.49, 3.00–3.24, below 3.00:** 3.50–3.74
Graduate institution and GPA, if applicable: University of Wisconsin
    at Madison; 3.50–3.74
**LSAT Score listed by percentile—99–95, 94–90, 89–85, 84–80,
    79–75, 74–70, 69–65, below 64:** 99–95
Hometown and high school: Waukesha, WI; Waukesha South High
Types of recommenders, i.e., professors or employers: One
    professor and two former employers
Race, sex, and class: White, male, upper-middle

Major undergraduate activities: I was involved in a lot of musical ensembles as well as some political activities.

Major scholastic or academic honors: History Department Prize; Phi Beta Kappa; Department Honors; Polanki Arts Achievement Award

Work experience (including summer) prior to HLS: Two and one-half years' work as a labor union contract negotiator (SEIU Local 399); six years' work as a freelance musician (classical singer and conductor) as well as work as vocal music director and conductor at a private prep school.

Parents' occupations: Father—College professor, Mother—Housewife, part-time teacher

Legacy factor: N/A

Questionnaire

1. When and why did you apply to Harvard Law School? Was your application completed early, late, or in the middle of the rolling admissions process?

I decided that I didn't really identify myself as a musician and found that elements of logical analysis were not challenged through teaching in the same way that law does. I had been active in public-interest activities in college and worked for a labor union when I graduated. I decided to go to law school because I wanted to apply my intellectual and analytical abilities to problems in a way unavailable to me through music. I made this decision at the end of April 1993, when it was too late to apply for the following fall, so my application was completed early the following year.

2. How would you describe the undergraduate institution that you attended? Does it have a strong reputation and a solid track record of sending lots of its graduates to Harvard Law School?

I carefully read all admissions materials from the various schools to which I was applying, including the lists of colleges represented on the student body. I never saw my college listed, even once! I think Wooster is a wonderful college and I learned a great deal there. It doesn't seem to send a lot of graduates to law school in general. It is a small liberal arts college with a dedicated and excellent faculty.

3. Did you think, prior to being accepted, that you had a decent chance of being admitted to Harvard Law School?

Before I took the LSAT, I had no idea how the school would view an older student. When I scored well, I figured I had as good a chance as anyone, given the huge numbers of applicants rejected. I didn't know how the admissions committee would view my previous career—whether they would be excited at the prospect of having the views of a musician among the political scientists, economists, and historians in the student body, or if they would think I was completely confused, without direction, and deserving of contempt!

4. Did you take any time off prior to applying or matriculating at HLS? If so, why did you take time off and what did you do?
I had no reason to go to law school until quite recently. I didn't take "time off"—I was just minding my own business, living my life. (I'm not good at planning particular jobs/activities for professional benefit.) (See above for specific jobs at labor union and as a teacher/musician.)

5. What were your strongest assets when applying to Harvard Law School? Grades? LSAT score? Extracurriculars? Personal statement? Recommendations? Family connections? Personal background? Work experience?
All were strong, though I had no family connections.

6. What type of courses did you take as an undergraduate to prepare yourself for Harvard Law School?
I was a history major and took a wide variety of courses in all other areas, including math, music, philosophy, and other social sciences. I later received a master's degree in music. I can't talk about this as a carefully planned "preparation" for Harvard Law School, but these were the areas I was interested in.

7. What was your LSAT score(s)? How did you prepare for the test? If you took an LSAT prep course, which one, and did it help?
171 out of 180 (99th percentile). I took several practice tests and used materials from Princeton Review, though I didn't actually take their course.

8. How long did you spend on your personal statement? What did you write about and how did you decide on the topic? Did anyone help you with your statement? If so, who?
I spent a lot of time on my statement, since it seemed a crucial way to distinguish my application from others. I wrote about a major accomplishment I had and leadership skills that I learned in an experience conducting a group of student musicians. I asked several friends/colleagues to

read and comment on my statement. Their suggestions were very helpful.

9. *Who wrote your recommendations for Harvard Law School and how did you choose them? How much notice did you give your recommenders and when were the recommendations completed?*

I asked a college professor from the olden days way back when I was a student, and I asked my supervisor at the labor union and the prep school to write. I gave them plenty of time (six weeks?).

10. *What type of extracurricular activities did you participate in during your undergraduate years that you feel were beneficial to your being admitted to Harvard Law School, and why?*

None, I've been out of college for ten years, so I don't think I even put any of these on the application.

11. *Do you feel that your race, sex, or class played a role in the admissions process? If so, explain.*

Not as far as I know.

12. *Do you think that your political ideology played a role in the admissions process? If so, explain.*

I don't know. Since I worked for a labor union, the committee could have inferred certain political views from that, but I don't think it really had much impact. I do think that the views of my colleagues are not representative of the population at large (though they might be representative of law students who scored well on the LSAT). The views tend to be very mainstream, liberal, but not at all radical. Much less fundamental questioning than I hoped for (maybe that will happen more in second or third years).

13. *Did you see the Harvard Law School campus prior to applying or being admitted? If so, what arrangements did you make for the visit, what were your initial impressions, and have your impressions changed very much? If you didn't visit the campus prior to being accepted, why not?*

No. I was going to law school for the faculty and the education; not the architecture or the "atmosphere" I might find on a particular day's visit.

14. *When did you receive your letter of acceptance from the Dean of Admissions and what were you doing?*

January (I think). I was teaching prep school.

15. How are you paying for Harvard Law School? Parents? Loans? Savings? Work?

Loans, some savings; I'll probably work next year.

16. What do you plan to do in the immediate years following Law School graduation? What are your long-term career goals?

Public interest—I'm interested in Native American law, labor law, international law. I hope the LIPP (low income protection plan) will make it possible. Long-term, I hope to be able to pursue both my interests in law and music. Thus far, I have found no way to actually combine them (and I don't expect to), but I would like to have both a part of my life.

Profile

Name Withheld
Harvard Law School class: 1995
Undergraduate institution: Harvard/Radcliffe
Undergraduate GPA listed by category—3.75+, 3.50–3.74,
    3.25–3.49, 3.00–3.24, below 3.00: 3.75+
Graduate institution and GPA, if applicable: N/A
LSAT Score listed by percentile—99–95, 94–90, 89–85, 84–80,
    79–75, 74–70, 69–65, below 64: 99–95
Hometown and high school: Cerritos, CA; Whitney High School
Types of recommenders, i.e., professors or employers: Two
    professors
Race, sex, and class: Asian American, female, middle
Major undergraduate activities: Public service, minority recruiting for
    the admissions office, teacher education program
Major scholastic or academic honors: Phi Beta Kappa,
    Harvard/Radcliffe National Scholar; John Harvard Scholarship and
    Elizabeth Cary Agassiz Scholarship
Work experience (including summer) prior to HLS: Public-interest
    Work-abroad Fellow, English teacher in Indonesia; Intern at Asian-
    Pacific American legal center in Los Angeles; Work at District
    Attorney's office, Los Angeles; Intern at Los Angeles city
    councilman's office (These are all summer jobs, most unpaid.)
Parents' occupations: Mother—Computer analyst for County of
    Los Angeles, Father—Works at a science technology company
Legacy factor: N/A

Questionnaire

1. When and why did you apply to Harvard Law School? Was your application completed early, late, or in the middle of the rolling admissions process?

I applied in my senior year of college. Application was very end of December 1991. I applied to law school because I did not want to work/did not know what kind of work I wanted to do; because I thought a law degree would be "useful" for a lot of the things I was interested in; and because I didn't want to stay in school long enough to get a Ph.D. (As you can see, very generic and bad reasons.) I guess late December would be considered in the later part of the rolling admissions process.

2. How would you describe the undergraduate institution that you attended? Does it have a strong reputation and a solid track record of sending lots of its graduates to Harvard Law School?

Harvard/Radcliffe sends a lot of folks to HLS. It's a good school.

3. Did you think, prior to being accepted, that you had a decent chance of being admitted to Harvard Law School?

Yes.

4. Did you take any time off prior to applying or matriculating at HLS? If so, why did you take time off and what did you do?

No.

5. What were your strongest assets when applying to Harvard Law School? Grades? LSAT score? Extracurriculars? Personal statement? Recommendations? Family connections? Personal background? Work experience?

I think I was a package of different things—none really unique but all had a fairly high level.

6. What type of courses did you take as an undergraduate to prepare yourself for Harvard Law School?

I didn't take any undergrad courses to prepare for law school.

7. What was your LSAT score(s)? How did you prepare for the test? If you took an LSAT prep course, which one and did it help?

I can't remember my exact score; I think it was a 170 out of 180. I prepared by studying on my own for a month. I didn't take a prep course.

8. *How long did you spend on your personal statement? What did you write about and how did you decide on the topic? Did anyone help you with your statement? If so, who?*

I did my personal statement over winter vacation senior year. I'm not sure how long it actually took to write. The topic was why law school was for me. My sister read my statement when it was done.

9. *Who wrote your recommendations for Harvard Law School and how did you choose them? How much notice did you give your recommenders and when were the recommendations completed?*

My recommenders were two professors at the college, one whom I had for junior tutorial (a small course in my department) and one whom I had for two anthro courses. I'm not sure about the second part of the question—I can't remember! Sorry.

10. *What type of extracurricular activities did you participate in during your undergraduate years that you feel were beneficial to your being admitted to Harvard Law School, and why?*

Many of my extracurriculars were service-oriented. I worked with two programs at Phillips Brooks House, working with Chinatown residents and with Southeast Asian refugees. I also was a minority student recruitment coordinator for the college admissions office. I served on the Harvard Foundation's Academic Affairs Committee, which dealt with issues of minority and women faculty hiring and ethnic studies courses. I also was in a program of the college and the school of education to get public high school certification, and taught at Dorchester High School as a student teacher my senior year fall semester. I think these different activities all were consistent with my interest in going to law school—to provide better opportunities for low-income people of color, to change the structure of opportunity in society. . . .

11. *Do you feel that your race, sex, or class played a role in the admissions process? If so, explain.*

My race explains many of the extracurricular activities I chose to do in college, so I think it played a role that way. I think being a qualified woman of color did play a role.

12. *Do you think that your political ideology played a role in the admissions process? If so, explain.*

If it played any role at all, I'm surprised that it would be considered a positive one at HLS. I wrote one of my essays on essentially the subjectivity/culturally situated-ness of truth, and how treating law (or anything for that matter) as neutral, objective truths was dangerous.

13. Did you see the Harvard Law School campus prior to applying or being admitted? If so, what arrangements did you make for the visit, what were your initial impressions, and have your impressions changed very much? If you didn't visit the campus prior to being accepted, why not?

I had seen the HLS campus prior to applying and being admitted, having been here as an undergrad. I was not very impressed with the facilities, and I'm still not.

14. When did you receive your letter of acceptance from the Dean of Admissions and what were you doing?

My application was complete (all recommendations in and scores sent from LSDAS) in late January, and I received my acceptance letter in early February. I think I was just at school, checking my mail.

15. How are you paying for Harvard Law School? Parents? Loans? Savings? Work?

I'm paying for HLS through a combination of parents' contribution, loans, and work, both summer and term-time.

16. What do you plan to do in the immediate years following Law School graduation? What are your long-term career goals?

I will be returning to Los Angeles in June and beginning a district court clerkship in August. I don't know what my long-term career goals are. . . .

Profile

Name: Tania Tetlow
Harvard Law School class: 1995
Undergraduate institution: Newcomb College, Tulane University
Undergraduate GPA listed by category—3.75+, 3.50–3.74, 3.25–3.49, 3.00–3.24, below 3.00: 3.50–3.74
Graduate institution and GPA, if applicable: N/A
LSAT Score listed by percentile—99–95, 94–90, 89–85, 84–80, 79–75, 74–70, 69–65, below 64: 99–95

Hometown and high school: New Orleans, LA; Benjamin Franklin (public magnet)

Types of recommenders, i.e., professors or employers: Profs and an employer

Race, sex, and class: White, female, middle

Major undergraduate activities: President of College Democrats, New Orleans Symphony Chorus, chair of Student Government Multicultural Affairs Committee, student representative to University Affirmative Action Committee

Major scholastic or academic honors: Truman Fellowship, Dean's Honor Scholarship, National Merit Scholar, Dean's List, various honor societies

Work experience (including summer) prior to HLS: Assistant to former Congresswoman Lindy Boggs for two years; Worked in various roles for congressional, gubernatorial, and legislative races, research coordinator, running phone banks, etc.; Candidate for Democratic State Central Committee, fundraising, media work; Internships with my congressional delegation, state senator, and city councilwoman.

Parents' occupations: Father—Psychologist, Mother—Lawyer (disabled, not working)

Legacy factor: N/A

Questionnaire

1. When and why did you apply to Harvard Law School? Was your application completed early, late, or in the middle of the rolling admissions process?

December.

2. How would you describe the undergraduate institution that you attended? Does it have a strong reputation and a solid track record of sending lots of its graduates to Harvard Law School?

Tulane sends anywhere from none to two grads a year to HLS. It has a strong, second-tier school reputation, but is not an elite institution by Harvard's standards (although it costs as much.)

3. Did you think, prior to being accepted, that you had a decent chance of being admitted to Harvard Law School?

No. But I wasn't sure. I originally did not want to apply because the name Harvard puts an instant wedge between you and most people for the rest of your life. I did not want such an ostentatious name associated with me.

4. Did you take any time off prior to applying or matriculating at HLS? If so, why did you take time off and what did you do?

No.

5. What were your strongest assets when applying to Harvard Law School? Grades? LSAT score? Extracurriculars? Personal statement? Recommendations? Family connections? Personal background? Work experience?

I really don't know, but probably the Truman Scholarship, and perhaps regional diversity.

6. What type of courses did you take as an undergraduate to prepare yourself for Harvard Law School?

I never took a course with law school in mind. I majored in American studies, so my courses were in a variety of departments, from English and history to art and architecture.

7. What was your LSAT score(s)? How did you prepare for the Test? If you took an LSAT prep course, which one, and did it help?

172. I took an LSAT course at a local college, much cheaper than Kaplan. I tended to skip a lot of the sessions, but it did make me practice so my score went up a bit.

8. How long did you spend on your personal statement? What did you write about and how did you decide on the topic? Did anyone help you with your statement? If so, who?

Maybe a week. I wrote about my experience running for a little Democratic Party office the fall of my senior year, and what it taught me about politics. The experience itself really shaped me and I thought it might sound impressive that I ran for office at 19, even though I lost. Nobody helped me.

9. Who wrote your recommendations for Harvard Law School and how did you choose them? How much notice did you give your recommenders, and when were the recommendations completed?

My academic advisor, another professor, and former Congresswoman Lindy Boggs, whom I worked for. I gave plenty of notice and got the recs early.

10. What type of extracurricular activities did you participate in during your undergraduate years that you feel were beneficial to your being admitted to Harvard Law School, and why?

Most of my college activities were overtly political, and relevant to law school because of my knowledge of government. The multicultural stuff I did has not been terribly relevant here, because racial issues are discussed by student groups made up of members of that racial group. Some openly accept white members, some seem happier to avoid them. But of course the issues of group membership are something I have taken courses on, and will always think about.

11. Do you feel that your race, sex, or class played a role in the admissions process? If so, explain.

No.

12. Do you think that your political ideology played a role in the admissions process? If so, explain.

Probably. The student body seems to be fairly liberal here, and everything on my application had a liberal spin to it.

13. Did you see the Harvard Law School campus prior to applying or being admitted? If so, what arrangements did you make for the visit, what were your initial impressions, and have your impressions changed very much? If you didn't visit the campus prior to being accepted, why not?

No. I didn't think I wanted to go here and I didn't have money to fly to Boston. I did come visit once I had accepted, because I didn't want to move here without seeing the place once. I came during Accepted Applicants weekend, and stayed with a friend of my parents. I don't remember learning very much about the place while I was here, but sitting in on a class made me realize I would not have problems with the work. I couldn't wait to talk in class.

14. When did you receive your letter of acceptance from the Dean of Admissions and what were you doing?

The weekend before Mardi Gras, so March?

15. How are you paying for Harvard Law School? Parents? Loans? Savings? Work?

Loans!! Truman Scholarship pays for a third, and my parents contribute a few thousand every year. Some of my summer earnings help.

16. What do you plan to do in the immediate years following Law School graduation? What are your long-term career goals?

Clerk, perhaps work in a firm, and eventually run for office in Louisiana.

Profile

Name Withheld
Harvard Law School class: 1995
Undergraduate institution: Harvard/Radcliffe
Undergraduate GPA listed by category—3.75+, 3.50–3.74, 3.25–3.49, 3.00–3.24, below 3.00: 3.25–3.49
Graduate institution and GPA, if applicable: N/A
LSAT Score listed by percentile—99–95, 94–90, 89–85, 84–80, 79–75, 74–70, 69–65, below 64: 99–95
Hometown and high school: Littleton, CO; Heritage High School
Types of recommenders, i.e., professors or employers: Two professors, one thesis advisor, one a music professor
Race, sex, and class: Mexican American, female, lower-middle
Major undergraduate activities: H–R Collegium Musicum, undergraduate mixed choir, president, tour manager, sales manager; Response, rape hot line; worked ten to twenty hours a week at a women's library
Major scholastic or academic honors: Dean's List (four years), Harvard College Scholarship (four years), Elizabeth Cary Agassiz Scholarship (four years), Charles Warren Fellowship for Thesis Research (summer 1991); National Hispanic Scholarship Award (1988); *cum laude*
Work experience (including summer) prior to HLS: The summer before law school, I waited tables. I didn't take any time off to have other work experience. I have worked in various part-time and full-time jobs continuously since the age of fifteen.
Parents' occupations: My mother is the director of a senior citizens' center. My father is a piano tuner.
Legacy factor: N/A

Questionnaire

1. When and why did you apply to Harvard Law School? Was your application completed early, late, or in the middle of the rolling admissions process?

I applied early (before December 1) in order to avoid paying a higher fee since Harvard was the only school to not give me a fee waiver.

2. How would you describe the undergraduate institution that you attended? Does it have a strong reputation and a solid track record of sending lots of its graduates to Harvard Law School?

Harvard/Radcliffe has a great reputation, especially here at the law school. As you know, there are a *huge* number of Harvard grads in our class at the law school (I heard that there were over seventy).

3. Did you think, prior to being accepted, that you had a decent chance of being admitted to Harvard Law School?

Yes, I really didn't think I would have much of a problem based on my extracurricular activities and work experience while an undergrad. Also, my brother assisted with admissions at Boalt Law School (Berkeley) and he didn't think I would have much of a problem.

4. Did you take any time off prior to applying or matriculating at HLS? If so, why did you take time off and what did you do?

I did not take time off.

5. What were your strongest assets when applying to Harvard Law School? Grades? LSAT score? Extracurriculars? Personal statement? Recommendations? Family connections? Personal background? Work experience?

I think that my best assets were my extracurricular activities, personal background, and work experience. Although I did well as an undergrad, I did not do as well grade-wise as others who were admitted to the Law School and had a lower GPA than many who were rejected. But, I believed that my other experiences would override those differences (at least, I hoped they would!). I guess I had faith in the admissions process— I felt that, if they looked at what I overcame to come here (financial pressures, discrimination, etc.), they would recognize my real desire to be a lawyer and that I could do the work.

6. What type of courses did you take as an undergraduate to prepare yourself for Harvard Law School?

None, really. I felt like I wanted to be true to myself in my course selection and have any law school accept me for that rather than based on some stereotypical classes. I also felt I would do better if I took what I wanted rather than the standard pre-law courses.

7. What was your LSAT score(s)? How did you prepare for the test? If you took an LSAT prep course, which one, and did it help?

You know, I don't remember my actual score (it was not on my application) but I do remember that I was in the 97th percentile. I did not take a prep course (too expensive), but I did buy a book to give me an idea of what the test would look like. I looked at it the night before the test. I think that it helped in being familiar with the format, but not much else. In retrospect, I think that a course would have helped me, but the cost really is too prohibitive.

8. How long did you spend on your personal statement? What did you write about and how did you decide on the topic? Did anyone help you with your statement? If so, who?

I spent a lot of time on the personal statement in that I could not figure out which tactic to take. I finally decided to write about my management experiences in the Collegium Musicum because my pre-law advisor thought that would be the best way to go. He looked over the statement before I sent it in and suggested adding some language about the difficulties of the projects I worked on, etc. Now that I look at the statement, I am pretty embarrassed because it is so self-promoting! Not really my writing style at all.

9. Who wrote your recommendations for Harvard Law School and how did you choose them? How much notice did you give your recommenders and when were the recommendations completed?

I decided to have my thesis advisor write me a recommendation and the director of my choir. I chose my thesis advisor because he was at least a little familiar with my academic accomplishments although I had not known him long. My choir director was my first choice because he knew me really well and knew about how much work I put into my extracurriculars and my family background. I gave them about a month to fill them out.

10. What type of extracurricular activities did you participate in during your undergraduate years that you feel were beneficial to your being admitted to Harvard Law School, and why?

As I said before, I was really involved with the Harvard/Radcliffe Collegium Musicum which is the undergraduate mixed choir. Since it was completely student-run, I had a lot of opportunities to learn management, fundraising, and social skills. I was also a peer counselor on a rape hotline my senior year. Although I am not sure, I feel like my activities in the Collegium were the strongest part of my application. I was the most proud of my accomplishments there and I think that it showed in my application. Also, it was pretty clear in my application that this was the thing I spent my most time on, so I figured that it would make or break my application.

11. Do you feel that your race, sex, or class played a role in the admissions process? If so, explain.

Yes. Since my academics were not as strong as others from Harvard, I think that my being Latina might have made a difference. I also base this conclusion on how I was admitted. I was admitted off the waiting list on the last day they admitted people into the class. Out of that group of about fifteen people, four were Latino which, although not conclusive, says a lot to me about their wanting to increase the numbers at the last minute (since they had only had twenty-four Latinos prior to our admittance). There were also many women admitted at the last minute. I also base my assessments on various conversations I have had with Dean Curll regarding how she takes ethnicity into account. Since it was very clear in my application (both in my personal statement and in my essay question) that my ethnic identity was very important to me, I am sure that it was factored into the decision. I also think that my financial situation played a part in that, since my mother was raising four kids on less than $20,000/year, I had to overcome a great number of financial hurdles to even get to undergrad.

12. Do you think that your political ideology played a role in the admissions process? If so, explain.

I am not sure since my application did not demonstrate a clear political ideology (as I was not involved in any political organizations as an undergrad). There may have been assumptions by some admissions officers that I was liberal because I am a Mexican American. It is true that I am very liberal, so this would not be a mistaken assumption. But, I am still not sure that it came in as a factor in my admissions.

13. Did you see the Harvard Law School campus prior to applying or being admitted? If so, what arrangements did you make for the visit, what were

your initial impressions, and have your impressions changed very much?
If you didn't visit the campus prior to being accepted, why not?

I saw the campus often because I went to undergrad here and my
fiancé lived in the grad school dorms across the street. My initial impression of the law school is that it was very corporate and very unfriendly
towards minorities and women. This idea was made more concrete in my
mind during the 1991–92 school year during the uproar about Professor
Bell, the Griswold Nine, and the Law Review parody of Mary Jo Frug.
Although I knew that the Law School was not friendly, I decided to apply
anyway because I was excited by the activism displayed by the students
and the possibility to change the school. After attending here, I still think
that this is a very unfriendly institution in that there are very few professors of color, no women of color, no Latinos, and no openly gay professors. I also think that the academic environment is very hostile towards
those who bring up race and gender theory in class and much of this is
attributable to the student body. But, I have been impressed with the
students in general and was surprised to find that so many of them were
so nice.

**14. When did you receive your letter of acceptance from the Dean of
Admissions and what were you doing?**

Dean Curll called my home in Colorado the day I left to go to Cornell. My mother reached me at the airport in Boston and told me I had
gotten in. I went to the law school the next day and accepted.

**15. How are you paying for Harvard Law School? Parents? Loans? Sav-
ings? Work?**

Mainly loans because my family is not well off. My mother does not
make a contribution because of her financial situation. I didn't have any
savings, so my other main source of income has been from summer and
term-time work.

**16. What do you plan to do in the immediate years following Law School
graduation? What are your long-term career goals?**

I am going to work for a large firm in Boston doing litigation. I plan
on being there for a couple of years while my fiancé finishes his Ph.D. At
that point, I will reconsider the large law firm practice. Eventually, I would
like to work for the U.S. Attorney's Office and then work for the Mexican-
American Legal Defense and Education Fund doing employment litigation.

Profile

Name: Rory E. Verrett
Harvard Law School class: 1995
Undergraduate institution: Howard University
Undergraduate GPA listed by category—3.75+, 3.50–3.74, 3.25–3.49, 3.00–3.24, below 3.00: 3.50–3.74
Graduate institution and GPA, if applicable: N/A
LSAT Score listed by percentile—99–95, 94–90, 89–85, 84–80, 79–75, 74–70, 69–65, below 64: not given
Hometown and high school: New Orleans, LA; St. Augustine High School (home of the national champion Purple Knight basketball team!)
Types of recommenders, i.e., professors or employers: Dr. Dale Sinos, chair, classics department, Howard University; Dr. Tsomondo, professor of English, Howard University
Race, sex, and class: African-American, male, middle
Major undergraduate activities: Undergraduate Trustee, Howard University Board of Trustees; director of Student Grievances; Undergraduate Student Assembly representative; Undergraduate Student Assembly founder and president; Howard University Environmental Association Campus Pals (peer counseling)
Major scholastic or academic honors: Phi Beta Kappa; *magna cum laude*; Howard University Honors Program; Harry S Truman Scholar; National Environmental Management Fellowship, U.S. EPA; Patricia Roberts Harris Public Service Fellowship; Golden Key Honor Society; Howard University National Competitive Scholarship; National Achievement Scholarship; Dean's List (four years)
Work experience (including summer) prior to HLS: Office of Congressman William Jefferson (D-LA), legislative aide; National Environmental Education Foundation, policy analyst; U.S. Environmental Protection Agency, policy fellow; International Health Network, legislative aide.
Parents' occupations: Mother—University administrator/professor, Father—Cement mason/union president (retired)
Legacy factor: N/A

Questionnaire

1. When and why did you apply to Harvard Law School? Was your application completed early, late, or in the middle of the rolling admissions process?

I applied to Harvard because of its outstanding reputation as a law school, its diverse course offerings, diverse student body, and diverse faculty (NOT!). I was very encouraged that, among the nation's top law schools, HLS had a large, diverse student body. Coming from a predominantly Black undergraduate school, I felt student diversity at HLS was a *big factor*. I applied late in the rolling admissions process (surprised? . . . I just roll like that . . .).

2. How would you describe the undergraduate institution that you attended? Does it have a strong reputation and a solid track record of sending lots of its graduates to Harvard Law School?

Howard University is the nation's preeminent African-American university, boasting an impressive list of famous alumni, including: Justice Thurgood Marshall; former Virginia Governor L. Douglas Wilder; former Senator Edward Brooke (R-MA); former New York Mayor David Dinkins; Andrew Young; Sharon Pratt Kelly. Its faculty has included the likes of: Alain Locke, first black Rhodes Scholar; Toni Morrison, Pulitzer Prize–winning author; Frederick Douglass, etc., etc. Needless to say, getting in and succeeding at HLS is a given for such esteemed students.

3. Did you think, prior to being accepted, that you had a decent chance of being admitted to Harvard Law School?

Pretty much (ya know how I do it).

4. Did you take any time off prior to applying or matriculating at HLS? If so, why did you take time off and what did you do?

No.

5. What were your strongest assets when applying to Harvard Law School? Grades? LSAT score? Extracurriculars? Personal statement? Recommendations? Family connections? Personal background? Work experience?

1. Grades 2. Extracurriculars 3. Work experience 4. Personal statement (n.b.: I think I was "well-rounded").

6. What type of courses did you take as an undergraduate to prepare yourself for Harvard Law School?

I was a pre-law student: English major; poli sci minor; most courses in those areas.

7. What was your LSAT score(s)? How did you prepare for the test? If you took an LSAT prep course, which one, and did it help?

I took Kaplan, and yes it helped me tremendously.

8. How long did you spend on your personal statement? What did you write about and how did you decide on the topic? Did anyone help you with your statement? If so, who?

About two weeks (seriously). I wrote about the tension of living in poor, blighted areas and going to prestigious academic institutions. I also wrote about how this tension affected my decision to get involved in the environmental justice movement and public service generally. No one helped me on my statement.

9. Who wrote your recommendations for Harvard Law School and how did you choose them? How much notice did you give your recommenders and when were the recommendations completed?

Two professors whom I had studied under in two classes each. Two weeks.

10. What type of extracurricular activities did you participate in during your undergraduate years that you feel were beneficial to your being admitted to Harvard Law School, and why?

My fellowship at the Environmental Protection Agency—I authored the first major policy report on environmental inequity in federal environmental policy.

11. Do you feel that your race, sex, or class played a role in the admissions process? If so, explain.

In the sense that I brought a different perspective and interesting experiences to the law school, I believe my race played a role in my admission to the law school.

12. Do you think that your political ideology played a role in the admissions process? If so, explain.

In the sense that environmental justice was a hot, new policy topic, perhaps.

13. *Did you see the Harvard Law School campus prior to applying or being admitted? If so, what arrangements did you make for the visit, what were your initial impressions, and have your impressions changed very much? If you didn't visit the campus prior to being accepted, why not?*

Yes. I did not arrange anything formally with the Law School.

14. *When did you receive your letter of acceptance from the Dean of Admissions and what were you doing?*

April 4, 1992, the anniversary of Dr. King's assassination. What a coincidence, two historic moments on the same day!

15. *How are you paying for Harvard Law School? Parents? Loans? Savings? Work?*

Parents—⅓; scholarship—⅓; loans—⅓.

16. *What do you plan to do in the immediate years following Law School graduation? What are your long-term career goals?*

I am working at Howrey & Simon, a Washington, D.C., law firm. I intend to become involved in politics someday, either at the federal level or at the local level in my hometown of New Orleans, Louisiana.

Profile

Name Withheld
Harvard Law School class: 1995
Undergraduate institution: Wheaton College
Undergraduate GPA listed by category—3.75+, 3.50–3.74, 3.25–3.49, 3.00–3.24, below 3.00: 3.75+
Graduate institution and GPA, if applicable: University of Washington, MA, in Asian art history, 3.8
LSAT Score listed by percentile—99–95, 94–90, 89–85, 84–80, 79–75, 74–70, 69–65, below 64: 99–95
Hometown and high school: Kingston, MA; Silver Lake Regional High School
Types of recommenders, i.e., professors or employers: Professors (undergraduate and graduate)
Race, sex, and class: White, female, middle
Major undergraduate activities: Editor of college magazine which published outstanding student papers; dorm staff; head of campus writing tutoring program

Major scholastic or academic honors: Valedictorian, Phi Beta Kappa, recipient of national Beinecke Scholarship; Dean's List

Work experience (including summer) prior to HLS: Worked at a local plant nursery each summer during college; Teaching assistant while in graduate school; Worked for a year as an office manager at a small medical software company before coming to law school.

Parents' occupations: Father works at a local plant nursery; mother is deceased but while alive she was a housewife.

Legacy factor: N/A

Questionnaire

1. When and why did you apply to Harvard Law School? Was your application completed early, late, or in the middle of the rolling admissions process?

I applied to HLS in early October of 1990. I applied to HLS because I knew I wanted to move back to Massachusetts. I applied early in the process.

2. How would you describe the undergraduate institution that you attended? Does it have a strong reputation and a solid track record of sending lots of its graduates to Harvard Law School?

While I was at Wheaton College it was still an all-women's college. It is not well known because it is a very small school and I would guess only a handful of graduates have come to HLS.

3. Did you think, prior to being accepted, that you had a decent chance of being admitted to Harvard Law School?

Yes, I knew my grades and LSAT scores would stand me well. I also felt that I had a good chance because I had gone to grad school, had attended Middlebury Chinese school for two years, and had spent a year at the Stanford Center for Chinese in Taiwan.

4. Did you take any time off prior to applying or matriculating at HLS? If so, why did you take time off and what did you do?

Yes, I deferred for a year. I worked as an office manager during that time. I felt that I wanted a break from school because I had been a student for too long.

5. What were your strongest assets when applying to Harvard Law School? Grades? LSAT score? Extracurriculars? Personal statement? Recommen-

dations? Family connections? Personal background? Work experience?

I would say that my strongest asset was probably the fact that I had lived abroad in Taiwan for a year and done a lot of stuff related to East Asian studies in grad school. I know that top grades from my undergraduate institution would not have been enough.

6. What type of courses did you take as an undergraduate to prepare yourself for Harvard Law School?

I did not think I would ever want to go to law school while I was an undergraduate so I did not take any classes "to prepare" me. I was an art history major and also took a number of English classes. I think they helped me to learn how to write well and I think that skill is one of the most important for attorneys.

7. What was your LSAT score(s)? How did you prepare for the test? If you took an LSAT prep course, which one, and did it help?

I scored a 47 (on the old system) which put me in the 99th percentile. I took Stanley Kaplan. I think the class helped me in that the course was expensive and I paid for it myself so I was intent on doing all of the homework and all of the practice tests to get my money's worth. I think the class helped me take preparation seriously.

8. How long did you spend on your personal statement? What did you write about and how did you decide on the topic? Did anyone help you with your statement? If so, who?

I spent a good deal of time writing the statement. I wanted to make it as concise as possible so I rewrote it many times to pare it down. I also showed it to my graduate advisor, my best friend, and my Kaplan teacher for feedback.

The topic of my statement was how I wanted to pursue East Asian law. This was not quite true but I felt this topic would allow me to talk about what I thought to be my most unique qualities.

9. Who wrote your recommendations for Harvard Law School and how did you choose them? How much notice did you give your recommenders and when were the recommendations completed?

This information is hard for me to remember. I asked two of my undergraduate professors and two of my graduate professors. I chose people who I felt knew me best and whom I knew could write specific and positive letters. I think I gave each person about three weeks to respond and they all finished the recommendations within about two weeks.

10. *What type of extracurricular activities did you participate in during your undergraduate years that you feel were beneficial to your being admitted to Harvard Law School, and why?*

Honestly, I do not think my undergraduate activities were probably all that significant in HLS's decision. As I mentioned above, I think they were probably more impressed by the things I did after graduation—studying Chinese at Middlebury/living in Taiwan.

11. *Do you feel that your race, sex, or class played a role in the admissions process? If so, explain.*

It is possible that my class had some impact. I mentioned in my application that I was the youngest of four, the only member of my family to go to college, and a child of working-class parents.

12. *Do you think that your political ideology played a role in the admissions process? If so, explain.*

No. My political ideology was not clear from my application.

13. *Did you see the Harvard Law School campus prior to applying or being admitted? If so, what arrangements did you make for the visit, what were your initial impressions, and have your impressions changed very much? If you didn't visit the campus prior to being accepted, why not?*

No. I grew up in Massachusetts so I was familiar with Harvard and the surrounding area. Besides I knew I wanted to go to the best law school I could get into and my first choice was to move back to Boston to be near my family.

14. *When did you receive your letter of acceptance from the Dean of Admissions and what were you doing?*

It was December 29th and I had just returned to Seattle where I was living from being at home in Massachusetts for Christmas.

15. *How are you paying for Harvard Law School? Parents? Loans? Savings? Work?*

I am paying for HLS with a combination of grants, loans, and money from my dad.

16. *What do you plan to do in the immediate years following Law School graduation? What are your long-term career goals?*

I am going to a Boston law firm. I would eventually like to work in some private public interest firm or maybe for the DA or Attorney General.

Profile

Name: Christopher Shang-Yung Yeh
Harvard Law School class: 1996
Undergraduate institution: Harvard College
**Undergraduate GPA listed by category—3.75+, 3.50–3.74,
    3.25–3.49, 3.00–3.24, below 3.00:** 3.75+
Graduate institution and GPA, if applicable: N/A
**LSAT Score listed by percentile—99–95, 94–90, 89–85, 84–80,
    79–75, 74–70, 69–65, below 64:** 84–80
Hometown and high school: Honolulu, HI; Punahou School
Types of recommenders, i.e., professors or employers: Professors;
    law school advisor (an HLS student who received free meals in
    return for advising undergraduates about their law school options)
Race, sex, and class: Asian, male, middle
Major undergraduate activities: Wind ensemble; jazz band;
    community tutoring
Major scholastic or academic honors: *summa cum laude*; Phi Beta
    Kappa; Briggs Price (top thesis in English Department); John
    Harvard Scholarship (nonstipend); Detur Award (for academic
    achievement)
Work experience (including summer) prior to HLS: Staffer in Hawaii
    House of Representatives, wrote press releases, speeches, and
    articles; organized bill lobbying; Teacher at Punahou School, taught
    composition to 11th and 12th graders; Summer intern at *Honolulu*
    magazine, wrote articles and essays for monthly city publication.
Parents' occupations: Father—Professor of sociology at the University
    of Hawaii, Mother—Dietitian at the university-affiliated Cancer
    Research Institute
Legacy factor: N/A

Questionnaire

1. When and why did you apply to Harvard Law School? Was your application completed early, late, or in the middle of the rolling admissions process?

I applied to law school because the study of law seemed a somewhat logical application and extension of the research and writing skills I had developed as an English major. I also anticipated that the profession would be both intellectually challenging as well as social/interactive—two qualities that I sought. Quite honestly, despite the affirmative advantages of law school noted above, I also chose law school as a matter of default—it was the most glaring option left after the process of elimination. (I discounted graduate studies in the humanities because of a fear of the prolonged Ph.D. track with little prospect of employment afterward. I was also under some tacit pressure from my parents to pursue a fairly well-salaried profession; I wasn't a good enough musician to consider seriously going to a conservatory.)

I applied to HLS in particular because of its reputation and because I learned (during my undergraduate years) that I liked the university, Cambridge, and Boston (weather notwithstanding). I was not at all deterred by HLS's larger size, partially because I was used to a much larger student body (1,600 per class) and partially because I wanted a broad and diverse environment.

This being said, my first choice for law school was, without a doubt, Stanford because of its strong program as well as its temperate climate and proximity to San Francisco. Since I turned down my admission to Boalt, however, geography alone was not a compelling criterion.

My application was completed in the middle part of the application process; however, it was not sent off until the late part because of bureaucratic holdups and inefficiencies by the Harvard supervisors (my house tutor and my law school advisor) assigned to approve the application and recommendations.

2. How would you describe the undergraduate institution that you attended? Does it have a strong reputation and a solid track record of sending lots of its graduates to Harvard Law School?

Harvard College sends many students to HLS.

3. Did you think, prior to being accepted, that you had a decent chance of being admitted to Harvard Law School?

I felt that I had a decent chance, principally because I knew that HLS accepted a large number of Harvard College students and my college grades were strong (see #5 for more).

4. Did you take any time off prior to applying or matriculating at HLS? If so, why did you take time off and what did you do?

I took one year off between college and law school and did a number of things. The summer immediately after graduation, I taught composition at my high school in Honolulu. The following fall, I did some volunteer work (clerical and caller intake) at the Hawaii ACLU, and also did some travelling in East Asia. I also took advantage of my relatively flexible schedule to engage in some self-study of jazz theory (I play the saxophone and have a strong interest in jazz).

In the spring, I worked at the Hawaii House of Representatives for a very conservative representative, which was interesting given my liberal tendencies. Despite our ideological differences, I enjoyed the work in the office (which for the most part did not involve any divisive political hot-buttons).

I took time off (1) to confirm that I wanted to go to law school; (2) because I felt that being away from school was necessary to give me a better perspective on school and work; (3) because I needed a break from school and the East Coast, and wanted to be back in Hawaii with family and my girlfriend. Interestingly, the people with whom I most closely associate now at HLS have all taken at least one year off—I'm not sure exactly what this means.

5. What were your strongest assets when applying to Harvard Law School? Grades? LSAT score? Extracurriculars? Personal statement? Recommendations? Family connections? Personal background? Work experience?

My strongest single asset was grades. My LSAT score was certainly sub-par for applicants to HLS, so I assume my grades were strong enough to counter that. I believe I also had a strong personal statement and essay on the "World of Ideas" (although I have no way of independently verifying this) and strong recommendations from professors. It is possible but I am not sure that being Asian or from Hawaii had any positive effect on my admission.

6. What type of courses did you take as an undergraduate to prepare yourself for Harvard Law School?

I was an English major, and loaded up heavily on English courses (which obviously had a strong research- and writing-intensive bent that might be seen as good law school preparation). However, I *never* took a class specifically to prepare myself for law school or to make myself more attractive to a law school admissions board. I merely took the classes that I thought I would enjoy and/or were required by the English department.

7. What was your LSAT score(s)? How did you prepare for the test? If you took an LSAT prep course, which one, and did it help?

I think my score was 160 out of 180, and that my percentile was 80. I did not take an LSAT prep course; rather, I studied a Princeton review book for about a week and a half before the LSAT.

(The night before the LSAT, I was stressed and miserable and only slept a few hours.)

8. *How long did you spend on your personal statement? What did you write about and how did you decide on the topic? Did anyone help you with your statement? If so, who?*

My personal statement was based on an essay that I had written the previous summer for *Honolulu* magazine, and that I adapted for law school purposes. Thus, during the actual law school applications process, I spent only a moderate amount of time revising the statement (although I did spend considerable time in the summer writing the original). I chose to use my magazine essay because it dealt with the importance of remembering one's humble roots and the importance of empathizing with one's client when providing a service—ideas which seemed appropriate to the legal profession.

No one helped me with my statement, but I was encouraged to use it due to the positive reception it received during the summer from the other magazine editors.

9. *Who wrote your recommendations for Harvard Law School and how did you choose them? How much notice did you give your recommenders and when were the recommendations completed?*

My recommendations were written by two professors who taught classes not only in which I did well grade-wise but also in which the enrollment was small enough so that I had a lot of interaction with the professor. One professor taught an English tutorial with eight students (my first year in college). The other professor taught a Beowulf class with only about a dozen students (my last year in college). I believe a recommendation was also provided by my law school advisor (an HLS student) who wrote a statement based upon a review of all recommendations in my student file as well as his informal discussions with me.

I believe my recommenders had at least a month's notice, and I believe the recommendations were completed before Christmas.

10. *What type of extracurricular activities did you participate in during your undergraduate years that you feel were beneficial to your being admitted to Harvard Law School, and why?*

I participated in mainly musical activities—the wind ensemble, the jazz band, and some smaller musical combos. I feel it was beneficial to have some focused, sustained extracurricular activities, but I don't believe that any law school admissions board would view an interest in music per se as indicative of an applicant's success in law school.

In my particular case, however, my musical interest was helpful in one regard. For my "World of Ideas" essay (required during the year I applied to HLS), I wrote about the abstract and expansive world of jazz theory, and how I tried to make that world concrete by applying those ideas in my playing. I felt that the essay was helpful because it showed my sustained development in an intellectual (non-legal) field, and thus hinted at my ability to succeed in diverse, challenging pursuits.

11. Do you feel that your race, sex, or class played a role in the admissions process? If so, explain.

I am not entirely sure of HLS's position on affirmative action. The only relevant factor under which I would benefit from such a program would be race; it is possible, given my low LSAT, that race was a positive, counterbalancing factor. Then again, grades and recommendations may have been sufficient to overcome my LSAT disadvantage. Thus, I am not entirely sure if race played a role in my admissions process.

12. Do you think that your political ideology played a role in the admissions process? If so, explain.

I don't believe that my political ideology was manifest in anything that I wrote or that my record showed. (I applied to law school before working for the ACLU and at the Hawaii House of Representatives.)

13. Did you see the Harvard Law School campus prior to applying or being admitted? If so, what arrangements did you make for the visit, what were your initial impressions, and have your impressions changed very much? If you didn't visit the campus prior to being accepted, why not?

Even though I was a Harvard undergraduate, I really only toured the HLS campus once (with my law advisor, the HLS student). I didn't even attend the reception day for admitted students (which for many admittees involved a plane commute, and for me would've required only a few minutes' walk). By that point, I had already decided I would go to HLS (Stanford already negged me) and saw no point in a prolonged tour. One valuable piece of advice, however, which I did learn prior to attending HLS was this—don't live in the Gropius dorms. Next year will be my third year in Hastings. Oh yes, I was also warned during my tour of the cafeteria that the food was barely edible.

My initial impressions of HLS (based upon my one tour) was that it was a fairly large, attractive campus (I believe it was a warm sunny day and people were sitting outside the Hark). I was also shown some of the empty classrooms, and tried to imagine what it would be like to sit in one of them anticipating being called on. Seeing the seating charts against the wall and hearing my law advisor speak of Miller and Areeda in hushed, reverential tones, I was under the impression that classes were more Socratic than they actually are.

14. *When did you receive your letter of acceptance from the Dean of Admissions and what were you doing?*

My application was sent off fairly late (see #1)—I believe early February—but I heard quite soon thereafter, about two or three weeks later.

After returning to my dorm room from class, I found a manila package placed outside my door by one of my suitemates (I can't remember how he got a hold of it first). Anyway, I was fairly excited and my suitemates congratulated me.

15. *How are you paying for Harvard Law School? Parents? Loans? Savings? Work?*

Parents.

16. *What do you plan to do in the immediate years following Law School graduation? What are your long-term career goals?*

After graduation, I plan to work for a private law firm, either in San Francisco or Honolulu. Because of my lengthy stay at Harvard, I had considered working in Boston, but at the close of the interviewing season opted instead for a summer job in San Francisco and Honolulu (due to the better climate, what I believe are the friendlier people, etc.).

Right now, my long-term career goal is to remain at a private law firm.

6

Fifty Successful
Personal Statements from
Harvard Law School Students

Personal Statement

Raquel E. Aldana

My primary motivation for receiving a law degree surfaces from my personal experiences with the struggles of the Latin American immigrant in the United States. My family and I have lived as immigrants in the United States for the past twelve years. In 1980, we left El Salvador because my father feared for our lives due to his refusal to allow the political ideology of the guerilla movement to infiltrate the church that he pastored. In less than two months, we sold our belongings and left for Guatemala, my father's birthplace. There, commonplace armed confrontations, bus takeovers, and the mandatory recruitment of young boys into the military or guerilla forces convinced my parents to file for legal residency status to the United States. We entered Miami, Florida, on May 10 of 1982.

Since our entry to the United States, we have lived in predominantly Latin American communities in the cities of Miami, Los Angeles, and Phoenix. From the first time my brother and I were called "wetbacks" (a derogatory term referring to someone who has crossed the border illegally), I became aware of the discrimination and the difficulties immigrants face in adjusting to a different lifestyle, culture, and language. I also became aware of the vast presence of a large group of immigrants who are undocumented and who must and do make a living in this country in violation of the law and under conditions which go against U.S. civil rights and labor protection laws.

Especially in Arizona, my contact with this large immigrant population has been very personal. I have learned to appreciate the perspective of the individual who has very few skills, who is sometimes illiterate, and who speaks very little English. Often this individual has come escaping horrendous human rights violations and the harsh economic realities of third world countries. In the process, he or she has had to face the persecution and often abusive treatment of the U.S. border patrol and to live under conditions which legally deny him or her the right to procure safe and adequate living conditions.

So far, my work with the Latin American immigrant community has been primarily in education. At South Mountain High School, I volunteered to teach citizenship classes to candidates of naturalization. Through my employment as a peer advisor at ASU [Arizona State University] I gave motivational workshops for higher education to high-school and junior-high-school students, especially in schools with a high Latin American population. Since my sophomore year in college, I have been working as a bilingual instructor with a nonprofit organization, Unlimited Potential. Its primary vision has been to develop the skills of low-income immigrants, mostly Mexican women, to help them become self-sufficient. We function as a support group to build self-esteem and a sense of family among the participants; we stress awareness and participation in the community (especially in the issues affecting the lives of the participant's children); we develop basic skills in the areas of literacy and English as a second language; we teach the survival skills necessary in adapting to America.

I am also currently a volunteer with Tonatierra, a nonprofit organization which actively seeks to ensure that the human rights of all residents in the United States, regardless of their legal status, are not violated. With other Tonatierra members, I have been drafting a document to the Arizona INS [Immigration and Naturalization

Services] Department in which we will be asking for policy reforms in their handling of deportation arrests. We hope these changes will rectify some of the patterns of abuse which have been a part of the agency, most of which have been handled in the past with impunity.

In addition to my strong commitment to the Latin American community, my personal achievements as a student make me a strong law school candidate. I will graduate from Arizona State University *summa cum laude* with a concurrent degree in Spanish and English literatures. I will be the first in my family to graduate with a B.A. I am especially proud of this accomplishment because I began my studies in the United States in the seventh grade, not speaking English, and attended schools in low-income communities which lacked strong academic programs. I have also had to work while attending school, sometimes full-time simultaneously, to supplement my parent's limited income. Although this created for me a very rigorous and demanding lifestyle, I gained tremendous satisfaction working with diverse groups of all ages as a teacher or tutor or peer advisor to children, college and high school students, professionals and mothers returning or going to school for the first time.

The strengths I will bring to the law school are exceptional communications skills, a tremendous sensitivity to diversity, a strong dedication to hard work, a unique background, and a surpassing willingness to learn. I am certain about my commitment to bettering the conditions of the Latin American immigrant in this country and am increasingly conscious of the limitations my lack of a degree causes. I wish to contribute to the inclusion of rights to the marginalized members of society.

Personal Statement
Stephanie Barnes

Every summer I go home to the Delta of Mississippi to teach a band camp at my alma mater, Greenville High School. Initially, I thought that my instruction was limited to the intricacies of baton twirling. However, I was soon to find that I am more than a majorette instructor, but a symbol for those students who follow and want to succeed. This revelation came to me when one of my students expressed to me how she "looked up to me" and that when she went to college she wanted to "be like me." This elementary utterance revealed to me that I am a symbol for what the rich Delta soil produces from the depths of its poverty, high teenage-pregnancy level, rampant drug abuse, and other oppressive phenomena. I have risen like a phoenix from the ashes of the Delta mud to become the queenly woman that I am today.

As a young girl, I was exposed daily to the "queens" of my community. There were the teachers that taught at my high school, the ladies at my church, and the sundry women that inhabited the streets of Greenville. The most influential "queen" in my life is my mother. For twenty-one years, I have watched in amazement as she has struggled and overcome the task of providing a nurturing environment for me and my younger brother. She has endured the hardships that accompany the absence of a man in the household. By watching her fight, I am inspired to become an independent woman who is capable of providing for herself with or without the presence of a male provider.

My developing years were characterized by the rebellious antics of a teenager trying to attain independence in an adult world. That impetuous rebellion has cooled down into the feisty determination that is evident in my every action. I am moved by an unfaltering faith in myself, my abilities, my God, and my people. My mother's struggles are ongoing and not in vain. I am the embodiment of my mother's tears as she has labored in the hot cotton fields of survival.

As I strive to understand the power of my mind, I also debate how I will use my knowledge to serve my community. The formative years of my college career exposed me to many diverse and appealing subjects from which I could choose my profession. My initial business law course introduced me to the complexities of the legal text. More than any other course, that challenging atmosphere served as the impetus of my yearning to become a lawyer. The passion that I have for law is as powerful as the defiant spirit of my youth. I am the product of six generations that have endured and overcome the dehumanizing institution of slavery. I will use the lesson that my ancestors taught me to teach the inhabitants of the Delta how the law works for them and not against them. Just as my foremothers toiled in the blazing Mississippi sun, so will I toil in the heated debate of the courtroom. I am a symbol of all that the Delta soil produces. I am the queen that will provide for all future generations that reap the benefits of my fruit and labor.

Personal Statement

Name Withheld

Human interactions can be reduced to a number of interconnecting, complex games if you really isolate their components. For instance, relationships are games in which people, by following social rules, try to produce favorable by-products for themselves and the other participant. School is a game in which individuals compete against subject matter and other students. Knowledge and competency are only by-products of the process.

Traditionally we have thought of games in terms of the outcomes, winning and losing; or the players, how they choose to play or how much skill they possess; but what's important to me is the game structure itself. The rules, the history, and nature of development of the game itself is the most fascinating facet. I appreciate the structure partly to understand how to better play and win, but mostly so that every human interaction can be as intricate and fun as possible.

In high school an overdeveloped sense of competition overshadowed my love of games and I wanted to be the best point guard during basketball season and the best lineman during football season. I wanted to write the best stories in our newspaper, win the most scholarships, and date the prettiest girls. Wanting it made me work and I was successful in a lot of ways. I won the Alpha Phi Alpha Recognition Award, the Outstanding African American Student of Syracuse Award, a National Merit Scholarship, and a Syracuse University Outstanding Achievement Award. I was an editor for the newspaper, on the staff of the literary magazine, the sixth man on the basketball team, and a starter on the football team. These were successful games for me. However, as I began to see other interactions in life as games, I realized that for each of those successful games, I probably lost a thousand less identifiable competitions. Identifying and understanding the other games became important.

I entered Cornell as an engineering major because I was interested in the consistent rules of science and mathematics. My coursework taught me that there were as many exceptions and rulebreakers in science as there are among people and I became annoyed and frustrated. It seemed to me that the physical sciences were less logical than the chaos of human behavior. An engineering internship at United Technologies Carrier Corporation further convinced me that engineering simply wasn't that interesting.

If I was going to have to give up the notion of stable rules in the science of my lifelong occupation, I had to at least pick something fun. I had to pick something with a great deal of conflict, a little confusion, and a complex set of rules. I chose communication science because it was an exciting approach to the only arena that seemed to speak to my preferences. The arena of human behavior and interaction reintroduced me to the notion of gaming and I experienced renewed success. I have been on the Dean's List every semester since I left engineering, I won an Alumni Federation Scholarship, the Kenneth Bissett Communication Award, and I was a semifinalist in Cornell's McKnight Moot Court Competition. I also held leadership positions on a campus newspaper and a literary magazine. I found a healthy connection between my love of games and the writing and speaking skills that I have been working hard to develop since high school. The overall result has been the second great leap in confidence and personal strength that I have experienced; the first coming at the end of a fifty-pound weight-loss drive I put myself through in high school.

The only drawback to my new academic orientation, in my view, was its inability to help me make a consistent and lasting impact on the conditions of my African-American community. I selected a concentration in African studies to better understand the specific nature of the problems of African America and arm myself with relevant history. Political struggle is a game that requires a great deal of preparation to play, and I insist on participating. Up to now I have only been able to participate through campus activities and volunteering my time as a tutor or a big brother to African-American youth in Ithaca. I decided that further education was necessary, but it had to be something that could be comfortably added to the developing pieces [me]. It struck me that the law was the most complex set of rules dealing with humans, who are primarily random in their behavior, that I could involve myself with. I could be a writer, a speaker, develop the power to fight for my community, and have my grand game all in one shot. This is a challenge and opportunity I can't ignore.

Personal Statement

David Buckner

I have always believed that a balanced life is a successful one, and I have accordingly tried to maintain that balance in everything I do. My collegiate career reflects this goal, because it is through a combination of scholarship and leadership that I have achieved my greatest successes. No personal history would be complete without an account of the roles these two concepts have played in my personal and intellectual growth.

Early on I departed from the normal course of undergraduate education to pursue unusual and challenging opportunities. I have been a member of the Rutgers College Honors program for four years, which has given me access to a number of seminar courses not available to all undergraduates. I am presently an undergraduate associate of the Eagleton Institute of Politics, a program that admits only twenty political science students at Rutgers University annually, and is by no means a standard part of a major in political science. Membership at Eagleton entails intensive study of domestic American politics and the completion of an internship, which I will undertake next semester. In my junior year I was selected for membership in Phi Beta Kappa.

Another atypical facet of my education is my work on a Henry Rutgers Senior Honors Thesis. This academic option involves a year-long research project resulting in a published paper. My research deals with the role of the United States Department of State during the Vietnam War.

It is my theory that State Department decision making was greatly influenced by domestic politics, specifically by the fear of a return of McCarthyism. I will establish this through personal interviews with former department officials.

My extracurricular activities have been an equal partner with my academic endeavors in my personal and intellectual development. I am presently in my fourth term as the president of the Rutgers College class of 1991, which has given me the opportunity not only to lead a class of nearly three thousand people, but also the chance to develop a role for myself in working to help improve the university as a whole. The class presidency traditionally involves fundraising for and planning of the commencement exercises and other related events, but I have redefined the position to include greater involvement in university politics. A prime example of this occurred this year when Rutgers banned homecoming festivities for undergraduates. I worked to unite organizations from all of the colleges, the fraternities and sororities, and the alumni organizations into a cohesive force, the Student Homecoming Committee, which from now on will be a permanent body at Rutgers. I then drafted a new plan, and after discussions with a number of university officials, was able to get the university to change its policy and to help us establish a new tradition at Rutgers in the form of a more organized and responsible student homecoming celebration. This new unity will continue to help us solve problems facing our University. Of all of the things I have done during my college career, I believe that my tenure as class president has taught me the most about what it takes to lead, how to deal with people, and the best ways to attack and solve problems.

My membership on the Dean's Cabinet has allowed me to further my goal of being an active participant in campus life. This body meets to discuss campus issues and to begin the steps to solve the problems that members identify. In my four years on this committee I have expanded my knowledge of student and administrative concerns and developed an ability to reconcile disparate interests. Many issues that could have led to conflict on campus were resolved in these face-to-face sessions. A dispute over access to a new campus aquatic facility, for example, was arbitrated in this way.

In writing a political column for the *Rutgers Review* and *The Medium* I was able to tie my academic work to an extracurricular interest. Political science is one of my hobbies as well as my major, and I have found an excellent place to express this in the campus papers. The effort needed to create a written work often differs from that needed to lead a group, and writing provides me with a break from my other activities.

I have received a number of honors for my efforts on campus. In my junior year I was selected to be a member of Cap and Skull, an honor society composed of eighteen student leaders chosen by their peers to be the vanguard of student leadership. I have received the Dean's Award for Excellence, which recognizes those who have combined high scholastic achievement with excellence in leadership. My greatest honor has come recently, as I was appointed to be a Rutgers College Fellow. This group, consisting mainly of faculty, is charged with deciding the policies and course of Rutgers College. My position on the Student Life Committee will give me an even greater voice in policies directly affecting my peers. My undergraduate activities and my participation in a number of political campaigns have led me to seek a role in the service of others.

My selection as a 1989 Truman Scholar is a demonstration of this commitment. The Harry S Truman Scholarship is awarded nationally to those who demonstrate leadership and who plan to become involved in public service. I intend to do this as an elected official at the national level.

Personal Statement
Craig Buckser

Most law school applicants dream of enjoying successful careers in the skyscrapers of New York or the halls of Congress. Not I. I simply aspire to inhabit ivory towers—as a law school professor.

I did not make my decision to become a law school professor overnight. Indeed, this idea developed over several years.

I can recall that as far back as elementary school I was interested in being a lawyer, largely because my sister, whom I admired, wanted to be one. In high school, after taking American history and government classes, my admiration of law extended beyond a mere childhood infatuation. I first studied constitutional law, the first subject I had ever explored which fascinated me, in the government class.

Since I was in twelfth grade, I have worked for a civil rights attorney, Arthur Graseck. Immediately after I started working for him, I became further interested in practicing law. As I saw him try to check widespread police abuses, including police brutality, I understood how the law could be used as a vehicle for achieving social justice.

In the summer of 1992 I worked for him on a constitutional

law case. A woman had been fired from her deputy-tax-receiver post because the Conservative Party, of which she was a committee-woman, did not support the Republican candidate for town supervisor. She claimed that her First Amendment rights were violated. Having lost in district court, she retained Mr. Graseck for the appeal, and he gave me the responsibility for researching the issue and writing a brief to the United States Court of Appeals for the Second Circuit. Creating and arguing the legal theories of the case was a tremendous challenge, but I enjoyed writing the brief, which was submitted with few changes made by Mr. Graseck. Although the client lost, Mr. Graseck was pleased with my effort. Working on this case reaffirmed my love for constitutional law.

My college experiences refined my interest in law and convinced me to enter academia. Since my freshman year, complex, intellectual discussions with students and professors have enthralled me. I realized that students, whose diverse backgrounds brought different perspectives into the dialogue, could significantly contribute to the learning process by sharing their views. Professor William Muir, who taught an American legal system course I took in the summer of 1991, often told the students that each class was a thrilling learning experience for him. His message impressed me. In my opinion, an intelligent class discussion is the biggest attraction in spending a career as a law professor.

Researching for my honors thesis has had the largest effect on shaping my career decision. I began my research this summer because I won an Institute for Labor Relations Undergraduate Research Assistantship. I am studying the history of the prosecution of a Communist labor union president which occurred in the mid-1950s. I chose this topic because, as a civil libertarian, I am repulsed by the restrictions on free speech and association that accompanied the Red Scare. From my experience I have learned that doing my own research and personally pursuing knowledge is interesting and exciting. The autonomy is terrific. Also, I enjoy sharing the fruits of my research with interested people. In addition, I could use my scholarship to advocate the expansion of civil liberties or to find new ways of achieving social justice. So, I think that I will relish performing the research aspect of being a law professor.

Moreover, I eagerly anticipate getting embroiled in intellectual debates, which I believe are essential to understanding all the ramifications of any issue. At every opportunity I engage in political and philosophical arguments, and afterward I always have a greater knowledge of the subject than I had beforehand.

In conclusion, while my classmates will be seeking to make the connections that will guarantee them jobs with prestigious law firms or prominent politicians, I will be expanding my knowledge of constitutional law, or perhaps another law discipline that I may find even more fascinating, as I ride the road toward academia.

P e r s o n a l   S t a t e m e n t
Name Withheld

I have scars on my face, the reminders of a nearly fatal car accident in which I was involved when I was ten years old. While barely perceptible today, the scars were painfully noticeable during my image-conscious pre- and early-teen years. Fortunately, I have no lasting impairments. But the accident and my resulting disfigurement was one of the defining experiences of my life, playing a central role in the development of my character and values.

In particular, the car accident instilled in me a tenacious enthusiasm for life. The experience of nearly dying at such a young age left me with a precociously profound appreciation for life and a determination to make the most of life's opportunities.

The accident also gave me a strong and healthy self-confidence. My disfigurement forced me to derive confidence from internal attributes, rather than from external characteristics.

In addition, the car accident gave me a heart for people in need and a burning desire to do what I can to help them. During my youth I experienced a degree of loneliness, embarrassment, and pain because of my scars. Through my own suffering, I developed a strong sense of empathy with those who must endure sometimes far greater forms of suffering.

As a result, I am not a conventional person. Certainly, I am an achiever, thanks in large part to my ingrained love of life and self-confidence: I set and attained ambitious educational goals at Stanford and the Kennedy School of Government, and have enjoyed extraordinary success in my work in and with the United States

Congress. But the car accident inspired me to live boldly and to define success broadly, in terms of internal happiness and personal fulfillment, instead of solely in more orthodox ways like money or raw power.

More than simply achieving stereotypical notions of "success," I seek a challenging and adventurous life, and a career which grows out of my dreams; I want to travel unusual paths requiring unconventional risks. For instance I want to have the professional flexibility to take a sabbatical and start a community development corporation, or to stop practicing law for a year and sail around the world, or to combine part-time law practice with volunteer work.

Indeed, I am willing to take risks to follow my dreams: I left a high-level position in Seattle, for example, to move to Washington, D.C., without a job because I wanted to fulfill my lifelong goal of working on Capitol Hill. (The gamble paid off spectacularly— please see my resume, included in my application, for more details about my accomplishments in Washington.)

I also trace my fundamental commitment to public service to the car accident, for this commitment grows directly out of my strong sense of empathy with people in need. Devotion to public service has been and will remain a cornerstone of my personal and professional life. For years I have volunteered weekly in homeless shelters, and after college I spurned more lucrative opportunities [in order] to teach English in a Hong Kong Vietnamese refugee camp. My commitment to public service led to my studies at the Kennedy School, to my five years' work in legislative politics in Seattle and on Capitol Hill, and to my issue specialization in housing and social policy.

My desire to go to law school emanates from these fundamental aspects of my character, as well as from the simple fact that I am intrinsically drawn to law and want to be a lawyer (I work closely with attorneys, and often feel comparatively limited without a law degree). Law will empower me to make a difference in people's lives while giving me the tools to achieve my personal goals and dreams. With my educational and professional background, a law degree will exponentially expand my public service opportunities in both the private and public sectors. And law provides the flexibility to fulfill my goal of an accomplished yet unorthodox life.

Can I really trace my desire to go to law school to a car accident which occurred when I was ten years old? Maybe not completely. But clearly the car accident, which seemed so horrific at the time, played a crucial role in shaping my fundamental values and goals, which will now be immeasurably enhanced and enabled by a law degree.

Personal Statement
Helen Virginia Cantwell

I wanted to study law, economics, and music in college. It was not easy. A liberal arts education, however, has given me the freedom to prepare for a legal career while pursuing my love for playing the organ and studying economics. Wellesley College was an excellent choice as it offers strong departments in my fields, a unique baroque organ, and plenty of professional advice specifically for women. This support and commitment to women's education has been invaluable to me in making important decisions. Outside employment at the Federal Reserve Board and as a local organist allowed me to explore my majors in more depth, but made me aware that these careers were not for me. I kept returning to the law and its relationship to society as a future focus.

During my junior year, this harmony of academic interests was disrupted. Extracurricular activities and increased academic obligations demanded more of my time, leaving less energy for organ practice. Economics classes seemed drab compared to the lively pace of the summer in Washington, D.C. Finally, the biography of Morris Dees, a civil rights attorney in Alabama, caused me to question who was being served by our judicial system and to think about my future role in it. I needed to decide if I would spend my senior year writing a thesis or practicing every day for a senior organ recital in addition to thinking about the different types of law I might study. My commitment to law school was firm, but including all three options would not be possible.

Last summer I decided that despite the benefits gained from an intensive study in one's field, I did not have a firm topic and did not want to compromise other academic experiences for the sake of a thesis. I also wanted to take advantage of a last opportunity to give a performance on an instrument that I love. All the while I was working for CONNPIRG [Connecticut Public Interest Research Group] (in conjunction with the National Environmental Law Center) to enact tougher legislation penalizing toxic waste dumpers. Through this I saw a great need for reform in the public sector concerning issues like the environment. It's frustrating and merits attention from the legal establishment. Though environmental law is not a potential specialty for me, the areas of public interest and policy are very attractive.

I still have a considerable amount of exploring to do before I decide my specific future. Choices along the way may be confusing, but I feel confident that I will be able to balance my priorities. Music and reading the Wall Street Journal each morning will always be a part of my life, but not integral to my professional career.

Personal Statement
Catherine Caporusso

As I began to think of how to write my personal statement, I asked my family how they would describe me if they had the task of introducing me to the Admissions Committee. Their responses, together with my own thoughts, provide a good basis for explaining the choices I have made in my life, and the goals that I hope to achieve with a law degree from Harvard.

I am very competitive. In academics, I tend to compete with myself, to the point of being a perfectionist. My parents knew, for example, that I would not be satisfied with anything less than a score of 180 on my LSAT. They described me as being "focused" and "intense," and are very confident that I would succeed in anything that I chose to do. Indeed, I set very high goals for myself, and work as hard as I can to achieve them. When I fail, I double my efforts and try again.

I am a Cancer. This description comes from my younger sister, who is currently fascinated with astrology. Although I do not share her belief in horoscopes, I agree that I possess one main characteristic of Cancers: a strong attachment to my home and family.

I am fascinated with law, politics, and government. When I was twelve years old, I brazenly announced to my family that I wanted to be president when I grew up. I got the impression that to be a politician, I must become a lawyer. At that time, law also appealed to me because of its theatrical aspects, as I was very involved in the school plays.

My preoccupation with current events and political figures continued. During my sophomore year in college, I took a class called "Crime and Punishment," where we studied cases such as *Texas v. Johnson* and *Webster v. Reproductive Health Services*. I realized that law was not a means to an end, but an end in itself. Classes in constitutional law, civil liberties, and philosophy confirmed my interest in legal reasoning and argumentation.

I am a feminist. Unfortunately, many women my age are unwilling to give themselves this label. Throughout my childhood, however, I wondered why it was that the overwhelming majority of the politicians that so intrigued me were men. My parents gave me the confidence that my gender would not stand in the way of achieving my dreams, but I came to realize that this was not entirely true. I concluded that I must knock down any barriers of sexism that I encountered on the path to fulfilling my aspirations. Feminism flowed easily out of these beliefs.

My choice of undergraduate education reflects many of these aspects of my personality. The University of Illinois at Chicago Honors College offered me a full scholarship. Knowing that I would be going on to law school, I realized that free tuition would give me the opportunity to devote more time to my studies and to save money for my legal education. The Honors College also offered me the chance to compete with other students in specialized honors courses. Finally, I did not feel that I was quite ready to move away from home, and UIC was close by.

Because of my competitiveness, I have set very high goals for myself. My fiancé states it simply: I would like an entry in the encyclopedia. Although I would not put it in this manner, I do know that I want to "make my mark upon the world." I would be interested in serving as a legislator, a trial lawyer, a lobbyist, a professor, and a judge—in any order. In whatever occupation, I would take particular interest in so-called "women's issues": abortion, sexual harassment and discrimination, child care, rape, pay equity, etc. In any way I can, I would like to change the status quo. A degree from

Harvard Law School would allow me the opportunity to pursue these lofty ambitions, and I hope that you will give me that chance.

Personal Statement

Name Withheld

During my junior year at Stanford, I spent spring quarter studying in Tours, France. After three months of being inundated with the French language and with the accompanying disdain of native speakers, I longed for any easy reading in English. My search of the local library produced a book from a dusty shelf entitled *Major Issues in Public Policy*. The book's title was not exciting, but it was written in English and that was all that mattered. To my surprise, however, I was instantly captivated by learning that small adjustments to the law could have a huge impact on society. For example, the book pointed out how a state's welfare policy encouraged the disintegration of two-parent families by giving more money to single mothers than to married couples. If the state's welfare policy were slightly changed to keep monetary benefits marriage-neutral, thousands of families would be affected. After reading the book, I saw important issues such as poverty and substandard education in concrete policy terms instead of as vague situations that I wanted to change. Thus began the transformation of a naive college student into an avid follower of socioeconomic issues.

During my senior year, my desire to learn more about the law and public policy led me to participate in the Stanford Alternative Spring Break Project. This project combined direct experience with policy exposure by enabling the volunteers to work in homeless shelters and to speak with advocates and city officials involved with combatting the homeless problem. The experience strengthened my belief in the need for change in current policies and in the idea that change could be effected if the proper motivation, strategy, and resources were implemented.

The summer after I graduated from college, I volunteered as an intern at Public Advocates Law Firm, Inc., one of the lobbying groups that we visited during the spring break project. My assignment at Public Advocates was to explain why, in the past twenty years, the percentage of African Americans in the homeless population has drastically increased. My study of newspaper articles, books, and government reports determined that the disintegration of African-American families and communities, due to destructive welfare policies and to the influx of highly addictive drugs into black communities beginning in the late 1950s, was ultimately responsible for the increase in African-American homelessness. In order to remedy the situation, I concluded that a multifaceted solution was needed that included not only more low-income housing, but also free drug-treatment and family-planning programs. Thus, I progressed from simple awareness of "major issues in policy" to the actual development on a novice level of practical solutions to socio-economic problems.

My interest in public policy came full circle when I became a legislative analyst at New York City's Office of Management and Budget (OMB). Working at OMB gave me the opportunity not only to see how policies were formulated, but also to get involved in the fight for their implementation. Victory in these battles was often determined by which side had the best legal expertise. Therefore, in the same way that my experiences since France have increased my *desire* to help change laws for the better, attending law school would improve my *ability* to do so.

Personal Statement

Michael Lee Castellano

I would not guess that my high school soccer coach was an avid reader of Nietzsche, but he did have his own version of the phrase "wretched contentment." During especially rigorous workouts he was fond of lecturing us, in proper athletic-coach-speak, "If you always do what you have always done you will always get what you have always gotten." At the time, undefeated, out of breath, and sore from what seemed like our one-hundredth sprint, the team did not particularly care to hear our coach's maxim. Still, his point was well taken as we would somehow find the energy to turn an above-average workout into an exceptional one. By now you may be wondering whether or not I somehow mixed up my personal statement with a philosophy paper (or perhaps a coaching guide), but I have not. I included the two quotations above as an introduction to part of my credo. I believe in putting in extra effort and seeking to get more out of life. On the most elementary level this credo manifests itself in my approach to life's mundane tasks. It is during these periods— walking to and from class, waiting in lines, or doing daily chores— that it is easiest to slip into wretched contentment and settle for the ordinary. Rather than trudging mindlessly through these chores, I make the most of my time.

My chief response to tedium is to challenge myself with intellectual questions. When things tend towards mindlessness, I use the time for contemplation. Take, for example, mowing the lawn, a chore that is neither intellectually nor physically challenging. Instead of "zoning out" in the repetitive back and forth of lawn mowing, however, I take advantage of this free-time as a means of philosophic exploration. I have spent many an hour pondering race relations, questions of sexuality, and Western values to the smell of freshly cut grass. I used to collect the products of time spent mowing the lawn in a binder appropriately labeled, *Thoughts While Mowing My Lawn*. Lately, though, I have been keeping the "Thoughts" in mental storage until presented with the opportunity to incorporate them into a paper or a discussion.

These thought processes do not cease after the LawnBoy is quiet. I use many other monotonous periods as opportunities to consider competing arguments I have encountered. I also try and engage friends in debate on these topics. While walking on campus, doing dishes, or eating lunch, I am often deep in thought or discussion. Recently I have been most concerned with the issue of Third World development and its relation to global capitalism. I have especially considered the arguments of the Austrian school, as embodied by F. A. Hayek, on the one hand, and the dependency theorists, such as Andre Gunder Frank, on the other.

My response to the mundane takes other forms as well. I do not like to fall into patterns of behavior, to always do what I have always done, if you will. A daily necessity while I studied abroad in Cambridge, England, was the forty-five-minute walk to the Marshall Economics Library. I made it a point during my stay to get lost at least once a week on my way to the library and to use that opportunity to explore new places around the university as frequently as possible. There is always more to be discovered.

I followed this rule later when I traveled around Europe. When returning from somewhere I always took a route different from the path of arrival. This got me lost a number of times, but in the process I stumbled across some wonderful sights. Also, I spent as little time sleeping on trains as my body would allow, instead using the time to "experience" Europe. I will never forget taking the night-train to Barcelona when an Italian student and I discussed the recent Italian political turmoil over a bottle of wine. I do not like to look back only to realize that time and opportunity have passed me by while I was inattentive.

It is not just in Europe that I rebelled against monotony by going out of my way. Even at Hopkins I try to take different paths to and from classes. Each path offers its own perspectives. I also go out of my way by helping people and being considerate. Sometimes this takes just a little extra effort—holding a door or greeting a stranger; other times it is more involved, such as organizing the participation of my fraternity brothers in the Special Olympics or in neighborhood projects. This type of effort can turn an ordinary day into an exceptional one.

These have been some of the methods with which I parry life's thrusts of tedium. They reflect just one subset of the ways in which I challenge myself. On the athletic field, in the classroom, spending time with friends, or performing the most mundane of chores, I try to get the most out of all of my endeavors. I am rarely gripped by the "wretched contentment" of which Nietzsche spoke; I have always done a little extra and I think this is reflected in what I have always gotten.

Personal Statement

Laura R. Cheng

Clients in troubled situations will find me easy to talk with, for I know what it feels like to have no voice. As a child, I was shy and isolated from my peers. Day after day I came home from school and cried, wondering if anyone would ever take the time to understand me. Eventually, with the help of my father, I began to work on my social skills. I practiced asking people questions about themselves, looking people in the eye, and speaking assertively. My parents hoped that boarding school would help me break out of my shell, and they sent me to Exeter for my last two years of high school. My new classmates found me to be a good listener, and they often told me what was on their hearts. Through a speech class at Exeter I discovered that I enjoyed talking to groups, and that I could even make an audience laugh. In college I went on to speak before church groups in both English and Chinese. While working on my own expression, I also continue to practice listening. At Northeastern I am studying in detail the effective listening techniques used in counseling psychology. My desire is to hear the cries of people in need and help them find their own words.

My experience with other cultures gives me sensitivity to the voices of today's international America. Even as a child in Louisiana, I wrote to twenty-two pen pals from across the globe. At Exeter I had the privilege of meeting international students in person, and their stories followed me to Harvard. For four years I worked at the Harvard International Office, helping the staff give visa advice and process immigration paperwork. Throughout my time at Harvard I studied Chinese history, culture, and language. I have also experienced Chinese culture through my husband, whose family immigrated to the United States from Taiwan when he was a child. Presently I edit a student newsletter and arrange field trips for the international community at Northeastern's English Language Center. I am also studying multicultural theories of counseling through my graduate coursework.

Both at Harvard and now at Northeastern, I enjoy spending time with the people I meet at work, informally tutoring them in English. The summer before my senior year, I taught English to a class of refugee youth. Two years before that, I helped teach computer science at a Duke program for advanced junior-high-school students. Some of my favorite memories have been working with those students; I have the heart of a teacher. As a lawyer I want to educate people about their legal options and constitutional rights. I am also interested in academic law, in changing the future of my profession by instructing new lawyers.

The intellectual challenge of law appeals to me. I have a strong academic background, especially in areas which require analytical skill. Since childhood I have been an excellent student. The puzzle of language intrigued me; I studied French, Latin, Greek, Russian, and Spanish, all before college. At Harvard I took time to explore a broad range of subjects, from astrophysics to anthropology. My junior year I joined the linguistics department, where I learned to logically break down the syntax, phonology, and historical patterns of language. In each of my linguistics classes I received an A grade, including graduate seminars in phonology and psycholinguistics.

Through my current graduate studies I am learning that, although some problems can be settled on an individual level, society and legal issues play a large role in the unhappy situations of many clients. My goal as a lawyer is to serve this population in a personal and meaningful way. I am especially interested in helping internationals and refugees as they struggle to work, study, and make their homes in America. Because of my personal experiences, teaching skill, and academic background, I feel I can be sensitive to the needs of the unempowered and act as their articulate advocate.

Personal Statement

Tim Corriero

It wasn't the Mafia, it was just a way of doing business. There were no double-breasted suits or red sport cars, just my Levi's and my mountain bike.

I flew to Italy to work with an international real estate firm in Rome. It was the summer of 1992 and I had just graduated Phi Beta Kappa from Colgate University. It was a job I had pursued since my junior year when I first approached the director of the company and I couldn't have imagined a better position. I had spent a year in Spain between high school and college and then a junior semester abroad in Venice. Since these experiences, my most powerful impetus and motivation had been to return to live and work in Europe. Through some persuasive letters and nervous phone calls, I had managed not only to land a job, but land one in *Italy! La dolce vita*, at the age of 22, how much better could things be?

Much better. All preconceived notions crumble eventually, and in proportion to my enthusiasm, mine did as well. There is more

than distance and language separating the worlds of Colgate academia and Italian business and I found myself swimming in the gap.
My first lesson was to arrive at Fiumicino Airport to be greeted by
the company driver in a Mercedes, only to be charged almost a hundred dollars for the service a half hour later. Two weeks later I ran
across a computer file that contained a list of names that included
my own: everyone who had used our "taxi" service. The company
was taking kickbacks from the driver.

Within the first hour of my arrival in Italy, the company had
managed to take money from my pocket. I had worked two jobs my
senior spring in order to afford the one way ticket to Rome. They
knew that. The sign over the airport gate read: "Welcome to Italy,"
but in retrospect, I could swear it was printed in perfect Dantesque
script: "Abandon All Hope . . ."

My introduction to business "Italian Style" is a good representation of my experience in long-term Roman rentals—my area
of specialty—and the situation seemed only to steadily deteriorate.
Clients would call about security deposits that were over a year old,
and I did not know what to tell them. The policy of misrepresent-
ing a rental price to a client would often times lead to an uncomfortable situation, leaving us . . . the company . . . *me* . . . caught
in a lie. I was in Italy, but if this was the price, I was not prepared
to pay.

I began to truly appreciate honesty in business. I recognized
the importance of a carefully constructed contract and the danger
of naive trust. What I learned was not "How to effectively write a
rental contract," or "How to treat a client" but rather how *not* to
do these things. I left Italy with an appreciation for the importance
of virtue in any professional transaction, be it law or business. I
would never work like this. I could not. It was just a way of doing
business.

My time in Rome was not ill-spent. I learned as much about
myself as I did about Italian business. The memories of my time in
real estate have had a great effect on me and it was a far better lesson for having learned it in the negative.

I am now a year older, a bit wiser, and fluent in both Italian
and Spanish. Having banished some of the demons of unrealistic
expectations, I have for the past eight months been employed in a

law firm in Washington, D.C. Law is my interest and I am looking forward to starting law school in the fall of this year. I would like one day to work again in an international context, but this time as a lawyer.

Personal Statement
Brooke Melisse Deratany

1992 has been quite a year. In fact, since May 1991, when I graduated with high distinction from the University of Virginia, my life has been one growth experience after another. There is just no way to compare the person I was fresh out of college with who I am now.

I knew that before embarking on my law school education I would have to travel, the taste for which I had developed studying a semester in Valencia, Spain, and a summer in Fortaleza, Brazil. Although my parents financed my semester in Spain, all future study/travel I was to pay for myself. With my savings from summer jobs, I toured Western Europe after graduation, spending some extra time in Slovenia to marvel at the enthusiasm of this newly independent country.

My travels had just begun. I had won a Rotary International Ambassadorial Scholarship to do a year of graduate work in the country of my choice. Having majored in Latin American Studies and Spanish, I chose Argentina. School in the southern hemisphere does not begin until March, so I started my master's degree in the Center for Latin American Studies at the University of Florida, where I supported myself as a graduate assistant.

I also applied and was chosen for a Fulbright–Hays fellowship to study Portuguese and Brazilian culture in Belo Horizonte, Brazil, the two months preceding my arrival in Buenos Aires. What I learned and saw complemented and expanded upon my earlier Brazilian experience.

In Buenos Aires, aside from speaking at Rotary Club meetings and other ambassadorial activities, I studied Latin American economic and international relations, and Argentine foreign policy at the *Facultad Latinoamericana de Ciencias Sociales*. I also studied French six hours a week at the Alliance Française. I worked six to ten hours a week as an English professor to pay for my travels through Argentina, Chile, Bolivia, Paraguay, Uruguay, and Brazil. These experiences afforded me great learning and insight for my graduate studies—and for life.

I am now back as a graduate assistant at the University of Florida. Before starting law school this fall, I plan to return to South America to write my thesis on South American economic integration.

My dream since the sixth grade has been to be an attorney, but I have defined this goal more clearly through the years, ultimately deciding upon public international law, and concentrating in developing countries. Although no one can "save the world," I do know that as an attorney I will have the critical abilities, skills, and professional influence to make my contribution.

Personal Statement

Donald R. Esposito, Jr.

I am applying to Harvard Law School because of the intellectual and personal challenges that it would provide, and because of my desire to play a part in the decisions that will govern the United States in the 21st century. My career goals are to teach law and to advise government on public policy issues. I hope to someday establish a career in Washington, D.C., because I want to be on the cutting edge of legal scholarship and public policy decision-making. I am especially interested in constitutional law and the manner in which political theories and legal opinions reflect a continuum in Western intellectual thought.

In addition, I have an obligation to repay those people—namely, my family, teachers, neighbors, and friends—who have pushed me and sacrificed for me, and who have enabled me to achieve what I have. The best way to repay this debt is to utilize my talents and energies in public service. Furthermore, I am attracted to public service, perhaps as a judge, because of my desire to demonstrate that government can play an active role in improving society, my own family serving as an example. My grandfather's family first received governmental assistance while establishing themselves in the United States, and he now owns a successful business in Tallahassee,

Florida. My father, benefitting from government assistance, was the first in our family to graduate from college, and now I intend to be the first to graduate from law school.

My interest in public service formerly included a desire to hold political office; I dreamed of being a United States senator or the governor of North Carolina. My aspirations have changed, however, as a result of my experiences in the UNC Student Congress. At times, I have had great difficulty reconciling my beliefs and positions with those of my constituents, especially when I supported funding for the Carolina Gay and Lesbian Association. Then and now I refuse to compromise my beliefs for political expediency. I was also dismayed by my colleagues who saw government and the Student Congress not as a way to benefit others, but as a way to secure power and prestige for themselves. Finally, I was disheartened by the 1990 North Carolina Senate campaign. I am still proud to be a North Carolinian, but I am disgusted and frustrated by the tactics of my elected representatives and the values of some of my fellow citizens. I refuse to enter a career where I must work with such people or deal with such frustration and dismay.

My interest in constitutional law and political theory has been reaffirmed by my work on my senior honors thesis. My topic is the secessionist strategy in North Carolina, especially between February 28 and April 13, 1861. In the course of my research, I have come across the debate in the North Carolina General Assembly over the means by which the state could leave the Union. The debate centered upon the right of revolution versus a right of secession, and questioned the permanence of the independent states' ratification of the United States Constitution. I am fascinated by such historical questions, and relish the prospect of a career that would expose me to similar issues.

I am attracted to Harvard Law School because of the excellence of its legal instruction, the diversity of its course offerings, and its strength in constitutional law and in judicial clerkship placement. Furthermore, being from a small town in North Carolina, and having attended the University of North Carolina at Chapel Hill, I seek to "get away" for law school and to interact with a diverse, talented, and ambitious body of peers with backgrounds and views different from my own. Finally, I have always been motivated by the desire to test and exceed my personal limitations—whether by completing a police cadet-training program, by working on Wall Street, or by climbing Mount Kilimanjaro—and I eagerly anticipate the challenge of Harvard Law School.

Personal Statement

Name Withheld

"It is the rare cucumber who can emerge from the vinegar vat as anything but a pickle." (per my 'Psychology I' professor, Philip Zimbardo)

I have long valued pursuing my own path, often deliberately setting my agenda at least somewhat apart from that of my peers. In keeping with this effort, I now seek complementary degrees in law and public affairs in order to lay a broad foundation for several career ambitions. In addition to learning to think in American legal terms, I hope to ground myself thoroughly in international affairs and domestic education issues, in methods of substantive and quantitative analysis, and in the procedures and institutions which shape international relations and education policy.

My curiosity about foreign cultures, particulary European ones, began early. Though I was born in Philadelphia, my parents arrived in this country in 1957 as refugees from Hungary. I developed my interest in international affairs further during an eight-month junior-year stay in central Europe, which included an internship arranged through my own initiative in the Austrian Federal Education Ministry. The considerable personal effort that enabled me to obtain this meaningful work in Vienna reinforced my faith in my capacity for achievement. If international relations, my undergraduate major, were an exclusive academic preoccupation for me, I would now likely advance my study of it through another extended visit to Europe. Instead, however, I seek the more flexible academic and vocational preparation which a joint program in law and public affairs would provide.

At present, I work as a foreign affairs analyst for a member of Congress, a role which immerses me in a great variety of global and regional matters. In any given week, it is not unusual for me to draft an op–ed article on international population growth, write a memo on Middle East peace talks, summarize a bill on Chinese human rights, and respond to constituent letters on Mexican free trade. I have also had the good fortune to participate in a number of exceptionally interesting events, including a Congressional delegation to Saudi Arabia and Israel one month prior to the outbreak of war in the Persian Gulf. Unfortunately, the breadth of material for which a legislative assistant in Congress is responsible frequently necessitates relatively shallow familiarly with the issues; too often, the tasks are miles wide but only inches deep. Nonetheless, my experience on Capitol Hill has taught me a great deal about politics and legislative procedure, two factors with at least as profound an influence on Congressional activity as that of the underlying issues.

This international concentration shares my attention with an interest in education policy and administration, which may one day send me to work for an educational foundation, a school district, or a university. It is clear to me that access to quality education at a young age is the key to future success because it prepares individuals to open the doors that lead to progress—at the personal, community, and national levels. My senior year included two activities in which I provided educational services; in one, I served on the national board of the American Association of University Students, gaining an understanding of the constraints of working within an extended bureaucratic structure; the second experience, volunteering as an upper class advisor for five first-year students, showed me the reward that came come from direct service in education. Both activities confirmed my intention to work to make quality education more widely available.

The same desire to have a tangible constructive impact which attracts me to education also steers me toward the judiciary; in fact, one of the few distinct occupations to attract me consistently is that of a federal or state judge. Even if not headed for a career on the bench, however, I recognize that a legal education would enhance my qualifications for the majority of my ambitions. John Gardner (founder of "Common Cause"), Franklin Thomas (president of the Ford Foundation), and Thurgood Marshall are just three of many individuals who have used their law degrees to make significant societal contributions in ways that appeal to me.

Though I admit to already being slightly pickled, I nonetheless strive to maintain enthusiasm and to keep my career options open. With one degree in public affairs and another in law, I hope to do all this and more, because that suits the kind of unusual cucumber I would like to remain.

P e r s o n a l   S t a t e m e n t

Name Withheld

As the child of Paraguayan immigrants, I too occupy a borderland. Even after four years at the University of Michigan, a personal statement remains a challenge. Always Latina to Americans, always American to Latin Americans. I have attempted to establish an identity between these two "worlds." Although often difficult, through my academic choices, my commitment to extracurricular activities and community involvement, and my work experience at the University of Michigan, I have successfully forged a shifting and multiple identity in the borderland between two cultures.

Surrounded by Spanish and reminders of my parents' country, I grew up with an undeniable sense of being Paraguayan. However along with the appreciation of their culture and history, my parents also conveyed the reality for Latinos in the United States. Burdened with accents and alien status, they insisted on the use of English. I was to be an American to succeed. Confronted with these contradictory messages, I retreated to the safe "world" of being American.

My experiences at the University of Michigan however have changed this view. As a whole, I have attempted to blend these two cultures. In academics, I have consistently selected classes that both enhance my understanding of my Latin American heritage as well as those that broaden my knowledge of other areas. As a student, I have mixed traditional classes in history, communication, and English with Latin American studies and American culture.

I have similarly blended identities in my extracurricular activities. Along with my commitment to Amnesty International and Alpha Phi Omega, a co-ed service fraternity, I have been involved in the creation of a chapter of Sigma Lambda Gamma, a Latina sorority on campus. Aware of the difficulties of living in the borderland, I, along with my fellow co-founders, are attempting to bring women together for cultural, academic, and social support. Our hope is that by making ourselves and the general community sensitive to and aware of the diverse cultures and issues among Latinos, incoming Latinas at the University of Michigan will feel pride in maintaining a multiple identity.

As an intern at the Washington Office on Latin America prior to my junior year, I fully realized my own Latina identity by working for an office that concentrated on Central and South American issues. My decision to intern in a "non-traditional" agency emphasized the new direction my interests had taken in college. The experience, as well as my interaction with other Latin Americans in the office, highlighted the importance of understanding the concerns among the various cultures in Latin America. As a resident assistant, I rely on counseling, communication, and discipline skills. However, the single most important tool is tolerance and understanding of diverse cultures. This sensitivity allows for the resolution of conflict because it forces the involved parties to appreciate each other's opinions. In a multi-cultural community, this skill proves invaluable. My multiple identity allows for multiple understandings.

In a world that is rapidly changing and in a country where minorities will become a majority in my lifetime, the appreciation of diversity will be more important than ever. Since I possess this advantage, I will be uniquely qualified to practice law in the twenty-first century. Due to my cultural heritage and previous travel experiences in Europe and South America, I am drawn to the study of immigration law.

Therefore, I have used and I intend to use my tenuous existence in the borderland to aid myself and others in dealing with the challenges and problems arising from an increasingly diverse nation.

P e r s o n a l   S t a t e m e n t

Name Withheld

I have consistently made my career choices knowing that in order to be fulfilled, I have to work in an area where both my mind and heart are engaged. During my senior year in college, I investigated the types of jobs traditionally chosen by economics majors and concluded that, for me, they would not inspire the level of dedication I deemed necessary. Instead, the passion for music I developed through many years of piano study and choral singing led me to pursue a career in concert production. As the manager of a concert series and coordinator of logistical and public relations details for orchestras' and solo artists' tours, I was immersed in music-making at the most essential level. Although I continued to acquire additional responsibilities over the course of five years, I eventually recognized that my work involved little intellectual challenge and that a significant move was necessary.

The Population Council has proven to be just such a change, providing a stimulating, academic atmosphere where the object of our efforts is interesting and important to me. When I came to the Population Council I already had been a supporter of reproductive rights, both as a matter of personal freedom and for the vital role that contraception plays in enabling women to control the course of their lives. The insight offered by the public health and demographic perspectives has deepened and strengthened my conviction that access to high-quality reproductive health services—including safe and legal abortion, and screening and treatment for sexually transmitted diseases—must be granted to every woman. At the individual level, without adequate contraceptive services and information within reach, women in a variety of circumstances find it difficult to support the children they bear and to care adequately for their own health and general well-being. On the aggregate level, where high fertility contributes to rapid population growth that outstrips the pace of economic development, the difficulties developing countries face in providing sufficiently for their populations' most basic needs are exacerbated. Further, even in cases where population growth is not a problem, the hundreds of thousands of maternal deaths caused annually by complications from unsafe abortions and the alarmingly high adolescent pregnancy rate in the United States both illustrate the magnitude of the unmet need for contraception.

In seeking to reduce unwanted and unplanned childbearing, it is not sufficient to rely on the provision of reproductive health services. One also must consider the vast range of cultural and economic factors that influence individual behavior. If the status of women is improved, for example, through measures that aim to increase the levels of female literacy and women's participation in the work force, and to discourage marriage at an early age, and if the disparities that exist between men and women in shouldering the burden of childcare are reduced, women then can be valued beyond their capacity to bear children and men will take more responsibility for their offspring. When both women and men develop new roles that transcend the boundaries sustained by tradition, the demand for children is reduced, the incentive to use contraception increases, and fewer children are born, serving demographic and health goals, and furthering progress toward full equality between the sexes.

The work of the Population Council and organizations with whom we collaborate has made an impact on efforts to curtail population growth, improve reproductive health, and enhance the status of women, but greater advocacy measures on behalf of these issues are needed, both in the United States and abroad. Knowing that there is a role I could play in effecting political and legal changes, I have decided to study law. I look forward to examining the legal dimensions of access to reproductive health services and information, particularly as they relate to the questions of individual liberties and entitlements to health care, and to exploring how changes in laws regarding child support, widows' inheritance rights, divorce, and property ownership can enhance the status of women. Working as an advocate for access to a full range of reproductive health services or for legal remedies to the conditions that continue to limit women's emancipation, I will join a field where my mind will be challenged and my heart can endorse the value of my mind's efforts.

P e r s o n a l   S t a t e m e n t
Name Withheld

One day in early November of 1991, I found myself seated on a beige, vinyl sofa in my advisor's office at Princeton University. A week earlier I had delivered a thesis proposal before the faculty of the French section of the university's department of romance languages and literatures. At the time, the faculty had seemed excited by my proposal to write on the tombeau (tomb) poetry of

Stephan Mallarme, but, just one week later, my advisor informed me that although the faculty found the project fascinating and worthwhile of investigation, I needed to rethink, rewrite, and resubmit my proposal.

On the surface, my advisor's remarks were constructive. She reminded me that any project could benefit from further reflection. My advisor and I both knew, however, that the faculty's request for resubmission of my proposal presented me with the occasion to reevaluate my career. For several reasons, my years at Princeton had been a difficult time. Upon graduating from the University of Kentucky, the only career that I had even considered was college teaching. The prospect of studying at Princeton with well-known critics of French literature had thrilled me, and in the first two years leading to the master's degree I had worked diligently. Yet my advisor saw clearly, and I had begun to perceive, that I was unhappy with my chosen career. Although I wanted nothing more than to throw myself into my studies, I was not emotionally prepared to undertake the long haul of an intense, four-year Ph.D. program. I enjoyed reading and researching and I spent innumerable hours in the library, but I could not present the results of that research. I found no authoritative position from which I might cast my critical voice. Writing became increasingly difficult as I felt myself called to be an authority on subjects that I had only begun to discover.

That afternoon in November, the beige, vinyl sofa held enormous meaning. Every other time I met with my advisor, I had sat in a cold iron chair next to her desk while the sofa was used only for stacking piles of books. She would often interrupt our meeting to answer phone calls. That day the books were piled elsewhere and the phone went unattended. We sat next to each other on the sofa and through the course of the afternoon talked sincerely about me, my future, my career.

My advisor thought that I would benefit from further study abroad or from working temporarily in a non-academic setting. She and I both felt that academics left too little time to devote to social causes that we nominally supported. Before graduate school I had been an active participant in political and social causes in Kentucky. Graduate school had been an almost religious calling that required total commitment. My advisor and I agreed then that I would resubmit my proposal in January and begin looking into other options.

By the time the faculty had accepted my proposal I had already begun an aggressive job search. I focused primarily on law-related jobs in New York City. I was already considering the possibility of law school, so in February of 1992 I took the LSAT, having spent a few weeks of self-study to prepare. By April I had decided to accept a position as a legal assistant in the corporate finance group at the New York office of Sullivan & Cromwell.

As an adolescent I had often thought of becoming a lawyer, but I never saw myself working in a large, Wall Street firm. As is typical of young students, I had very idealistic notions of justice and equality which drew me to the legal profession: fighting prejudice and discrimination which I, having been raised Catholic in the Bible Belt, feared; defending the poor, which included most of my extended family; and representing the interests of the working class whom my own father, having dropped out of high school to become a unionized factory worker, seemed to epitomize. At age twenty-two those ideals still appeared noble, but I had grown and changed, thus new areas of the law had begun to interest me. After years of studying a foreign language and the experience of living in Europe, I now wanted to apply myself to international issues. After seven years of secondary study in the humanities, I wanted to do something else, to learn something about business and to apply myself to real-life problems. Working at the firm proved to be very educational and because of my language skills I was named a specialist for foreign companies, a position which granted me excellent opportunities to learn about and to work on international finance deals at both the governmental and corporate levels.

I have waited almost two years to commit myself to law school. I am certain of this decision, not only because I have learned from and appreciated my job as a legal assistant, but because a legal education, unlike the Ph.D. in French literature, opens many career paths, many of which I now find worthwhile. Two years later, I now know that the unease I felt sitting on that beige, vinyl sofa was due, in part, to the feeling that I was making a mistake by pursuing an academic career. I have come calmly and seriously to the decision to pursue a legal career and I look forward to starting that career in law school.

Personal Statement

Name Withheld

Although it involves a significant career change, my decision to pursue a legal career reflects a continuity with interests I have had, and skills I have demonstrated, throughout my adult life, both at work and in community activities. Often, I have been involved in creating orderly processes for resolving disagreements, and in using language (both written and spoken) to present a position or to establish a common understanding.

I have had three distinct careers since my college graduation in 1971. I spent two years researching and writing a biography of the late rock 'n' roll singer Buddy Holly. *Buddy Holly: His Life and Music* was published in 1975; it was later revised and republished twice, as *The Buddy Holly Story* (1979) and *Remembering Buddy* (1987), and has also been issued in British editions and in a German translation. The book served as the basis for the Academy Award–nominated film *The Buddy Holly Story*, as well as PBS and BBC documentaries on Holly. Writing the book required that I research documents, locate and gain the cooperation of many individuals (who were sometimes antagonistic to each other), weigh the credibility of conflicting recollections, and write for an audience previously unfamiliar, for the most part, with the early years of rock 'n' roll. It also gave me experience in public speaking, through appearances on radio and television and before live audiences.

After obtaining a master's degree in regional planning, I worked for three years at a regional planning agency on an EPA-funded water quality planning project. I coordinated our program with those of federal and state agencies, helped communities and private businesses implement new regulations, and drafted town ordinances on land use and water quality. I also wrote lengthy plans and impact statements, and made numerous appearances before groups of town officials and private citizens. Later, in 1980–81, a private consulting firm hired me on a part-time basis to manage a study, funded by the Department of the Interior, evaluating similar planning programs nationwide. I also wrote the final report.

In 1979, I joined family members in opening a bookstore on Cape Cod. By operating the store, I have become familiar with corporate accounting principles, while continuing to exercise many of the same interpersonal communication skills as before, in dealing with customers, employees, and other business people. I appear regularly before civic groups and on radio and television to promote the store, and I write a monthly book review column for a local newspaper.

Within my community, I have spent much of my spare time serving in leadership positions in town government and in youth sports organizations. During years of fiscal crisis for many Massachusetts towns, I was chairman of my town's finance committee, which prepared the annual budget. In that position, I negotiated with public officials and employees competing for limited funds, and tried to establish a consensus where possible. I was responsible for explaining and defending the budget recommendations before an open town meeting of several hundred voters. I like to think that I was respected for fairness, objectivity, and candor, even by those who disagreed with me on specific issues.

My other volunteer activity has involved youth sports. Since 1976, I have been a soccer coach and referee. I served two years as president of the town soccer league and also as treasurer of the regional league, during the formative years of both groups. As a league official, I drafted detailed by-laws to forestall the problems that commonly arise among adults in such associations, trained new coaches and referees, and organized the activities of dozens of volunteers. As a coach—almost exclusively of girls' teams—I have learned to be sensitive to the needs and aspirations of my players, and to be available to them as a friend, mentor, and advisor. The many hours that I have devoted to this activity have given me more pleasure and, I think, had a more beneficial effect on others than anything else I have done in my life.

Whatever legal specialty I might eventually pursue, my prior experiences and my personal habits of mind and conduct make me particularly interested in the use of mediation and other alternative dispute resolution methods. In all my activities, I have tended to seek out common ground, and to institute procedures that anticipate and defuse potential conflict.

My breadth of experience in the workplace and in my community would, I believe, allow me to contribute positively to the diversity of the Harvard Law School student body. I am confident that I have the energy, intellectual ability, and maturity to meet the challenges of a legal education and a professional career.

P e r s o n a l   S t a t e m e n t

R. Jordan Hall

My infancy played out before the backdrop of the two major events of the 1970s: Vietnam and Watergate. Shortly after my birth, my father was shipped off to Thailand to help bomb the Vietnamese. As soon as I was out of the hospital, my mother and I followed him. Vietnam, the locus of the struggle between the ideal and the real in America, had my toddling self right at the center of it. If I had missed the heat of the fighting, I was the offspring right in time for the national soul-searching after the conflict. As a child I was, of course, not embroiled in the problems of the war. But I could not hope to avoid its effects: the cynicism, the loss of hope.

Watergate, another grand reflection of the era, was further fuel for the cynicism of the '70s. The scandal can also be taken as the beginning of the advanced manipulatory culture. Everything became a great commercial, exercises in persuasion advanced by catchy tunes and colorful, beautiful salespeople. Presidents and cartoons were hard to distinguish: both seemed hard to believe and a little bit irrelevant. My impressions of the heads of state were limited to chance glitz and sketchy conversation between adults, the gist of which was that the government was filled with incompetents whose only predilections were lying or stealing, or on occasion, both.

Cartoons were the real life of the children of the '70s. Saturday mornings were religious holidays, rituals that animated the age of manipulation. No single cartoon could go for as much as ten minutes without breaking for commercials filled with vast promise and desire. My world was constructed by vague, empty promises from every corner. A child of the '70s grew up with the knowledge that you couldn't trust the commercials on TV, just like you couldn't trust the leaders of the nation. Is it so hard to understand then why we find it difficult to believe in anything at all? They call us the thirteeners, generation X, the generation of apathy.

Strangely, this apathy might very well be our greatest strength. It is more than a simple disgruntlement with our vanishing opportunities; a reflection of our defeated hopes of getting a fair share. It is instead a sign of a great discontent, a disdain for the goals, not merely the methods, of our parents. The metaphors of yester-year simply have no power over us. If we do not choose to define ourselves, it is because we are wary of the transient definitions that dotted our childhood. If we show little motivation towards our education, it is because we realize that we are not being taught, but told. We are a generation that had been suckled on illusion: we can see only too clearly through the truths of our forefathers. We might be the first generation to "get" Dostoyevsky as a generation. He echoes *our* hearts. Perhaps one would be hard-pressed to characterize this wasteland as a positive, but I think it is; or, rather, it can be.

Things aren't working. "This generation is the first in American history that will do worse than its parents." That factoid must elicit a characteristically derisive laugh. I don't need statistics, economics or CNN to know *that*. Look around, when I see the world around me, I know that things simply aren't working out. Moreover, I recognize that the hypocrisy and deceit that was the foundation of my childhood is a symptom of a much larger disease: self-deception. A denial of the death of our American vitality. America, and perhaps the rest of the world with us, must face this deception and reinvent itself.

My education has culminated in this dawning realization. I have been the beneficiary of numerous 'advanced' or 'gifted' programs, one of which was the Talent Identification Program at Duke University. It was at TIP that I first discovered philosophy and the awakening recognition that there might be something behind the tremendous yawning apathy that I had owned all my life. I chose philosophy as an undergraduate major. Now I come to the end of my undergraduate career and I find myself moving from simple efforts to undo cynicism, to understanding it and coming to guess at its power. My generation stands at a terrifying, but perhaps exhilarating, point in history: our utter loss of faith in the old gods might lead us to discover a new tablet of values for America *or* it might complete its task of denial and devastation and turn our cleared cropland into desert.

It is my task to bring about the former. My generation's apathy is the recognition of the bankruptcy of the old ideas. Whereas the generations before us have labored to resurrect dusty dreams, we tire of the ancient game. We are perceived as apathetic because we do not struggle to recast the world in our own image. Perhaps because we recognize such a struggle is pernicious and doomed from the start. We know too well the effects of such a struggle—we were born into them. This does not mean, however, that we have resigned ourselves to deadening and helpless passivity, but that the dialectical relationship between man (and I do mean "Man") and nature that has dominated the American mind simply does not appeal to us. The question that we now face is this: do we endeavor to create for ourselves a new dialectic, or shall we search for a language that might allow us to escape from the spirit of dialectic itself.

Personal Statement

Name Withheld

Imagine growing up without language. Imagine yourself without this basic human right, without an essential part of what makes us human. Imagine being excommunicated from words and from the world. How would you find your voice?

I imagine that such an experience would be terrifying. But the tragedy of the above scenario is that it is not imaginary. Too often, it is the legacy of deaf American children and it is one of the concerns which led me to seek a career in legal public service.

As a linguist at the University of Texas, I studied American Sign Language (ASL) and was introduced to Deaf culture. The language and history I learned were colorful but painful at times: too many case histories of deaf children denied education; too many children growing up illiterate—or without any real language at all; too many efforts to make deaf children "normal," whatever the cost.

I had hoped to become part of a solution to these problems by working at the Texas School for the Deaf. I applied, only to be told that the administrators were seeking someone who would use Signed English, not a language per se, but a rough and unwieldy hybrid of English words and ASL handshapes. Instead, during the interview, I alternated my use of ASL and English, explaining my belief that while both languages are valuable, their grammars are so divergent that to attempt both at once makes English awkward and ASL unintelligible. Rather than use a confusing code, I suggested, deaf children would be best served by use of ASL, a natural language they can easily understand.

"Thank you, —. We'll call you."

As I later discovered, the reason Signed English was preferred over ASL was so that the teachers and administrators, most of whom were hearing, could communicate without speech. Their justification for using English over ASL was the hope that their students would be able to assimilate into hearing culture and "pass." This method of instruction is in line with current professional theories about deaf education. Members of the Deaf community, however, view deafness entirely differently.

Deaf community? Some hearing people are surprised, as I was at first, to learn of its existence. Imagine deafness as a source of connection! Imagine growing up with a beautiful language, visual literature, humor, and theater. Imagine taking pride in your identity without any desire to become a member of the majority culture. For many deaf people, their community is a comforting relief from the isolation and condescension of the hearing world. Inside this community, deaf people become *Deaf*, proudly capitalizing their culture. Hearing people suddenly find that they are handicapped: "deaf-impaired."

As a hearing person, I do not aim to become a member of the Deaf community. I do, however, have several obligations as an ally. The first is to treat deaf people as human beings, not freaks. Currently, deafness is considered an illness by many hearing doctors, audiologists, and teachers who work passionately to make deaf children speak; to make these children "un-deaf." They try hearing aids, lip-reading, speech coaches, and cochlear implants. In the meantime, many deaf children grow out of the crucial language acquisition phase. They become disabled by people who are anxious to make them "normal." Their lack of language, not of hearing, becomes their most severe handicap.

While I support any method that works to give a child a richer life, I think a system which focuses on *abilities* rather than deficiencies is far more valuable. Deaf people have taught me that a lack of hearing need not be disabling; in fact, it need not be considered a "lack" at all. My second obligation, therefore, is to follow the suggestions of deaf adults and work for both the use of ASL and a positive portrayal of Deaf culture in the classroom.

Finally, I believe my place is behind the scenes, in the courthouse or the statehouse. Deaf people themselves are the appropriate leaders of their own liberation movement, as shown by the actions of Gallaudet students in 1988. My legal service commitment is not to give a voice to an oppressed population—it is to make sure that the voice already present is heard.

Personal Statement

Name Withheld

By the time I entered college, I had mastered the language of three communities: the Paraguayan Spanish spoken by my mother at home; the profanity-laden slang of our poor, all-Black Washington, D.C., neighborhood; and the textbook English enforced in the private schools which I attended with children from neighborhoods far wealthier than my own. These three communities—my home, neighborhood, and school—taught me lessons as diverse as the physical environments in which I learned them.

At home, I saw that the hard work of my parents could do little to overcome the barriers imposed by my immigrant mother's ignorance of the English language and my father's lack of education. Outside our home, the Spanish language was a barrier that relegated my intelligent mother to a lifetime of domestic work. I regularly helped my mother clean houses after school, often resenting the loss of those hours which, for many students, were carefree ones. Several of the houses which I helped my mother clean belonged to the families of classmates. Scrubbing the bathroom of a teenager with whom you share homeroom is a humbling experience.

The neighborhood which we left shortly before I entered college was a lesson in the problems of the urban poor. It teemed with both children and petty drug dealers. Nevertheless, we were not *truly* poor, as my father, who is Black, had been. He often described the poverty that forced him to begin working in a factory at the age of eleven. Many of his brothers and sisters never overcame their impoverished beginnings—today, several of my aunts and cousins are on welfare.

In school I studied the gaps that existed between my family's modest life and the lives of my wealthier classmates. I realized that, while I may have been economically inferior to them, I was by no means the intellectual inferior of my classmates. I learned that only through education could I and others like me achieve the economic and social equality that had eluded our parents.

I entered college acutely conscious of the separate worlds of the wealthy and the poor. The disparity between the two pained me and drove me to committed action. I got involved with a program in which law students and undergraduates worked together to find homeless people in New Haven permanent apartments. I soon was spending at least as much time apartment-hunting and accompanying clients to interviews with landlords as I did on my own studies. I felt more responsibility toward the people we were trying to help than I did toward my own academic success. At the time, the immediate problem of getting someone off the streets outweighed in importance that night's reading assignment. After only limited success, however (the task of finding fellow undergraduates willing to take on a job that was not fun and infrequently rewarding was almost as daunting as finding indigent men and women places to live), the group eventually disbanded.

While I subsequently reduced the numbers of hours I spent volunteering (working only weekly in a New Haven homeless shelter), my responsibilities in other areas increased. Among other activities, I was a varsity hurdler during the winter and spring track seasons, co-edited a science magazine, and became a freshperson counselor. While I value those experiences, I regret that my energy was constantly focused outward. I now intend to keep the remaining years of my formal education free of major non-academic responsibilities.

Activism, however, is still a part of my life today. I helped to found and am now president of the Alumni Association of the Black Student Fund. The BSF largely funded my high school education, making it possible for me to attend Sidwell Friends. If it had not been for the BSF, I and many others would not have enjoyed the intellectual opportunities that we did. To say that I feel a need to repay this debt is a gross understatement. Through the Alumni Association, I have organized a mentoring program and am a mentor and tutor to other Black students.

Whatever professional path I take, I intend to work so that others are given the same opportunities that were given to me. However, I must first focus on reaching my goals. I can only be fully effective in helping others to achieve their potentials when I have reached mine.

Personal Statement

Matthew T. Henshon

Like most Americans, I was riveted to the television by the testimony of Anita Hill and Clarence Thomas before the Senate Judiciary Committee. And like many Americans, I could empathize with Professor Hill's conflict. Until forced into the public eye, Professor Hill had decided that the cost of bringing sexual harassment charges was too high, as measured in the loss of privacy, public embarrassment, and the closing of career options.

Professor Hill recognized the consequences of her unfortunate set of choices—silence meant internalizing the damage done to her, while speaking out was, in effect, professional suicide. Like Professor Hill and others, I have faced, at times, difficult choices; like Professor Hill in the past week, I am confident that in times of crisis, I can put higher principle ahead of self-interest. While the weighing of choice and consequence is part of maturity, I know that I have consistently made these choices throughout my life.

An early choice I remember making was relatively simple. A lifetime (and long-suffering!) Red Sox fan, I had the good fortune of being invited to Hall-of-Famer Carl Yastrzemski's final game at Fenway—a once-in-a-lifetime experience. However, earlier that year I had been elected an officer in a music club (I played classical piano throughout my childhood). Although I could have missed the October meeting, I had given my word that I would be there if at all possible, and so I turned down the invitation to the game and watched the highlights on television.

While that choice was straight-forward, other choices have been less so. As a columnist for the *Princeton Alumni Weekly*, I had freedom to select subjects that I felt would interest my readers.

When I wrote articles about the real effects of Princeton's budget-cutting to alleviate a deficit, or the efforts of a tiny minority to increase the rights and visibility of homosexuals on campus, no one told me to do so; nor did those columns endear me to the administration or to Princeton's primarily conservative student body. Yet I felt those subjects were newsworthy and interesting, no matter what the potential backlash.

Sometimes a choice involves weighing the risk of consequences. One of the defining activities of my life to date has been basketball. Since the night in 1979 that I watched Magic Johnson beat Larry Bird in the finals, my highest goal was to play in an NCAA tournament game. That goal inspired as I sought to overcome my lack of quickness, a shattered arm-bone, and the problems of adjusting to a new position in college. When I chose Princeton, I did so with the goal of becoming an important player (as opposed to just a guy at the end of the bench) of a good team that could go to the NCAAs. Yet I have always recognized the need to balance my love for the game with the rest of my interests.

Basketball at Princeton is the will and whim of Coach Pete Carril. He has absolute authority in the gym and recruits ten or more players per year to insure competition for each of the five positions. While it is important to stay in Carril's good graces (especially if one wants meaningful playing time), I knew that basketball was just a part of my total education.

When I took electives in the Wilson School that made me late for practice, I risked my basketball career by risking Carril's unprovable, but nonetheless real, wrath. When I spent the summer of 1989 in Mexico, teaching English, I risked my career again; Carril had wanted me to play in the best summer leagues and spend hours in the weightroom—and these were not available in rural Mexico. But that summer taught me about friendship, and a different culture, and the fear of living in poverty—such as the night that I was woken by a scorpion's sting, knowing that the nearest medical clinic was an hour away. (Fortunately my 6'5" size dispersed the poison and prevented dire consequences.) And I used the experiences and contacts that I had made when I returned to do background research for Professor Volcker's conference on U.S.–Mexican economic relations the following year.

Even recently I have been making choices. I was offered two jobs in Washington, D.C., last spring. If had taken a (relatively) high-paying position at Health and Human Services, I would be drafting position-papers that would help the Administration to stonewall on health care reform until after the 1992 elections. But I am instead working for Independent Sector—a coalition of 850 nonprofits and foundations like American Red Cross and the Ford Foundation—to protect and strengthen the charitable sector. My most interesting assignment here has been to help formulate I.S.'s response to the Supreme Court's *Rust v. Sullivan* ruling, commonly referred to as the abortion gag rule, that in effect gives the state power to muzzle those nonprofits that accept grant money. Another project has been to develop a strategy to encourage the use of the Peace Dividend to replenish the neglected social services.

Throughout my life, I have put principle above self-interest. At this time however, I realize that in order to continue this pattern, I need to be as well-prepared as those on the other side of the aisle; in that pursuit, I want to study law at Harvard.

Part of standing for principle, however, is risking failure, as I did in my final college game. In March, we played Villanova in the Syracuse-Carrier Dome in the NCAA tournament, and I played well. But with 0.7 seconds left, we trailed by two points, with the ball 94 feet from our goal; barring a miracle, our season was over.

We called timeout, and confusion reigned. I tried to block out the noise of 25,000 screaming fans and think of a plan. If I could get fouled, I reasoned, I would have a much better chance of making two free-throws, despite the overwhelming pressure, than anybody would of making a heave-shot from half-court. I thought about all the games I had seen before, and diagrammed in the huddle a way to draw a charging foul on a Villanova player.

The timeout ended. We returned to the floor, aligned ourselves, and started the play. I stepped in front of the defender, we collided, and I fell to the floor. I looked to the referee, and he caught my eye. And then looked away. There would be no foul called against a Big East team in a Big East gym. There would be no chance for me to make two free-throws to force overtime.

Our season ended a few seconds later with a half-court shot, but as I lay on the floor, I thought of what might have happened: if I had made the foul shots, they would be long forgotten in excitement of the overtime; but if I missed, I would have had to face my teammates as the goat. I swallowed and wished he had blown the whistle.

Personal Statement

Name Withheld

Two years ago, I read an article in the *Houston Post* about a San Francisco city planner and gay activist who had been an advisor and friend to Harvey Milk. In an interview, the man said that no matter how far he had travelled from Texas, he was still being affected, if not haunted, by the memory of his hometown. "I'm as much a product of Port Arthur as Robert Rauschenberg, Jimmy Johnson, or Janis Joplin," he said. "It made me what I am, though I am not sure it knows how to deal with me yet."

I remember his quote because I am also a product of the oil producing industrial coastal town in Southeast Texas. I grew up in Port Arthur, where the stench of emitted chemicals and the "Port Arthur—We Oil the World" signs greet one as one enters the city. It is the place that *Newsweek* once described as a blue-collar, self-righteous, beer-drinking town with a church on every other corner, and bars on all the rest. Even though I always knew I would leave the area, I know that my decisions and choices at Yale have always been guided by my background.

Located across Sabine Lake from Louisiana, Port Arthur serves as the westernmost boundary of Cajun territory. Despite the city's racist reputation, African Americans make up a third of the population. In the past twenty years, Vietnamese immigrants have flocked to the city, attracted by its proximity to the Gulf of Mexico and the shrimping industry. The growing Hispanic population is divided into two segments, an English-speaking Mexican-American populace whose relatives settled in the area in the late twenties and early thirties, and a younger group of Central Americans and Mexicans who came looking for employment and opportunities in the last ten years. Despite this array of ethnicities, Port Arthur is not a "diverse" place. For the most part, racial and ethnic lines are distinctly drawn; only the white Cajuns and some of the more established Mexican Americans have moved from the realm of bad "ethnics" to that of good "ethnics."

I am a fourth generation Mexican American with Cajun ancestry. My Mexican ancestors came to the area from other parts of Texas in search of jobs in the oil industry early in the twentieth century. My mother's generation grew up speaking only English and were expected to intermix with the "white" populations. Port Arthur's ethnic mosaic and my own Mexican-Cajun heritage motivated my decision to major in American studies. I have concentrated a great deal of my work on ethnic studies because I am aware of the importance of maintaining one's ethnic heritage. While I know mostly my Mexican heritage, I belong to two distinct American enclaves with rich histories. By majoring in American studies, I could explore these cultures through academics.

While my studies have been important to me, my grades have not been my only priority. There are not many people from Port Arthur who go to Ivy League schools.When I arrived in New Haven my first year, there were a lot of opportunities for me. So I took advantage of as many as I could; I joined the newspaper, did intramural sports, became involved with minority issues and participated in various other things. I wanted to prove that I could work, study, and become involved with activities as much as I wanted. After leaving Port Arthur, I wanted to show that not only could I survive in a more competitive and different environment, but I could excel.

Port Arthur no longer oils the world; perhaps it never did. People who had once graduated from high school and proceeded to high-paying jobs at the oil refineries are now encouraging their kids to go to college or to join the military. Many residents are not really sure what the city will have to offer in the future. Despite all the problems I see in Port Arthur, I know that I can never say I have succeeded in spite of where I have grown up. In many ways, I am very similar to the San Francisco city planner. I know that I am a product of my hometown and that the memories of the bayous, the refineries, and the racial tensions will always be with me.

Personal Statement

Scott Humphries

Growing up in Texas as an Australian immigrant has not been particularly difficult. After extensive summer tutoring corrected academic deficiencies stemming from a shoddy Australian school system, no language barriers or cultural gaps existed to harass me. However, even having long lost that peculiar accent, my foreign citizenship remains an oddity that often prompts new friends into lengthy, lackluster performances of Paul Hogan's best film lines. That substantial benefits are to be gained by dispelling "G'day mate!" stereotypes is a lesson that goes hand in hand with the *Crocodile Dundee* quotes. Financing all of my undergraduate expenses left me little spare time at the University of Texas, but during my junior year Rotary International's generous award enabled me to fully appreciate this lesson as I traveled throughout sixteen countries in Europe, North Africa, and Asia, speaking publicly in England, France, Holland, and Belgium. Having now seen both sides of the coin, I endeavor to follow a simple rule which I hope to find as applicable to the study of law as to my exploration of foreign cultures: take a long look at what it appears to be, then discover what it is.

Despite my undergraduate government major, philosophy is my academic passion. I understand that the mechanics of philosophical training, dissecting complex texts, for instance, are handy law school skills, and the work does seem not unlike the deciphering of some Supreme Court cases I've attempted. However, I find the content of the discipline engaging as well. Specializing in the application of logic, I recently completed a lengthy examination of William of Ockham's attempt to bring Aristotle back to Aristotelianism, and I am currently finishing a personal project, an attempt to reconcile Ayn Rand's Objectivism with the Aristotelian roots to which she clings so tightly.

Philosophy is not something I abandon upon leaving the classroom, either. Political philosophy first drew me toward privatization law, and Akin Gump's extensive practice in that field enabled me to examine the particulars of a subject in which I am now keenly interested. Likewise, debating for the University of Kent and judging numerous high school debates while at the University of Texas necessitated the production and evaluation of formal arguments that one could diagram symbolically in the syllogistic form if called upon to do so. Finally, while working for the Texas legislature, it was logic's rational approach which led me to the inescapable conclusion that precious little rational activity occurs on the floor of the Texas House. Seriously, though, I do value the application as well as the study of philosophy.

Friends tell me that I only want a law degree in order to bring capitalism to the masses. While I agree with them that I find privatization law appealing now, it would be naive to presume that three years of school might not change my mind in some manner. An alternative aspiration is the union of law and philosophy, perhaps in an academic arena. The possibilities are endless. Regardless of the application to which I lend my legal education, the knowledge inherent in the title juris doctor, as Socrates said, is good in and of itself.

Personal Statement

Name Withheld

A Chinese friend of mine recently told me that he thought the Chinese, who are fiercely individual, are much closer in thinking to the Americans than our common hosts, the Japanese. When I asked him how, then, he felt we are different, his reply was quick and fairly simple: Americans, he said, seem to have an ingrained faith in the system of laws that upholds their society. Neither the Japanese nor the Chinese share that faith in the law, he told me. His remark, defining the differences in our societies by our different attitudes and uses for the law, however generalized, started me thinking once again about the essential, reciprocal relationship between a society and its laws.

My friend's remark inadvertently underscored the most important theme of my Japan experience: the process that redirected my interest in law as an approach to understanding society and in turn shaping it. During college, I thought I wanted to be a lawyer, but after two and a half years as a legal assistant in a Miami law firm, I became discouraged; so many of the attorneys I met seemed personally lost and professionally unsatisfied. A six-month stay as an exchange student and several years of Japanese in college had fostered my long-standing and, at times, inexplicable fascination with the language and culture of this—in my ignorant view—mysterious people. Having won a Rotary Scholarship, I decided to spend two years pursuing these interests while I reconsidered my legal career.

After the first year of intensive language study and a growing respect for and understanding of Japanese society, I had to decide what to study as my research topic. Trusting my past interests, I returned to what had always fascinated me about law: studying society through its legal framework. Specifically, I chose to study a uniquely Japanese bureaucratic enforcement technique known as "administrative guidance"—unique because of its reliance (like so much else in Japanese society) on mutual understanding between regulators and offenders, reluctance to commit anything to paper, and a tendency to avoid outright conflict in the form of formal administrative orders. The direct correspondence between social values and the legal system astounds me, but nowhere near as much as the growing rift between the rapidly changing society—evidenced by the election of the new Hosokawa government and the push for political reform—and the entrenched legal and bureaucratic system.

My goal in returning to the United States and entering law school now is to acquire a solid understanding of our legal system and a fundamental understanding of the law. Ultimately, of course, my desire is to explore my even greater interest in our own society and, as my Chinese friend noted, its faith in the legal framework that supports it.

I hesitate to commit myself to a particular career path until I have had an opportunity to explore some of the possibilities at law school, but I believe in no less than creating a role for myself in those areas that continue to fascinate me. Two years of lectures from my Japanese hosts on the sanctity of the Japanese rice market, observing the GATT negotiations, and enduring the outrageous cost of living here have interested me in the volatile trade relationship between our two countries, and I can imagine myself in government or trade negotiation. A broad legal education from Harvard Law School will provide the basis for the role I eventually undertake.

Personal Statement
Name Withheld

As I cross the bridge that takes me from Virginia to work in Washington every morning, I look for inspiration out of the left-hand side

of the train. This is no superstitious ritual, but instead a glance—
sometimes a pensive stare—at the monument to perhaps the most
learned figure in American history, Thomas Jefferson. Many experiences and desires have led me to pursue a legal education. But
what undergirds them all is the search for what I see every morning in the Jefferson Memorial—the rarely executed combination of
study and practical action that I can only hope to approach.

A few of my experiences—most notably those in the recent
presidential campaign and graduate study of political thought and
constitutional law—represent my attempt to combine the pursuit of
academic knowledge with practical action particulary well. They
reflect the same principle that prompts my daily look to Jefferson,
the core conviction that each individual has a personal responsibility to better himself or herself in service to others. I have felt this
duty for as long as I can remember, and believe that law school will
help me fulfill it by deepening my exploration of the law and its
relation to the philosophical concepts that have guided American
politics from its inception.

Working for the Clinton/Gore campaign and the new Administration illustrates the more practical side of my obligation to better myself. Though I find the solely academic life attractive, I have
not been content only to consider the problems America and the
world face from afar; I need to participate in the concerted action
leading to the political triumph of socially beneficial ideas. As the
1991 academic year progressed, I became more involved in the
Clinton campaign—helping to set up the campus organization at
Yale, passing out literature in the icy cold of New Hampshire and
Connecticut, and eventually taking a full-time policy position with
the campaign. Since the election, I have served on the presidential
transition, at the White House Domestic Policy Council, and at the
Department of Education.

Over this period, I have sharpened my interest in building the
political and legal structures needed to make government work
again. I have learned with excitement throughout because the goals
of the Clinton campaign and Administration accord well with some
of my longest-held beliefs: that America has an abiding obligation
to build equal opportunity for all, and that all have an obligation to

America, and that politics should be a positive, constantly innovative enterprise that does not descend into demagogy or rely on simple solutions from the left or the right. I have relished the ability to contribute to the political process. Now I look to reflect on what I have learned from politics in practice by again pursuing my academic interests.

My graduate studies reflect the academic effort I have already made at self-improvement. Because understanding one's social environment plays a major role in serving effectively, and because of my continuing fascination with the ideas that have shaped America and the world, I was drawn to a graduate program focused on political thought. Throughout my academic career, I have kept an eye on how the subjects I have studied affect the ideas the American founders and their forebears articulated, and that so many in today's world are trying to interpret for their own circumstances. My work in graduate school enhanced my ability to contribute to resolutions of controversies in American political thought and constitutional law that have brewed from the early days of the Republic, such as the place of the judiciary in the political order, the integration of traditionally excluded groups into our society, and the proper role for religion in politics.

The nexus between my academic and political interests lies most clearly in my dedication to bringing political and legal philosophy to bear on practical questions. Two of the issues I would like to focus on in law school exemplify this particularly well: constitutionalism and the transformation to democracy in Eastern Europe, and the political philosophy of the American legal system. These are topics that, when examined carefully, take highly theoretical issues about the nature and meaning of law and politics and make them relevant to everyday issues in peoples' lives. Practical interests such as these reflect the broader version of my personal dedication to self-improvement in service to others. We all must constantly be examining the social and political systems of America and the world, in and out of the political arena. Where there needs to be change, each person should articulate his or her vision so that we all may be enriched, and can get on with the process of improving society. My academic time has been and will be dedicated to building a personal vision and understanding, one which I plan to continue both constructing and presenting to the political and legal communities all my life.

The major experiences I have had each prepare me for a life in political and legal philosophy at their best—building shared visions of community. Though I do not know whether my involvement will be primarily academic or as a more deeply involved participant in political debates, I feel that I am now ready to take a significant role in this overall enterprise that blends deep study with practical action. I do know that the learning I need to do is still great, and that I will never be done learning; it is that understanding that prompts my daily look to Thomas Jefferson, and my desire to bolster my skills with a formal legal education. A formal legal education would be another step in my search for the ideal that Jefferson reminds me of every morning on the way to work.

P e r s o n a l S t a t e m e n t
Name Withheld

For a long time, I have been interested in pursuing a career in international relations. My parents tell me that I was probably bitten by the "international bug" when I was a child. We moved to France when I was three months old and lived there for four years. After I had learned English, my Haitian-born mother taught me French and I attended school with French children.

We moved back to the States after a one-year stay in New Brunswick, Canada. In choosing what school I would attend, my parents wanted to make sure that I did not forget my second language and that I continue to be exposed to both the American and foreign culture. They enrolled me in the Lycée Français de New York, a French school for francophone children.

In my first years at the Lycée, I did not realize the impact that the school had on me. Children are required to attend school and I thought that one institution was as good as the next. Not until I reached high school did I come to understand that I was getting more than an education at the school. I had been exposed to the customs and ways of life of Europeans, Africans, Latin Americans,

326 HOW TO GET INTO HARVARD LAW SCHOOL

such agencies and chosen for their credentials and not their social connections, we would see more results from the UN. It is for this reason that I am applying to Law School. I want to pursue an education in international and comparative law in order to put my interest in international relations to work toward a greater role for these organizations in the international system.

Personal Statement

Just over a year ago, I requested applications from several law schools. At the time a senior at Princeton, I used my personal statement to reflect on transitions I had made over the course of an undergraduate education. I wrote about serving as a resident adviser, helping to make freshmen feel more comfortable in an academic community. But perhaps even more significantly, I wrote about how I had matured in academic settings. At Princeton, and more specifically in the Woodrow Wilson School, I learned how to synthesize complex material, assimilate information quickly, and think critically in order to reconcile conflicting viewpoints on a broad range of policy and legal issues. In the twelve months since that personal statement, I have continued to develop and implement these analytical skills.

At school, I completed my thesis and my undergraduate focus on domestic education policy. More than an academic rite of passage, my thesis was an opportunity to combine both theory and practice by examining a management reform pilot project in the Dade County Public Schools. In addition, during my senior year I served outside the classroom as a student member of the Discipline Committee. A role that is part judge, part advocate, and part counselor, this position required a steadfast commitment to academic integrity as well as a compassionate heart. While my senior year marked the culmination of my Princeton experience, the year also provided numerous opportunities for personal and intellectual growth.

Since graduation, I have been fortunate enough to get two

and Asians. This realization is what led me to want to pursue a career in a field where I would keep meeting and interacting with people from different backgrounds.

One of the main factors that I considered in choosing colleges was whether the school allowed study abroad. I wanted the chance to live in a foreign country for an extended period of time at an age at which I would be able to appreciate it more. I chose Amherst College and spent my junior year abroad in Madrid, Spain. I think that I got more out of studying abroad than most people. I of course got to travel, meet new people, and experience new things. But because I knew that I eventually want to work abroad or at least deal in foreign affairs, I was anxious to see not only how I interacted with foreigners, but also how I exchanged ideas and presented my point of view of various subjects.

To get a better idea of what work in the international arena entails, I interned this past summer at the Human Rights Center of the United Nations at Geneva. In my first few days there, I was filled with a sense of awe. I found myself "inside" the place to which so many important heads of state had come, where the leaders of the Serb, Muslim, and Croat people were negotiating peace treaties, where decisions that affected the world at large were taken. After a couple of weeks at the UN however, my impression changed. I came to see the inefficiency of the organization, the bureaucracy that surrounded simple procedures, and the employees' numerous coffee breaks. In some of the meetings on different topics of international concern, I felt that the speakers spent more time dispensing with formalities than really addressing the issues. I was disappointed to see that the UN, this organization that to me epitomized international relations, was to a certain extent a "debating club on the East River," the expression often used to criticize the New York branch. It seemed to me that in this aftermath of the Cold War when the UN is enjoying rebirth, more positive activity should be coming from the organization.

I still want to work in such an international organization. It is not that I naively think that one person can change the whole system. I do, however, think that if more people who are really committed to the idea of international organization were employed in internships—one in business and one in government—that have related to my undergraduate field of study. Over the summer, I returned to Monsanto to undertake an assessment of state educational programs and policies in Missouri. Designed to help build a consensus for educational improvement, the report will enable Business Roundtable companies and other stakeholders to measure their progress in achieving educational reform. At the same time, the report also offered tremendous insights into the state lobbying and policy-making process.

Similarly, my internship at the White House this fall has provided valuable insights from a government perspective. Nearly every day, I am applying the skills I learned in school to ongoing political debates. Working on the President's domestic policy staff has shown me the role of critical analysis and political compromise in improving the way a government serves its constituents. In many ways, the internship has bridged the gap between hypothetical academic ideas and the actual making of public policy.

Certainly, public policy has been a consistent theme of my experiences in the past year. However, I have also become increasingly aware of the interrelatedness of public policy and law. For example, one issue my department at the White House recently addressed—how to justly provide adequate health and pension benefits for union employees of now-bankrupt coal companies—required a familiarity in both bankruptcy and labor law. Over the course of my work in education policy, the constitutional relationship between federal, state, and local governments has often been directly at issue. While my experience is certainly limited, I am hopeful that my experience and skills in public policy can also be applied to the study and practice of law. Indeed, throughout all of my experiences, I have repeatedly found legal and policy issues to be both challenging and intellectually stimulating. Hopefully, formal legal training will allow me to continue to build on these experiences.

A year after I first applied to law schools, I am still unsure about my long-term career plans. Nevertheless, an additional year of experience in academia, business, and government has made me even more certain about pursuing a legal education.

Personal Statement

Sam Liccardo

A smutty, worn sneaker lands upon the first of nine wooden steps leading to the old church's attic. Like so many shoes that attempt this ascent, its soiled appearance tells of its repeated spanning of the dirt-strewn floors in the local state prison. The creaking of that first stair does not deter the shoe's owner from venturing farther, nor does the increasing whining of each of the subsequent planks of the aged redwood.

At that same instant, exactly two thousand four hundred and fifty-three miles east of those rickety stairs, eleven lobbyists with feet clad in Italian black leather hastily scale the marble steps separating an imposing edifice from a four-lane thoroughfare. The stairs' appearance boasts of their recent washing.

Simultaneously, the bare feet of a thin, pigtailed child manage the three steps reaching the cramped classroom of her local elementary school. Beneath the planks of these wobbly stairs, a chicken feeds on the edible remains of the previous day's trash. Though tardy, the student slows her advance upon hearing her teacher's voice within the chamber. She hesitates, peeks nervously inside, and scuttles toward her seat.

Each of these stairways stands as a monument to the power of human hope. The first lies behind a Catholic church in San Jose, California, where volunteers operate an employment program for people who have recently emerged from penitentiaries and substance-abuse clinics. Rarely have I witnessed the hope that I saw while working with these individuals, many of whom had seemingly little reason for such optimism. The second series of steps lead up to the Rayburn Building and the offices of members of the United States House of Representatives. My two-semester internship there granted me the view of a different thread of hope, one woven among strands of pragmatism and legalism that often conceal the existence of such hope from any discernible notice. Nonetheless, those marble stairs still provide, for the truly determined, the access necessary for constructing more equitable public policy. Finally, recollection of the child's ascent emerges from my experience as a volunteer teacher in Dangriga, Belize. The ambitions of the children there remained confined to that undeveloped seashore community, yet their enthusiasm for learning burned radiantly amidst the surrounding darkness of poverty, malnutrition, and disease.

The prospect of even marginally improving the lives of others has allowed me to discover a greater enjoyment and fulfillment in each of these activities. Whether by finding employment for a recovering alcoholic, by researching issues in defense, health, or foreign affairs for a Congressional staff, or by helping a Belizian child find skills and self-esteem in the classroom, hope serves as the impetus of my endeavors.

Hope bares itself in my current employment as well. My work for a plaintiff's attorney at a San Jose firm has given me newfound respect for the legal profession. Despite the often justified criticism expressed by the media and public regarding this nation's judicial system, I have found that when the law is used with competence and a hopeful spirit, the courtroom stands as society's last bastion of justice. I feel that my investigatory and legal research in cases involving issues of negligence, product liability, and fraud has made me a participant of this struggle toward a more just society.

As an attorney, obviously, I can better serve those who struggle against unjust circumstance. I apply to Harvard because I aspire to make my sense of hope contagious, thereby empowering others to improve their own lives. With Harvard's assistance, I can make this aspiration a reality.

Personal Statement

Erik Lindseth

In 1978, my parents resigned long-standing professional careers to undertake a manual arts project in the Tanzanian public schools. At nine, I saw such foreign service as a dramatic commitment to everyday principles: A Lutheran Sunday school appeal to "do unto others," a parental plea to "be kind and fair," a teacher's request to "share." I saw my parents—though sensing a divine "call to serve"— reject what I'd now call enlightenment Prospero-style in favor of attempts to negotiate social energies—African-determined needs and American-derived training—into just, visible change in villages outside Moshi. To a third grader, it looked easy. I soon learned it was not.

During rhetorical criticism in college, I put together a Neo-Aristotelian analysis of Martin Luther King's 1967 address "A Time to Break Silence." From the pulpit in New York's Riverside Church, he had argued that "every man of humane convictions must decide on the protest that best suits his convictions, but we all must protest" especially, in this case, for "peace in Vietnam and justice throughout the developing world." I thought of my parents in Africa. Had they, as King apparently encouraged, turned inward to their "conviction" for an understanding of "justice" and, thus, a suitable "protest" in Tanzania? I had hoped not, for such action avoided negotiating the nature of "justice" and "protest" with those to whom injustice was committed and for whom protest should work.

Yet, even King seemed to rely on his own conviction when choosing a protest. Still, offering, as he recalled, "the sentiments of my own heart"—that civil rights and Vietnam "are inextricably bound together"—provoked abuse from all sides: *"Persona non grata* to Lyndon Johnson," he hampered negotiation and, in turn, legislative advancements for American blacks and for those in war-torn Vietnam; a "lost ally" to the civil rights movement, he came close to "betraying the cause"—almost one in two blacks polled after the address disagreed with his means and message. I was troubled by this effect. Heeding his own advice, King had chosen a protest "suitable" to his conviction. But, it seemed, the only "peace" and "justice" he achieved were internal: "I was politically unwise," he later admitted, "but morally wise." It seemed like a cop-out: Wouldn't broader social negotiations—what I saw as the crux of "politics," yet a frequent complaint of "morality"—have without ignoring his "moral wisdom" brought more justice and peace to the "movements" and their actors? I sought clarity in King, but found complexity: in my own service, how could I reconcile the knotty relationship between politics and morality, between negotiable factors and necessary principles?

Reading for American Public Address, Frederick Douglass's 1850 "Lecture on American Slavery, No. 1" confirmed that such reconciliation would not likely be neat. In 1839, William Lloyd Garrison had recruited Douglass to recount with the Massachusetts

Antislavery Society his experience in and escape from bondage. Troubled by the confines of mere description, though, Douglass in his 1850 lecture sought to express the slaves' larger, more prescriptive social interests, but still clung as well to Garrisonian concerns: his call for militant resistance to oppression, for example, was mollified by stressing non-violent action to "awaken conscience"; his support for Machiavellian political pressure as an abolitionist tactic was soothed by highlighting the value of "moral suasion." Here, I thought, was masterful social negotiation: Douglass managed, as a biographer noted, "to express convictions plausible to most blacks yet consistent with Garrison." Had he both turned inward, like King, to his own "sentiments" and turned outward to the "convictions" of those social actors—mostly abolitionists and slaves—whom he presumed to serve with his lecture? Such a move made sense, I thought, because it seemed to recognize—perhaps as my parents did—a symbiotic relationship between the server and the served. Still, it seemed problematic: Wouldn't the *nature* of the social convictions impact on negotiation? Douglass, I learned, was "at war with himself" as he underwent a split with the Garrisonians in 1850: was his would-be skillfully-negotiated lecture, then, only a fluke, a necessary by-product of a set of moral codes and political processes so in flux as to allow such diverse expression within one speech? Though rightfully, I thought, an advocate for hearing the convictions of those for whom one protests, Douglass made the issue even more uncertain. In my negotiating efforts in campus politics, in government and, soon, in law, what would happen when the nature or substance of the social actors' requests—using certain political processes, say, to pursue particular ends—clashed with my well-established moral sensibilities?

I found out, not first but most dramatically, last summer at the Department of Health and Human Services in Washington, D.C. I was working as a Truman Scholar intern in HHS's then-named, but as-yet designed Administration for Children and Families (ACF). Veteran civil servants from the emerging agencies, Human Development Services and my "side of the house" the Family Support Administration (FSA), were drawing up a reorganization plan; upon its release, I was to contribute my conception of the "ideal" ACF Ethics Office, including Congressionally-mandated ethics training materials for some 300 employees. As I began preparing recommendations including—like King and Douglass—my own notions of federal government "ethics"—a term which has, I imagine, taken an odd turn after the Thomas-Hill "hearing"—and ideas from employees in-house and ethics "experts" in other agencies, I faced what I thought was a direct challenge to my moral compass, to my belief that "public service" involves real efforts to negotiate social convictions into a mandate for just changes or products. While negotiating the proposal, upper-level FSA ethics officials were concentrating more on their personal advancement—as manifested in their desire to keep it in-house and in their hands—than on designing an ACF Ethics Office which would best serve both merging agencies and, in turn, the public.

Evidence, I thought, was abundant: attempts to spurn the "other house's" case studies while crafting joint training materials, to keep editorial control in FSA, to deny extra-agency comment on the draft, to steer its passage to the Assistant Secretary. How much of this, I wondered, was conditioned by reorganization jitters, including position or building changes? Probably some; still, such political posturing promised greater focus—to the point of irregularity—on those who would control the information than on the nature of its content. Had we lost the "public" in "public policy?" I was in a difficult position from which to negotiate: intern with agitated moral convictions in a well-defined pecking order undergoing massive overhaul. Thus, it seemed, my only tool—the one I must use to navigate abused political processes which countered my understanding of public service—was authorship: did I capture through my own thinking and interviews the nature of the convictions of those social actors the Ethics Office must serve? And would the proposal, then, survive ethics officials struggling to make with it their own agency—and, in turn, career-minded mark? Here, the resolution, like that for other such conflicts, was uneasy: I left to study in London frustrated with agency politics, but fairly comfortable with my own service in such a context. My ethics supervisors, in our last meeting, begrudgingly noted that "that other house" had just lodged my proposal in a larger memo to the Assistant Secretary. "Erik," they then reminded me behind forced chuckles, "information is golden."

I am, of course, facing new social negotiations in Europe this semester. Like my attempts in the United States, these, too, are complex, filled with perhaps even greater contradictions given the continent's vast cultural distinctions. Yet, I write seriously about them here—especially in terms of the difficult relationship between moral principles and political processes—because they seem so central to my intellectual and practical interests: cultural studies, public policy, politics and the law, particularly public interest law. I don't have a guidebook to navigate these issues, but for me negotiating mandates for change, with all the conflict that necessarily implies, is an exciting, though somewhat daunting, prospect. It is certainly not easy, as I had thought in Tanzania. But I genuinely welcome the challenge.

P e r s o n a l S t a t e m e n t

David J. Markese

If accepted, I will bring to Harvard Law School a very rich and diverse background. I spent many of my formative years overseas, living in France, New Caledonia, Vanuatu, French Polynesia, and the Philippines. As an expatriate I developed a keen awareness of cultural diversity by actually being a part of different cultures. I also learned to speak, read, and write fluent French at an early age. During this time I attended French, British, and international schools, where I was consistently at the top of my class. During my time overseas, I had the privilege of visiting South Korea, the People's Republic of China, Malaysia, Fiji, Australia, the Netherlands, and many other Asian, European, and Pacific countries. And in the United States, I have lived in the South, the Midwest, the Southwest, and the Northwest. My travels have helped me learn to be adaptable to my surroundings, no matter how diverse.

While at Southern California College, I studied history and political science. With this blend, I specialized in the Kennedy era, writing papers and presenting speeches on the Kennedy assassination, the Bay of Pigs, the Cuban Missile Crisis, and the erection of the Berlin Wall. I plan to expand my personal study to include Martin Luther King, Jr., and Malcolm X as part of the Civil Rights movement of the 1960s, a topic with which I have been fascinated since junior high school.

As well as having a rigorous academic schedule, I was busy with extracurricular activities at SCC. As a member of the Constitutional Review Committee, I was able to take advantage of the unique opportunity to apply my study of political science in a practical effort, as I aided in the revision and rewording of the school constitution, including the bylaws. I was a charter member of the tae kwon do class, and participated in a regional tournament and did several demonstrations with other class-members. I currently hold a class-4 blue belt. I was also involved in the international students' club. This was an opportunity for those of us students with an international background to get together for activities and share our personal experiences. The group represented, among other countries, Japan, Nigeria, Australia, Germany, Zaire, Korea, the Philippines, Cyprus, and Italy.

Since I began my college career, I have gained a wide variety of work experience. My most interesting job was as a French translator. Working for a large television production, I monitored the dubbing of the program into French, and was even able to do many voiceovers myself for syndicated telecast in Francophone countries. In addition to this job, some of my most rewarding work was as a tutor at SCC. I worked in the Writing Center, assisting students with writing assignments, and tutoring English and U.S. Government.

Throughout my young adult life I have enjoyed working with the community. One rewarding experience was as a volunteer for Jumpstart. This was a Saturday School program for Los Angeles youth in predominantly Hispanic and Chinese neighborhoods. I also participated in Hands Across the Border 1992. This was an organization of several teams of volunteers that went into Mexico during spring break to work with people of all ages, including unschooled children, people with medical problems, students at a deaf school, and even members of a local street gang. And currently, I enjoy going to an American Indian school here in Oregon and talking with troubled teens from across the country. This is a great opportunity for me to learn of the unique problems faced by Native Americans in the United States.

In conclusion, I believe that my record indicates that I am very capable of successfully completing the J.D. program at your superior institution, and that I would bring a rich and well-rounded background to the study of law at Harvard.

Personal Statement

Robert A. McCarter

Introspectively, his eyes wander around the room focusing on dreams of childhood, memories of the past, and the significance of the present. These walls represent what has been, is, and might be; they are the history of a young man who has worked to get to the point that he has just reached and now realizes that his task is not yet completed.

He looks to his right and sees a box of baseball cards of men who were one day to be his teammates. He glances behind him to a poster of Michael Jordan and sees a basketball legend who would have been the second-best player in the history of the game if this twenty-year-old had played. Looking left, he rereads a newspaper article, which has long since turned brown from age, featuring himself after scoring the championship-winning goal as a junior in high school. Far above, he peers at Michelle Pfeiffer, who was once going to be (and still may be) his wife.

The other side of the room is filled not with childhood dreams, but current aspirations. On one wall rest posters of Jack and Bobby Kennedy, men who lost their lives fighting for that in which they believed. Next to them hangs Old Glory, still vivid despite her age, still inspirational despite past setbacks, and still symbolic of the American dream despite today's crime, poverty, and despair.

In the center of the room sits a desk, at which the young man sits in his Boston College T-shirt and hat. Above him is a personal letter from the President, which thanks Bob for his support; below that is a picture of the young man (or so he claims, since the picture is of the back of his head) shaking hands with the Vice President. Staring him in the eye as he ponders his past and his future is the man from Hope giving him confidence that he can reach his goals, overcome any challenge, and live the American dream.

Finally, he glances down at the Harvard application in front of him. As his eyes wander, his mind wonders how he can describe himself to the men and women of the admissions board. Then he realizes that these four walls paint him as the child he was, the student he is, and the person he hopes to be.

Personal Statement

Erin McPherson

One year ago, I set off with a backpack, an around-the-world ticket, and a friend who shared my desire to "see the world." Fortunately, I don't think either of us quite realized the magnitude of our undertaking. I left full of unbridled enthusiasm, with a supportive family and limited funds. And I returned ten months later, my money gone and a little worn out, but much wiser. I've decided to write about this trip because it has had a profound impact on my present attitudes and future goals. I had heard the adage that travel is one of life's greatest teachers; it proved itself true. The trip allowed me to role-play, to become an observer of life from a foreign perspective, and to depend on myself as I never previously had. Travelling solidified my career goals. My half-glorified, half-terrified visions of law school became more realistic ideas of what I could do with a career in the law.

I believe that my post-graduate indecision was a good thing, for it allowed me to explore my options, and to look for my own priorities as I looked at the world around me. The mystique of the traveller, from Odysseus to Jack Kerouac, has long fascinated me. What is it about the extensive voyager, or the footloose vagabond, that so captures the human imagination and spirit? I think in part it is a longing for no responsibility, few material possessions, and a continuous sense of adventure. I definitely had my share of these elements, but I was also tested in unexpected ways. I discovered that I could be strong when my travel partner was not, that I could travel alone, protect myself, handle tense situations, and stay motivated and determined. I brought more of my academic skills with me than I thought I would; self-reliance, responsibility, consistency, and unending curiosity—all of these qualities helped to make my experience successful. Yet I also saw many of my weaknesses surface on the road. I learned that I can procrastinate, stopping to smell the flowers for too long. I can also spread my attentions in all directions, trying to accomplish too many projects or activities at once. These are things that sometimes impeded the daily lifestyle of the trip, facets of myself I want to work on and improve.

This opportunity to learn about myself, and to discover who I want to be, is one of the most valuable results of my travel experience. In this sense, the trip was like a giant global theater, where I was able to try on different perspectives as an actor puts on costumes. I could role-play and test my values, while simultaneously peeling off the layers of my own cultural wardrobe. I believe the most successful lawyer possesses this mobility, this personal and intellectual flexibility. He/she must weigh every possible outcome in a situation, seeing conflicts from every angle. Gradually, travelling became my metaphor for legal study. Every day was a new series of problem-solving tasks. Planning and preparation became more important than they ever had been. I found myself weighing the consequences of spot decisions, whether it was deciding to stay with a friendly Indonesian family, or whether to take a later train to a different French village. Travelling, I was constantly receiving new information and finding meaning, fitting it into the jigsaw puzzle that would become my complete experience. I see parallels in these processes with the way a law student must try to fit individual concepts into the larger context of the law.

And the trip was certainly not solely an inward journey. Before my time abroad, I did not have a real concept of the vast differences that comprise the nations and characters of the world. The trip provided me with the opportunity to gain perspective about the "larger picture" of life, and to imagine my place within this picture. Interacting with individuals was the key in my attempt to understand the countries I visited. I still write to the small group of Balinese jewelry craftsmen we met, and I remember being intrigued by the Japanese musician who has travelled and studied various cultural music for ten years. These individuals were the separate colors in my larger picture of travelling.

I saw only a minute portion of the world this past year; but what I did see motivated me to become involved with the processes that shape relations between individuals and nations. My interests expanded as I lived in a variety of cultures; I believe that it would be both challenging and rewarding to work in international or comparative law. Our national and global challenges in trade, in environment, and in human rights, were all brought into a sharper focus during my time travelling. I am particularly interested in Harvard's East Asian Law program. The Asian countries we visited were my favorite stops; the culture and people are as inscrutable as they are entrancing. The East is also a region we must recognize more fully, as the widening role of Japan has so forcefully demonstrated in the past decade. There are so many options in legal study, so many problems to be solved, so many fields to explore. I am anxious to become a part of it all, to be active in my profession and community, and to use the skills that I will gain at Harvard Law School in shaping an increasingly complex world.

Personal Statement
Christopher Messina

This essay provides me with an opportunity to express to you, the selection committee, a side of myself which may not have been revealed through my responses on the application. It is a chance for me to expound upon any topic I desire, so that I may be considered as more than just an LSAT score and a transcript in your file. Two areas where I believe consideration is necessary but was not afforded space on the application are my studies in Italy and my passing of the CPA exam. Both are important events in my life that I believe merit more than one line on a law school application.

While attending Notre Dame I was given the unique opportunity of spending my sophomore year in Rome with the Saint Mary's College Rome Program. I understand that studying abroad is not necessarily a unique experience for college students, as many universities offer such programs. However, what made it a unique experience for me was the courses I took while in Italy and their relation to my chosen course of study, accounting. Due to the course curriculum and the focus of the program, I was able to attend classes across a large spectrum of disciplines including in-depth art history and archeology courses which would not have been available to me at Notre Dame. I have always had a great passion for the art, architecture, and history of the Roman Empire (probably dating back to the first time I saw *Ben Hur*), but, because of my decision to major in accounting, it would have been difficult for me to take upper-level classes in those subjects as the classes are generally reserved for Arts and Letters majors. Studying in Rome gave me the opportunity to take the types of classes I desired, however remote from my intended area of study.

In addition, it has long been my belief that there is no better teacher than experience, and words cannot express what a magnificent experience it was to learn about the illustrious history of Rome in the shadow of the monuments erected to document its greatest triumphs. To study the language, history, and culture of a society from its very core is truly enlightening.

The second topic on which I wanted to elaborate is my passing of the CPA exam. I am very proud of the fact that I passed all four parts of this extensive exam on my first attempt. It not only has allowed me to register as a CPA in the state of Illinois, but I believe it is an attestation to my abilities to understand and disseminate large amounts of difficult material. The exam is not an aptitude test or an exam where rote memorization is particularly useful. Instead, it is an exam which requires the recognition and application of complex theories and formulas. Preparation for the exam is an exhaustive process which begins many months before the exam. Many people find it difficult to handle the responsibilities of both studying for the exam and preparing for graduation. I feel that my high levels of comprehension, discipline, organization, and success in managing the pressure were reflected in the grades I attained.

I realize that success on this exam does not necessarily equate to success in law school, but I feel that many of the qualities I employed to succeed on this exam will be the same qualities I use to carry myself to equal or greater heights in law school.

Personal Statement
Kevin Mohr

When I was a little boy, I frequently argued with my mother for hours on end, until I finally convinced her to give me what I wanted. She often said in exasperation, "You should become a lawyer." It seems fitting that today, so many years later, I have an opportunity to fulfill that prophecy.

Yet, like many people my age, I am not certain of just what I want to do with my life. I could pursue a career doing something I really enjoy, such as basketball, but I don't think I would eat very well if I did. On the other hand, I could strive for a career doing something that I'm good at. Unfortunately, I don't enjoy doing many of the things that I do well, such as solving problems in physics or calculus.

Thus, my dilemma boils down to this: what do I enjoy doing that I also do well? I believe that practicing law is the answer. Of course, having never been a licensed attorney, I can not say with absolute confidence that I will make a good lawyer or that I'll enjoy being one. But after examining my own skills, experiences, and ambitions, I believe that the law is my calling in life.

Throughout my education, I have performed well in most courses. However, I have excelled in courses that rely on logical reasoning and critical analysis. My study of political science has tested and honed my ability to analyze public policy and political theory within a variety of contexts. Inasmuch as logic and critical thinking are indicative of the skills of a good lawyer, I believe that my academic interests suggest I am suited for a career in the law.

My abilities of oral presentation also strengthen my confidence in my future as a lawyer. After many courses in communication, and after participating on my high school's speech and debate team, I have become very comfortable speaking in front of groups. In 1990, I was an Ohio finalist in the Veterans of Foreign Wars' Voice of Democracy speech contest. My experiences in the Honors Tutorial College (HTC) at Ohio University have further honed my speaking skills. In HTC, one class each quarter is a one-on-one tutorial with a professor. As the only student in the room, it was impossible to hide when I did not know the answer to a professor's question! Those many rewarding tutorials have forced me to think quickly, and then to quickly translate my thoughts into articulate speech.

I'm also confident that I will enjoy being a lawyer. I have always been fascinated by the role of law in society, and by the relationship between law and politics. In high school, I participated for three years on our mock trial team. As I argued cases that lawyers had created to demonstrate the intricacies of the law, I relished the search for fact, the application of logic, the courtroom oration, and the art of persuasion. During my final year, I received the outstanding attorney award at the Ohio state finals. During my years at Ohio University, I have taken almost every class that directly involves the law, and I have prospered in and enjoyed each one.

It is hard to make a decision that is certain to affect the rest of my life, but I am confident with my decision to go to law school. I have always enjoyed the study and practice of law, and I believe I have the skills necessary to be a good lawyer. I don't know what I want to do once I have a law degree, but I don't believe I need to know that right now, and I certainly don't need to fret about it. I should just be thankful that I am lucky enough to have so many options available to me.

Personal Statement
Timothy E. Moran

Although the strong pool of applicants for law schools warns of the difficult task of gaining admission, it also testifies to the increasing desirability of a legal career. I first wanted to be a lawyer in emulation of my father, a lawyer himself. My mother still has pictures that I drew of myself in first grade, sitting behind my father's big oak desk at the office. I continued to plan for my future career all through high school. Soon, however, aspects of the legal world began to bother me: excessive litigation and the increasing number of attorneys, for example. I came to realize that a six-year-old's naive ambitions should not necessarily hold very much weight a dozen years later.

Fortunately, during college I have had the opportunity to view the law from a closer perspective. My sophomore year I began counseling inmates in decision-making skills at the Hampshire County jail. My first client, a man only a few years older than I, who could have been me if not for one mistake (albeit a great mistake), reminded me that ordinary, even decent, people can go to jail. The next two summers I worked as a sheriff in New Haven County. One morning especially stands out in my memory because a man was sentenced to fifteen months on a motor-vehicle violation, which ordinarily carries no threat of jail time, and a failure to appear. The prosecutor even had "nulled" the original charge which had started the trouble. It struck me that with better legal assistance, this poor man could have avoided over a year in jail. People may joke about the number of lawyers, but that day taught me that there is always a need for another good attorney.

My studies, especially my senior honors thesis on the role of virtue in the framing of the Constitution, have given me a deep appreciation for the function that law serves: to provide an important guide on how to live as an upright, honest individual as well as a firm grasp of right and wrong. This assertion often provokes a great deal of debate, yet I have learned that the main responsibility of the law is to codify those values and morals which then can be applied equally to everyone. This regard drives my desire to be a lawyer.

The law has always intrigued me; I have never seriously considered doing anything else. Interest in other professions which my friends are pursuing—banking, consulting, medicine—has been only a passing fancy. The more realistic view of the law which I have acquired over the past few years has taken away much of its glamour, but none of its appeal. Now more than ever before I aspire to become a capable and accomplished lawyer and I am confident that I will reach this goal.

Personal Statement
Robert Musslewhite

Despite the attacks levied against trial lawyers by George Bush during his presidential campaign, I still maintain that law is a worthy avenue of public service, and my lifelong interest in the profession remains undeterred. From childhood, my father's profession has led me to understand that nothing is a more lucid manifestation of the values and beliefs at the heart of American society than that the letter of the law. Generations of East Texas lawyers, judges, and politicians on his side of the family have demonstrated how the study of this law leads to a greater understanding of the ways in which we, as a society, expect people, lawmakers, and leaders to interact, and they have translated this enhanced perception into careers of public service. My great-grandfather was known for his fairness on the bench and his advocacy of individual rights, and both my father and my grandfather have served clients who were wronged and entitled by the law to restitution. One uncle lost his bid for Congress when publicity about my father leading a sit-in at a diner that refused to serve African Americans reached his rural district; however, his support for the civil rights movement, politically unpopular in the area, improved racial relations there. What these men exemplified was service to others in some capacity, and they helped show me at an early age how an understanding of the law would aid my own pursuit of public service.

Though I have always remained open to the attractions of other professions, two summer experiences were instrumental in maintaining my focus on law. In 1986, I lived with a French family as part of an exchange program. Though the French are indeed proud of their own culture, the French students I met expressed admiration and even envy at the amount of individual freedoms Americans are granted by our Constitution and the degree of power lawyers possess to protect those freedoms. My impressions of our occasionally maligned system were again very positive after that summer. While I continued to participate in school leadership and community service activities, it was not until 1990 that I directly experienced law as a public service. During that summer I took a break from year-round swimming training to work as a full-time volunteer criminal investigator for the Public Defender Service in Washington, D.C., assisting an outstanding defense attorney aid indigent clients. While volunteers often questioned the ethics of assisting people who, in many cases, admitted their guilt of violent crimes, I learned how important this assistance was to maintaining the validity of our entire legal system and hence in upholding the beliefs at its roots. And my attorney's expert function of her fiduciary role demonstrated just how important her position was, not only to her individual clients, but to the community and to society. My respect for her work and its results intensified my desire to pursue a career in law.

My enjoyment of economics at Princeton likewise stemmed

from the discovery of the way in which it contributes to my ability to positively influence my community. My first course in econometrics introduced me to the multivariate linear regression which, along with the several other related tools, can provide detailed analyses of public policy initiatives that often impact our society extensively. From advocating a tax increase by demonstrating the beneficial behavioral effects on the consumer to discouraging nationwide implementation of a pilot program to reduce unemployment by signalling its significant societal cost (both issues about which I conducted independent research), econometric analysis, and economics in general, provides a unique way of examining how policy affects people. Hence, studying economics allowed me to pursue my interest in public service in a worthwhile and intellectually stimulating way, and the benefits I gained from it will be invaluable to my career.

My other activities during school also have endowed me with a desire to enter a profession of public service. I spent one semester of my senior year as a full-time high school social studies teacher, fulfilling the education program requirements at Princeton and certification requirements in New Jersey. I also served as the head teaching assistant for Princeton University's financial accounting course and spent three of the past four summers teaching children's swimming lessons in Dallas. This extensive teaching experience has instilled in me a love of sharing my knowledge with others, which I feel is a vital aspect of public service and will translate into using mastery of law to help others. Also, out of my sixteen-year swimming career, nothing was so rewarding as service as team captain during my senior year. While of course I will always remember victories and awards, the most valuable part of the sport was the formation of valuable friendships with teammates, and serving as captain was the best way to help my friends gain as much satisfaction from the sport as I did during my career.

It is thus with enthusiasm that I seek to begin the study of law next fall. Apart from its merits as an intellectual test and as a way to expand upon a liberal education, the study of law is the way by which I want to pursue a career in public service. Through my association with those who have studied law in my family to my own positive experiences with public interest law, I have determined that I have chosen the correct path by which to most effectively fulfill my aspirations. Whether I serve through practice or I ascend to elected or appointed positions, my goal will remain constant: to use my knowledge of the law to serve the good of others.

Personal Statement

Name Withheld

We were in the sixth hour of deliberation. The day had been one of the longest and most exhausting experiences of my life, yet I had never felt so alive. As a member of the Undergraduate Judicial Board, I had been slated to sit on what promised to be a difficult case involving an accusation of date rape within the Duke community. Although each of us on the seven-member panel expected an unusually long hearing (most last about three hours), we certainly never imagined the ten hours of emotionally wrenching testimony and six hours of closed-door discussion that had brought us to the final vote. The arguments on both sides were compelling and the decision was one of the most difficult I have ever had to make. In my tenure on the Board, I had served on cases which, while certainly important to the operation of a civilized university community, were comparatively sterile. The gravity of this case, which took place during the last week of my undergraduate career, went beyond the bounds of Duke, highlighting both the lessons I had absorbed there and the many questions I have yet to answer.

Student writers often jokingly refer to Duke as "The Gothic Wonderland." The bite of the joke, of course, is its element of truth. Life at Duke, not unlike that at many undergraduate institutions, often loses any connection to the events taking place beyond its walls. Even the most level-headed student may have difficulty establishing meaningful priorities. Life moves from deadline to deadline as this week's exams flow into next week's papers. The interim is filled with the intensity of life in a community that places countless demands on a student's time. It is easy to forget that the topics discussed in the classroom—the suffering of the homeless, the crime on American streets, and the daily violence in South Africa—

are not just additions to a syllabus but rather a part of some individual's real life.

The four years I spent in this wonderland were ones of immense change for me. A late bloomer, my personal development had lagged behind that of my peers. As a freshman, I lacked the interpersonal skills, self-reliance and basic good judgment that marks the exceptional individual from the average. I had only one goal in high school—an acceptance at Duke University. With that goal achieved, my purpose was unclear. I had no sense of priority, no sense of commitment, and certainly no sense of direction.

I am a completely different person today. The lessons I learned at Duke were part of a long and often painful path towards increased self-respect and achievement; my learning curve was steep. The assimilation of those lessons, however, could not have happened as quickly or as productively without the influence of a professor, whom I met during the first semester of my senior year when enrolled in his course. The class itself was an incredible learning experience, but it is the impact the class has had on my approach to life that has permanently committed it to my memory. My professor tried, in those ten weeks, to give us some of his hard-earned wisdom. He taught us that life is a struggle. He taught us that leadership meant more than making decisions; it meant understanding that a leader has a responsibility to the people he or she leads. He taught us that taking responsibility for other peoples' lives means making a commitment to yourself and to others, and should be done with care and understanding. Yet the lessons of the classroom were only theory. I could comprehend the difficulty, but I could not feel it.

The Judicial Board case taught me that I could feel it. I could make the lessons of the classroom become a part of not only my mind, but also of my heart. None of us had wanted to be there. As a board, we had been charged with a responsibility that we were uncomfortable accepting, yet one that we had no choice but to shoulder. During that day, I accepted the full burden of that responsibility. I experienced moments of fear, frustration, sadness, fatigue, relief, and anger coming in rapid succession. The case was complex, the truth almost indecipherable, and a decision inevitable.

When it was over, I couldn't think about the logic anymore. I could only cry. But in the months that have followed that day, my mind has often returned to that decision. I will never know if I was right. Sometimes I feel that by making my decision based on the rules, I was hiding behind them. But when I remember the moment that I cast my vote, I know that I did what I thought was right. I know that the decision I made was made with care, and that was the best I could have done.

It was only one case, and it was only one day, but it was also the summation of what I had learned at Duke and what is now important to me. It is a symbol of the effect my lessons at Duke have had on me, a symbol of how those lessons have changed me and given me substance. It reaffirmed my belief in the process and thus my desire and my commitment to go to law school.

Two months have passed since I first sat down to write this essay, and the experience of those months has given an element of reality to this case that I never expected. During that time, I moved to Washington, D.C., to intern for the Senate Judiciary Committee and found myself in the eye to the storm. Hired as permanent staff two days before Professor Anita Hill's allegations became public, I spent my first official weekend mired in the sleepless nights of the Clarence Thomas confirmation hearings. While those historical hearings certainly did not afford me anything close to the personal responsibility I experienced last April, they bore a striking resemblance to that Judicial Board case. Many of the emotions I shared with my fellow board members during that one long day last April—tension, frustration, anger, and fatigue—I saw again in the faces of the Judiciary Committee staff. My job, however, gave me more than a backstage pass to the drama showing on our nation's televisions. It gave me a renewed sense of purpose in my pursuit of a legal education. I was with dozens of bone-tired lawyers working for low pay and relatively little thanks, and felt no pity for them because I knew only that I would have traded places with them in a blink of an eye.

Even as the excitement of the hearings wanes, my enthusiasm for the job has not. I am ready to accept not only the intellectual demands of law school, but also the personal ones. I am confident that I can be a successful law student, but more importantly, that I will be a successful lawyer. I am ready for Harvard. I hope Harvard is ready for me.

Personal Statement

Name Withheld

Master architects have understood for centuries the profound and intimate connection between the human soul and its physical surroundings. Our ideas often seem less the product of mental energy alone than the unique convergence of intellectual creativity and sensory perception which merge to shape consciousness. In like fashion, the structural limits of human society exert an influence upon thought and action similar to that of physical structures. . . . The daily challenge of those who make and apply laws is to forge a legal framework which fosters opportunity and creative growth for all members of society.

As a history major at Williams College, I studied the lives of nineteenth-century mill workers who struggled to maintain and adapt a cultural identity in the face of evolving societal constraints. Now, as I engage in this exercise in personal self-definition, my mind settles on a few special moments in my own past which have contributed to an understanding of my place in society. Three such experiences occurred in very different settings during the summer of 1989, each associated with a particular time and place.

June of that year brought me to Washington, D.C., as an advisor to the Presidential Scholars program. My duties on one typically sweltering summer day included leading a group of students on a tour of the capitol's landmarks. The first stop was the Jefferson Memorial. As I mounted the steps of this impressive edifice, I reflected on the nature of Jefferson's uniquely diverse talents. John F. Kennedy once remarked at a state dinner for Nobel laureates that the White House had never before witnessed such an assemblage of genius, with the possible exception of when Thomas Jefferson dined there alone.

Displayed on the inner walls of the Memorial are several of Jefferson's writings, speaking eloquently of human rights, religious freedom, and the ideal of good government. His words portray a deep understanding of the role of law in society. Although his personal ownership of slaves was inconsistent with much of his writing about freedom, Jefferson was otherwise a fervent defender of individual liberty in a society which even two hundred years ago was developing a nascent rigidity and impersonalization. In the wake of two centuries of industrial expansion and governmental bureaucratization, his example of rational thinking, open-minded toleration, and aesthetic innovation is all the more meaningful. The study of law at Harvard will enable me to further my pursuit of such ideals within the academic world as well as in society at large.

Another episode which touched a part of my character that summer was a pilgrimage to a shrine of a different sort, built not for a national hero but for a national pastime. Bathed in sunlight on a crisp July afternoon, Wrigley Field in Chicago fulfilled every expectation I had harbored for this jewel of America's ballparks. I was immediately struck by the tangible sense of history which pervaded the distinctive green grass and ivied brick of the stadium. Decades ago my grandparents, or even great-grandparents, might have enjoyed substantially the same experience.

Wrigley Field with its ageless charm is the perfect setting for a sport which defies the passage of time. Indeed, the great triumph of baseball's laws resides in their timeless and carefully measured balance of past, present, and future. Each game replicates countless actions and procedures from its nineteenth-century roots, yet beneath the familiar rhythms of every contest lies a latent seed of novel immortality, available to any who can subdue the normal boundaries of human ability to grasp for new levels of achievement. Baseball's structure allows for such transcendence through a wonderful irony of its laws—by constraining its players to a mere 90 degree slice of the universe between the foul lines, it provides a universal common ground on which its participants may strive for perfection. In a rare marriage of equality and freedom, players compete under identical regulations, differentiated only by physical ability and psychological resolve. Like all truly inspired systems of law, its rules and limitations exist solely for the purpose of enhancing, rather than denying, the shared creativity and accomplishment of its citizens.

The final weeks of my summer of 1989 were spent with my "little brother," a ten-year-old in the Williamstown Big Brother Program. We lived for several weeks in August in a cabin, owned by his grandfather, on a tiny Carleton Island at the eastern end of Lake Ontario. The two of us passed the time leisurely—reading, playing catch, swimming, fishing—all set against a lyrical backdrop of deep blue water and pale blue sky. Surrounding us always was nature, at once awesomely powerful and sublimely beautiful.

Like most Americans, I am an urban (or at least thoroughly suburban) creature, often too far removed from the elemental forces of this earth. Being on the island brought me in touch with a rule of law infinitely more ancient than that of human society. To this day, I find an interest in the natural world enlightens my efforts to comprehend the problems of this post-industrial world. The eternal laws and subtlely balanced relationships of nature inspire me to imagine a more perfect legal order for our own society. Perhaps in this light it is fitting that I should also be inspired by Jefferson, a naturalist philosopher, and baseball, the most pastoral of sports. I hope to infuse some of this naturalism into my pursuit of a legal career, and I seek admission to Harvard Law School in order to do so.

P e r s o n a l   S t a t e m e n t

Name Withheld

Many life experiences have crafted my desires. Which one can most fairly explain myself?

My friend distracts my daydream by engaging his common, yet irritating habit of channel flipping. Thanks to modern technology and human impatience, . . .

[ON]:   Channel 2:   My Home

"Never run away from policemen, they are your friends, they want to help you."   —My Father

My father was a policeman, his brother, a criminal defense attorney. My uncle drove a new car, my father carried a gun. Both positions were respected within my close, traditional family. I was taught to trust policemen but grew distrustful of lawyers. It seemed that attorneys were rewarded for undoing the work of policemen, for undoing justice. I could not understand how my father and uncle remained such close personal friends despite their opposing occupations. My curiosity was aroused.

When I was in the ninth grade, the sudden death of my eighteen-year-old cousin brought me very close to my uncle. My parents encouraged me to spend time with Uncle Joe, he lives only one-half mile from my home. I was uneasy when I first arrived. I felt like a small child forced to play in a room crowded with delicate crystal, warned not to break anything. As my resistance eased, I began to enjoy our evening together. We discussed several topics but law inevitably crept into the conversation. Every Sunday soon found me testing my uncle's knowledge and patience. I became fascinated with the law and prompted my uncle to explain my rights on every topic which could possibly affect a ninth-grader and on many issues which bore no direct relevance to my surroundings. I prided myself on being the most knowledgeable "lawyer" in my class and was frequently consulted by my classmates. My relationship with my uncle helped me realize that the work of lawyers is complementary to the work of policemen; the police safeguard my person and property, while lawyers protect my civil liberties.

[ZAP]:   Channel 4:   Delta Sigma Phi

When I returned from my semester abroad, I did not aspire to the presidency of my fraternity. I decided to run because I feared that if I did not, much of the progress (stronger fraternal bonds, greater involvement in community service, and a more active social calendar) made during my previous three years would be jeopardized with complacent leadership.

Serving as president has been extremely challenging. At times the frustration of the job has driven me to question the basis of our group's existence. On other occasions, the experience has been tremendously rewarding: observing the group come together and succeed with the help of my leadership is a memory that I will always hold dear. Perhaps my favorite role is one which I did not anticipate, that of counselor. As president, I have become a confidant of many of our younger members. They have shared many of their fears and successes with me. Though I have often been the "teacher," I have learned as much as I have taught.

[ZAP]:   Channel 5:   Old No. 7

Old No. 7 is an intramural basketball team comprised of several friends from my freshman dorm. This year Old. No. 7 will begin its fourth and final season. Playing on the team is among my favorite activities at Duke. We play with tremendous enthusiasm despite winning only five games in three seasons. Team practice has done little to improve our winning percentage but the team is a great success nonetheless.

[ZAP]:   Channel 7:   Partnership for Literacy

Partnership for Literacy (PTL) is a program that I co-founded during the spring of my sophomore year. The student-run program helps university employees to improve their reading skills. Tutoring began during my semester abroad and I returned to find a maturing program, which surpassed my highest expectation. Though I was offered the job, I passed up the opportunity to be president of the group. Much had changed in my absence, but the program was running smoothly. I feared a sudden change of leadership could only harm PTL.

Declining the offer was difficult for me, but I do not regret my decision. In fact, I am proud of it. I was able to place the group needs ahead of my own desires. I know that I would not have made such a decision only a few years ago, and realize how much I have grown.

[OFF]

Personal Statement
Alexei M. Silverman

For some American students the third year abroad is an exotic summer camp; for me it was a year of growth and accomplishment. Above all, it was during the two semesters that I spent in Milan, Italy, that I exercised the self-motivation that seems to me a prerequisite for the study of law. When I selected my foreign-study program, after only one year of Italian instruction at Rice, I rejected the more touristed cities, as Florence or Rome, because I knew that native Italians in those urban centers would be less likely to speak Italian to a foreigner. I didn't want to squander my opportunity to learn the language. Study in Milan offered me the benefits of a small program, a city that was not focused on catering to the needs of foreigners, and the choice of sharing both an apartment and pasta 'sciutta solely with Italian students.

Once there, I was unyielding in my refusal to speak English to my roommates (which in fact my roommates would have welcomed). I tested into the most advanced language class, on the basis of my intensive summer of independent study. I joined four experienced students, who were more facile speakers than I, as well as better versed in the grammar. But by the end of our three-week orientation session I felt their equal.

Reassured by my progress I supplemented my studies with a course at the Universita Cattolica, Milan's oldest and most highly regarded institution. I was one of the few students eligible to attempt the entrance interview and subsequently was able to enroll. I chose an art history course on the topic of Impressionism in sculpture, taught by Lucien Caramel, the foremost expert on the subject. Once I adjusted to his spirited commentary he won my esteem as one of the most outstanding lecturers I have encountered. At the end of my second semester I was required to take an oral examination covering the entire year, exactly as required of all Italian students.

My only previous experience with oral exams consisted of the two-week battery of tests administered by the International Baccalaureate Program at the end of high school. Nonetheless, more than three years later, the pressure induced by facing a renowned professor in front of a room full of students and having to rely on Italian as a second language was extraordinary. To my pleasure I communicated effectively during the forty-minute cross-examination. Professor Caramel was astonished at the level of my Italian and complimented me on the apparent passion I had displayed in my coursework. I received a thirty with honors or the equivalent of an A+ in our grading system. That grade was more meaningful to me than any other I received in my undergraduate years, because it symbolized both my mastery of the material and the end of a long and determined quest for fluency.

In many ways the first year of law school is akin to full immersion in a foreign, sometimes hostile, environment, and demands the learning of what is essentially a second language—the language of the law. The self-discipline and commitment with which I plunged into my junior year abroad I intend to bring to my legal education. In particular, the global perspectives and cultural understanding I acquired bolster my interest in international law. Finally, I am convinced the law profession will provide the day-to-day challenge that I invariably demand of my pursuits.

Personal Statement
Kristen Smith

At the conclusion of my undergraduate experience, there is one thing in particular that makes me feel that I am ready to move on to law school. That thing is the satisfaction I feel from knowing I have taken advantage of the resources and opportunities found at Brigham Young University. I have personally gained and given all I could from this experience. Looking back on the things that I have been involved in, I would say that as an undergraduate, over three-quarters of my education has come outside of the classroom.

I have always been involved in student issues and activities at college, but the one that probably set the greatest precedent for my experience was one that I had as a sophomore. At that time I was serving as a representative on the Student Advisory Council, which is the student's legislative body. I was selected to chair a committee that would look into various aspects of the BYU Honor Code which encompasses both the values we uphold at BYU as students and the principles that are encompassed in our religion. This particular document had not been altered for over twenty years and the opinion at that time was that it probably would not be changed, at least not by students. However, my committee and I took the initiative to go through twenty years of research and I embarked on a year-long process with students, faculty, and administration, which eventually produced a new Honor Code that was approved by the Board of Trustees. This taught me several significant lessons, not only those dealing with leadership and administrators, but also lessons on public values, the difference between lasting principles and changing attitudes, and the ways in which individuals come to own and uphold their own personal value systems.

This leads directly to my interests in the study of law. As an undergraduate, I have studied political science and economics, which have allowed me to explore matters of public policy and have given me some simple tools for analyzing choices. I have no current interest in serving the public as an attorney, but I desire to study law to increase my understanding of the principles and precedents upon which our society is founded. I perceive law as both the source and reflection of many of our public values and I am particularly interested in the basis of our interpretations of Constitutional law.

Another unique aspect of my experience here has been the framework within which student leadership is taught. Instead of functioning in a political model, our issues and activities take place in what would be better entitled a "cooperative model," in which disagreements may be had, but motives and agendas are not competitive in nature. It is a different framework than that which occurs in the majority of universities. It has given me a different perspective in working with others that I notice I take with me whether I am working at BYU or with entities outside of the university. As a student representative over issues, an associate vice president over programs, and a current student body vice president, I have learned that service is given through a variety of means. When one's focus is on performing work as a service, one gains greater personal benefits than if the work comes from one's own self-interest.

I may sound like an idealist, but I have learned that personal value systems and motives distinctively color the environments in which public policy takes place. I am fascinated particularly with the way in which young college students form and solidify their value systems after they leave their homes. I have had the opportunity to watch this as a student, as a teaching assistant, and as a student leader. People act upon their beliefs, and values form the attributes that they take into every experience they enter. My intention is to study law, issues in higher education, and to return to the university setting as an administrator so that I can continue to work with young people.

My experience in college has been hard as well as exciting. The fact that there are only twenty-four hours to a day has been a particularly hard fact to swallow. Experiences in classes, in leadership, in clubs and organizations, and in work have taken my full attention these last four years. I am grateful for the opportunities that I've had and the education that I've received. I hope to use my education to benefit others. For me education is not gained solely for one's own use, but for the use it can provide in serving others.

Personal Statement

Name Withheld

My decision to attend law school reflects my own life experiences, and particularly, my exposure to several influential role models. Two such role models in the area of the law are retired Supreme Court Justice Thurgood Marshall and Justice Constance Baker Motley. Their ideals and accomplishments have been a source of inspiration for me. Their careers, dedicated to their hope for change in regard to human rights, have led me to ask—what can I do to help?

I first learned about the contributions of Thurgood Marshall and Constance Baker Motley when I studied the history of the civil rights movement in junior high school. That study convinced me that this nation could flourish and remain strong only by raising the status of oppressed people. Thurgood Marshall has done just that. He fought injustices against the poor, minorities, women, and many other oppressed groups in the United States. Many of the battles he fought have led to the improvement of society as a whole. Justice Marshall served the public well, bringing compassion for the common people into the law field. To me, this is what makes a difference. As a young adult, I constantly had negative images of society thrust at me. I found strength in knowing that changes could be made. I have always wanted to help people and it was important for me to know that it was possible for me to correct the wrong that I saw.

Justice Constance Baker Motley has affected me in a similar way. She is a local heroine to me; while she grew up in Connecticut, her legal career flourished in my hometown of New York. She devoted herself to public service from the outset of her career. She worked with the NAACP and was one of the courtroom tacticians during the civil rights movement. As a female African-American role-model, Justice Motley has made a profound impression on me. She was willing to engage the essential issues and tackle the adversity that she saw around her. Her ability to argue effectively and initiate change is something to which I aspire. Both Justice Thurgood Marshall and Justice Constance Baker Motley have shown that through education, study, and commitment, inequality can be overcome.

Throughout my college career, there have been many experiences that have reinforced my initial desire to serve the public through the judicial system. As I pursued my studies at USC, I became very active in the local school systems, contributing to the education of disadvantaged students. Tutoring for the Joint Educational Project as well as my current involvement with the USC Neighborhood Academic Initiative Program have allowed me to experience what "unequal education" can actually be. I have seen the expectation and desire to learn on the faces of the students that I have tutored. Unfortunately, some of these students will not obtain the knowledge that they need. These students have to struggle to get through basic skills such as algebra and grammar because their classrooms are overcrowded and lack essential resources such as books. I have learned that many of the policies that have led to the condition of the school systems are often intricately linked to decisions and policies that are inappropriate. I have grown to understand that the law and its interpretation often drive policies that shape educational institutions, and it is only through the law that these policies can change.

Another experience that has strongly influenced my desire to study law was an internship at the New York County District Attorney's Office. The summer before my junior year in college I obtained this internship and expected that I would finally get a glimpse of the law in action. I wanted to work in the prosecutor's office to get an idea of how people are processed through our legal system. The District Attorney's Office has an enormous caseload to process each week. Too often, I saw people being treated not as individuals, but as numbers. On one hand, the prosecutors were doing their job by getting through the cases as quickly as they could. On the other hand, the individuals were not defended equally. I witnessed trials where people were convicted without full knowledge of due process or time to have an adequate defense. It seemed that the people who could benefit the most from legal help often got the least.

Whether I become involved in law that impacts public policy, or the practice of criminal law, I know that for me the study of the law is a must. I want to be in a position to make a difference in the lives of people who become the victims of our political, social, educational, and legal systems. Like Justice Thurgood Marshall, Justice Constance Baker Motley, and so many others who have dedicated their careers to public service, I would like an opportunity to make a difference. While much progress has been made since the civil rights movement, there are many new issues and challenges to face. As I conclude my undergraduate studies, my direction is clear. I know that I must prepare myself by studying the laws that exist. This knowledge in combination with my compassion for underprivileged people, will allow me to fulfill my mission to devote myself to public service.

Personal Statement

Joe Stuligross

Art and law? What can they possibly have to do with each other? In fact, leadership, courage, justice, and beauty are interrelated in important ways. I discovered something of the nature of these relationships in a musical challenge I faced in my third year of boarding-school teaching.

I met the singers for a "preseason" before school started and they had, as a group, daringly composed a wonderful piece of avant-garde twentieth-century music. For educational reasons, I was certain both that the entire school community would learn from hearing this piece, and that the students would benefit from performing it. Unfortunately, the students, though proud of their work, were dead set against performing for a wider audience. Public performance for any composer is daunting, often causing cold sweats, nausea, or other symptoms. For a group of kids who barely know each other to get up and perform their composition for a community that is less than encouraging of the arts would require an infusion of courage that would demand my greatest persuasive and motivational skills.

The fifty or so of us had a remarkable discussion, at the conclusion of which all but two singers voted enthusiastically to perform. They didn't feel pressured to do something they were unsure of. They craved performance—to show the school the adventurous spirit of the arts, to prove something to themselves, and to reveal a part of themselves which could not be expressed in any other way. Their tremendous energy led to a vigorous performance of a piece they had truly come to believe in. To be sure, the performance was controversial and the campus was buzzing for days afterward, but it was a success partly because the school began discussing issues of artistic expression in a way which had never happened before.

From this experience, I learned, in a practical way, the importance of some fundamental concepts of leadership:

1. Listen. Ask questions until you understand each subtlety of every member's concerns. Sometimes a leader must respond to facial expressions, shrugs, and vague phrases to unearth things which are difficult to express. The singers were worried that their composition was just a mediocre piece, but were hesitant and embarrassed to express this verbally. By using skills of intuition and observation, I anticipated their concern. I offered a professional evaluation of the wonderful structural ideas they had employed and the striking way the musical devices worked together to convey some quite perceptive thoughts.

2. Respect their concerns. They are valid. The students overwhelming emotion was fear. Fear that the performance would flop. Fear that their friends would laugh. Fear that they would embarrass themselves. These are legitimate concerns. Taking this risk is a palpable danger for a student who must spend the next nine months living and working with members of the audience. They are feelings that performers frequently experience and are quite natural.

3. Offer advice and counsel (but not a lecture). Although fear is perfectly legitimate, it can be directed in positive directions. Fear provides energy. By channeling, focusing that energy, a greater performance will result. Part of the reason the students' fear was so intense was that they really felt vulnerable. They had put a great deal of themselves—their own ideas, personalities, and sweat—into composing. I suggested that this possibly made this event more personal than any performance in their lives. Because they put so much

of themselves into the work, it expresses them—directly and honestly—in a way that no dead composer's piece possibly can. That is what makes it scary, but that is also what makes it beautiful.

4. Recognize free will. No one likes to be coerced. In a free society in which individual rights are jealously guarded, pressure tends to evoke resentment, even rebellion. In this case, any hint of pressure would have been ludicrous. The students, after all, were the ones taking this risk. Their friends were in the audience, their "rep" at stake. Further, a successful performance of such an unusual and difficult piece would require absolute commitment and tremendous energy. People can be pressured into many things, from cleaning their rooms to paying taxes, but pressure cannot make people believe in what they are doing or commit fully to an act. I was convinced that pressure would ultimately lead to a failed performance. In turn, such failure might damage the ability of these students to take risks (of whatever sort) in the future. People enjoy being courageous and want to do the right thing. Given freedom of choice and good advice, they usually will.

Students learned some remarkable things from this experience—and I learned at least as much as they did. I rediscovered a natural ability to listen to people and to respond in such a way that their concerns are validated and their worth esteemed while maintaining my ideas of what is necessary. I also discovered that leadership requires listening, respect for others, and thoughtful counsel. Applied without pressure, leadership can help a person find the courage to be expressive artistically (or to undertake other courageous acts). It is these leadership skills which I want to combine with my analytical and reasoning abilities in a legal career. Justice, as beauty, requires courage and leadership.

Personal Statement

Name Withheld

"What's the point of graduatin'? Gettin' a high school diploma ain't gonna make no difference in what happens to me anyway. It's all gonna end up the same no matter what." "Troy," echoing the sentiments of many of his classmates, articulated as well much of my own frustration and disillusionment while student-teaching this fall. Admitted in my sophomore year to a teacher-education program of Harvard College and the Graduate School of Education, I requested placement in an inner-city high school during my senior year in fulfillment of my final requirements for certification. Full of optimism and enthusiasm, I hoped to put into practice many of my long-held yet untried ideas of what could be done to correct a system that, while celebrating the ideals of equality of opportunity and upward mobility, kept so many in our society marginalized and disempowered. Yet it was just a few short weeks into my assignment that Troy's matter-of-fact statement during class discussion crystallized the strong ambivalence I had come to feel toward our educational system.

Student-teaching represented the culmination of my efforts while in college to address some of the inequities and injustices I saw around me. Despite my past experience, however, nothing I had done until then prepared me for what I was to see in our urban schools—not my work in Boston's Chinatown, with a population that felt in many ways similarly frustrated with their lives and opportunities; not my student recruitment through Harvard's Office of Admissions, during which time I visited predominantly minority lower-income urban schools and spoke with students who shared some of my students' hopelessness; not my internship at the Asian-Pacific American Legal Center, when I saw the myriad ways that seemingly small legal matters confounded and frightened people unfamiliar with the system; and not my teaching experience with Vietnamese immigrants who faced the seemingly insurmountable obstacles of a past torn by war and flight and a present of slow and painful language and cultural adjustment. My classroom and students confirmed—indeed, surpassed—many of my worst images of inner-city schools: the facilities were old and in need of repair, textbooks were outdated and limited in number, classroom size exceeded the number of available seats (only a problem, however, when the students came to school, unexpectedly, on the same day), and students were frequently absent for welfare-eligibility or parole matters, or "simply" because their baby had kept them up all night.

What was common among my varied experiences, however, was

the sense of helplessness and disillusionment that many of the people with whom I worked felt. I was struck by the extent to which most of them believed that things in life just *happened* to them, inevitably and irrevocably. They spoke often, many times bitterly and more matter-of-factly, about what was being done *to* them and seldom about what they could do and wanted to do. At the same time, I found that the most widely publicized impressions of urban students missed much of what was rich, worthwhile, and touching in their lives. Whether it was my SAT class students dancing listlessly to traditional Vietnamese music and then exploding spontaneously and joyously to Michael Jackson's latest, or my high-school students listening with uncharacteristically rapt attention to a panel of Harvard students of color talk about the importance of college, urging them to "go for it" no matter what anyone else told them, I saw that students, despite their cynicism, could allow themselves to laugh freely and with a pure heart, and even more rarely, permit themselves to dream. How could I move students away from the easy and self-reinforcing excuse of victimization to a more productive and truly transformative orientation? It is this commitment to empowerment, enabling people to feel some sort of mastery and control over their lives, that has guided all my undergraduate interests. It is this same passion that impels me now toward the study of law. Law seems to me to be the next natural extension of my deepest commitments.

    At the end of my college career, after having spent a sustained amount of time dedicated to and deeply involved with children and families in urban areas, I am confronted with my own personal dilemma regarding education and teaching. I have always been a strong believer in the power of education to change lives, hence my devotion to teaching. By opening minds to different points of view, by presenting alternatives and offering up possibilities, by celebrating diversity, I hoped to enable students both to embrace and participate in a more equal, more just, and more inclusive society. But in doing this, wasn't I teaching my students about a world that wasn't yet out there? I was torn between on the one hand preparing them, poor students of color, for the types of lives they could "realistically" expect to have and on the other, educating them to take part in creating a vision of society that I believe can and should be. How was I to make the promises of education more than just empty promises?

My pursuit of the answer drew me to law. I feel that fundamental change in the structure of opportunity is impossible without working through the legal system. I believe, then, that it is on this front that much work needs to and can be done to help realize the ideals of and potential in education. Knowledge of the legal system takes empowerment one step further by giving us the tools to take control of our lives, offering us a greater degree of mastery over outside forces, and providing the power to effect change so that perhaps one day, students like Troy can believe that education does make a difference.

Personal Statement

Name Withheld

I was orphaned August 10, 1979, upon the death of my mother. She was thirty-nine years old when she died, and had been left alone to raise four children two months earlier when my father died unexpectedly from heart failure. Emotionally exhausted, she had been admitted to a private hospital a few days prior to her death for rest. A mistake was made in the administration of her medication, and she was overdosed. They were unable to save her.

My parents were young and had not even contemplated an estate plan. My sisters, brother, and I had no relatives willing or able to take on the burden of raising four more children, the youngest of whom was only five. As the oldest, the responsibility fell to me; overnight, I acquired three children, two car payments and a mortgage. And I had just turned seventeen.

Our aging grandfather agreed to become our legal guardian. Although he didn't live with us, his guardianship allowed us to remain together in our home. (When I became of age I petitioned for and was granted the legal guardianship of my siblings.) There was, as could be expected, a great deal of initial pressure from neighbors and church members to split us up, especially to take away my five-year-old sister. The townspeople argued that a teenage girl could not properly raise three children and manage a home. I countered that I could, arguing that the community, being relatively small and upper-middle-class, had just never seen it done before. I appealed to them emotionally as well, pointing out that my siblings and I had just lost our father and our mother; all we had left was each other. To separate us would be more damaging than giving me a shot.

The naysayers backed down, but while no one ever called the child welfare authorities, we lived under the scrutiny of the community for years. In all honesty, however, I really didn't have time to care how it all "looked"—I was far too busy working for our survival. Being fearful of the welfare system, I never asked for outside help. I worked every day, day and night. I was not without advocates, though, among them my high-school principal. He allowed me a schedule of two classes in the morning so I could work the rest of the day. My senior year did suffer a brief interruption, but I graduated just one semester behind the rest of my class.

Full-time higher education was now out of the question. Until the day of mother's death, the summer of 1979 had been for me a typical one of a college bound senior—looking at schools and planning a future. While I was not quite sure what I wanted to pursue as a major, I did know that after college I wanted to join the Peace Corps. My upbringing had instilled in me a desire to help people in whatever way I could; my circumstances gave me that chance a little sooner than expected.

By 1986 I was earning enough to work a more reasonable forty to fifty hour week. I was finally able to begin my higher education in Harvard University's extension program, where I had taken courses whenever my schedule permitted since 1981. It was also around this time that my interest in law and government developed, so in 1987 I became a paralegal. My respect for the law and the humanity it serves has had an influence on my family as well. I have raised three fine human beings. Each has an unshakable set of values, and the desire and personal strength to reach for his or her dreams.

During the twelve years of my role as surrogate parent I necessarily developed an ability to negotiate and solve problems. We were four children, with no one but ourselves to mediate our differences. I have learned more from my experiences of the past twelve years than many people do in a lifetime, and I have put that experience to effective use in my career, academic work, and family life. I am now married and have two children of my own. With the youngest of my siblings now in her freshman year of college, and the support and encouragement of my husband, I am at last able to devote myself full-time to the study of law. The knowledge and discipline I have gained from my experiences will be a tremendous benefit to me at Harvard Law School and in my legal career.

P e r s o n a l S t a t e m e n t

Tania Tetlow

At twenty, I was probably the youngest person on Louisiana's ballot this fall. We elect representatives to our Democratic State Central Committee, and I ran from my legislative district for a seat. I have never been as intimidated as the first time I had to knock on someone's door and ask for their vote, or worse, call a friend and ask for money. I raised almost two thousand dollars, got the endorsements of most of the elected officials in my district, and garnered 2,700 votes. Unfortunately it wasn't enough to win, but I learned more than I ever wanted to know about the political system.

I was active in government long before I was old enough to vote, interning everywhere from city hall to Congress, and working in campaigns. I have seen the power of the law to shape people's lives, and I want to learn how to use that power constructively.

Louisiana ranks last among the fifty states for many things, including the percentage of women in our legislature. Two years ago legislators almost laughed out of the capitol a law making it illegal to rape your wife. While we have one of the most sophisticated political systems in the country, elected everything from insurance commissioner to assessor and consistently producing very high voter turnouts, we have a rather unsophisticated government. Perhaps because of our poverty and resulting lack of education, Louisiana has suffered at the hands of backward legislation. As someone attuned to women's concerns and to the needs of society, I want to get involved with the law here to preserve a state wealthy with culture and diversity.

I don't know how much I will be able to accomplish, and I realize that there is more involved in change than the legal system, but with the help and encouragement of women like my mentor, former Congresswoman Lindy Boggs, and the Truman Foundation, I have hopes that I can make a difference.

Personal Statement
Rory E. Verrett

In many ways, my commitment to a career in public service is a product of my personal history—people, places, and events that have motivated me toward improving society through the practice of law.

While my mother fought in a Louisiana court to pursue her doctorate at Tulane University, my father never had the privilege of a formal education, having to end his schooling in the seventh grade to work for the family's survival. This blend of scholarship and self-sacrifice produced a unique family environment, one in which cultural and intellectual enlightenment was combined with personal dedication to others. Growing up within a violent and drug-ridden community meant that, although I dreamed of Congress and the Supreme Court, I could not close my eyes to the despair of my friends and neighbors. Today, I am certain that the only barrier between myself and the turbulent streets was an education.

Throughout my life, I have consistently experienced this dichotomy: a rigorous academic life set amidst a sometimes hostile and indifferent external environment. Attending St. Augustine, a Catholic high school for African-American males, meant to some of my friends that I was "selling out" my race or acting "white." Inside, however, as student-body president and captain of our state-champion speech and debate team, I was learning how to be a leader, acquiring the skills needed to develop solutions to some of the pressing issues facing the African-American community.

As a student at Howard University in Washington, D.C., I have also experienced this tension. The university is located in one of the District's poorest and most violent areas; students cannot escape daily interaction with community residents. While pity or apathy may characterize some of my peer's attitudes toward community relations, I have found impassioned advocacy and intelligent action to be the best responses to those in need. Indeed, as I have matured and broadened my horizons, my achievements have become more service-oriented and less individualistic.

In my junior year, through a research fellowship in environmental policy at the U.S. Environmental Protection Agency, I completed a study that sought to fuse the perspectives of community organizations, the private sector, and government environmentalists on effective strategies in urban environmental policy. The eight-month project resulted in an increase in EPA funding for Historically Black Colleges and Universities (HBCU) to develop community-based environmental education programs in urban areas, as well as the formation of an Environmental Equity Task Force to monitor agency projects in urban/minority areas. The success of the report made me realize that, just as Dr. Martin Luther King envisioned, there is a table where disparate groups can sit down and reach consensus for improving society.

Intelligent action is another strategy that I have found to be successful in service to others. As the elected student trustee on Howard University's Board of Trustees, I am helping to develop the Community Outreach Program, which would make one semester of community service a requirement for graduation. Pending approval from the Board of Trustees, this program would be one of the first of its kind in higher education and should help to bridge the gap between Howard students and the D.C. community. Hopefully, such a project would also help to instill a sense of collective responsibility among the District's often racially divisive residents.

As I prepare myself for a career in law, I know that the challenge to forge consensus in an increasingly diverse society will not be an easy one. With a rigorous legal education, however, I am confident that I will be able to chisel my talents into razor-sharp weapons in the crusade for social justice. For only by lifting others as I climb will I truly become a public servant of my community, my country, and my race.

Personal Statement

Christopher Shang-Yung Yeh

I was seventeen when I found my first summer job—a position at the local movie theater. I started as popcorn guy ("extra butter, sir?") but through hard work soon became the guy who rings up the snack total ("$12.00 ma'am, enjoy the movie").

Despite this career advancement, my work remained constant in one sense: it kept teaching me how to interact with customers. Whether serving or selling popcorn, I tried to provide a good time for moviegoers. Sometimes this meant refilling a spilled bucket of popcorn. Other times it simply meant subsidizing the six-year-old who was a dime short of getting his soda. At all times, however, it meant keeping a sense of humor and humility. After all, if you're handling popcorn, how seriously can you take yourself?

According to my former high-school dean, not very. He once told me that everyone should perform a service-oriented job in his or her life. I wasn't sure what he meant at the time, but recently I think I've figured it out. All too often, people in glamorous or well-paid jobs take themselves a bit too seriously. They have never had—or have forgotten what it was like to have—a job helping others. Last summer, for example, I interned at the publishing house of Honolulu's city magazine. I needed some phone numbers for an article, so I called Mr. Sherman, a prominent local journalist. Although he has an impressive list of credentials and an understandable reason to be proud of himself, I didn't expect the kind of conversation that ensued.

"Hello, Mr. Sherman. I'm interning with *Honolulu* magazine, and I was wondering if I could get some phone numbers from you." I paused.

Silence.

I continued. "So, would you have Ms. ABC's num—"

"Never heard of her."

"Oh. How about the number of Mr. XYZ?"

"Call the *Star-Bulletin*." Click.

At the time, I didn't have the presence of mind to ring back and call him a rude S.O.B. And now I'm glad I didn't; he simply could've been having a bad day or a busy afternoon. But if our conversation in fact reflected his general attitude, then he has probably forgotten what it was like to serve popcorn, or bag groceries, or deliver newspapers.

Fortunately, it seems that many Honolulu careerpersons have not forgotten. When I performed clerical work at a law firm, an attorney appropriated for himself the title of my "Uncle Rick" and talked with me about everything from legal studies to college parties. When Iraq invaded Kuwait, I was interning at a local energy company. Although my boss was besieged daily by the media to discuss statewide gas prices, he put aside his work to make sure I was learning new things.

I'd be naive, of course, to assume that a summer of humble work necessarily makes a sympathetic person. But I do believe this: those who have served popcorn are more likely to see the next generation of popcorn scoopers as human equals. As Emerson said (kind of), we are defined less by our different jobs than by our common humanity. We should not have writers, but humans writing; we should not have popcorn servers, but humans serving popcorn. In the most important sense, the prominent journalist is no different from the newspaper delivery boy.

So, when I join the legal profession—whether as a corporate lawyer or as a public defender—and enter a new type of service work, I hope I do not acquire a new attitude about service. I hope always to remember that the human who is blessed with legal training is no different from the new kid at the publishing house, energy company, law firm, or movie theater.

Extra butter, sir?

Epilogue

Harvard Law School is a top-rated institution that expects its applicants to have excellent "numbers." But if you have read any of those general guides to law schools in the United States, you have probably noticed that the HLS admissions committee does not provide a profile chart of applicants considered and admitted because such charts are usually based solely upon the "numbers" (undergraduate GPA and LSAT scores). The HLS admissions committee decision-making process takes many factors besides undergraduate GPA and LSAT scores into account, and is too complex to be portrayed accurately by a two-factor profile. That is to say, the committee evaluates all information in each applicant's file including transcripts, extracurricular activities, recommendations, personal statements, LSAT scores, work experience, and community service. Also, background factors such as demonstrated societal, economic, educational, or personal disadvantage the applicant has overcome are noted by the committee to help it understand more fully the candidate's achievements.

In other words, there are no mathematical cut-offs at Harvard Law School based on grades and scores. If you have excelled based

371

on the opportunities available to you and the circumstances in which you have found yourself, HLS will strongly consider your application.

Applying to Harvard is usually worth a shot for talented students who want a solid legal education. After all, every year a number of applicants—from various racial, ethnic and economic backgrounds—are admitted with relatively low undergraduate GPAs or LSAT scores while a significant portion of candidates with very high grades and/or LSAT scores are rejected.

Best wishes for making the right decision for you!